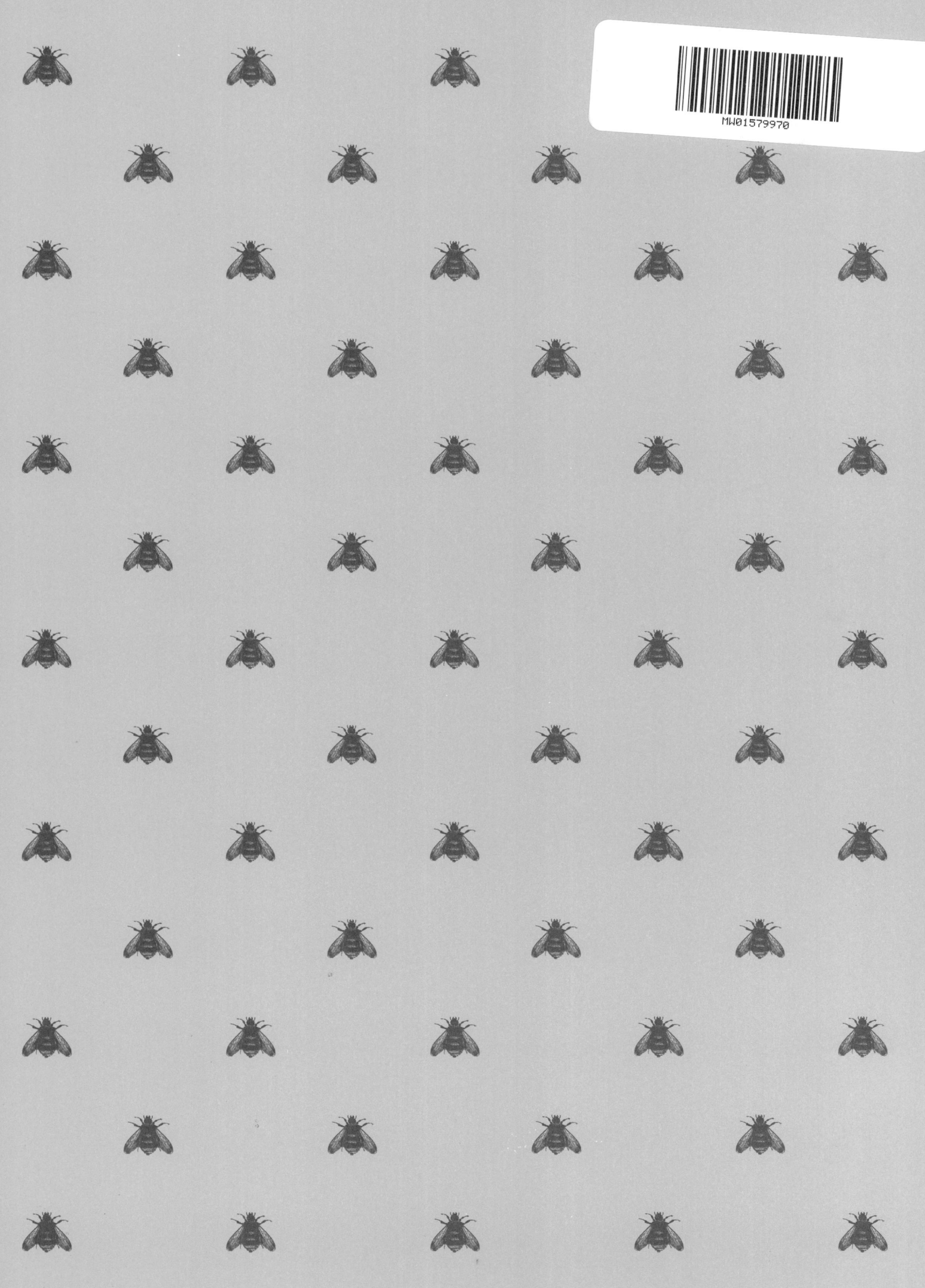

Joséphine and the Arts of the Empire

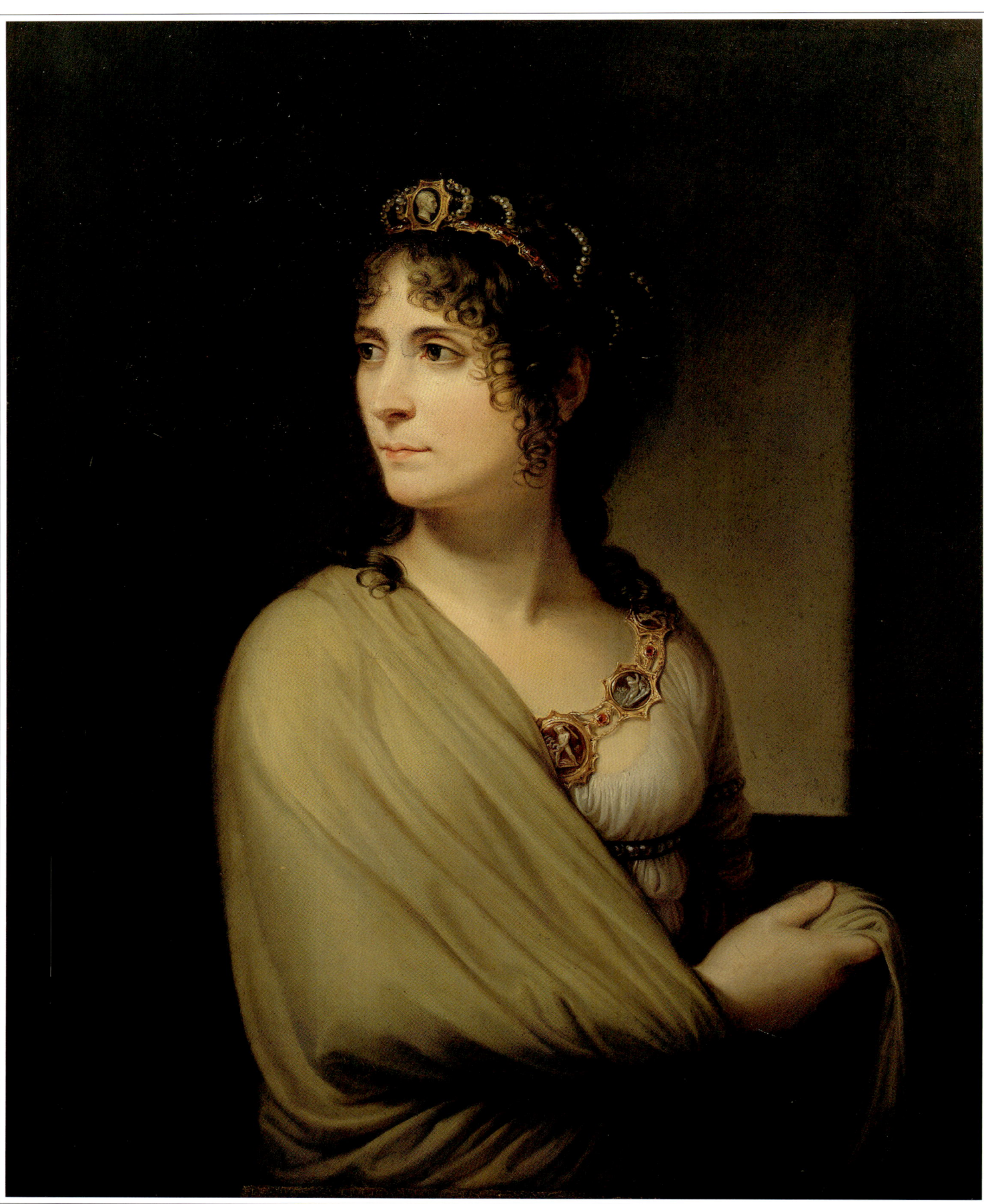

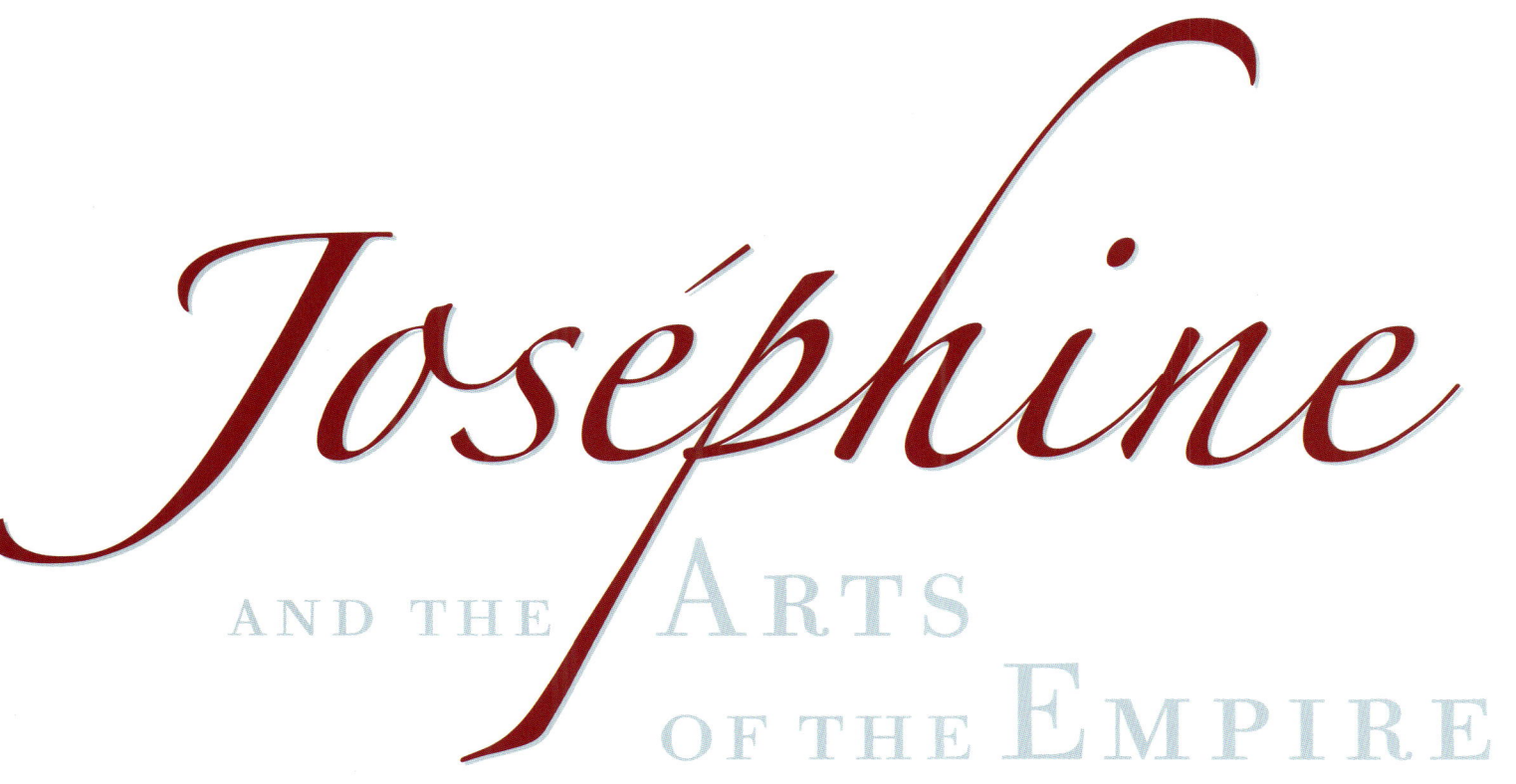

Joséphine
and the Arts of the Empire

EDITED BY ELEANOR P. DELORME

with contributions by
Bernard Chevallier
Kimberly Chrisman-Campbell
David Gilbert
Christopher Hartop
Peter Mitchell
Tamara Préaud
Diana Scarisbrick
John D. Ward

The J. Paul Getty Museum
Los Angeles

© 2005 J. Paul Getty Trust

Getty Publications
1200 Getty Center Drive, Suite 500
Los Angeles, California 90049-1682
www.getty.edu

Christopher Hudson, *Publisher*
Mark Greenberg, *Editor in Chief*

Dinah Berland, *Editor*
Charles Pearson DeLorme, *Developmental Editor*
Jim Drobka, *Designer*
Suzanne Watson, *Production Coordinator*

Typesetting by Diane Franco
Color separations by Professional Graphics, Inc., Rockford, Illinois
Printed by CS Graphics, Singapore

LIBRARY OF CONGRESS
CATALOGING-IN-PUBLICATION DATA

Joséphine and the arts of the Empire / edited by Eleanor P. DeLorme ; with contributions by Bernard Chevallier ... [et al.].
  p. cm.
  Includes bibliographical references and index.
  ISBN-13: 978-0-89236-801-3 (hardcover)
  ISBN-10: 0-89236-801-2 (hardcover)
  1. Art, French—18th century. 2. Art, French—19th century. 3. Decoration and ornament—Empire style. 4. Joséphine, Empress, consort of Napoléon I, Emperor of the French, 1763-1814—Art patronage. I. DeLorme, Eleanor P. II. Chevallier, Bernard, 1936– III. J. Paul Getty Museum.
  N6846.J67 2005
  944.05'092—DC22
                                     2005001019

FRONTISPIECE: Jean-André Appiani (Italian, 1754–1817), *Madame Bonaparte*, 1807. Oil on canvas, 98.5 × 74.5 cm (38¾ × 29⅜ in.). Private collection. PAGE viii: Jacques-Louis David, *The Consecration of the Emperor Napoléon* (detail, fig. 24). PAGE 6: Antoine-Jean Gros, *General Bonaparte at the Bridge of Arcole* (detail, fig. 9). PAGE 38: Joseph Chinard, *The Empress Joséphine* (detail, fig. 28). PAGE 56: View of the Salon de Saisons (detail, fig. 49). PAGE 76: August Garneray, *View of the Wooden Bridge* (detail, fig. 58). PAGE 90: Pierre-Joseph Redouté, *Hortensia, Jacinthe, Lis Saint Jacques, Chrysanthemum* (detail, fig. 67). PAGE 102: View of Joséphine's State Bedchamber at Compiègne (detail, fig. 82). PAGE 120: Plate for Knives (detail, fig. 88). PAGE 136: Cup and Saucer (detail, fig. 93). PAGE 144: Tureen and Cover (detail, fig. 103). PAGE 156: Antoine-Jean Gros, *Empress Joséphine* (detail, fig. 111). PAGE 174: Tiara (detail, fig. 117). PAGE 188: Dominique Doncre, *La Marseillaise* (or *The Patriotic Singers*) (detail, fig. 127).

PHOTOGRAPH CREDITS

Most of the photographs in this volume were provided by the owners of the works and are published by their permission. The following are additional credits.

Anne S. K. Brown Military Collection, Brown University Library, Providence, R.I.: fig. 128.
Archivio Fotografico Museo Napoleonico, Rome: fig. 14.
Art Resource, New York / Musée Correr, Venice: fig. 27 / Musée d'Art et d'Histoire, Nice: fig. 111 / Musée Ingres, Monauban, France: fig. 132.
Bibliothèque nationale de france, Paris: fig. 42.
The Bridgeman Art Library, London / Hermitage Museum, Saint Petersburg, color lithograph by Luigi Premazzi: fig. 41.
Cameraphoto Arte, Venice / Art Resource, New York / Hermitage Museum, Saint Petersburg: fig. 40.
Christie's Images, London: figs. 118, 119, 122.
Collection des Vélins du Muséum national d'histoire naturelle; photo Bibliothèque centrale: fig. 60.
From *Connaissance des Arts*, no. 196, June 1968: fig. 49.
Cooper-Hewitt, National Design Museum, Smithsonian Institution: fig. 95.
Getty Research Institute, Special Collections: figs. 43, 74.
Helen A. Ganser Library, Millersville University, courtesy of Archives and Special Collections: fig. 133.
James P. Boyce Centennial Library of the Southern Baptist Theological Seminary, Louisville, Kentucky; photo by Andrew B. Rawls: fig. 131.
Photo © Hubert Josse, Abbeville Press, New York: fig. 48.
Kunsthistorisches Museum, Wien oder KHM, Vienna: fig. 108.
Erich Lessing / Art Resource, New York / Musée Ingres, Montauban, France: fig. 132; Musée Massena, Nice: fig. 111.
Los Angeles County Museum of Art; photo © 2004 Museum Associates LACMA: fig. 112.
Mauboussin Archives, Paris / A. C. Cooper, London: fig. 123.
The Metropolitan Museum of Art, New York / Bequest of Edward S. Harkness, 1940 (50.135.2), photo © 1988 The Metropolitan Museum of Art: fig. 105 / Joseph Pulitzer Bequest, 1934 (34.17.1a-c), photo © 1997 The Metropolitan Museum of Art: fig. 99 / The Elisha Whittelsey Collection, The Elisha Whittelsey Fund, 1963 (63.535), photo © The Metropolitan Museum of Art: fig. 71 / Private collection, New York, courtesy of The Metropolitan Museum of Art: fig. 3 / The Thomas J. Watson Library, Rogers Fund, 1918: fig. 50 / Gift of Mr. And Mrs. Charles Wrightsman, by exchange, 1985 (1985.119), photo © 1985 The Metropolitan Museum of Art: fig. 86 / Wrightsman Fund, 2002 (2002.31), photo © 2002 The Metropolitan Museum of Art: fig. 106.
Napoléon Museum, Château d'Arenenberg, Switzerland: fig. 4.
National Gallery of Art, Washington, D.C.; image © Board of Trustees: fig. 107.
© PMVP/ Musée Carnavalet, Paris / photo by Joffre: fig. 104; photos by Toumazet: figs. 105, 134.
Private collection, New York; photo by Ann Grey: fig. 35.
© RMN / Art Resource, New York / Château Compiègne, France: figs. 81, 82 / Château de Fontainebleau: figs. 77, 109; photos by Gérard Blot: figs. 16, 76, 101, 102; photo by Lagiewski: fig. 100 / Château de Malmaison: figs. 20, 32, 43, 54, 55, 57, 59, 61, 92, 115; photos by D. Arnaudet: figs. 6, 28, 70, 83, 85, 87–89, 91; photos by D. Arnaudet, J. Schormans: figs. 29, 30, 52, 53, 58, 62, 90; photos by Gérard Blot: figs. 56, 110, 114, 120/ Château de Versailles: figs.1, 9, 19, 25, 72, 78, 84, 113, 130; photo by Arnaudet, Lewandowski: fig. 15; photo by Gérard Blot: fig. 12 / Musée de la ville de Paris, Musée Carnavalet, Paris; photo by Bulloz: figs. 11, 126 / Musée du Louvre, Paris: figs. 2, 7, 10, 23; photos by D. Arnaudet: figs. 75, 79; photo by D. Arnaudet, Gérard Blot: fig. 5; photo by Gérard Blot: fig. 17; photos by J.-G. Berizzi: figs. 21, 26, 98; photos by C. Jean: figs. 8, 27; photos by R.-G. Ojeda: figs. 22, 32–34, 124; photo by Franck Raux: fig. 129 / Musée national de céramique, Sèvres: fig. 93 / Musée national de Sèvres, Archives: fig. 94.
Scala / Art Resource, New York / Hermitage, Saint Petersburg: fig. 36.
Courtesy of Sotheby's, New York: figs. 63–68.
The State Hermitage Museum, Saint Petersburg: figs. 38, 39.
V&A Picture Library / Apsley House, London: fig. 18.
Courtesy of Wildenstein & Co., Inc.: figs. 44–47.

Contents

vi	ACKNOWLEDGMENTS
1	INTRODUCTION *Eleanor P. DeLorme*

CHAPTER 1	7	The Courtly, Heroic, and Romantic: Joséphine's Patronage of Painting *Eleanor P. DeLorme*
CHAPTER 2	39	A Taste for the Antique: Joséphine's Preferences in Sculpture *Eleanor P. DeLorme*
CHAPTER 3	57	Innovative Interiors: The Settings for Joséphine's Life *Eleanor P. DeLorme*
CHAPTER 4	77	Her Magical World: Joséphine's Gardens and Conservatory *Eleanor P. DeLorme*
CHAPTER 5	91	Redouté: Joséphine's Watercolor Garden *Peter Mitchell*
CHAPTER 6	103	From Mahogany to Gilt: Joséphine's Choices in Furniture *John D. Ward*
CHAPTER 7	121	The "Joséphine Taste": Porcelain for Her Table *Bernard Chevallier*
CHAPTER 8	137	On Her Majesty's Order: Joséphine and Sèvres *Tamara Préaud*
CHAPTER 9	145	Empire Silver: A Gilded Age *Christopher Hartop*
CHAPTER 10	157	The Empress of Fashion: What Joséphine Wore *Kimberly Chrisman-Campbell*
CHAPTER 11	175	Love and Glory: Joséphine's Jewelry *Diana Scarisbrick*
CHAPTER 12	189	The Music Joséphine Heard: From the "Plaisirs d'amour" to "Le Chant du départ" *David Gilbert*

204	INDEX
208	ABOUT THE AUTHORS

Acknowledgments

There are numerous people who have greatly contributed to the realization of this volume, and I extend my sincere appreciation to each of them.

At Getty Publications, Mark Greenberg, editor in chief, who championed the idea of the book from the outset and supervised its development at every stage; Dinah Berland, our superlative editor who is everything any author could desire and more; Jim Drobka, who produced the book's elegant design; Cecily Gardner, the photo researcher who persistently garnered most of the illustrations; Suzanne Watson, for shepherding the book into print; and ever-helpful Jesse Zwack, senior staff assistant, who kept the wheels turning. At the Getty Museum, the curators who gave valuable feedback on various chapters of the manuscript: in the Department of Sculpture and Decorative Arts, Catherine Hess, associate curator, and Jeffrey Weaver, assistant curator, and in the Department of Paintings, Scott Schaefer, curator; and Edward S. Harwood, associate professor and chair of the Department of Fine Arts at Bates College, who, while a scholar at the Getty Research Institute, offered helpful comments on Joséphine's gardens.

In France, at the Musée national des Châteaux de Malmaison et Bois-Préau, Director Bernard Chevallier, dean of Joséphine studies, for his warm encouragement and fine, comprehensive essay; at the Manufacture nationale de Sèvres, Tamara Préaud, who, with her accustomed authority, contributed an invaluable study of a little-known aspect of Joséphine's relationship to the Sèvres manufactory; and in Paris, Emmanuel Ducamp for contact information.

In London, at the Courtauld Institute of Art, Professor Aileen Ribeiro, who generously recommended Kimberly Chrisman-Campbell, to whom we owe an excellent essay on Joséphine's fashions. Diana Scarisbrick, who focuses her vast knowledge of jewelry history upon Joséphine's resplendent collection. Peter Mitchell, who, through his rich collection of Redouté watercolors, brings us an intimate experience of Joséphine's own vellums. In Norfolk and London, although usually on the road, Christopher Hartop, who sagaciously enlightens us about the wonders of silver-gilt and Joséphine's silver in particular.

In New York, at The Metropolitan Museum of Art, curators Gary Tinterow for his wise, valuable suggestions regarding the painting of the Empire, and Danielle Kisluk-Grosheide, for her unremitting support and enthusiasm for our project from its inception. I wish to thank Joseph Baillio of Wildenstein & Co. for providing me with transparencies of Pierre-Paul Prud'hon's decorative panels for the Salon de la Richesse in the Hôtel de Lannoy and of Jean-Baptiste Isabey's watercolor depiction of Napoléon placing the newborn king of Rome in the arms of Empress Marie-Louise. I am also grateful to him for sending me a copy of his recent monograph on the large marble reliefs that Pierre Julien carved for Marie Antoinette's Laiterie on the grounds of the château of Rambouillet. These sculptures were recently presented by Alec and Guy Wildenstein to the French nation as the "Dation Wildenstein" and will soon be reinstalled in the building for which they were executed. At Sotheby's, John D. Ward, for his perceptive, original analysis of Joséphine's taste in furniture. At Malmaison Antiques, Roger Prigent, for generously providing a photograph of his monumental Canova bust of Napoléon.

In Boston and Geneva, Professor William W. Park, for an indispensable reference book on the French Empire; and Doris Stone for her help with botanical information.

At the University of California, Los Angeles, David Gilbert, who responded in 1998 with gracious proficiency to my request for a crucial chapter on the music of Joséphine's day, which became the first contribution to this volume.

At Wellesley College, President Diana Chapman Walsh, for her generous support and her sustained encouragement; Professor Miranda Marvin for elucidating details of antique costume; Pamela Rogers, Visual Resources curator, who was always available to solve complex technical problems, and Maggie deVries, assistant Visual Resources curator, for her affable facility with graphics, recalcitrant computers, and even syntax; Lisa Priest and Nancy Bowman for dispatching documents and efficiently and genially attending to countless details; Mary Lee Mutch in computer services for her excellent professional help. In the Department of German, Isabel Geiger, for a priceless transparency from Queen Hortense's château of Arenenberg. Heartfelt thanks to two of my outstanding former Wellesley students: Rebecca Tilles, curatorial assistant, Musée national des Châteaux de Malmaison et Bois-Préau, 2003–4, a highly skilled liaison, for invaluable and timely assistance with manuscripts; and Isabelle Barber, now at Sotheby's, Department of European Decorative Arts, for patiently and capably unraveling some knotty editorial problems.

Finally, special gratitude is due to my developmental editor, Charles Pearson DeLorme, who was indispensable in editing my previous book, *Joséphine: Napoléon's Incomparable Empress*. For the present publication he has once again read, ameliorated, researched, clarified, reorganized, and augmented material; verified translations; met with and corresponded at length with various scholars; and contributed immeasurably to the volume's quality and substance.

"Everything comes from Thee, and we have given Thee only what comes from Thy hand" (1 Chronicles 29:14).

Eleanor P. DeLorme

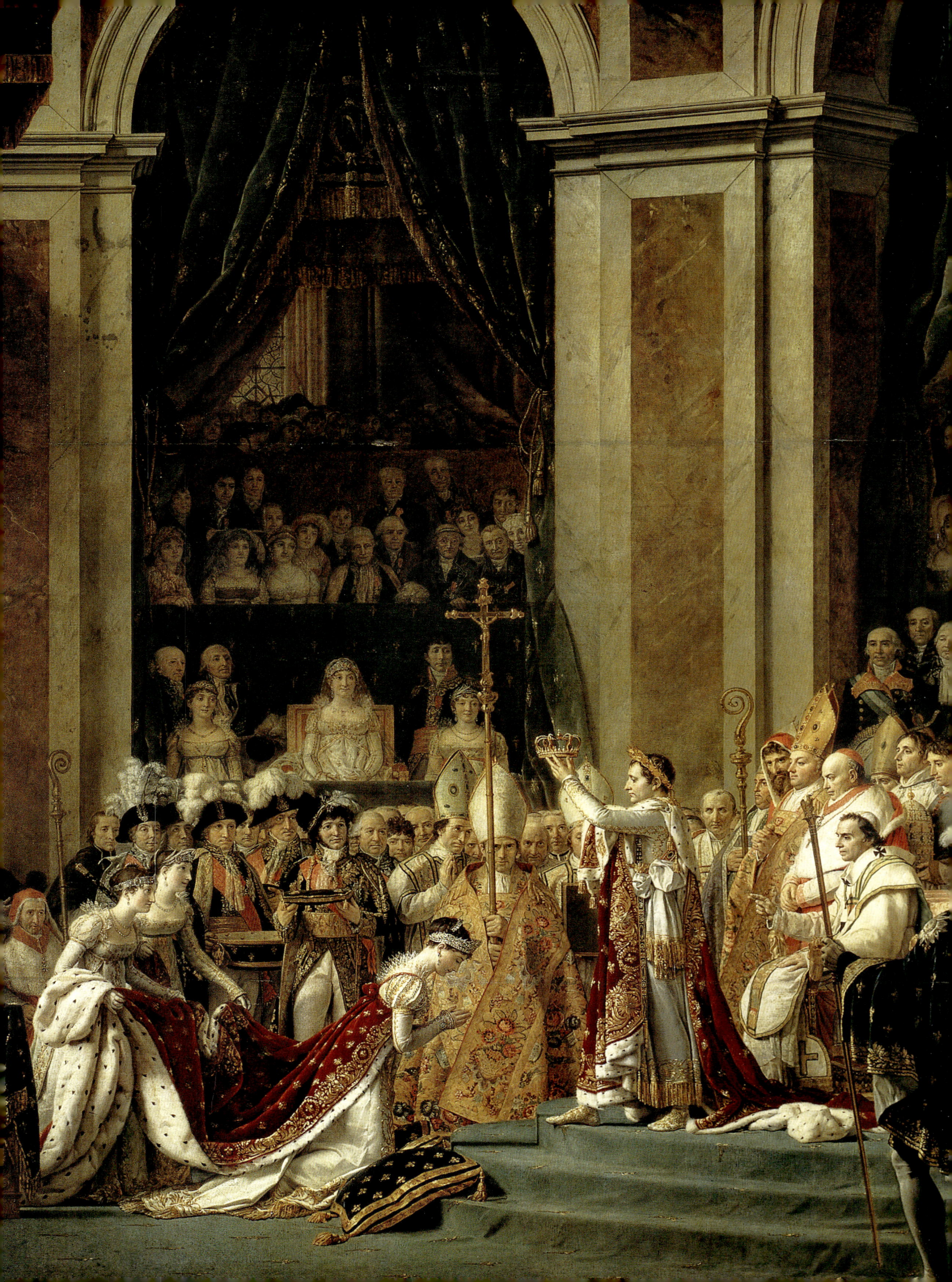

Introduction

ELEANOR P. DELORME

The pivotal age in which Joséphine lived witnessed profound and rapid social changes, tragedies on a grand scale, and personal triumphs. In 1795 a corrupt Directoire rule succeeded the Revolution, followed in 1800 by a more stable Consulate and then, in 1804, the expansive, opulent Empire period. The new world that emerged was principally shaped by Napoléon Bonaparte, the phenomenal personality who gave Joséphine her own momentous role in history. Perhaps no other woman has ever been required to play such an exhilarating, challenging, glorious but ultimately heartbreaking part as Joséphine, whose brief life was conducted to the counterpoint of legendary military campaigns that changed the map and culture of Europe. She carried it off, though, with conspicuous grace, elegance, acumen, and savoir-faire. Her luminous presence, refined manners, and unfailing tact mollified a stern, militant society, and her unqualified popularity significantly contributed to Napoléon's meteoric political ascension.

Joséphine was born Marie-Josèphe-Rose de Tascher de la Pagerie in 1763 on the Caribbean island of Martinique, where she was apparently charmed by the luxuriant flora and birds ablaze with color, judging by her later acquisitions. At sixteen she was catapulted into an arranged marriage with Alexandre, vicomte de Beauharnais, who moved in exalted social circles. Two gifted children were born of this union—Eugène and Hortense.

Thanks to Alexandre's position, Joséphine frequented the houses of people of ancient and illustrious lineage, bearing names such as de Caulaincourt and de Montmorençy, whose motto was "Naturellement." Their prestigious town houses represented a pinnacle in the art of living for the Western world—designed by leading architects; decorated with Lyons silks or *boiseries* (paneling) by master carvers and gilders; furnished by sought-after cabinetmakers; and garnished with priceless paintings, sculptures, and objets d'art. Her familiarity with these privileged environments and the eighteenth-century manners of their patrician owners were not lost upon the vicomtesse de Beauharnais, who was shortly to become the living link between the old court and the new.

After Paris erupted in 1789, Alexandre and Joséphine were thrown into prison. He was sentenced to the guillotine, but Joséphine, awaiting her own turn to mount the scaffold, was miraculously saved at the last moment by a strange turn of events. Released in a pitiable state from the sordid Carmelites prison in August 1794, she was nevertheless soon to be numbered among the Merveilleuses, pace-setters of Directoire society who tripped along the boulevards in daring, filmy gowns *all'antica* (classical style) and blond or blue wigs, although Joséphine never embraced their wilder excesses.

In August 1795, to provide a home for her two children, she leased a small house on rue Chantereine (later rue de la Victoire) from the estranged wife of François Talma, the theatrical legend who became an intimate of Joséphine's household. Naturally, she decorated her new pavilion with such stunning flair that Joséphine—along with Juliette Recamier[1]—virtually created the interior fashion of the day (see chapter 7).

That October, Joséphine was introduced to the man who would radically change her life—the twenty-six-year-old prodigy, General Bonaparte, who fell madly in love with the glamorous ex-vicountesse. When he proposed, Joséphine hesitated, but she finally agreed to marry him on March 9, 1796, never imagining the inconceivable heights to which he would bear her. Shortly afterward, Bonaparte was named commander of the Army of Italy, and after an unprecedented series of victories over the Austrians, he returned to Paris in December 1797 to be toasted as man of the hour.

Joséphine had visited her husband in Italy and—as wife of the conqueror—was luxuriously housed, fêted, and honored with lavish gifts of paintings, objets d'art, and jewelry. Here she first saw Antonio Canova's sculpture, and, typically, her discriminating eye noted two young artists soon to stand in the vanguard of French painting: Anne-Louis Girodet-Trioson and Antoine-Jean Gros, whose myth-making image of Bonaparte at Arcole was painted for her even before she left Italy.

Bonaparte's next adventure began on May 19, 1798, an amazing expedition to Egypt, which was the late eighteenth-century equivalent of going to the moon. Along with the army went experts from all disciplines and a team of artists under the direction of Joséphine's erudite friend Vivant Denon, whom she presented to Bonaparte as the one man who could coordinate the cultural aspects of this unparalleled enterprise. Denon recorded Egypt's antiquities on the spot and then published his drawings and text in the fabulous *Voyage de la Bas et de la Haute Égypte pendant les campagnes du général Bonaparte* (Travels in Upper and Lower Egypt during General Bonaparte's Campaigns, 1802). It revealed Egyptian art to France and the world. Later Champollion disclosed the mystery of the hieroglyphics on the Rosetta Stone that would be discovered by Bonaparte's army. So one might claim that it was Joséphine who indirectly prepared the way for Egyptology.

After the campaign, a wave of Egyptomania swept through the arts. Joséphine poured tea from her Sèvres *cabaret* (tea service) painted with hieroglyphs, and cultivated blue lilies from the Nile; Prince Eugène's candelabra were borne aloft by Nubian figures; in Girodet's scandalous *Mademoiselle Lange as Danaë*, the actress wears (only) a feathered turban like that of Bonaparte's Mamluk, Roustam; and Gros' *Napoléon Visiting the Plague-Stricken at Jaffa* is set in the exotic East.

In November 1802 Denon became director of the Musée Napoléon—his sure taste (and avarice) playing a capital role in forming its collections—and Joséphine made him her own artistic adviser. While Bonaparte was away, she purchased the château of Malmaison, where her architects would create suitable salons, an art gallery, a music room and theater for the essential concerts and performances, and a landscape garden with an immense conservatory to gratify her passion for horticulture.

After Bonaparte's return, the Directoire was overturned in an audacious coup d'état, and on November 9, 1799, Bonaparte was made first consul, with the Tuileries Palace their official residence. This inaugurated the brilliant Consulate regime (1800–1804), marked by Bonaparte's sheer creative energy and sweeping reforms, an achievement that Goethe compared to writing poetry. Thus Napoléon Bonaparte, the paradigmatic captain of modern times, also proved himself to be an administrator of the highest order. He had become so valuable to the nation that a new title had to be devised, so on May 18, 1804, Bonaparte ceased to be first consul and became Napoléon I, making Joséphine an empress.[2] During the glittering ceremony at Notre Dame on December 2, in which Napoléon became emperor of the French, he placed an imperial crown upon Joséphine's brow in the supreme moment of her astonishing career.

The Empire could be sustained, however, only by Napoléon's victories over France's enemies, who repeatedly formed mighty coalitions against him. So one way he sought to consolidate his position was by conferring kingdoms and/or titles upon his family, uniting some with royal or princely houses. Pauline became Princess Borghese, living amid the fabled collections of the Villa Borghese in Rome.[3] Jérôme's wife was Princess Catherine of the important duchy of Wurtemberg, Joseph later sat on the Spanish throne, and Louis was made king of Holland.

Especially favored were Joséphine's children, whom Napoléon adopted. Prince Eugène, Viceroy of Italy and an outstanding officer and art connoisseur,[4] married a Wittelsbach princess reared in the Residenz in Munich. Hortense, consort of Louis Bonaparte, became Queen of Holland. A painter, draftswoman, composer, and collector, Hortense also followed her mother's example, heeding the advice of her mentor, Mme Campan, who wrote to her former pupil, "Already you are justly renowned as a Princess friendly to the arts... made to judge and appreciate them. Be very attentive to artists... give [them] work. The power of this class is immense. It forms the renown of Queens, it uses marble... and the brush for... centuries yet to come."[5]

Now Joséphine became the principal ornament of Europe's leading court, arbiter of protocol, attraction and inspiration for the finest talent, and France's first female sovereign-collector on such a grand scale.[6] The Consular and Empire styles that now governed the arts were born of the classical ideal deeply imbedded in the French racial memory. The decorative vocabulary of the Consulate period had already been codified in the archaeological style of Louis XVI and Marie-Antoinette, a culmination of the Neoclassical taste that began to sweep over Europe around 1765. It followed the rediscovery of antiquity in excavations at Herculaneum (1719) and Pompeii (1750), augmented by publications such as archaeologist and architect Canaletto Piranesi's *Diverse maniere d'adornare cammini* (1769), featuring designs after Etruscan, Greek, and Roman styles—an aesthetic to which Joséphine always remained attached.

Although the Graeco-Roman lexis of Marie-Antoinette's delicate Neoclassical interiors of the 1780s still informed those invented for Joséphine and imperial circles, Empire reinterpretations of the ancient world were simpler, bolder, more dramatic, ponderous, formal, and assertive. The Empire style was especially manifest in interiors teeming with such symbols as laurel wreaths, triumphal arches, and winged victories and was devised by the pair of architects who had created Joséphine's decor at Malmaison and knew classical Italian models firsthand: Charles Percier (1764–1838) and Pierre-François-Léonard Fontaine (1762–1853).[7] Certain aspects retain the seductive charm of Hellenistic art, but they drew their principal inspiration from the decorative richness of the Romans.

Joséphine's proclivity for the arts has already been noted in my biography, *Joséphine: Napoléon's Incomparable Empress* (2002). In his introduction to that book, Bernard Chevallier announces the conception of this volume, "to provide...an essential work that explores the various artistic passions of one of the most extraordinary women in history." With this goal in mind, I invited outstanding international specialists and scholars to contribute their own expertise and to examine this vital aspect of Joséphine's captivating personality along with me.

Joséphine's aesthetic is revealed here through the environment in which she lived and the artists who owed their very careers to her largesse. Her rooms and gallery at Malmaison, where experts and critics gathered, displayed such an important collection of old masters and the modern school that it echoed the museum itself (see chapter 1).[8] Her sculpture was the most significant group by Antonio Canova to that moment and was augmented by works of the best French sculptors (see chapter 2). Joséphine's rooms in the Tuileries Palace and imperial châteaux were ornamented in the dynamic new style appropriate to heroes (see chapter 3). Her gardens and conservatory were recognized throughout Europe for their extraordinary specimens (see chapter 4), recorded by the immortal botanical painter Pierre-Joseph Redouté, as discussed here by Peter Mitchell (chapter 5). Her furniture by the Jacob Frères, presented by John D. Ward (chapter 6), was of regimented elegance and uncompromising geometry as foil for the architecture. Her table was set with magnificent porcelain, as described by Bernard Chevallier (chapter 7), much of it from Sèvres, as recounted by Tamara Préaud (chapter 8), and was highlighted by exquisite silver-gilt centerpieces featuring goddesses, swans, and garlands by renowned silversmiths, discussed here by Christopher Hartop (chapter 9). Joséphine's enthralling costumes, described by Kimberly Chrisman-Campbell (chapter 10), complemented by her dazzling jewelry collection rich in precious gems and antique cameos, presented here by Diana Scarisbrick (chapter 11), were imitated by Europe's most fashionable women. Theater and music were an indispensable part of Joséphine's life, and her staunch support for Gaspare Spontini made his *La Vestale* the operatic symbol of a decade, as revealed by David Gilbert (chapter 12).

Eugène Delacroix maintained that the life of Napoléon was the event of the century for the arts, and it is unquestionably true that the emperor's towering figure was the motivating force behind the artistic manifestations of the Empire. And yet there was Joséphine, with her love for the arts, her shining intelligence, her sure aesthetic instincts, her warm, personal relationships with the artists. It was she who recognized, befriended, introduced, encouraged, and patronized so many of the foremost personalities who conceived, crafted, and expressed with irrefutable distinction this last great French historical style.

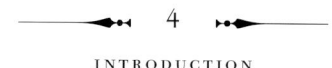

Notes

1. Mme Recamier engaged Louis Berthault in 1798 to design her Directoire bedroom with a bed featuring swan motifs (see chapter 6).
2. There had been numerous assassination attempts, so the senate proclaimed the Empire to be hereditary. Joséphine did not welcome this, as she was unable to produce a child by Napoléon, and, tragically, he was forced to divorce her for state reasons at the end of 1809.
3. Pauline's reclining image by Canova is among the most admired and was undoubtedly the model for Ingres' famous painting, *The Grand Odalesque*, commissioned by Pauline's sister, Caroline Bonaparte Murat.
4. Later, in exile, he formed one of the finest collections in Munich.
5. Mme Campan, letter to Hortense, Paris, January 23, 1809. Archives Nationales, 400 AP 31.
6. Alain Pougetoux, *La Collection de Peintures de l'Imperatrice Joséphine* (Paris, 2003), 42.
7. Fontaine said they owed their position to Joséphine. See Pierre-Françoise-Léonard Fontaine, *Journal 1799–1853*, vol. 1, 72. Malmaison interiors are usually said to be in the Consular style, but Bernard Chevallier (see chapter 7) recognizes two distinctive periods: the first, so-called Consulate, which is a prolongation of the 1780s manner, and the second, called Empire, which began around 1808. No style, of course, corresponds exactly to the dates of the period that gives it its name, for the elements of one style inevitably blend into the next.
8. Pougetoux, *La Collection de Peintures*, 65.

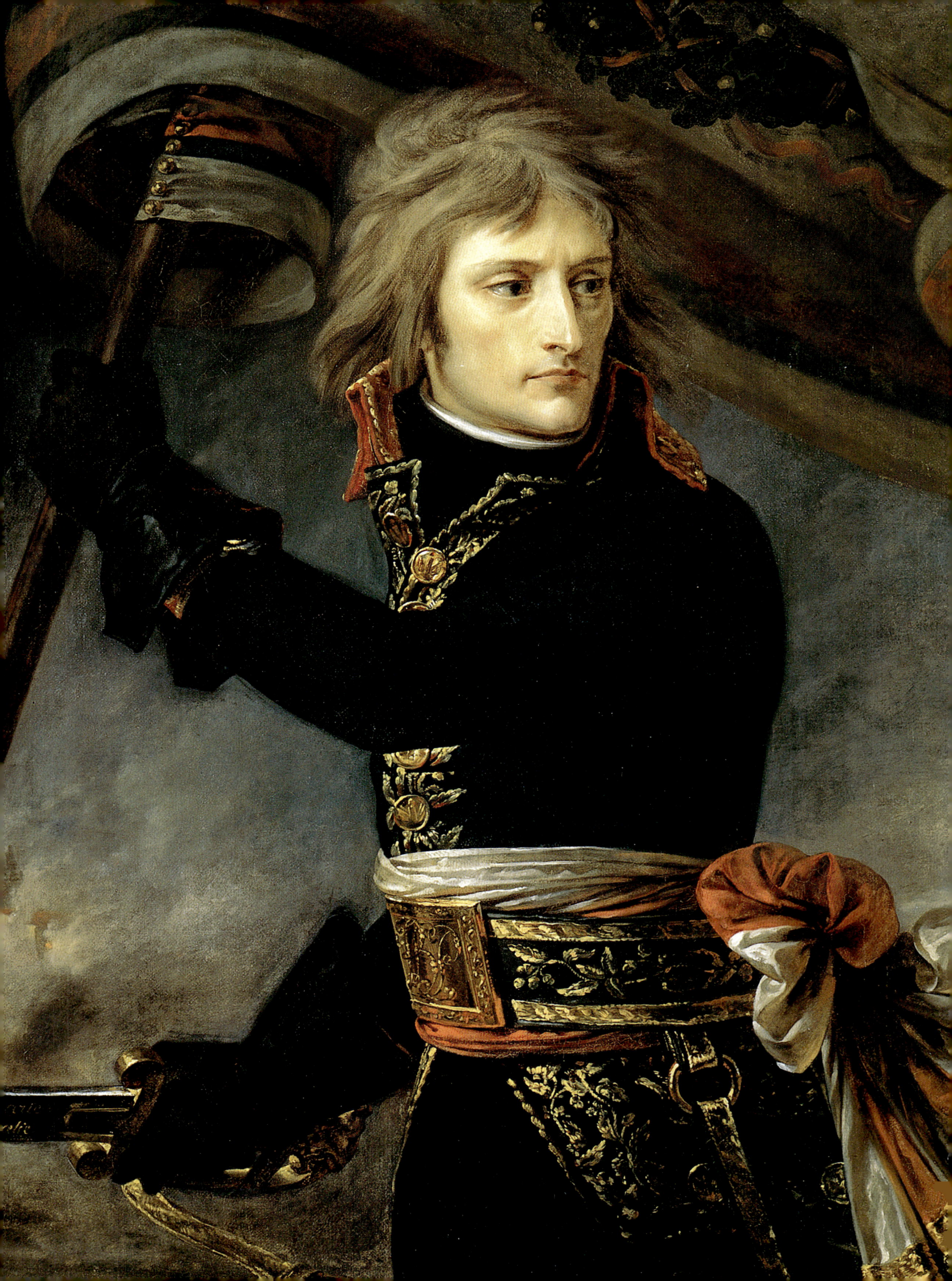

CHAPTER 1

ELEANOR P. DELORME

The Courtly, Heroic, and Romantic: Joséphine's Patronage of Painting

JOSÉPHINE'S PASSION FOR COLLECTING was perfectly aligned with the cultural and political climate of the Empire period. Her official residence, the Tuileries Palace, lay virtually at the doorstep of the Musée Napoléon (now the Musée du Louvre),[1] home to the greatest art collection ever assembled under one roof. The director was Joséphine's longtime friend Baron Dominique-Vivant Denon (1747–1825),[2] who supervised the entire beaux-arts complex. Napoléon Bonaparte and Denon shared a vision for the museum: that the French populace and international visitors have access to art in a worthy setting and learn history through the arts. No less significant was the unparalleled opportunity for artists to study world art, and Denon justifiably boasted that he could teach a course in art history without ever leaving the museum.

Denon was so driven by his quest for great art for his beloved museum that, although no longer young, he followed Napoléon's armies into Italy, Germany, Poland, Spain, and Austria in the face of grave danger to this end. Although the spoils were earmarked for the museum, in October 1806 General Lagrange, an officer in Napoléon's Egyptian and Prussian campaigns, sent masterpieces to Joséphine from the Prussian state of Hesse-Cassell. So, although Denon was one of Joséphine's principal advisers, an amicable rivalry sometimes existed between them.

The proximity of the museum allowed Joséphine to see the latest acquisitions as they arrived. On July 15, 1798, following Bonaparte's series of spectacular victories in Italy, a cortège bearing Italian treasures traversed the Champ de Mars to the museum, attended by a two-day celebration. Joséphine was especially attracted to the Dutch and Flemish schools, an interest spawned by the addition of a painting by Gerrit Dou (1613–1675), titled *Woman with Dropsy*, former gem of the royal collection in Turin and greatly admired by Napoléon. When traveling, she sought works by northern painters, acquiring as early as February 1797 a painting by the Flemish artist Adam Frans van der Meulen (1631/32–1690). She especially liked Paulus Potter (1625–1654), a taste stimulated no doubt by the Dutch artist's widely celebrated canvas *The Bull*,[3] then a major attraction at the museum. In 1806 she acquired two of Potter's strangest paintings, his earthy *La Vache qui pisse* (The Pissing Cow) and the eccentric *Vengeance of the Animals*.

In late July 1812 Joséphine traveled to Milan to be with her daughter-in-law and grandchildren while her son, Eugène, was with the Grande Armée in Russia. In Milan she visited the Brera Museum, recording her impression of frescoes by Bernardino Luini (1481–1532) in a letter to Eugène. What really caught Joséphine's eye, however, was a painting by David Teniers (1610–1690). She had written to Eugène on January 13, 1812, about a Teniers she was considering, "Since I know that you are a connoisseur of good painting, I want to mention an admirable Teniers which Constantin says is as beautiful as his [Teniers'] *Arquebusiers* that you saw in my gallery. . . . It was Mme de Souza who proposed it and who knows the owner."[4]

Joséphine also prized the work of living artists, regularly attending the important Salons at the Musée Napoléon and designating paintings she wanted to buy. Her commanding position, genuine interest in art, and patronage offered substantial encouragement to the artists, and her habitual presence at these Salons promoted attendance. Joséphine's relationship with young, talented members of the art world was warm and personal; she gave them commissions, visited their studios, and took a keen interest in their careers. She bought so many contemporary paintings that of the approximately 450 paintings at Malmaison one-third were modern. Joséphine was also the most prestigious and perhaps first collector of paintings in the avant-garde *genre chevaleresque*, or Troubadour style—small-scale works usually glorifying French history and produced with a precise, meticulous finish in the manner of the seventeenth-century Dutch masters she particularly admired.

Many previous rulers had distanced themselves from artists, relaying commissions to them through intermediaries, but this was not Joséphine's style. She included a number of painters in her entourage, among them Pierre-Paul Prud'hon (1758–1823), Jean-Baptiste Isabey (1767–1855), Baron François Gérard (1770–1837), and Antoine-Jean Gros (1771–1835). The imperial couple's interest was reflected in the improved fortunes of many artists, who now commanded higher prices. Jacques-Louis David (1748–1825) asked 100,000 francs for his painting of the coronation ceremony, while a Quentin Matsys (1465/66–1530) sold for only 1,800, and a Philippe de Champaigne (1602–1674) realized a mere 3,780.[5] Gérard, one of Joséphine's favorite portraitists, demanded 6,000 francs for a full-length likeness. Many painters prospered under the Empire and entertained extravagantly. Their burgeoning social and financial status brought legitimate social acceptance, and Joséphine patronized several even before they became well known.

JOSEPH BOZE

During the summer of 1787, Joséphine and her daughter, Hortense, then four years old, were living with Mme Renaudin, Joséphine's aunt, and the marquis de Beauharnais at Fontainebleau. At this time Joséphine paid 288 livres to the pastelist Joseph Boze (1744–1826) for portraits (presumably lost) of herself and Hortense, probably intended as gifts for Joséphine's parents the following year, when she and Hortense would visit them in Martinique.

Boze was not entirely unknown at this time, having exhibited pastels and miniatures in 1782 at the Salon de la Correspondence. Three years before Joséphine's commission he had painted a ravishing portrait of Mme Campan {FIGURE 1}, Marie-Antoinette's first lady-in-waiting. After the queen's tragic death in October 1793, Mme Campan opened a school for privileged pupils at Saint-Germain, which Hortense entered in the fall of 1795, becoming Mme Campan's most highly favored and gifted student. Not only did Mme Campan educate the younger generation, but she also became Joséphine's invaluable consultant in court protocol. Mme Campan's niece Adèle Auguié was Hortense's best friend.

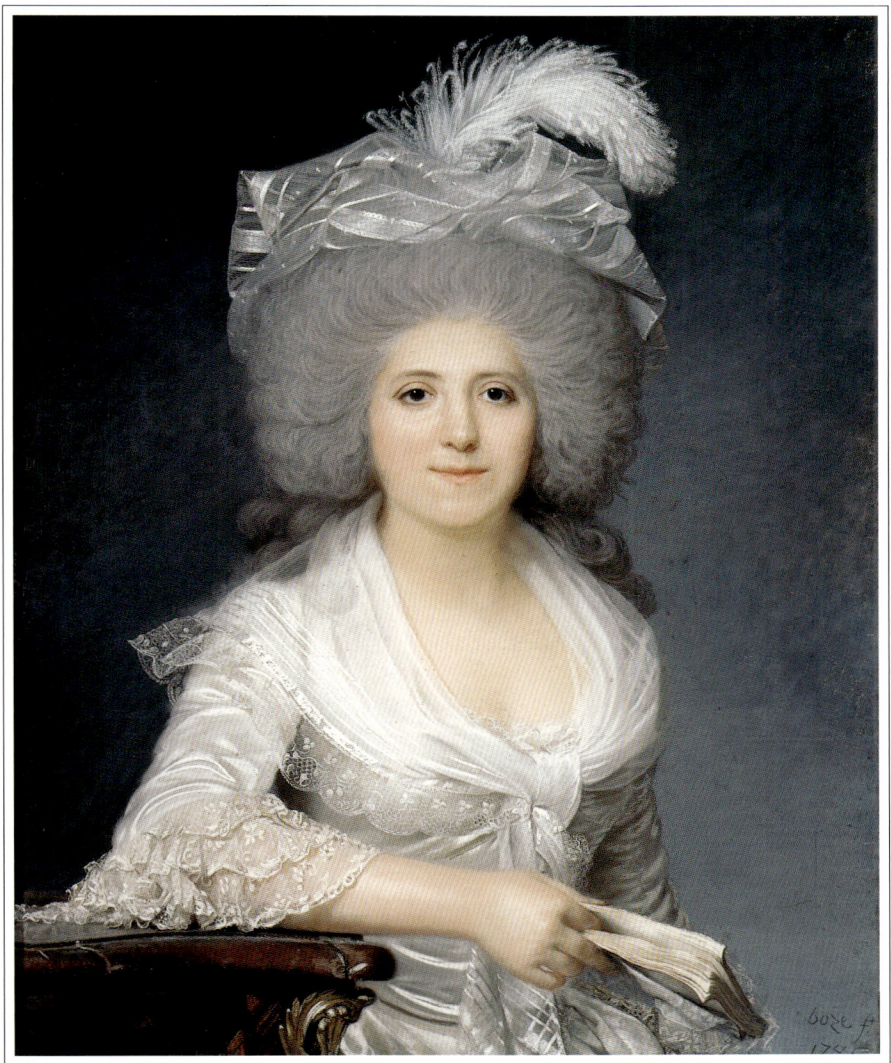

FIGURE 1.

Joseph Boze (French, 1744–1826),
Madame Campan, ca. 1784.
Pastel, 87 × 74 cm (34¼ × 29⅛ in.).
Versailles, Musée national des Châteaux
de Versailles et de Trianon.

• • •

Mme Campan intended that her school cultivate distinguished, well-mannered, articulate young women who could lend the proper tone to French society as well as all of Europe. She was conspicuously successful in this enterprise, made difficult by the fact that some students came from widely diverse economic and social milieus, with obvious lacunae in their educational backgrounds. Taught by an outstanding faculty, the young women were tutored in painting, drawing, music, religion, literature, languages, ancient and modern history, grammar, and Greek mythology — a classical education in the broadest sense.

Louis-Léopold Boilly

Having exhibited at the Salons since 1791, Louis-Léopold Boilly (1761–1845) was known to Joséphine as early as 1793, when she was still Mme de Beauharnais. In 1794, during the Terror, he sketched her just before her incarceration.

At the Salon of 1798, two years after Josephine's marriage to Napoléon, Boilly achieved considerable success with his *Reunion of Artists in Isabey's Studio* {FIGURE 2}. Most of the people portrayed belonged to Joséphine's coterie and were either prominent in the arts or friends of her brother-in-law Lucien Bonaparte, minister of the interior in 1800. They include the composer Etiènne Nicolas Méhul (1763–1817), whose "Le Chant du départ" (Departure Song) became the most famous military hymn of the Empire (see chapter 11); Prud'hon, Joséphine's favorite artist; Martin Drolling (1752–1817), the genre painter who shared Joséphine's and Boilly's taste for Dutch art; Isabey, Joséphine's indispensable friend and court artist, who designed gardens, fêtes, costumes, and more; François Gérard, her portraitist; Jacques-François Swebach (1769–1823), whose paintings adorned her porcelain vases; Horace Vernet (1789–1863), renowned battle painter; Charles Percier and Pierre-François-Léonard Fontaine, her architects; Jan Frans van Dael (1764–1840), whose master-

FIGURE 2.

Louis-Léopold Boilly (French, 1761–1845), *Reunion of Artists in Isabey's Studio*, 1798. Oil on canvas, 71.5 × 111 cm (28⅛ × 43¾ in.). Paris, Musée du Louvre.

· · ·

This distinguished assemblage is composed of the leading artists, composers, actors, and other members of the cultural elite, each of whom was or would become associated with Joséphine's own artistic enterprises. Boilly portrays them as erudite members of a salon, engaged in animated discussion. During the Empire, the status of artists was markedly ameliorated, and this is part of Boilly's message.

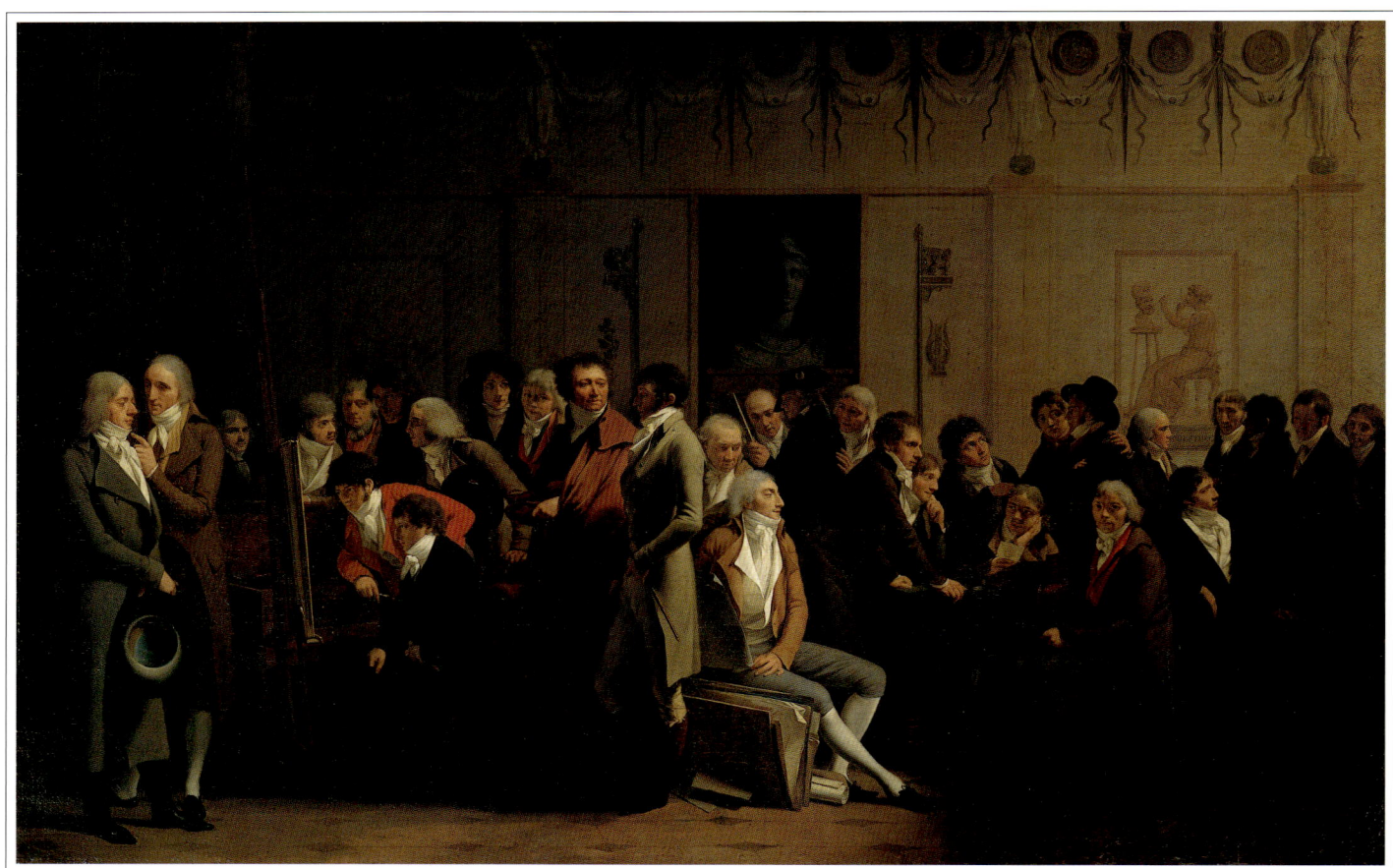

piece, *The Tomb of Julie*, and its pendant Joséphine owned; Pierre-Joseph Redouté (1759–1840), her official flower painter (see chapter 5); legendary tragedian François Talma (1763–1826), member of the Malmaison clique; the illustrious Anne-Louis Girodet-Trioson (1767–1824), whom Joséphine patronized; and, seated cross-legged in the foreground, the famous actor Nicola-Pierre-Baptiste Anselme (1761–1835) of the Théâtre Français—who, it was said, enunciated everything, even the periods and commas.

With the goddess Minerva presiding, Boilly's *Reunion* pays an oblique compliment to the sophisticated group. Percier and Fontaine's decoration is the ne plus ultra of Consular decor, and an elevation of the room is shown in their book *Receuil de décorations interièures*,[5] which marked the birth of the Empire style for interior decoration (see chapter 3).

After painting Napoléon as first consul, Boilly's career flourished, and he became a principal chronicler of Joséphine's age. Like Gabriel de Saint-Aubin (1724–1780) before him, Boilly was an inveterate observer of Paris life: people gathered on the boulevards to watch Savoyards and puppets, viewers at museum Salons, affluent citizens at the

Figure 3.

Louis-Léopold Boilly (French, 1761–1845). *The Grand Salon of 1810, Viewing the David "Crowning of Napoléon,"* 1810. Oil on canvas, 60 × 81 cm (23⅝ × 31⅞ in.). New York, Private collection.

. . .

When David's huge canvas of the coronation was finally unveiled to the public, everyone flocked to see it, for until this moment they had only journal accounts of the splendid event. Boilly's paintings always abound in human interest. At the right, a little girl looks up at her brother, transfixed before the canvas; one group is deep in critical discussion; a young woman in muslin dress (seen from behind) and her male companion study the Salon *livret* (exhibition list). At the far left, a girl with a shawl on her arm, utterly oblivious to her escort, gazes in admiration at the officer in uniform, for the military were society's heroes.

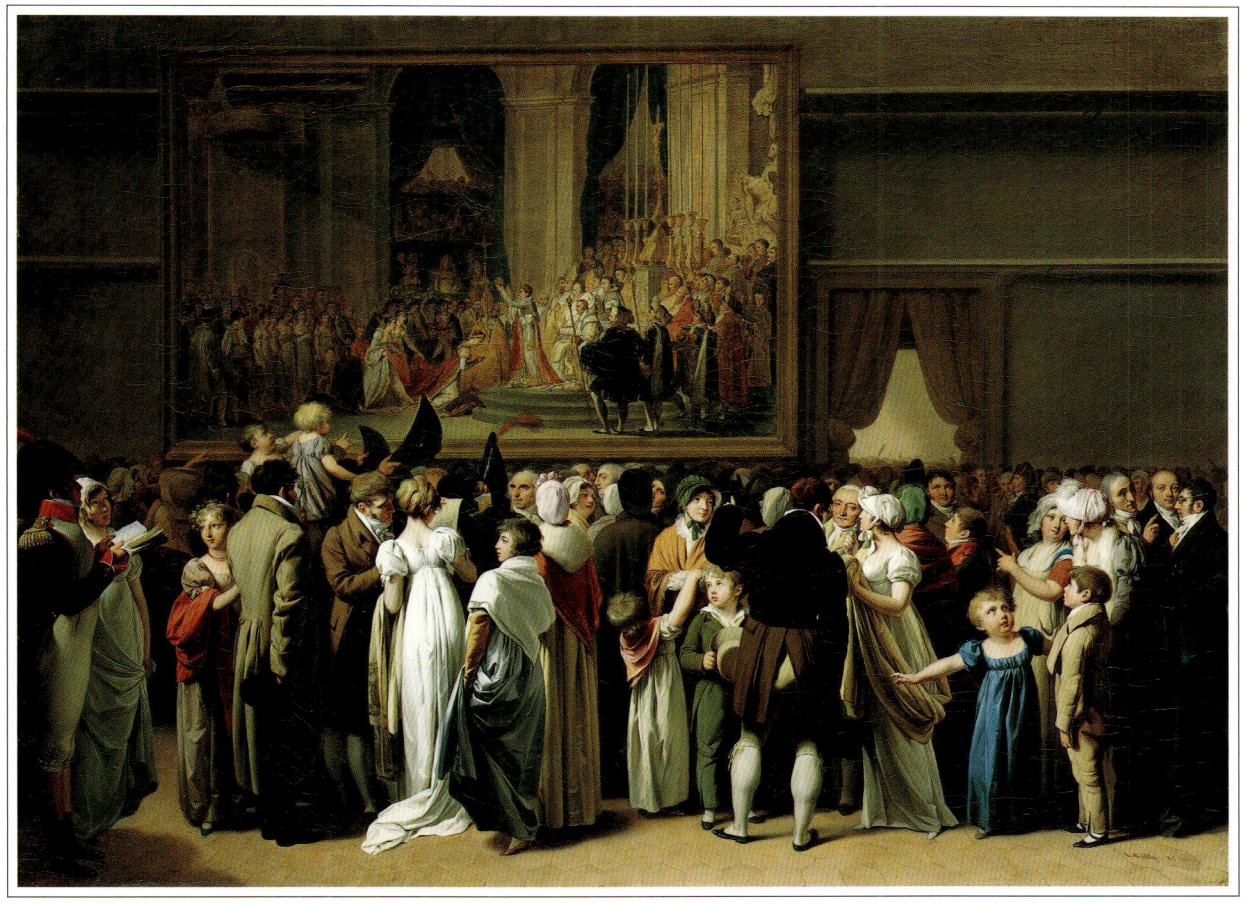

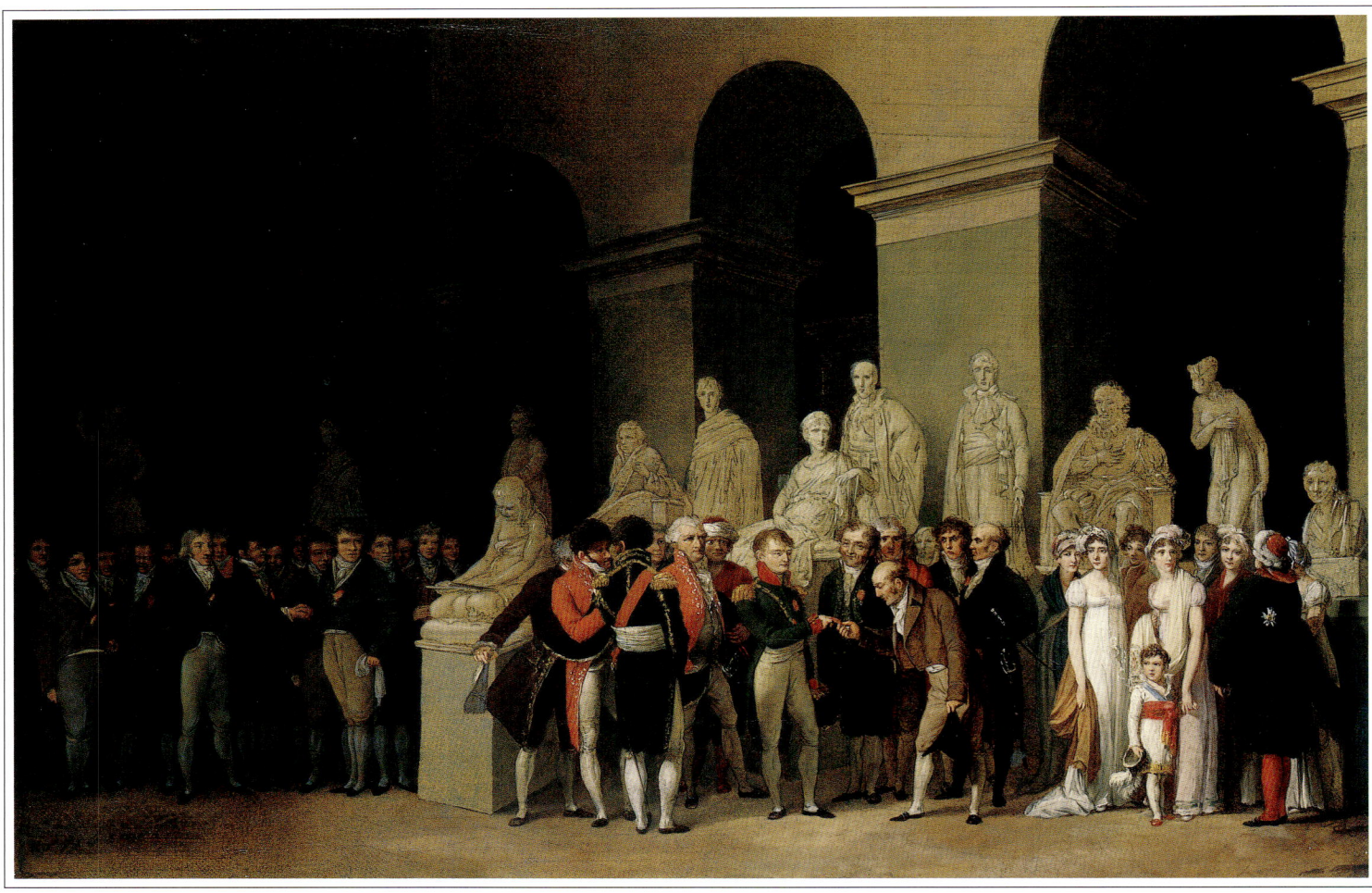

FIGURE 4.

Louis-Léopold Boilly (French, 1761–1845), *Napoléon Decorating the Sculptor Cartellier at the Salon of 1808*, ca. 1808. Oil on canvas, 42 × 61.5 cm (16½ × 24¼ in.). Napoléonmuseum Schloss Arenenberg, Switzerland.

• • •

Boilly's painting portrays an important incident during the famous Salon of 1808, which Napoléon attended with Joséphine and Hortense, shown on the right in white dresses, Hortense holding her son's hand. As Pierre Cartellier (1757–1831) receives his decoration at the hands of the emperor, David (recognizable by his facial malformation) stands between the emperor and the sculptor. Behind them is Cartellier's *Modesty*, a statue Joséphine bought from the sculptor for her gallery. On the wall at the far left is Canova's *Hébé*, which Joséphine also lent to this Salon.

Café Turc, rowdy crowds at free theater performances. Boilly's precise technical skills and mannered use of color recall the seventeenth-century Dutch school. He collected Gabriel Metsu (1629–1667) and Gerard Terborch II (1617–1681), two Northern masters whose work was also represented in Joséphine's gallery.

The Grand Salon of 1810, Viewing the David "Crowning of Napoléon" {FIGURE 3} is quintessential Boilly. The attention of the crowd, which includes the sculptor Jean-Antoine Houdon (1741–1828) and the portraitist Elisabeth Vigée-LeBrun (1754–1842), is riveted on the painting within the painting. Salons were major cultural events, and the museum offered free days to the public. Another fascinating glimpse of the imperial family is Boilly's *Napoléon Decorating the Sculptor Cartellier at the Salon of 1808* {FIGURE 4}. Boilly's painting is one of several depictions of Joséphine's visit to this renowned Salon, where works by some of her protégés (Gros, Prud'hon, and Girodet-Trioson) were highly acclaimed.

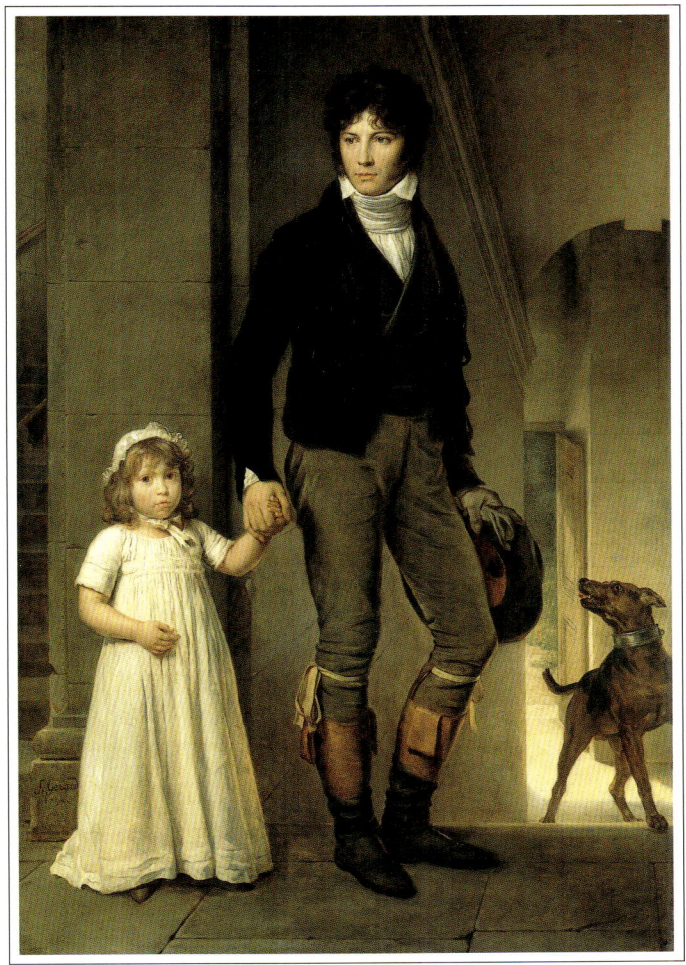

FIGURE 5.

François Gérard (French, 1770–1837),
The Painter Isabey and His Daughter Alexandrine,
ca. 1796.
Oil on canvas, 190 × 130 cm (74⅞ × 51¼ in.).
Paris, Musée du Louvre.

• • •

Gérard's large-format portrait of Jean-Baptiste Isabey was shown at the Salon of 1796 and is among the most sympathetic portraits of any major artistic figure of Joséphine's day. The painter stands at the top of a Louvre staircase, having just left his atelier, holding his daughter's hand. With exceptional talent, lively intelligence, taste, imagination, and the ability to work in many artistic areas, Isabey needed only a touch of genius—as Charles-Otto Zieseniss put it—to make him a great master. Although dressed informally, the painter carries his hat and gloves, the latter accessory symbolizing aristocracy.

JEAN-BAPTISTE ISABEY

It was inevitable that Joséphine and Isabey, another of David's students, should meet. Joséphine encountered Isabey at the salons of her friends Juliette Recamier and the writer Germaine de Staël, as well as in gatherings of other intelligentsia. They also frequently met at Mme Campan's academy, where Isabey was drawing master and Hortense his prize pupil.

In 1795 Isabey was promoting the career of his fellow artist François Gérard, then almost unknown, so Isabey asked Denon to lend his rooms at the Louvre for displaying Gérard's *Belisarius*. Joséphine, always solicitous of struggling artists, went to see the painting. It is a compelling vignette: the future empress of France visiting the atelier of Vivant Denon—soon to become director of the museum—to view the work of two artists destined for artistic stardom.

In appreciation for Isabey's help in selling *Belisarius* (eventually acquired by Prince Eugène), Gérard painted the delightful *The Painter Isabey and His Daughter Alexandrine* (Salon of 1796) {FIGURE 5}. Along with a portrait of the artist Pierre-Narcisse Guérin (1774–1833) by Robert Lefèvre (1755–1830), Gérard's portrait of the young Isabey is one of the most refined images of the Directoire period and the epitome of sartorial elegance.

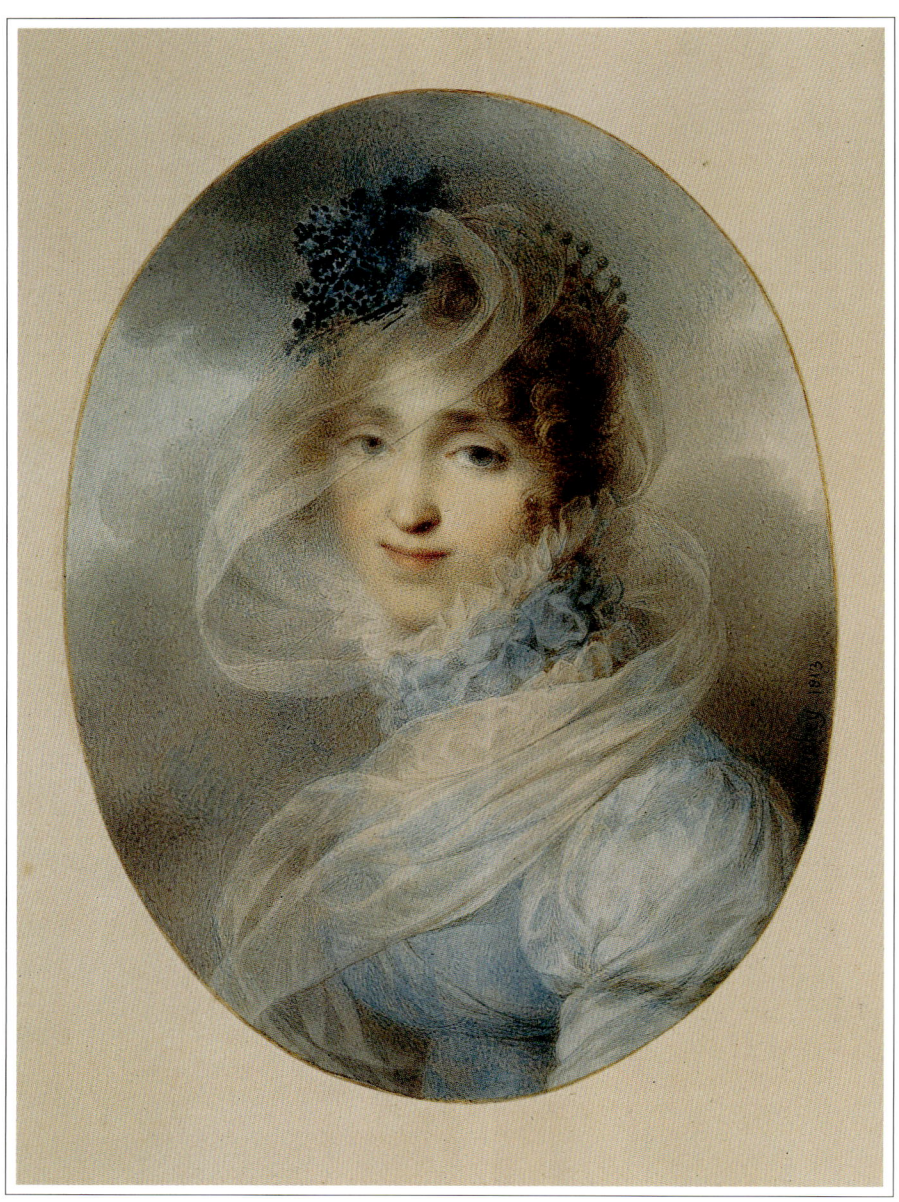

FIGURE 6.

Jean-Baptiste Isabey (French, 1767–1855),
La Reine Hortense, 1813.
Watercolor, 13 × 9.5 cm (5⅛ × 3¾ in.).
Rueil-Malmaison, Musée national des Châteaux
de Malmaison et Bois-Préau.

• • •

Hortense liked this particular watercolor by Isabey so much that she chose it to embellish her personal copy of her "Carnet de romances" (collection of illustrated songs). Hortense's "Romances" were illustrated by Joséphine's painter-friend, Count Turpin de Crissé (1782–1859), who accompanied her on a voyage to Savoy and made sketches of the trip, later conserved in an album. Isabey painted Joséphine, Hortense, and other European celebrities in this romantic manner, which became increasingly popular.

FIGURE 7.

Horace Vernet (French, 1789–1863),
Jean-Baptiste Isabey, 1828.
Oil on canvas, 81 × 64 cm (31⅞ × 25¼ in.).
Paris, Musée du Louvre.

• • •

Isabey in his later years is portrayed by Vernet in a touching manner: an aged man with only a fringe of white hair, stoic jaw, and eyes that reflect suffering, for Isabey lost his son during the war. The mantle with rich fur collar, the snowy white vest recall the finesse of the subject's youth, as Gérard's famous portrait had depicted him at the beginning of his career. Joséphine never ceased to appreciate the wide range of her devoted friend's gifts, his lively imagination, his loyalty, and his sense of the proprieties that contributed immeasurably to the cultural life of the Empire. When the court moved to Saint-Cloud, Isabey happily announced, "Etiquette has arrived!"

Isabey remained close to his pupil Hortense, leaving several portraits of her as the Queen of Holland, including a miniature, *Queen Hortense* {FIGURE 6}. In this watercolor her hair is romantically swathed in filmy material encircling her neck and secured by sprays of myosotis and hortensia.

The versatile Isabey assumed multiple roles. He produced the decor for the Tuileries theater; he designed the costumes for the coronation, illustrated in the magnificent *Livre du Sacre de S. M. l'Empereur Napoléon*; he orchestrated Joséphine's private fêtes; he decorated Sèvres porcelain, like the superb plate for his patroness in 1807 and a table service; he provided thirteen excellent portraits of Napoléon's lieutenants to adorn the huge Sèvres plaque atop the precious *Table des Maréchaux*;[7] and he planned several gardens, including a small formal garden at Épernay for Napoléon when he visited his comrade Jean-Remy Moët, of champagne renown.

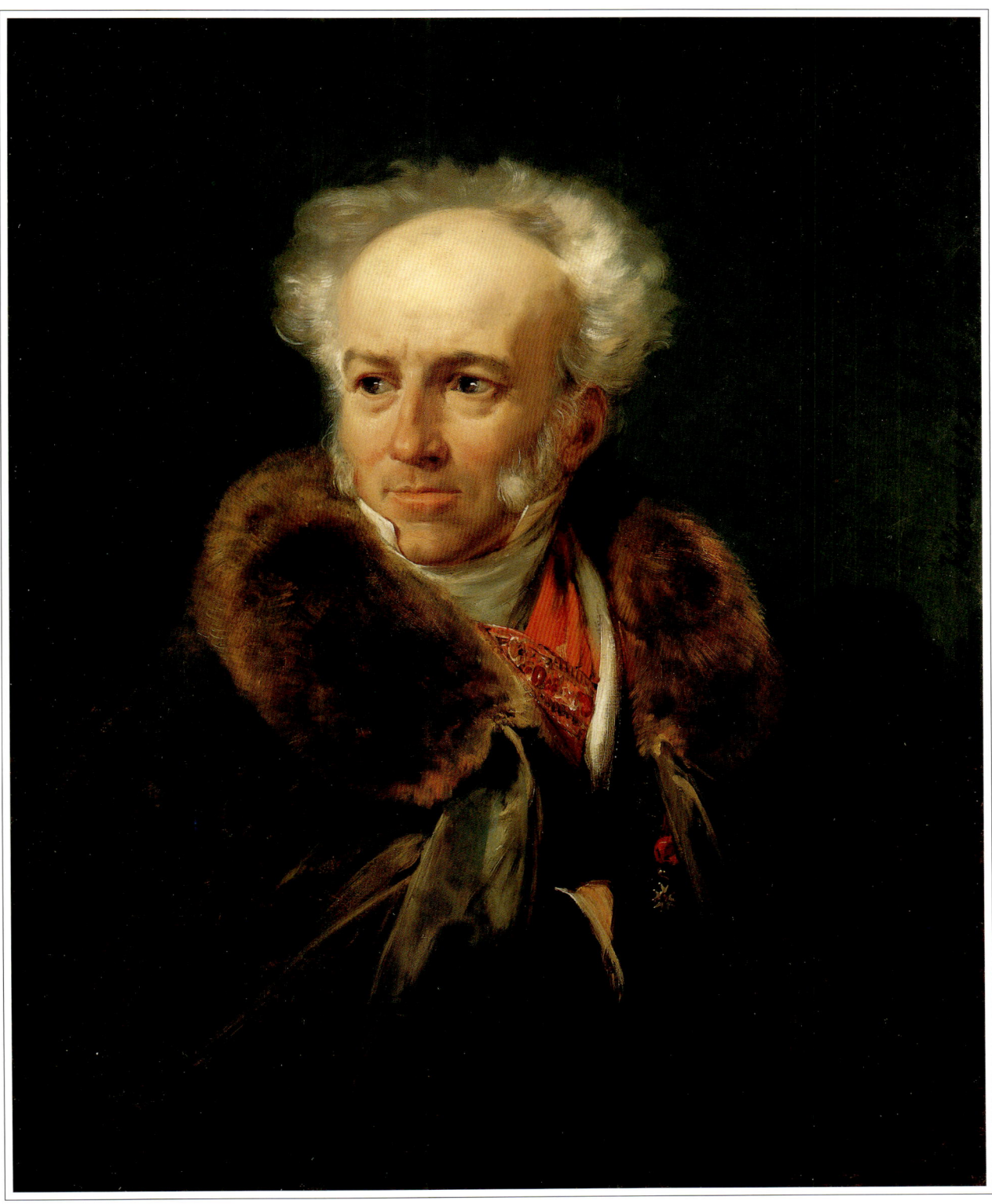

Joséphine's death in May 1814 was a blow to Isabey, who had become her cherished friend. The following year tragedy struck his own family. During the campaign of France, he lost his eldest son, a boy of seventeen, and Vernet's *Jean-Baptiste Isabey* {FIGURE 7} reveals the father's deep anguish. Happier times came at the end of his life when Hortense's son mounted the throne as Napoléon III. Two years before Isabey's death in 1855, that emperor bestowed on the aged artist—who had been so close to both his mother and grandmother—the Commander's Cross of the Legion of Honor, which Isabey himself had designed.

Joséphine's patronage of Antoine-Jean Gros (1771–1835) — generally regarded as the finest of David's pupils — may have begun as early as 1792, for in that year the young Gros apparently painted her portrait (now lost).[8] In any case, they certainly met in Italy at the end of 1796 during the first Italian campaign, when Joséphine departed Milan for other parts of the peninsula. In late December she made a quick trip to Genoa, where Gros happened to be staying.[9]

As one of David's favorite students, Gros had obtained a passport through his teacher to study at the French Academy in Rome. While there in 1793, at the height of revolutionary fervor, Gros encountered a demonstration so fierce that many terrified French students fled for their lives. Gros escaped to Genoa, where he befriended another student who had fled Rome — Anne-Louis Girodet-Trioson (1767–1824). It was there that Girodet-Trioson was most likely introduced to Joséphine, for he was known to the Swiss banker M. Meuricoffre, a friend of Joséphine's.

Gros could not have chosen a better place to be at that moment than this port city with its French colony of bankers, rich merchants, shipping magnates, soldiers, and French diplomats, all eager for portraits of themselves and their families. Gros' talent was soon discovered, and he quickly established an enviable reputation, acquiring many patrons among the leading personages of the day. All of them revolved around Mme Bonaparte, whose husband's rank and military prowess had thrust her into social and political preeminence.

At Mme Meuricoffre's costume ball Gros created a stir with his flamboyant costume. Mme Berthier introduced him to Mme Faipoult, who presented him to Joséphine. Délacroix called Joséphine Gros' "fairy godmother," for she whisked him straight to the center of power in Milan.

The French community in Genoa provided Gros some of his most attractive models, such as Mme Pasteur, the beautiful wife of a French banker. In her portrait {FIGURE 8}, the sitter's sparkling eyes are highlighted by curls falling over her forehead. Her dark hair is held by a gold arrow that picks up the glint of gilt tassels attached to her belt and gold chains around her neck. Gros conducts a symphony in brown, black, white, and gold — one of his richest coloristic achievements despite its subtlety. *Madame Pasteur* loses none of its artistic value by being also a noteworthy piece of decoration.

In André Barret's view, Gros owed his new-found elegance — refinement in work as well as dress — to moving in Joséphine's orbit.[10] Her promotion of Gros proved one of her most impressive cultural coups, opening new doors for the artist in Milan, a city that was even more exciting than Genoa. This was the Milan of Stendhal and Denon, who was now charged by the Directoire government with selecting works of art bound for Paris, and in 1797 Gros himself joined this commission.

Gros was also privileged to accompany Denon to the Brera Museum, where Denon, an excellent engraver, discoursed on the relative merits and styles of the Italian painters Mantegna,

FIGURE 8.

Antoine-Jean Gros (French, 1771–1835),
Madame Pasteur, 1796.
Oil on canvas, 86 × 67 cm (33⅞ × 26⅜ in.).
Paris, Musée du Louvre.

• • •

Gros, who became known for his military paintings, could easily have had a successful career as a portraitist. This tantalizingly appealing image of a young woman in Joséphine's coterie derives its charm, in large part, from the coquettish yet enigmatic expression of the lovely sitter and the textural contrasts: the soft white dress, the gleaming arrows and brooch, the dark military sash wrapped around her shoulders and tied at the waist, and the luxuriant cascade of reddish brown hair tumbling over her left hand.

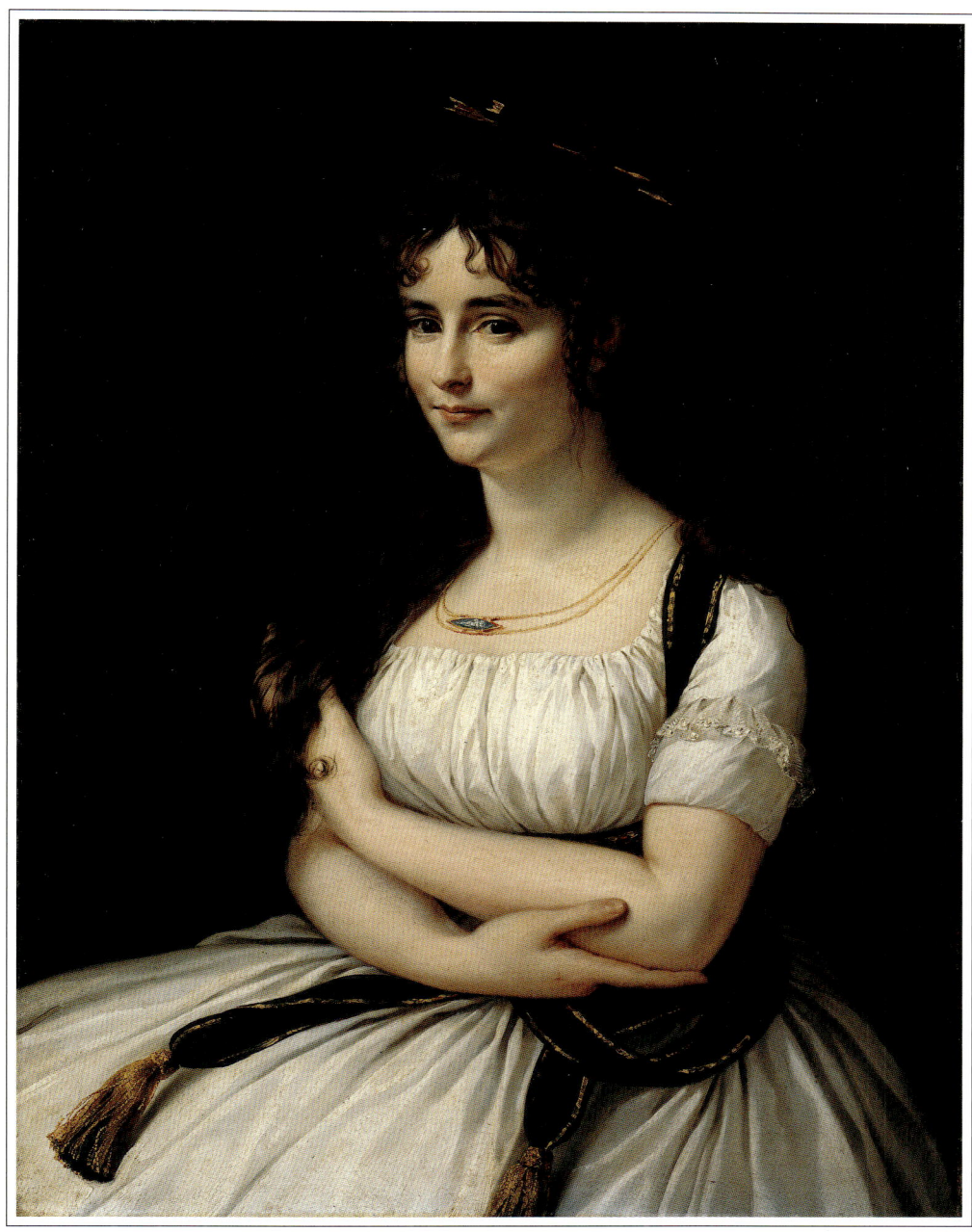

Bellini, Raphael, Tintoretto, and Veronese. During these idyllic days under Denon's tutelage, Gros reveled in the fashionable world of Milan over which his benefactress reigned. The sparkling society that gravitated to Joséphine was intoxicating enough, but when she presented him to General Bonaparte, the artist's wildest dreams came true. Although he knew the fabled general was only two years his senior, Gros must have nonetheless been shocked by Bonaparte's youthful appearance. Following his extraordinary military victories in the fall of 1796, Bonaparte had just won a decisive battle against the Austrians at Arcole on November 17,[11] a coup being toasted at Milan's salons and gathering places.

It was this pivotal moment at Arcole that Joséphine commissioned Gros to immortalize on canvas. But this presented a major problem: the general was always too preoccupied and impatient to pose, so Joséphine devised an ingenious solution. She asked the artist to arrive during breakfast, and — according to Gros' letter to his mother (confirmed by

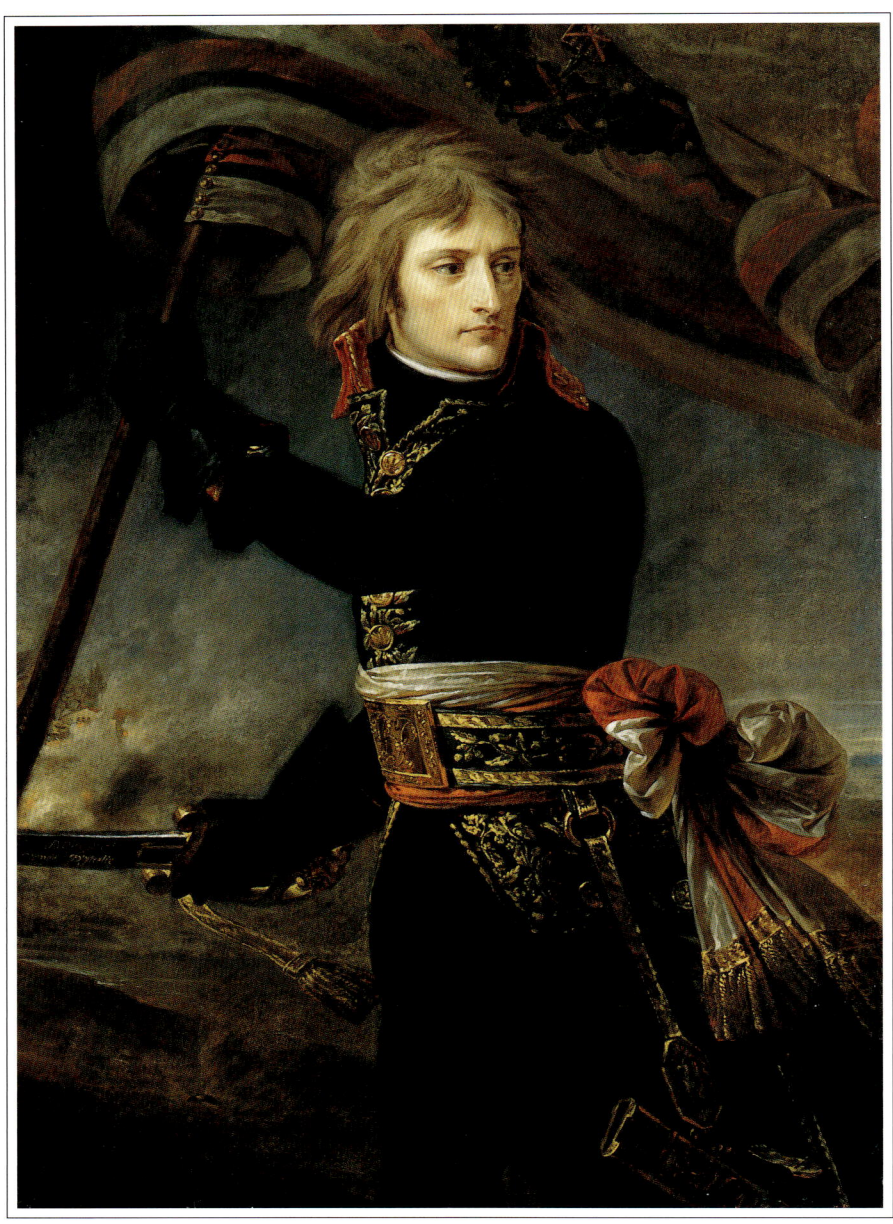

FIGURE 9.

Antoine-Jean Gros (French, 1771–1835), *General Bonaparte at the Bridge of Arcole, November 17, 1796*, ca. 1796. Oil on canvas, 130 × 94 cm (51 1/8 × 37 in.). Versailles, Musée national des Châteaux de Versailles et de Trianon.

• • •

This immortal image of Bonaparte came about through Joséphine's persistence, and it established Gros' reputation. The forward thrust of the tense, youthful figure, bearing a flag in one hand and a sword in the other, is accentuated by the sharp wedge created by the junction of flag and sword at the far left. The general, however, looks back, as if to encourage his troops to follow. The head is an excellent piece of portraiture, set off by the standing collar, dark uniform, and broad, gilt-laden belt and fringed sash. The uniform, which Gros delineates with such care in his military portraits, lends dash and vigor to this colorful but tragic age.

Bonaparte's aide-de-camp, Antoine Lavalette), Joséphine kept her husband seated on her knees long enough for Gros to work.[12] Several sessions were required, but the result was so arresting that *General Bonaparte at the Bridge of Arcole, November 17, 1796* {FIGURE 9} has become an integral part of Napoleonic iconography.

Arcole is surprising for its time. Gros' master, David, had painted figures from Roman history in his *Horatii* in a tightly structured, insistently geometric Neoclassical mode, as finely chiseled as marble statues, as heartless as automata. Gros departs from David's frigid manner to capture the flesh-and-blood hero of modern history at a momentous point in his meteoric career. In Delacroix's words, it is "animated by the sentiments of a young artist in the actual presence of the astonishing man whose first steps had just shaken the world."[13]

In this most "Beethovian" of Bonaparte's portraits,[14] Gros portrays the twenty-seven-year-old general charging across the bridge in the face of murderous Austrian fire, a tricolor standard in his hand. With fresh concepts, the sheer bravura of rich, lively brushwork, and ardent lyricism, Gros achieves "la vivante image de l'héroisme" (the living image of heroism), in Delacroix's opinion.[15]

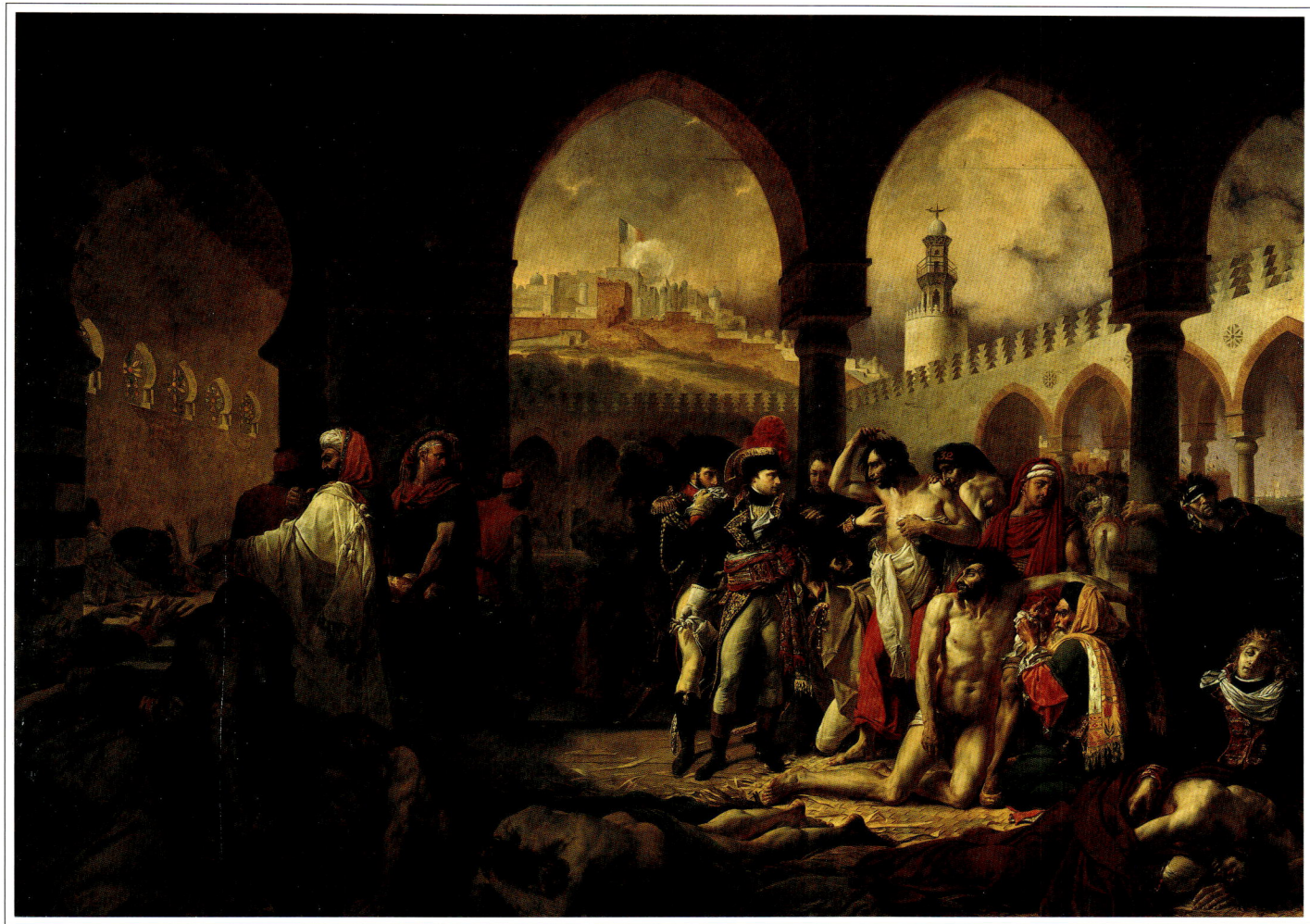

FIGURE 10.

Antoine-Jean Gros (French, 1771–1835),
*Napoléon Bonaparte Visiting the Victims
of the Plague at Jaffa, March 11, 1799*, 1804.
Oil on canvas, 523 × 715 cm (204 × 278⅞ in.).
Paris, Musée du Louvre.

· · ·

This celebrated painting, hailed as a triumph at the Salon of 1804, principally appealed to the public because of its subject matter—an incident during the Egyptian campaign. The critic Étienne Delécluze considered it Gros' masterpiece, and others also acclaimed it for the artist's rich and varied use of color, no doubt informed by his lengthy stay in Italy, where he studied Rubens and the sixteenth-century colorists. Gros also experienced military life, which prepared him to execute details of uniforms with meticulous exactitude and to realistically interpret the Empire's battles, as he did in *The Battle of Aboukir*, *Napoléon Visiting the Battlefield of Eylau*, *The Capture of Madrid*, and *The Battle of the Pyramids*.

So far-reaching were his innovations that Gros was soon considered the leader of his generation, and *Arcole* is said to have "single-handedly . . . reoriented the direction of French painting."[16] Gros' portrait has become a symbol for the entire epoch and the best-known image of the general of the Army of Italy. Lavalette thought it an amazing likeness, although Bonaparte's secretary avowed that no artist, however able, could truly capture the "mobility" of that face, the "expression now tender, now stern, now terrible, at times even caressing."[17] *Arcole* manifests the *fougue* (fire and passion) to which artists of Gros' generation aspired and that would find its ultimate expression in the great Romantic rebels of the next generation—Théodore Géricault (1791–1824) and Délacroix, whose immeasurable debt to Gros they freely acknowledged.

Although disappointed at not being invited to accompany Bonaparte to Egypt in 1798, Gros was asked to depict an incident of the expedition, another commission that came through Joséphine. With directives from Denon's team of draftsmen, Gros finished *Napoléon Bonaparte Visiting the Victims of the Plague at Jaffa, March 11, 1799* (Salon of 1804) {FIGURE 10}. The painting marked another milestone in his career, for it also became a central part of the Napoleonic legend, representing a new approach to history painting and confirming Gros as a pioneer of the Romantic movement.

The subject is an incident that occurred March 11, 1799, after the bubonic plague broke out in Jaffa and many French soldiers fell ill. Bonaparte—who often recklessly exposed himself to danger in battle—visited the victims to encourage them, actually placing his finger on the lesion of a soldier infected with the highly contagious disease. The painting transforms the horror of reality into an image emphasizing the nobility and sangfroid of the young commander in chief, replicating the traditional gesture of French kings who would demonstrate the power of their royal compassion by purportedly healing the sick with "the royal touch."

Here again Gros diverges from the precepts of his teacher and inaugurates a concept novel for its time. David disposed his friezelike figures in the *Horatii* across the picture plane, on a shallow stage, against a closed backdrop of Doric columns (the masculine order). But Gros presents his hero against a deep mise-en-scène with Moorish arches, invoking at once Near Eastern exoticism and the cultural triumph of the daring campaign that unveiled the East to European eyes. The figures are arranged like spokes of a wheel, with the commander in chief at the hub, and the lively, impassioned brushwork prefigures Délacroix's dynamic hand.

At the Salon of 1804 the *Jaffa* created a sensation, with Vivant pronouncing it a masterpiece. Joseph Fouché, prefect of police, famously remarked that it was Bonaparte's most beautiful gesture, and Gros' fellow students were so excited that they hung a huge laurel wreath above it. A banquet was given in Gros' honor, presided over by his proud teacher, Jacques-Louis David.

When the Salon of 1808 opened on October 14, Denon wrote to Marshal Duroc, grand marshal of the Tuileries Palace, that "this year it will be the most impressive that has ever been.... By [the artists'] great talents, everyone will place His Majesty's reign in the front rank in the arts, as it is in warfare, science, and literature" {see FIGURE 4}.[18] It proved to be one of the happiest moments of Gros' life. The emperor awarded David the Legion of Honor; made Girodet-Trioson, Vernet, and Prud'hon chevaliers; and intentionally passed Gros several times, ignoring him. Then, apparently ready to leave, Napoléon quickly turned to Gros and presented his own decoration, the medal of the Legion of Honor, to the startled artist.

Gros was profoundly affected by Joséphine's death, and his attachment outlived her; each time he passed through the little town of Rueil-Malmaison where she was buried, he placed flowers at the tomb of his "good fairy." After Joséphine's death, and then Napoléon's exile in 1815, Gros was showered with commissions from the restored monarchy, but his inspiration had deserted him. He received well-intended but unwise advice from David, then in exile in Brussels. His teacher counseled him to abandon contemporary history in favor of subjects from Plutarch. Gros unfortunately complied, producing one dreary canvas after another. By 1835 he was utterly discouraged and had lost the will to paint, so he donned the old uniform he had worn at Joséphine's court and drowned himself in the Seine.

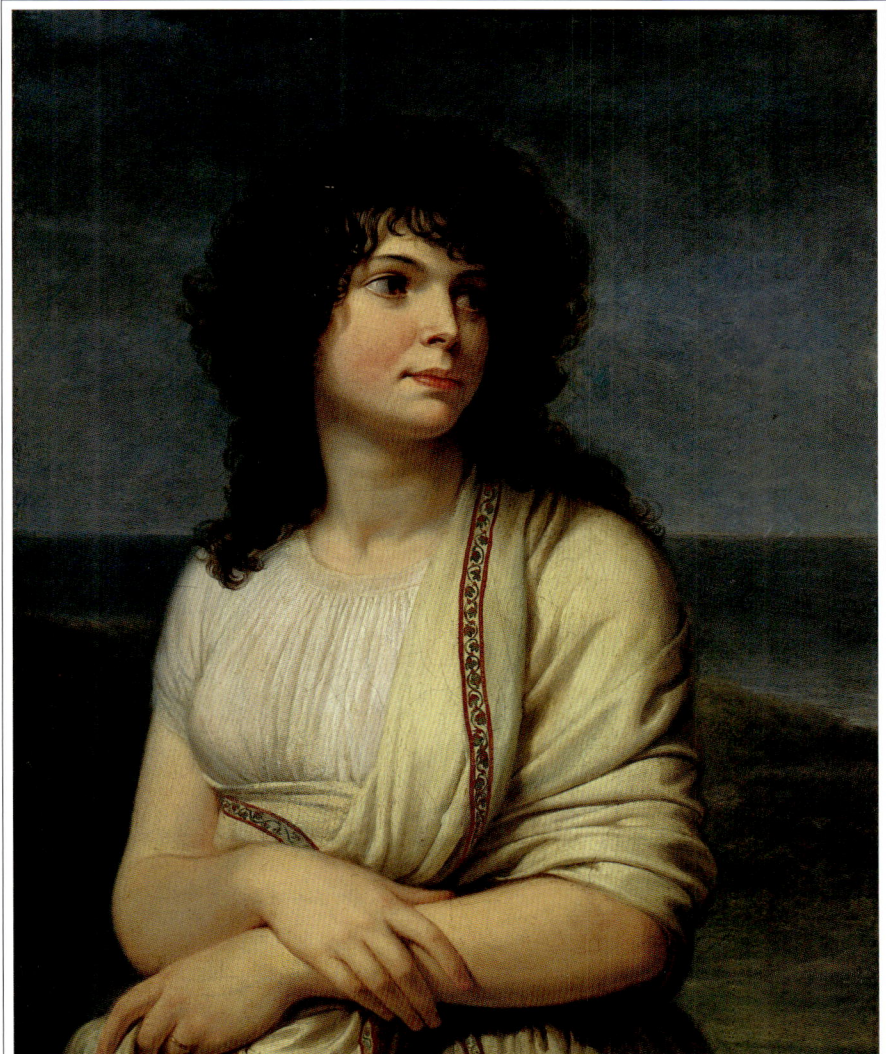

FIGURE 11.

Jean-André Appiani (Italian, 1754–1817), *Madame Hamelin, née Jeanne Geneviève Fortunée Lormier-Lagrave*, 1798.
Oil on canvas, 70 × 55 cm (27 5/8 × 21 5/8 in.).
Paris, Carnavalet Museum.

• • •

The dark-skinned beauty Fortunée Hamelin was among the most brazenly uninhibited of the fast set in Paris during the Directoire period (1795–99). The reign of the free-wheeling Merveilleuses (see introduction) came to an end, though, with the establishment of the Consulate, followed by Napoléon's disapproval of scantily clad ladies. It has even been claimed that Victorian prudery began with Napoléon.

— JEAN-ANDRÉ APPIANI —

Among the most intriguing artists of the Empire period was the Milanese Andréa (Jean-André) Appiani (1754–1817), who worked during the golden age of Milan, when Joséphine was in residence. Along with Stendhal were the poets Giovanni Berchet, Ugo Foscolo, Vincenzo Monti, and Carlo Porta, and it was from this world that Appiani drew inspiration.

In 1796 Appiani was already a successful painter when introduced to Bonaparte at a banquet in Milan, where Joséphine joined her husband in July of that year. Appiani's Neoclassical frescoes based on the Psyche theme were widely known. They were executed in 1789 for the villa at Monza, which would become the favorite Italian residence of Joséphine's son, Prince Eugène, after his promotion to viceroy of Italy in 1805.

The French colony in Milan was drawn to Appiani's atelier. One was the army supplier and chronic bankrupt, Antoine Hamelin, who had traveled in one of the carriages that brought Joséphine to Italy, hoping through her influence to profit from the Italian campaign (as he, indeed, did). He was accompanied by his wife, Fortunée Hamelin, a seductive

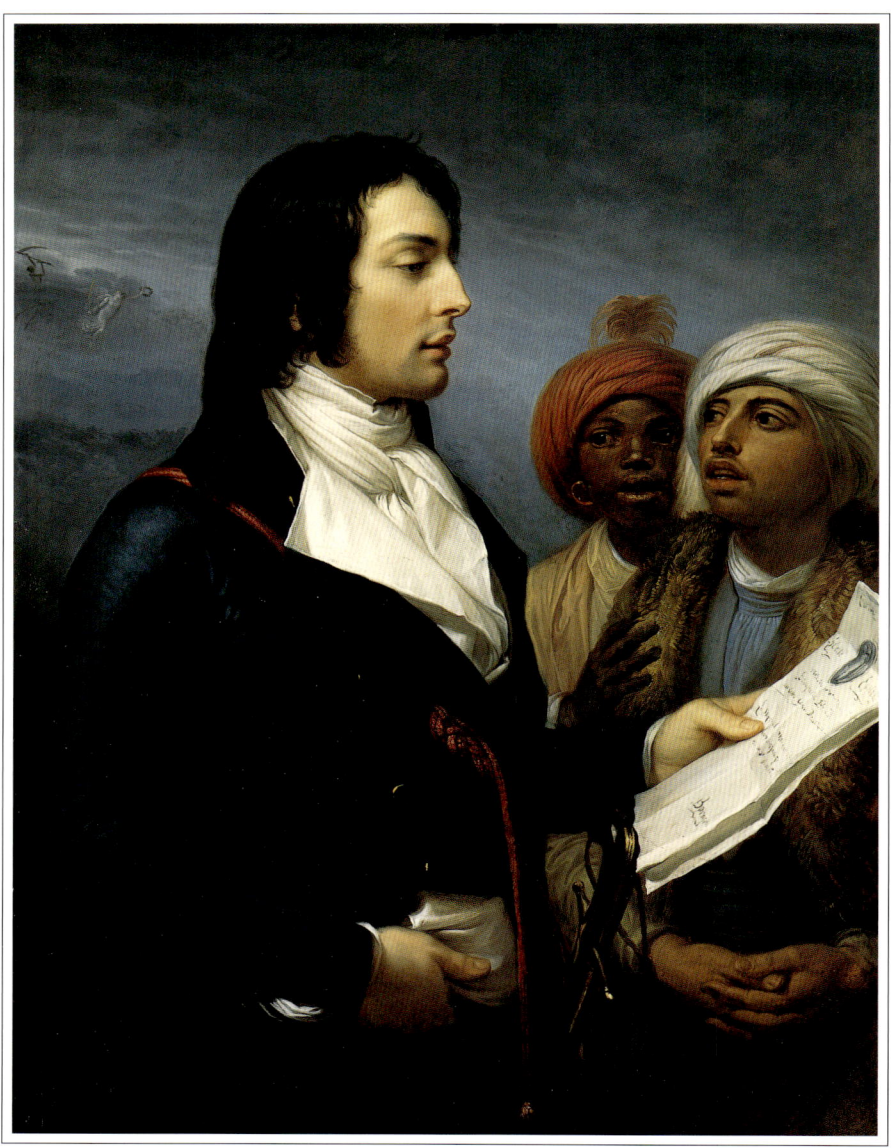

Figure 12.

Jean-André Appiani (Italian, 1754–1817),
General Louis-Charles-Antoine Desaix, Reading an Order from General Bonaparte to Two Egyptians,
early nineteenth century.
Oil on canvas, 115 × 99 cm (45¼ × 39 in.)
Versailles, Musée national des Châteaux
de Versailles et de Trianon.

· · ·

This striking posthumous image of the courageous soldier-scholar Antoine Desaix (1768–1800) was taken from his death mask made after the battle of Marengo. Appiani's replica of this painting belonged to Prince Eugène, who, like Napoléon, was Desaix' close friend. Desaix had an impressive knowledge of philosophy, strategy, tactics, and topography. After Joséphine's death Eugène took his painting to Malmaison, where it attracted special attention for the artist's arresting presentation of his subject and his technical prowess. Desaix' dramatic profile is masterfully delineated, and his charismatic personality is underscored by the addition of two admiring Egyptians.

creature and notorious Merveilleuse credited (or discredited) with introducing the *chemise transparente*. Mme Hamelin had known Joséphine in Paris, and it may have been Joséphine's idea to have Appiani paint her. *Madame Hamelin, née Jeanne Geneviève Fortunée Lormier-Lagrave* {FIGURE 11} is one of the Italian artist's most provocative portraits.

One of Eugène's best friends was the subject of a moving Appiani portrait, *General Louis-Charles-Antoine Desaix* {FIGURE 12}. Desaix and Eugène knew each other from the Egyptian campaign in which Desaix greatly distinguished himself and was killed at the battle of Marengo in 1800, a personal loss for both Napoléon and Eugène. This likeness of a fine scholar and exemplary soldier is among the most haunting of its time, visual testimony to Napoléon's description: "Desaix est tout à fait antique" (Desaix is totally classical), a description that applies to both his appearance and character. Appiani depicts a profile that could have been lifted from an antique coin, and the adoring figures allude to Desaix' reputation in Egypt as "the *good* sultan."

Appiani made a distinctly favorable impression on the Bonapartes, who heaped honors on him; he was appointed a member of the commission that arranged Napoléon's coronation as king of Italy in 1805, and he painted the official portrait: *Napoléon I, King of Italy*.

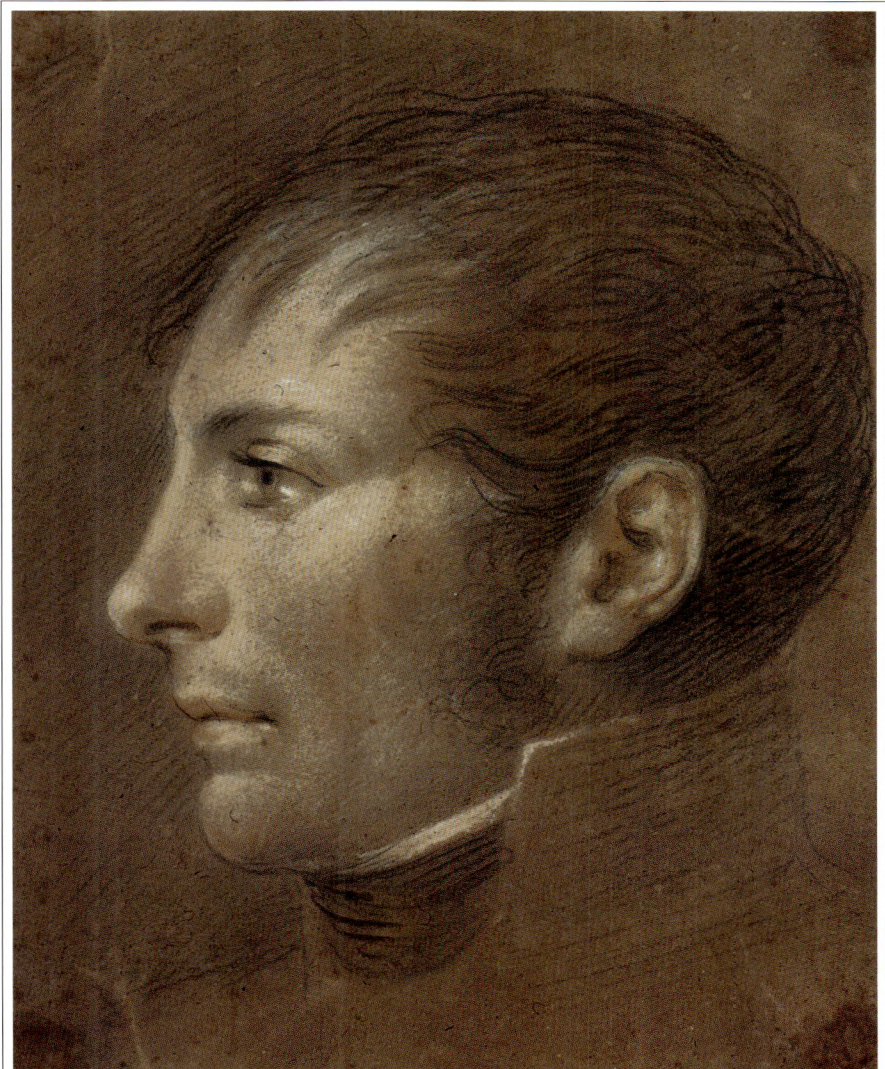

Figure 13.

Andrea Appiani (Italian, 1754–1817), *Portrait of Eugène de Beauharnais, Stepson of Napoléon Bonaparte,* ca. 1806. Album Cicognara. Black and white chalk on tanned paper, 15.9 × 11.9 cm (6¼ × 4⅝ in.). Venice, Correr Museum.

• • •

Eugène was one of those unforgettable personalities who flamed across the firmament of Empire history. Respected for his probity, courage under fire, and meticulous administration as the viceroy of a state of some four million inhabitants, Eugène was among the few who never disappointed Napoléon, as the emperor declared. Although Appiani painted Eugène in resplendent court attire with the iron cross and Legion of Honor, he also sketched him informally, as in this drawing in which the young prince appropriately wears his military uniform. Joséphine's aristocratic son was an elegant example of the two societies Napoléon wanted to reunite in his new regime.

During this time in Milan, Joséphine, queen of Italy, sat for Appiani's *Madame Bonaparte* (see frontispiece), which is quite unlike other portraits of her. Whereas Prud'hon's iconic image conveys melting femininity with a touch of fantasy, the Milanese painter portrays Joséphine at thirty-four in the guise of a Roman matron, a document of her unfailing sense of style and self-assurance. It is one of the most beguiling representations of her, free of the sentimentality found in some of her other portraits. Appiani presents her as a vivacious, seductive woman, capitalizing on her beautiful features, especially her large eyes highlighted by curling bangs. The fascinating diadem in her chestnut hair is centered with a precious cameo (see chapter 11).

Besides his official portraits of Eugène as viceroy of Italy, Appiani also executed a delicate chalk drawing of the young prince {FIGURE 13} that now hangs in the Correr Museum in Venice. Eugène commissioned Appiani to paint a series of Parnassus frescoes that are still in place at the Villa Bonaparte in Milan.

Joséphine sat for Appiani on other occasions, and he gave her Bernardino Luini's *Saint Catherine* for her collection. She also probably commissioned at least one of Appiani's portraits of her beloved daughter-in-law (Eugène's wife), Princess Auguste.

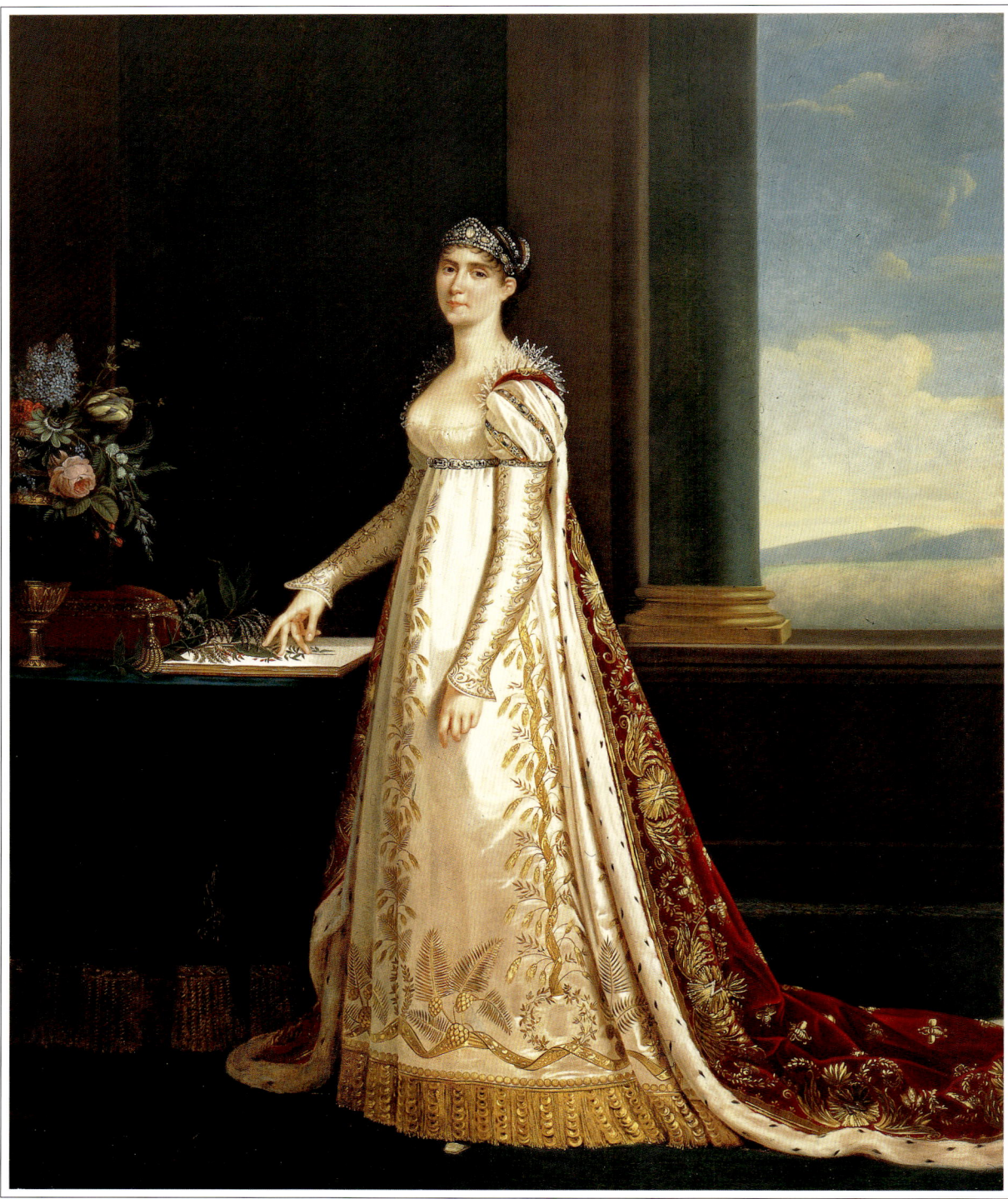

Robert Lefèvre

In 1784 Robert Lefèvre entered the atelier of Jean-Baptiste Regnault (1754–1829). Since Lefèvre was showing in the public exhibitions by 1791, Joséphine most likely knew him then and would have noted his avant-garde, Troubadour-style painting *Héloïse et Abélard* in the Salon of 1795. By 1801 Joséphine herself had taken the lead in patronizing this new historical genre.

It was as a portraitist, however, that Lefèvre acquired renown. One of the most informative paintings of the empress is his full-length *Empress Joséphine with an Herbarium on the Table beside Her* {FIGURE 14}. This work was supposedly commissioned in 1805 by Napoléon, who presented it to the city of Aachen. Since it was customary for the ruler's portrait to be displayed in cities allied to French interests, it is remarkable that Napoléon chose Joséphine's portrait rather than his own for this purpose. Yet she was, in essence, his best ambassador, and the artist discreetly advertised the supremacy of French fashion that Joséphine modeled so well, reproducing the rich details of her gown with meticulous precision. Moreover, the artist salutes her impressive knowledge of botany by placing her hand on an open herbarium.

Lefèvre also left the most compelling image of Denon {FIGURE 15}. The challenge of capturing the matchless art impresario's elusive, polyvalent personality was intimidating, but Lefèvre triumphed. Seated on a luxurious fur, directly confronting the spectator, leafing through an album of engravings, Joséphine's urbane friend and artistic adviser seems about to expound on the profundities of Nicolas Poussin.[19] In his commanding position as director of the museum and intermediary between Napoléon and the artists, Denon sent teams of draftsmen to the battlefield during campaigns. Their notations of costumes, disposition of troops, and topography were then sent back as instructions to the painters.

Denon also made certain that generous provisions were made for Joséphine's favorite artists, including Gros, Gerard, Prud'hon, and Isabey.

FIGURE 14.

Robert Lefèvre (French, 1756–1830).
Empress Joséphine with an Herbarium on the Table beside Her, 1805.
Oil on burlap, 216 × 175 cm (85 × 68⅞ in.).
Rome, Napoleonic Museum.

• • •

Lefèvre's portrait suggests that Joséphine is physically present in the city of Aachen, for she stands in a room from which a view of the old city may be seen through the window. Lefèvre's career had been launched by his successful portrait, titled *The First Consul and General Berthier at the Battle of Marengo*, for which Joseph Boze tried to take credit. Lefèvre executed forty portraits of Napoléon, some as miniatures, with interesting variations in each.

FIGURE 15.

Robert Lefèvre (French, 1756–1830),
Portrait of Baron Dominique-Vivant Denon, 1808.
Oil on canvas, 92 × 78 cm (36¼ × 30¾ in.).
Versailles, Musée national des Châteaux de Versailles et de Trianon.

• • •

Denon, the quintessential courtier, charmed such diverse personalities as Louis XV, Voltaire, Catherine the Great, Diderot, Emma Hamilton, Pope Pius VII, and Napoléon, who valued Denon so highly that he granted him direct access to his own rooms. Denon's watershed publication, *Voyage dans la Basse et la Haute Egypte* (1802), influenced René de Chateaubriand, Gustav Flaubert, Arthur Rimbaud, Gérard Nerval, and Edgar Allan Poe. Denon died in his apartment on Quai Voltaire with Antoine Watteau's (1684–1721) immortal *Pierrot* (called *Gilles*), only one of the many items in his celebrated art collection, before his eyes.

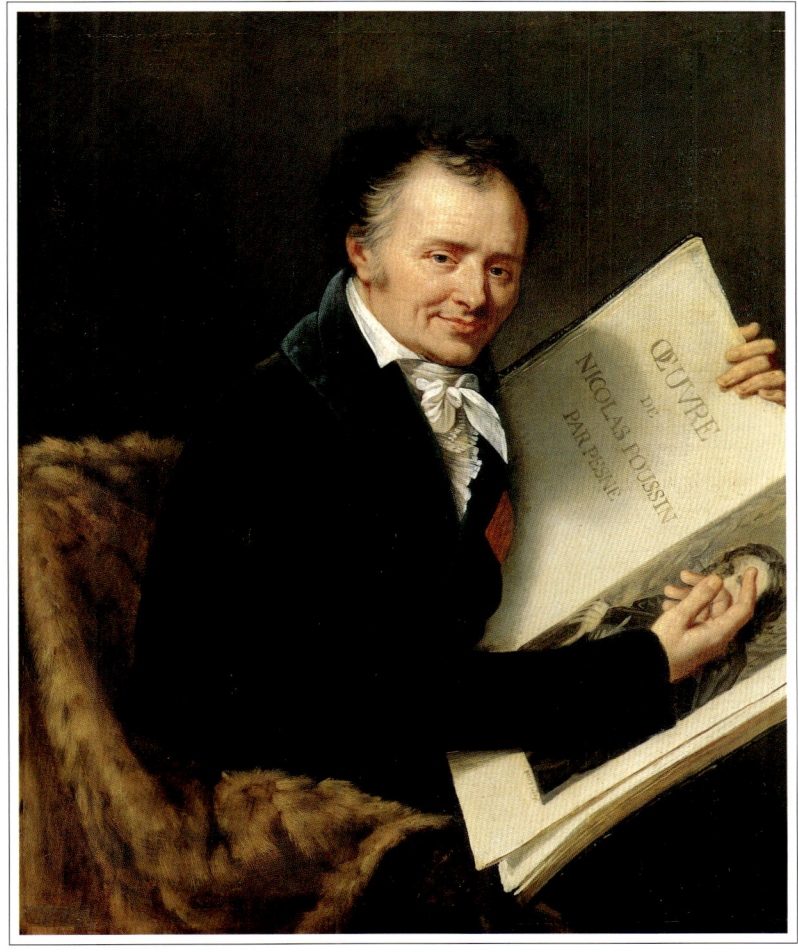

FRANÇOIS GÉRARD

It was Joséphine's protégé Isabey, as noted earlier, who launched the long, impressive career of François Gérard, the most sought-after, successful portraitist of his day, and perhaps the most expensive. Joséphine engaged the young Gérard to paint a now-lost portrait of the adolescent Hortense (1794/95),[20] so Joséphine was among his first patrons. It was at the Salon of 1798 that Gérard achieved his first real success, with the tactful *Psyche and Cupid* {FIGURE 16}. Two years later, Gérard's reputation was firmly established when he was commissioned to paint *Ossian* to decorate the principal salon, the Salon Doré, at Malmaison, later joined by Girodet-Trioson's version of the same subject.

Gérard exhibited his portrait of Joséphine seated on a divan at the Salon of 1801, and she most likely commissioned his sympathetic *Napoléon* {FIGURE 17}. Of all Napoléon's portraits, it most closely conforms to Sir Walter Scott's impression (verified by many contem-

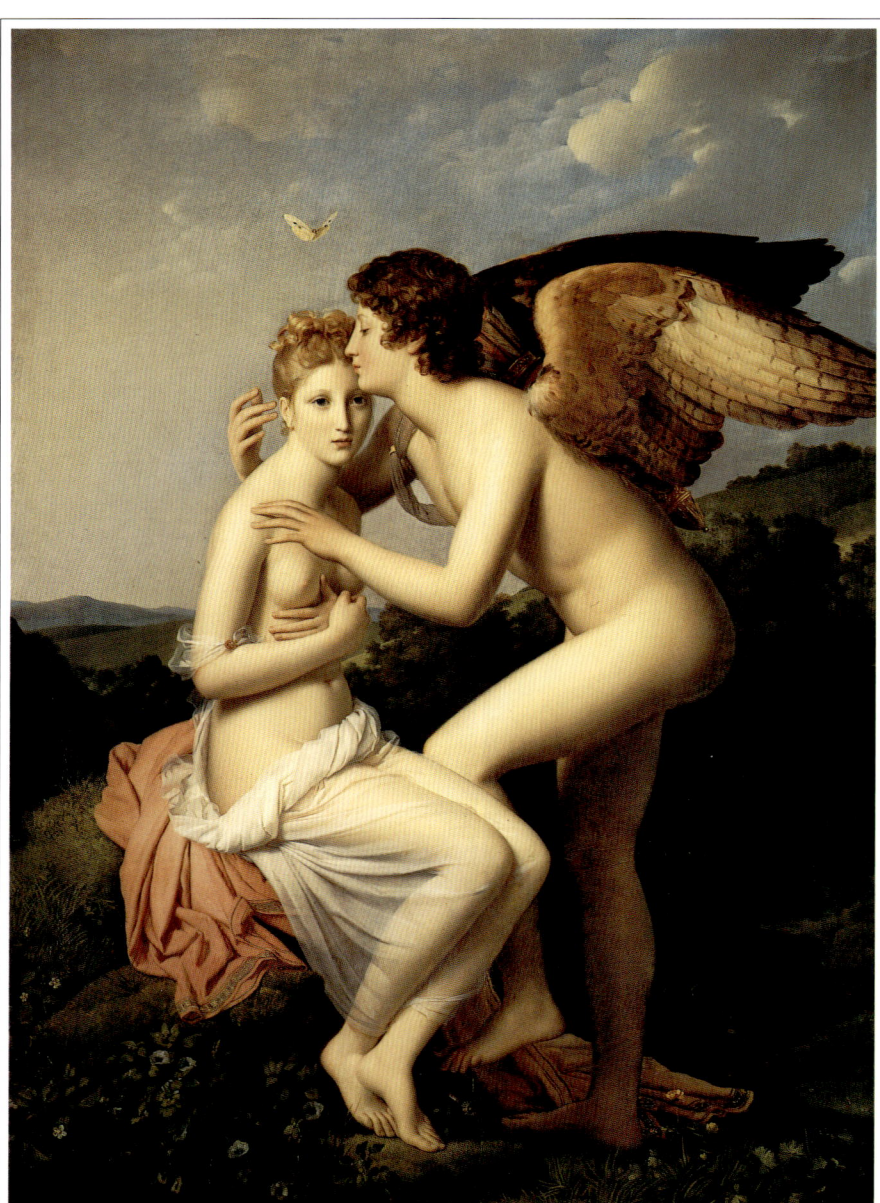

FIGURE 16.

François Gérard (1770–1837),
Psyche and Cupid (also called
Psyche Receiving Cupid's First Kiss), 1797.
Oil on canvas, 186 × 132 cm (73¼ × 52 in.).
Paris, Musée du Louvre.

• • •

Gérard's painting was presented at the same Salon in which Boilly showed his *Reunion of Artists in Isabey's Studio* (see FIGURE 2). Delicate, airy, and filled with light, its graceful lyrical spirit is akin to Canova's *Cupid and Psyche* (see FIGURE 36) in Joséphine's gallery as well as Chaudet's *Cupid Presenting a Rose to a Butterfly*. The svelte modeling of the figures is probably due to Gérard's two years in the atelier of the sculptor Augustin Pajou (1730–1809). Gérard's painting treats the erotic element of the Psyche legend with restraint, whereas David's later version of the same subject openly exploits it. Here, Cupid leans protectively over the chaste, naïve, adolescent Psyche, hardly daring to touch her.

FIGURE 17.

François Gérard (French, 1770–1837),
Napoléon, before 1830.
Oil on canvas, rectangular, framed to oval,
73 × 59 cm (28¾ × 23⅛ in.).
London, Apsley House, The Wellington Museum.

• • •

This portrait of Napoléon and its companion piece, *Joséphine* by Robert Lefèvre, are in the collection of the Duke of Wellington. These works would have been chosen not only for political reasons but also because they are among the most decorative paintings of the period. All Europe was enthralled by the Napoleonic mystique, and the artist expresses the emperor's charismatic power. Yet Gérard's portrait is also psychologically cogent, for it reveals the strain of leadership, recalling the emperor's poignant remark that whereas his brothers enjoyed the pleasures of kingship, he knew only its burdens.

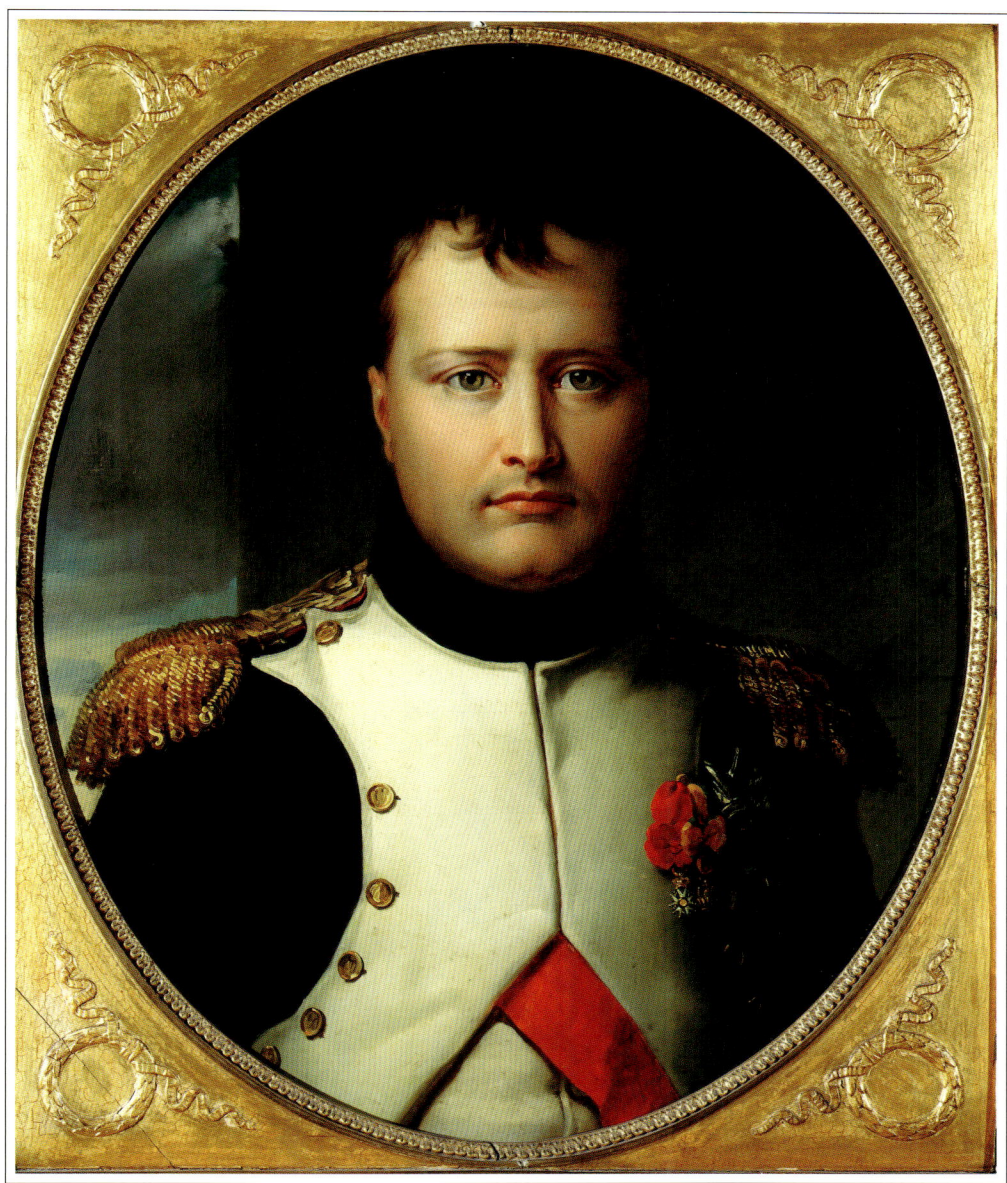

poraries): "'His eyes were grey and very expressive . . . he had a nose and mouth perfectly formed . . . his smile was of a rare sweetness, and one would say even irresistible.'"[21]

It was also Gérard whom Joséphine chose to portray her children, and his portrait of Prince Eugène in his deep green uniform of colonel of the *chasseurs à cheval* of the Consular Guard, in a private collection, is among his most appealing. Eugène was known for the probity of his character, a trait that radiates from Gérard's canvas. Around 1807, he painted Hortense and her son, Napoléon-Charles {FIGURE 18}. It evokes the quiet, distinctive elegance of Joséphine's daughter, a gifted artist and composer. Hortense's battle songs accompanied Napoléon's campaigns; one became a veritable Bonapartist anthem during the Restoration and Second Empire. One of her romances, "Bon Chevalier," inspired a Schubert piano piece, and another of her compositions was quoted by Saint-Saëns (see chapter 12).

Gérard proved his versatility with one of the finest military pieces, *The Battle of Austerlitz, December 2, 1805* {FIGURE 19}. This painting depicts the classic battle fought against the Austrians and Russians, the latter under Czar Alexander and the one-eyed General Koutouzov, hero of Leo Tolstoy's *War and Peace*.

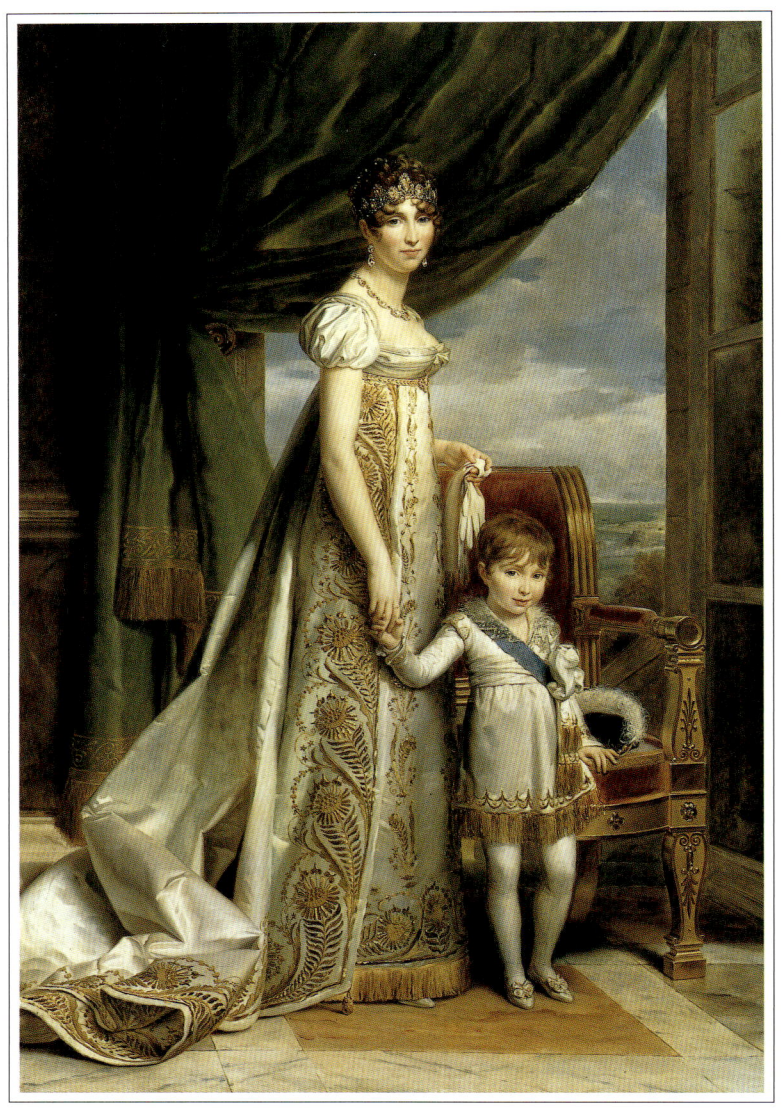

FIGURE 18.

François Gérard (French, 1770–1837),
Portrait of Hortense, Queen of Holland, with the Prince Royal of Holland, 1807.
Oil on canvas, 216 × 145 cm (85 × 57⅛ in.).
Fontainbleau, Musée national du
Château de Fontainebleau.

• • •

Napoléon liked this portrait of his beloved stepdaughter and nephew so much that it formed part of his family portrait gallery at Saint-Cloud. Its subsequent history is unsettling. In 1815 Prussian troops under Marshal Blücher looted the château, taking a group of choice Bonaparte family portraits, including this one. In 1975 they came to light in the Channel Islands, so Hortense's portrait now adorns the château of Fontainebleau, with its magnificent collection of arts of the Empire period.

FIGURE 19.

François Gérard (French, 1770–1837),
The Battle of Austerlitz, December 2, 1805, 1808.
Oil on canvas, 510 × 958 cm (199 × 373⅝ in.).
Versailles, Musée national des Châteaux
de Versailles et de Trianon.

• • •

Set against the clearing smoke of battle is, at left, a wedge of figures led by Eugène's comrade-in-arms, the ecstatic General Jean Rapp. He has just led to victory the Imperial Guard cavalry, headed by the Mamluks, and is bringing Prince Repnine, colonel of the Russian Imperial Guard, with other prisoners, to the commander in chief and his staff. At right, on horseback, is Napoléon, flanked by Marshal Berthier on his left and General Duroc on his right. At far right, in a plumed turban, is Napoléon's Mamluk, Roustam.

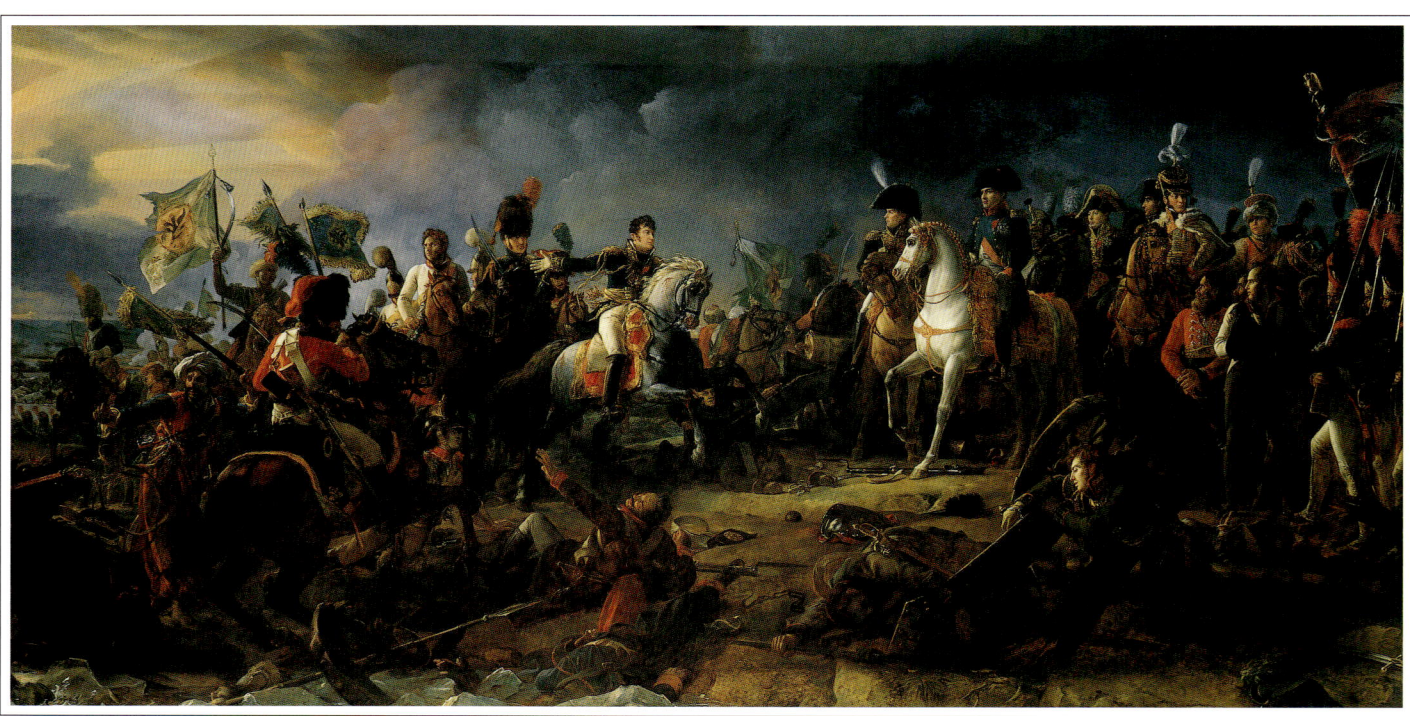

Pierre-Paul Prud'hon

Joséphine referred to her favorite artist, Pierre-Paul Prud'hon, as "mon ami (my friend), Prud'hon." His daughter was a boarder at the school of the Legion of Honor at Ecouen, where Hortense was protectress. Later, Joséphine and Prud'hon shared the agony of parents whose sons had fought in the tragic Russian campaign of 1812, but for Joséphine the outcome was happier. Eugène returned safely, despite the horrors of the retreat, but Prud'hon's young son was killed. It was but one of several tragedies that clouded the painter's life: First, his wife had an apparent nervous breakdown. Then Constance Mayer, Prud'hon's artistic collaborator, whose work hung on Joséphine's walls, dramatically took her own life in his presence. Joséphine was exposed to Mme Prud'hon's disturbing tirades, and, after a scandalous outburst in the empress's presence, she was committed to an asylum.[22]

Prud'hon received the Prix de Rome and became a friend of Antonio Canova (1757–1822) while in Italy.[23] After Prud'hon returned to Paris in 1798 Joséphine apparently

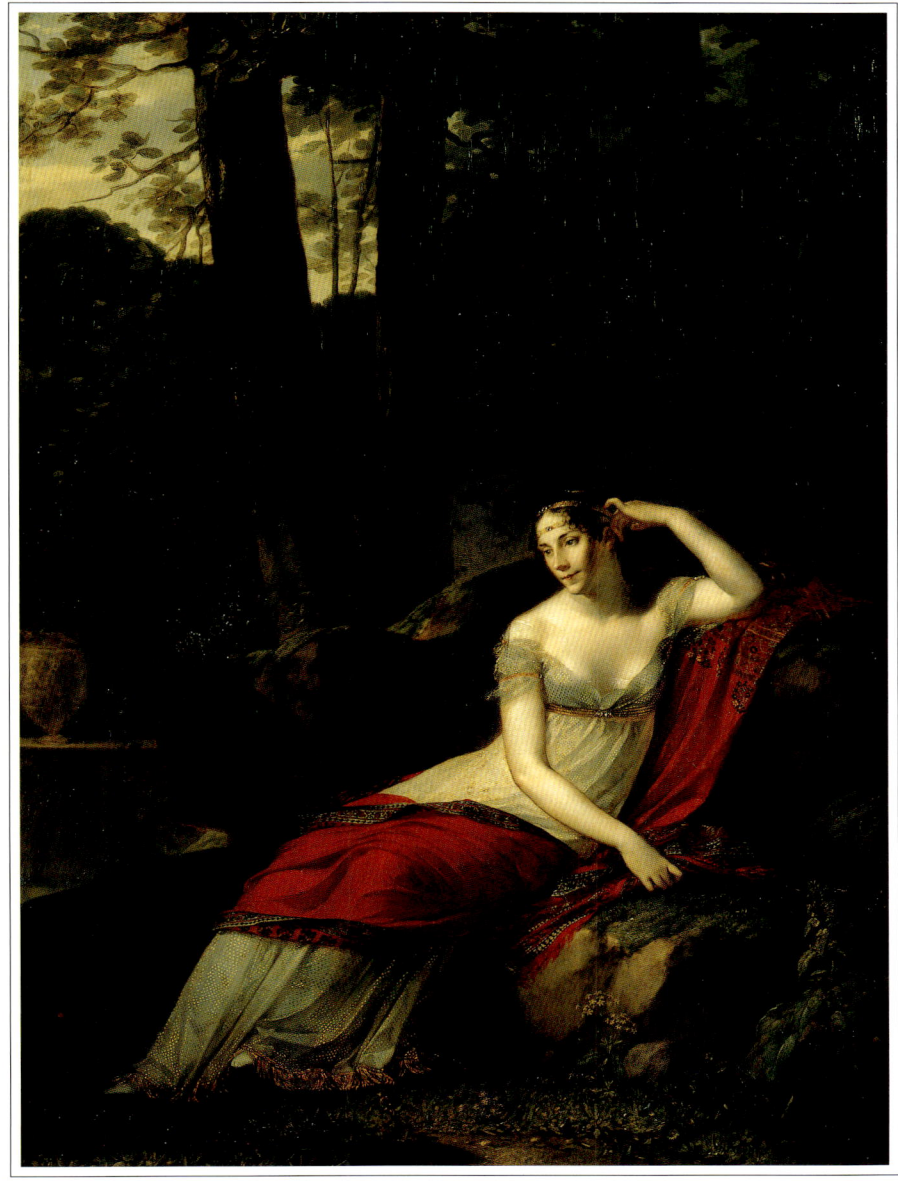

FIGURE 20.

Pierre-Paul Prud'hon (French, 1758–1823), *The Empress Joséphine*, 1805. Oil on canvas, 244 × 179 cm (96 × 70½ in.). Rueil-Malmaison, Musée national des Châteaux de Malmaison et Bois-Préau.

• • •

Joséphine sits on an amaranth cashmere shawl, an indispensable accessory that Ingres would artfully employ in 1806 to encircle the subject of his *Madame Rivière*. No jewelry interrupts the flow of the empress's shapely arms, which frame her upper torso and head within a rectangle. Although the simple white dress recalls the Alexandrine grace of antiquity, the sensibility is more typical of the late eighteenth century without descending to lachrymose sentimentality. Prud'hon's brushwork recalls that of Correggio, which doubtless provoked David's scathing comment that Prud'hon was "the Boucher of his time."

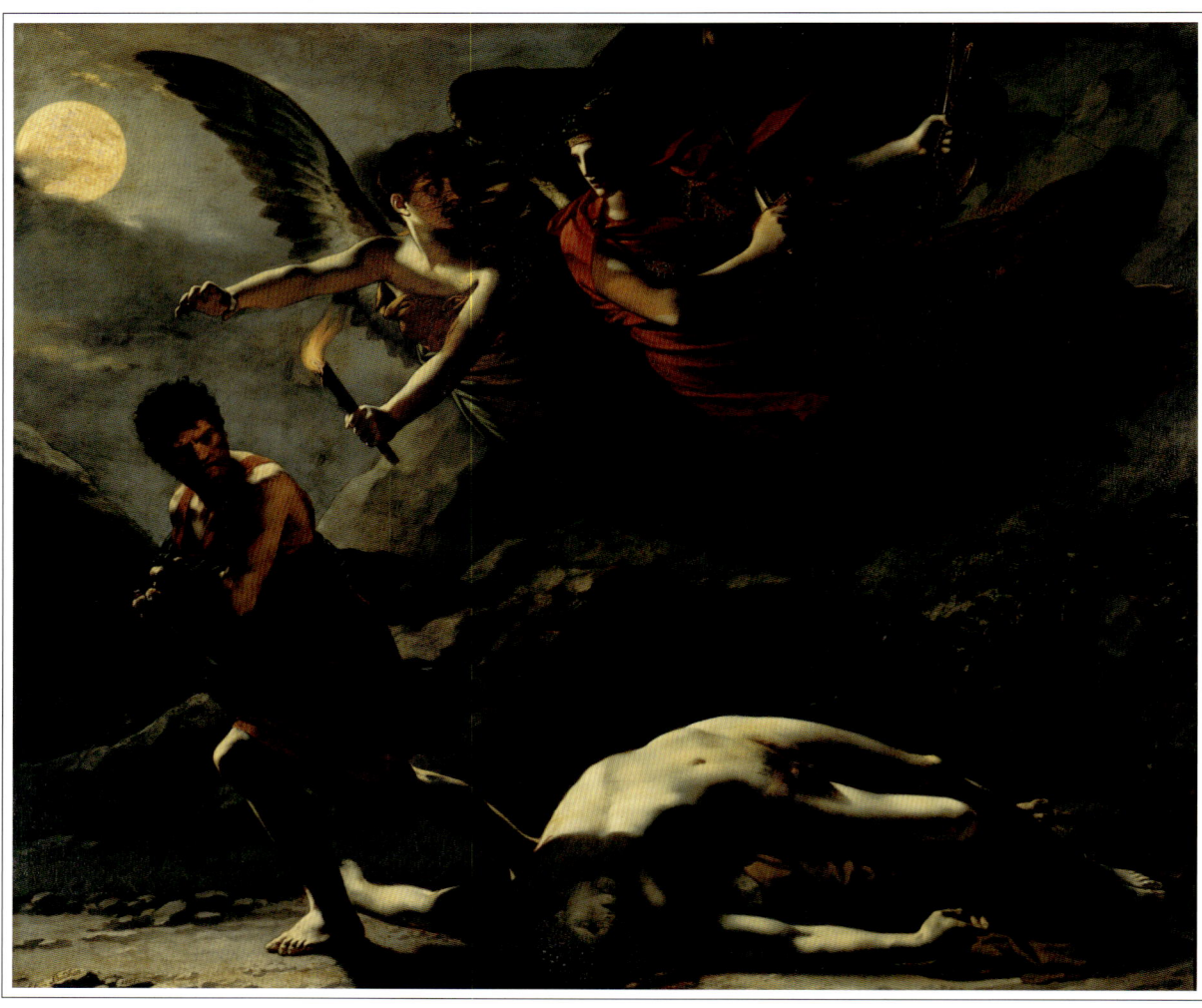

FIGURE 21.

Pierre-Paul Prud'hon (French, 1758–1823), *Justice and Divine Vengeance Pursuing Crime*, 1808. Oil on canvas, 244 × 294 cm (96 × 115¾ in.). Paris, Musée du Louvre.

・・・

Prud'hon's dramatic painting was shown at the Salon of 1808, which Joséphine and Napoléon attended on October 22, an event recorded by both Baron Gros and Boilly. Joséphine was especially gratified that this work by her favorite artist attracted the most attention at this historic Salon and that, on the same occasion, Prud'hon received the coveted Legion of Honor from the hands of the emperor. An oil-on-canvas study (1806) for this painting is in the collections of the J. Paul Getty Museum, Los Angeles.

engaged him to decorate the ceiling of her salon on rue Chantereine.[24] The same year he also executed a superb decor for the Hôtel de Lannoy, Hortense's Paris residence for ten years (see chapter 3). By 1801 he was lending his talent to allegorical compositions lauding the achievements of the first consul, and designing fêtes staged by the city of Paris, but his greatest opportunity came in 1805.

When Napoléon wanted an image of Joséphine, he selected Prud'hon on the recommendation of the painting expert and dealer Guillaume-Jean Constantin, a choice seconded by Isabey.[25] Being singled out by the emperor launched his career as a portraitist, and the poetic *Empress Joséphine* {FIGURE 20} became her best-known portrait. Both clothing and setting were probably her idea, a decision that Jacques-Philippe Voiart considered prophetic, for she knew that she might have to forfeit her imperial robes.

> To [Prud'hon's] brush we owe this fine portrait of a woman whom Fate had raised to great estate, and *who used her power only to support the arts* and to comfort the unfortunate. By a sort of premonition, Joséphine wanted her portrait to be free of imperial trappings. She sits on a rock shaded by dense foliage, surrounded by her beloved flowers, which she studied as an amateur botanist.[26]

When Mme de Chastenay visited Joséphine in 1810, she saw the painting in the empress's gallery and noted,

> This gallery was adorned with the finest works of the best-known painters. At the back of the gallery, a freshly finished painting stood on an easel; this painting was the portrait of the empress herself by Prud'hon. It showed her younger, and perhaps more beautiful than she was. Very graciously, she said, "This is more the work of a friend than of a painter."[27]

One of Prud'hon's admirers was Joséphine's friend Nicolas Frochot, prefect of the Seine since 1800, who assisted the empress in her official duties.[28] Perhaps she recommended Prud'hon to Frochot in 1804 for the important allegorical composition Prud'hon designed for the Palais de Justice: *Justice and Divine Vengeance Pursuing Crime* {FIGURE 21}. A graphic warning to criminals, *Justice and Divine Vengeance* is a theatrical drama in which a murderer, glancing back at his nude, prostrate victim, is about to be overtaken by the swooping, winged figures of Justice and Divine Vengeance, who are relentlessly pursuing him from overhead. This work certified Prud'hon's reputation as a history painter. The theme of the moonlit, recumbent nude would recur frequently in works by other artists and in other contexts. The grimacing face of the murderer was probably based on an antique Caracalla that Prud'hon could have seen in the sculpture galleries of the museum, another fulfillment of Napoléon's desire that the works of art in France's collection provide artistic inspiration.

ANNE-LOUIS GIRODET-TRIOSON

At the same exhibition in which Prud'hon's *Justice and Divine Vengeance* was shown hung *The Funeral of Atala* {FIGURE 22} by Girodet-Trioson, an artist who shared Joséphine's interest in mineralogy.[29] Joséphine then owned one canvas by Girodet-Trioson;[30] he made a copy for her of *Atala* (now lost) and also provided an exquisite portrait of Queen Hortense. Girodet-Trioson had been known to Joséphine since his days in Genoa with his friend Antoine-Jean Gros, but Girodet-Trioson's approach to his art and subjects differs markedly from that of Gros.

Baudelaire claimed that Girodet-Trioson always dipped his brush into literary sources. The springboard for this celebrated painting was a famous tale, also titled *Atala* (1801), by Vicomte François-Auguste-René de Chateaubriand (1768–1848), an illustrious member of Joséphine's circle. Like Prud'hon's *Justice and Vengeance*—in which the victim's livid, prostrate body is illuminated by the moon—the pathetic corpse of the Indian maiden Atala is also revealed by moonlight. So prominent is the moon in Chateaubriand's idyll that Chactas, Atala's lover, is described as keeping vigil by its light—"white as a vestal virgin"—before her burial.

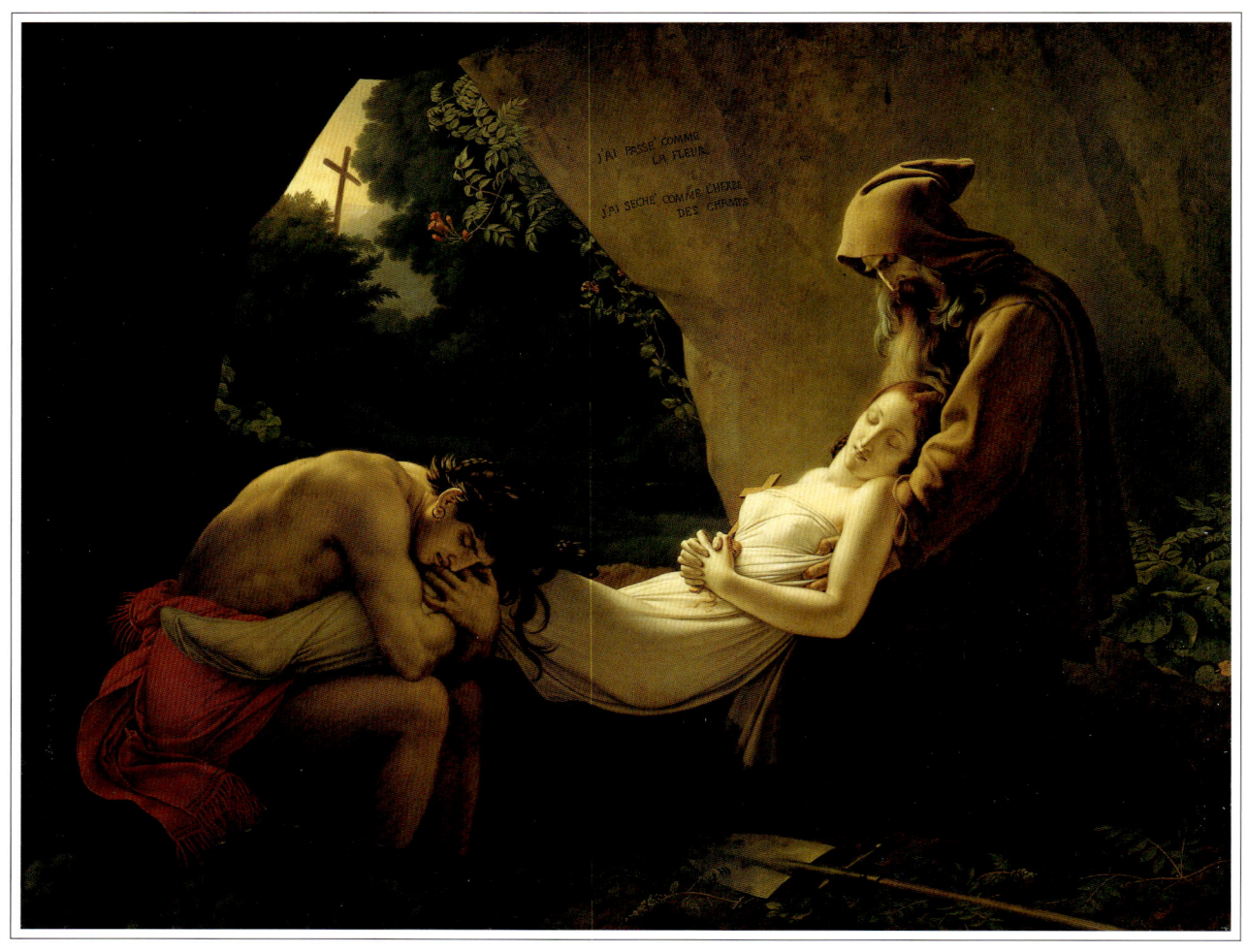

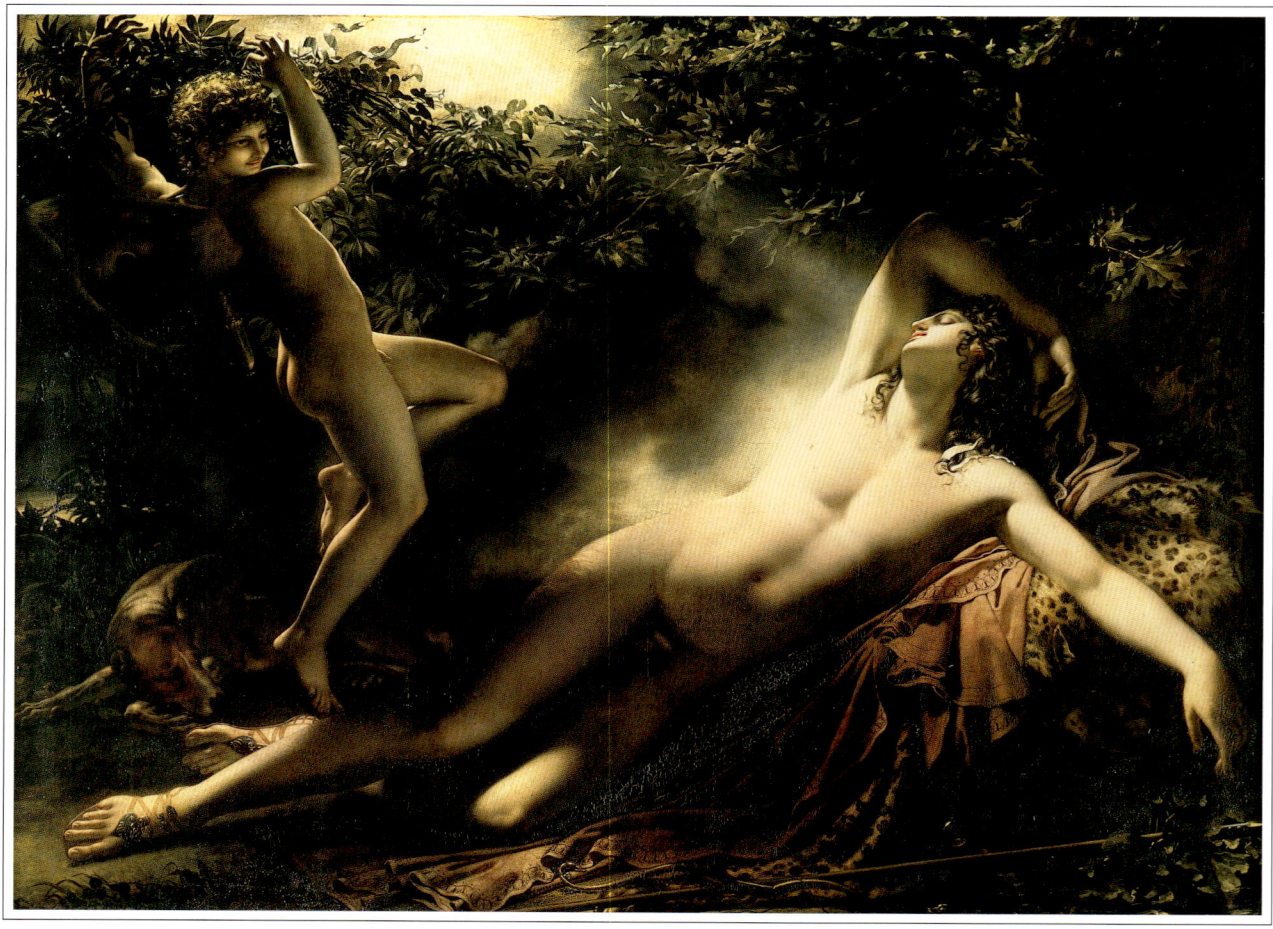

Figure 22.

Anne-Louis Girodet-Trioson (French, 1767–1824),
The Funeral of Atala, 1808.
Oil on canvas, 210 × 267 cm (82⅝ × 105⅛ in.).
Paris, Musée du Louvre.

. . .

After traveling to America in 1791, René de Chateaubriand was haunted by its wilderness. This story of the Indian maiden Atala, set against America's unexplored wilds, appealed to French taste for the exotic. Atala, who has committed suicide, is being borne to a cave by her lover, Chactas, and the priest Père Aubry. The untamed landscape reminded Joséphine of her island home, Martinique, and *Atala* is closely linked to Joséphine's painting, the renowned *Tomb of Julie* by Jan Frans van Dael. The subject of both is the death of a young woman, and both feature tombs with similar inscriptions. In *Atala*, Père Aubry intones an antique poem, "I passed like the flower; I withered like the grass of the fields," which Girodet-Trioson has incised on the young woman's tomb.

Figure 23.

Anne-Louis Girodet-Trioson (French, 1767–1824),
Endymion, 1793.
Oil on canvas, 197 × 267 cm (77½ × 105⅛ in.).
Paris, Musée du Louvre.

. . .

Girodet-Trioson claimed that this painting was inspired by a relief at the Villa Borghese in Rome, as well as an antique Endymion, of which there were many examples in that city. Endymion is reclining on a leopard skin and a cashmere shawl, two props hardly chosen by chance, as the former were placed under the saddles of mounted *chasseurs* and the latter were typically worn by fashionable women. A mischievous, moth-winged Eros pulls back branches to expose the sleeping androgynous figure.

Prud'hon's *Justice and Divine Vengeance* and Girodet-Trioson's *Atala* are but two examples of this nocturnal theme common to French paintings of the time.[31] Girodet-Trioson had exploited the motif as early as 1791 in *Endymion* {FIGURE 23}, which was such a major success at the Salon of 1793 that it established his reputation. The painting portrays the sexually ambiguous, dreaming Endymion being admired by the moon goddess Diana, represented by the atmospheric rays of moonlight.

What accounts for this odd convention mirrored in so many paintings of Joséphine's day?[32] It was probably a reaction of David's students against his Neoclassical principles that prescribed rational, overall lighting. David's followers favored mysterious illumination that imparted poetic, romantic coloration appropriate to the subject. Literature was also a compelling influence, especially Edward Young's popular book-length poem, *Night Thoughts* (1797), which was familiar to Joséphine.

Far more crucial, however, was the curious fad among European intelligentsia for the fictitious poet Ossian, supposedly the son of a Gaelic king, Fingal. Although Macpherson's *Fingal* may have been a literary hoax,[33] it nevertheless cast its spell over painting and was admired by Goethe, Ingres, Mme de Staël, Talleyrand-Périgord, and Napoléon, whose *Ossian*—illustrated with Isabey's watercolors—lay on his night table. Joséphine shared her husband's interest in the strange Caledonian bard, for she owned a painting of *Ossian* by the comte Auguste de Forbin (1777–1841),[34] and the previously mentioned pair of canvases by Gérard and Girodet-Trioson hung at Malmaison.[35]

The lunar vogue persisted late into the nineteenth century, which closed on the twilit gloom of Art Nouveau. It was not until the twentieth century—with its bright, optimistic Art Deco—that the sun finally emerged, as when F. Scott Fitzgerald's novel, ironically titled *Tender Is the Night*, is played out to the counterpoint of the blazing sunlight of Riviera beaches.

Jacques-Louis David

Considering Joséphine's relationship to the artists of her time, one can only imagine her feelings for the great master Jacques-Louis David, mentor to the younger generation. David returned to Paris from Rome in 1780, the first year of Joséphine's marriage to Alexandre de Beauharnais. A deputy to the National Convention of 1792, David voted for the king's death, was Robespierre's close associate, and in March 1794 signed (with others) the order

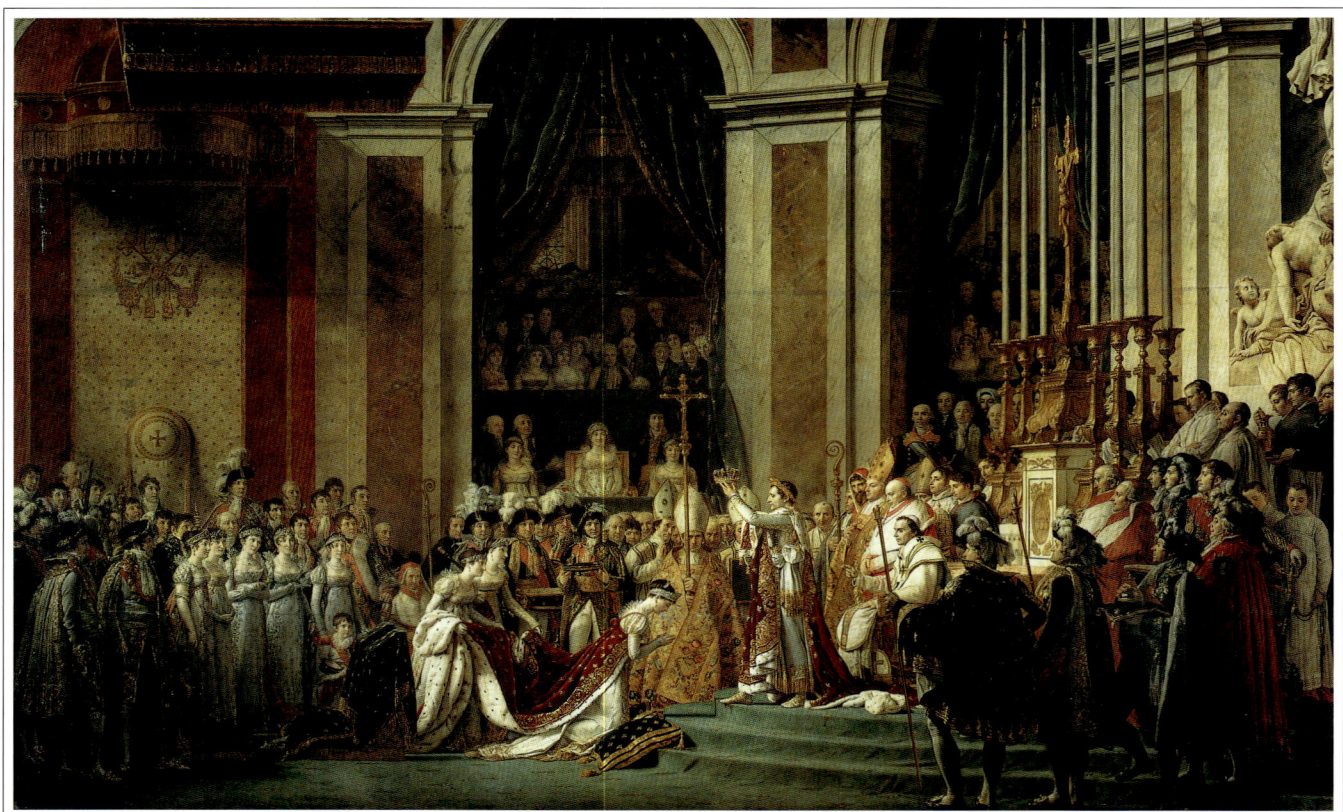

FIGURE 24.

Jacques-Louis David (French, 1748–1825),
*The Consecration of the Emperor Napoléon
and the Coronation of Empress Joséphine
(December 2, 1804)*, 1806–7.
Oil on canvas, 621 × 979 cm (242⅛ × 381¾ in.).
Paris, Musée du Louvre.

• • •

One of the devices uniting the figures of Napoléon and Joséphine is the confrontation of their profiles, with the emperor's Caesarean head providing a perfect foil for her delicate physiognomy. The emotions that bind them together in this highly charged moment are underscored by several devices: her diamond diadem, which corresponds to his gold laurel wreath by Martin-Guillaume Biennais (1764–1843); her folded hands that reflect his hands drawn together to hold the crown; and her ermine-lined, crimson train with gold embroidery, which is the female counterpart to the emperor's mantle.

for Beauharnais' arrest, which led to his death. Since Joséphine herself was saved only by Robespierre's fall, her sentiments concerning the "pageant-master of the Revolution" must have been ambivalent indeed.

She would have frequently encountered David after becoming, around 1795, mistress of the influential Paul Barras, who wore the director's costume designed by David. Then, in Barras' affluent company, Joséphine attended numerous republican events, orchestrated in large part by David. When she became Mme Bonaparte in 1796, however, her relationship with David assumed a different character. In 1797, when she ordered her architect Achilles Vautier to redecorate her house in rue Chantereine in the latest taste, Vautier asked David to design a frieze for one of the rooms. In December the painter was presented to Bonaparte at a dinner given by Joseph Lagarde, secretary of the Directoire. Here David found his "new hero," becoming Bonaparte's ardent supporter. Although a most reluctant sitter, the "hero" consented to remain quiet long enough for David to achieve a stunning, although unfinished portrait. This meeting with France's leader marked the beginning of an exciting phase in the artist's career and ushered David into Joséphine's immediate circle. They certainly met at the museum and at public exhibitions, and by 1798 David could even be counted among Joséphine's guests in her personal salon. This eclectic group included the daring Thérèse Tallien; captivating Juliette Recamier (whose portrait both David and Gérard painted); David's students Gérard and Girodet-Trioson; and an assortment of newly minted generals, as well as accomplished musicians, playwrights, and poets.

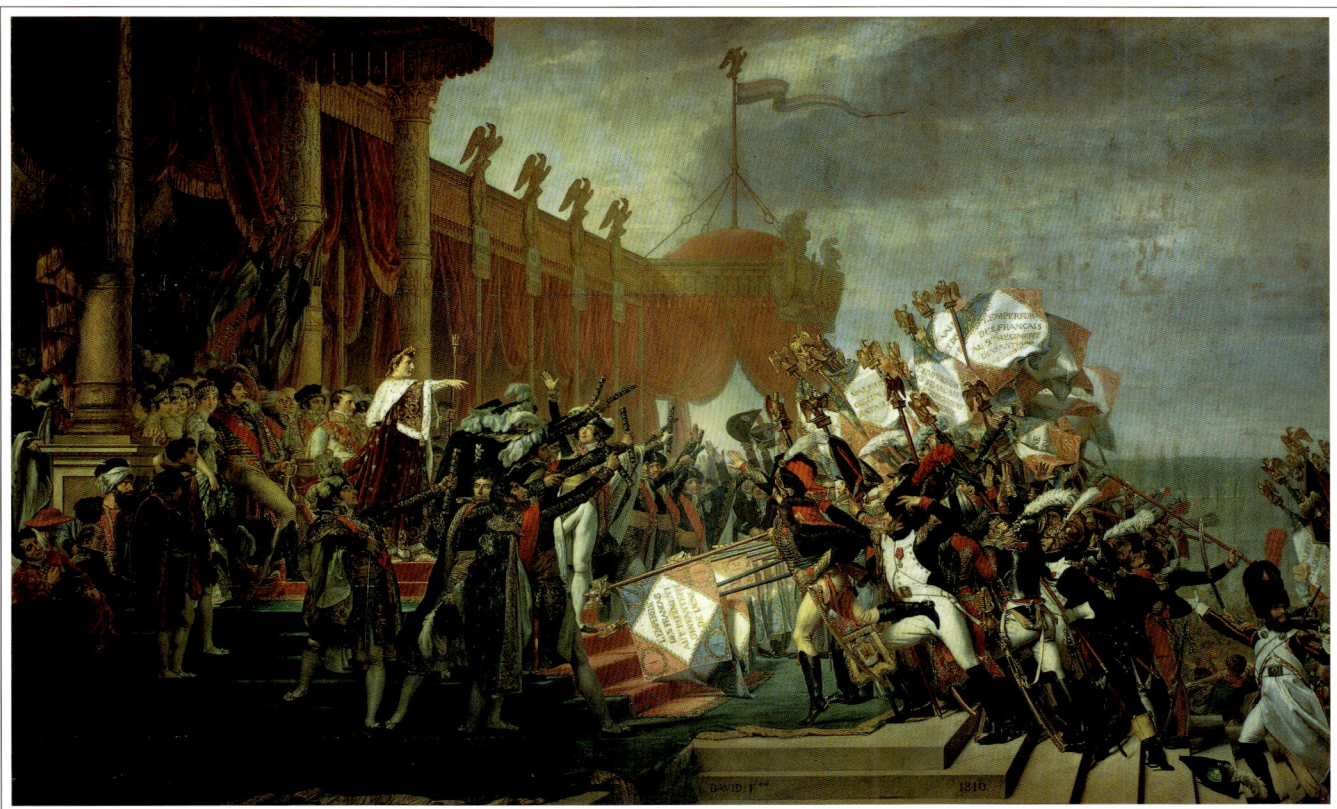

After the Empire was proclaimed in May 1804, Napoléon realized that the versatile David could be immensely useful, for he knew how to exploit the political utility of art. So David was made first painter to the emperor and received commissions for four large pictures to document the ceremonies of the reign, which, had they been completed, might have formed the Empire complement to Peter Paul Rubens's famed cycle in the Luxembourg Palace.

The first painting presented the formidable challenge of depicting the coronation of Joséphine and Napoléon, an ambitious piece requiring numerous, exacting portraits of the participants. The resulting work, *The Consecration of the Emperor Napoléon and the Coronation of Empress Joséphine (December 2, 1804)*, 1806–7 {FIGURE 24}, required many hours of sittings and countless preparatory drawings. As the complex composition began to evolve in David's drawings, Joséphine became the focus of attention, apparently due to Gérard's suggestion to his former teacher that the moment he should depict was Napoléon's courtly gesture as he bestowed the crown on Joséphine's head, and David agreed. As the emperor remarked to David on viewing the finished painting, "I am grateful to you for recording for posterity the proof of the affection I wish to give to the woman who shares with me the burden of office."[36]

When David had first met Napoléon, he was overjoyed by his hero's appearance, exclaiming to his pupils: "What a beautiful head he has! It is pure . . . beautiful like the antique."[37] So this is how David presents him—as an idealized head crowned by a victor's wreath. Since Joséphine was cast in the same mold, David was able to capitalize on the

FIGURE 25.

Jacques-Louis David (French, 1748–1825),
*The Oath of the Army Made to the Emperor
after the Distribution of Eagles at the Champs de Mars
(December 5, 1804)*, 1810.
Oil on canvas, 610 × 931 cm (240 × 367½ in.).
Versailles, Musée national des Châteaux
de Versailles et de Trianon.

· · ·

This ceremony recalls those of the ancien régime, for the architects Percier and Fontaine's sumptuous pavilion surmounted by eagles is in the tradition of those elaborate structures created for the royal fêtes. The military assume rather odd postures, such as the officer poised on one toe, as in Gianbologna's *Mercury*. The gilt eagles atop the magnificent gold-embroidered standards were designed by the sculptor Antoine-Denis Chaudet (1763–1810), whose work—along with paintings by his wife, Elisabeth Chaudet (1767–1832)—graced Joséphine's collection.

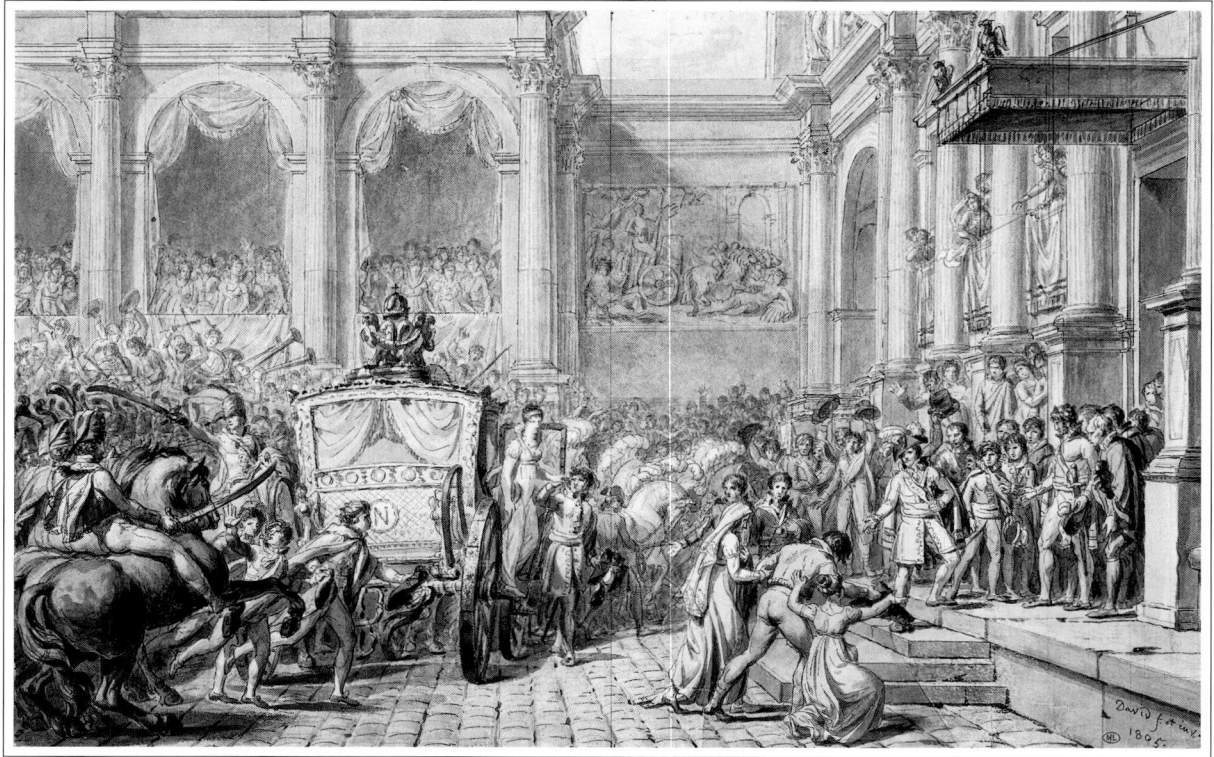

FIGURE 26.

Jacques-Louis David (French, 1748–1825), *Sketch for "The Arrival of the Emperor at the Hôtel de Ville, Paris (December 16, 1804),"* 1805. Brown ink, gray wash, white highlights, 26.2 × 40.8 cm (10¼ × 16⅛ in.). Paris, Musée du Louvre.

• • •

Although David's sketch is dated 1805, he did not produce the painting at this time, because Napoléon wanted him to execute the *Oath of the Army* (see FIGURE 25). Although there are images of the imperial couple in their carriage and of Napoléon on horseback at military reviews in the Tuileries courtyard, this is an unusual example of a portrayal of the sovereigns mingling with the populace. Joséphine's great popularity solidly contributed to Napoléon's meteoric political ascension, but her successor, Marie-Louise, was not enthusiastically accepted by the French people.

pleasing regularity of her features, turning the aquiline nose, slender neck, and well-shaped head into another classical profile. Her surprisingly youthful appearance is not entirely due to artistic license, however, for Claire de Rémusat recorded that the empress seemed to have been transformed into a girl of twenty-five on the day of her coronation.

The only works of the proposed series that David completed were the *Coronation* {see FIGURE 24} and *The Oath of the Army Made to the Emperor after the Distribution of Eagles at the Champs de Mars (December 5, 1804)* {FIGURE 25}. Despite her prominence in the *Coronation*, Joséphine's likeness had to be deleted from *The Oath of the Army*, for by the time David finished it in 1810, the divorce was a fait accompli—the sad consequence of her not bearing a child to the emperor. She is represented instead by her two children, Queen Hortense and Prince Eugène, whose leg juts forward to fill the awkward void at the emperor's side. Eugène is also a conspicuous figure in the *Coronation*; his handsome profile is seen at far right, and his hand thrusts out to hold a splendid sword that is distracting two choirboys.

The final piece in the proposed series is known only from David's *Sketch for "The Arrival of the Emperor at the Hôtel de Ville"* {FIGURE 26}. Here Joséphine is the central figure, descending from her carriage "like the life-giving sun," in David's words, greeted by a grateful populace.[38] Only later do we realize that the man at the top of the steps is Napoléon, for David has highlighted Joséphine, whose stately figure is aligned with a Corinthian column (the feminine order) and framed by the opulent carriage and gleaming white horses.

After *The Oath of the Army* was completed, a rupture occurred in David's relationship with the all-powerful Denon. By 1810 the artistic dictator of the Empire had come to prefer Joséphine's own protégés, Gros and Prud'hon, to the work of the first painter himself.[39]

Notes

1. The Musée du Louvre was called the Musée Napoléon from 1803 to 1815.
2. Joséphine rented quarters in 1794 from Mme de Krény, Vivant Denon's mistress.
3. This had been confiscated from The Hague by the Directoire.
4. Jean Hanoteau, ed., *Mémoirs de la reine Hortense*, 3 vols. (Paris, 1927), 95. Mme de Souza, mother of Charles de Flahaut, was rearing Hortense's illegitimate child by Flahaut. Guillaume-Jean Constantin restored Joséphine's paintings and was an adviser.
5. Bernard Chevallier, *L'Art de vivre au temps de Joséphine* (Paris, 1998), 143.
6. Charles Percier and Pierre François Léonard Fontaine, *Recueil de décorations intérieures : comprenant tout ce qui a rapport à l'ameublement : comme vases, trépieds, candélabres, cassolettes . . . miroirs, écrans, &c.&c.&c.* (Paris, 1812).
7. The title is a misnomer because Duroc, Caulaincourt, and Marmont had not yet become marshals.
8. André Barret, *Sautecoeur* (Paris, 1998), 122.
9. She was in Italy from July 10, 1796, until January 2, 1798.
10. Barret, *Sautecoeur*, 290.
11. Gros was apparently at the battle of Arcole on November 17, 1796. See Geneviève Lacombre entry, exh. cat., Paris Exposition 1974, 470.
12. Nicole Hubert, in *Dictionaire Napoléon*, Jean Tulard, ed. (Paris, 1989), 845.
13. Eugène Delacroix, *Ecrits sur l'art* (Paris, 1988), 177
14. Jean Massin, *Almanac du Premier Empire du Neuf Thermidor à Waterloo* (Paris, 1965), 63.
15. Delacroix, *Ecrits sur l'art* (Paris, 1988), 177.
16. Christopher Prendergast, *Napoléon and History Painting* (Oxford, 1997), 146.
17. Timothy Wilson-Smith, *Napoléon and His Artists* (London, 1996), 68.
18. Wilson-Smith, *Napoléon and His Artists*, 262.
19. Denon's collection included painting, sculpture, Egyptian artifacts, and death masks. It was catalogued and published by Firmin Didot in 1829, with illustrations by Ingres' pupil, Eugène Amaury-Duval.
20. Once in a collection in Maine (see Knapton, *Empress Joséphine*, figure 3.).
21. Quoted in Jacques Godechot, *Napoléon* (Paris, 1969), 250.
22. Charles Clement, *Prud'hon* (Paris, 1872), 293.
23. Joséphine's initial interest in Canova possibly came from Prud'hon.
24. *French Painting 1774–1830: The Age of Revolution*, exh. cat., Grand Palais, Paris, November 16, 1974–February 3, 1975 (Paris, 1975), 567. She rented the house on August 17, 1795.
25. Sylvain Laveissière, *Pierre-Paul Prud'hon* (New York, 1998), 193.
26. Jacques-Philippe Voiart, quoted in Wilson-Smith, *Napoléon and His Artists*; italics added. "Amateur" at the time meant connoisseur.
27. Mme de Chastenay, quoted in Laveissière, *Pierre-Paul Prud'hon*, 184.
28. Frochot had known Joséphine since *Brumaire* and supported Bonaparte's coup d'état.
29. Joséphine and Girodet-Trioson had a mutual acquaintance in the renowned botanist, baron von Humboldt, whose many studies in the field of mineralogy were of great interest to both Girodet-Trioson and Joséphine.
30. Syvain Bellenger's definitive study of Girodet-Trioson is forthcoming.
31. The same motif is seen in Guérin's *Iris and Morpheus*. It was owned by the Francophile collector Count Sommariva and then by Prince Yousoupoff.
32. Although Wilson-Smith claims that the painting had a "revolutionary pre-history" in David's *Death of Bara* of 1794, this is untenable, for Girodet-Trioson had finished *Endymion* three years before, in 1791 (see Wilson-Smith, *Napoléon and His Artists*, 174).
33. A schoolmaster, James Macpherson, heard fragments of Ossianic legends as he traveled through Scotland. He translated them from Gaelic into English, weaving figments of his imagination with the so-called poems of blind Ossian and published this work around 1765.
34. This was the comte Auguste de Forbin, whose *Interior of a Medieval Chapel* was bought by Vivant Denon and was among the first neo-Gothic paintings.
35. Girodet-Trioson's Ossian painting was condemned by his teacher David, who famously complained about Girodet-Trioson's "personnages de cristal" (crystal people).
36. Lee, Simon, *David* (London, 1999), 258–59.
37. E. J. Etiènne Jean Delécluze, *Louis David, son école et son temps: Souvenir de M. E. J. Delécluze* (Paris, 1855), 203.
38. Dorothy Johnson, *Jacques-Louis David* (Princeton, 1993), 189.
39. Fortunately, Napoléon continued to respect David's talent, and in 1812 David painted the likeness that the emperor considered the best, *Napoléon in His Study*, commissioned by the marquis of Douglas.

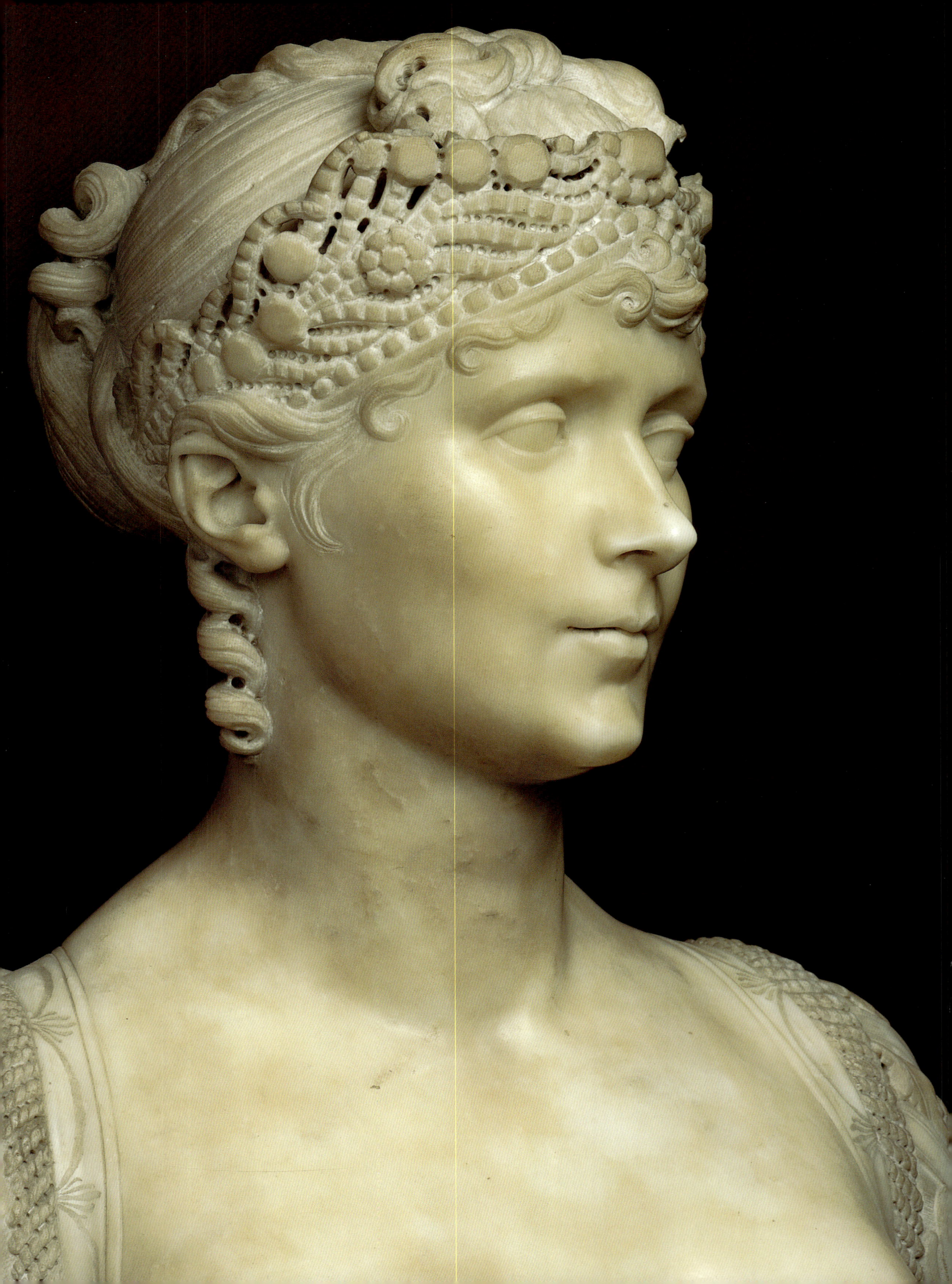

CHAPTER 2

Eleanor P. DeLorme

A Taste for the Antique: Joséphine's Preferences in Sculpture

Joséphine's taste in sculpture was determined by her aristocratic heritage, the ambience of her social position as viscountess and then empress, and her unique opportunity to study at will the unparalleled collection at the museum adjoining her official Paris residence, the Tuileries Palace. As a woman of the late eighteenth century, she was naturally drawn to sculpture in the classical tradition, especially pieces associated with the previous queen, Marie-Antoinette. Joséphine's apartments at the Tuileries were embellished with furnishings once used by the queen, her rooms at the summer château of Saint-Cloud held small bronzes from the queen's collection (including an Apollo Belvedere), and in 1803 Joséphine decorated her *laiterie* (dairy) with Pierre Julien's marble friezes based on stories of Jupiter from Marie-Antoinette's chillingly classical pavilion, the Laiterie at Rambouillet.[1]

Other bronzes in Joséphine's collection came from excavations at Herculaneum, contributed by Ferdinand IV, king of Naples,[2] and took their places beside numerous antique busts, reliefs, medallions, and "Etruscan" vases that Joséphine had been collecting since the Consulate regime (1800–1804).[3] Soon her Grande Galerie at Malmaison became so crowded that she had to add several salons to the great conservatory in her gardens to accommodate the overflow.

Joséphine's sculpture by contemporary French artists also celebrated classical themes in works such as *Cupid Playing with the Doves of Venus* by the ancien régime sculptor

Louis-Claude Vassé (1716–1772); *Modesty* by Pierre Cartellier (1757–1831), based on the antique Capitoline *Venus*; and *Cyparissus Mourning His Fawn* by Antoine-Denis Chaudet (1763–1810). Taking pride of place in Joséphine's personal gallery, however, was her collection by the undisputed master of Neoclassicism in all of Europe, the prodigious Italian genius Antonio Canova (1757–1822), who was to the sculpture of his day what Jacques-Louis David was to painting.

The revolutionary period had not been conducive to the production of fine sculpture, but with the establishment of Napoléon's Consulate regime early in 1800—when he and Joséphine moved into the Tuileries—it rebounded. Most French sculptors, already haunted by the French tradition of Cartesian rationalism, had been trained in Italy, where they copied ancient statuary. They must have been ecstatic in 1798, when Italy's best came to Paris. In that year, a cortège bearing eighty-three antique sculptures (including *Laocoön* and *Apollo Belvedere*) was paraded through Paris, destined for the museum, bearing spoils of Bonaparte's peninsula campaign. The splendidly refurbished galleries, which afforded a worthy mise-en-scène for these masterpieces {FIGURE 27}, were inaugurated in 1800 by Napoléon and Joséphine, and soon the museum was renamed the Musée Napoléon. It attracted such throngs—the general populace (Balzac's "grande troupe de Paris"), along with artists, students, and international visitors—that the architects Charles Percier and Pierre-François-Léonard Fontaine had to construct three large staircases to accommodate

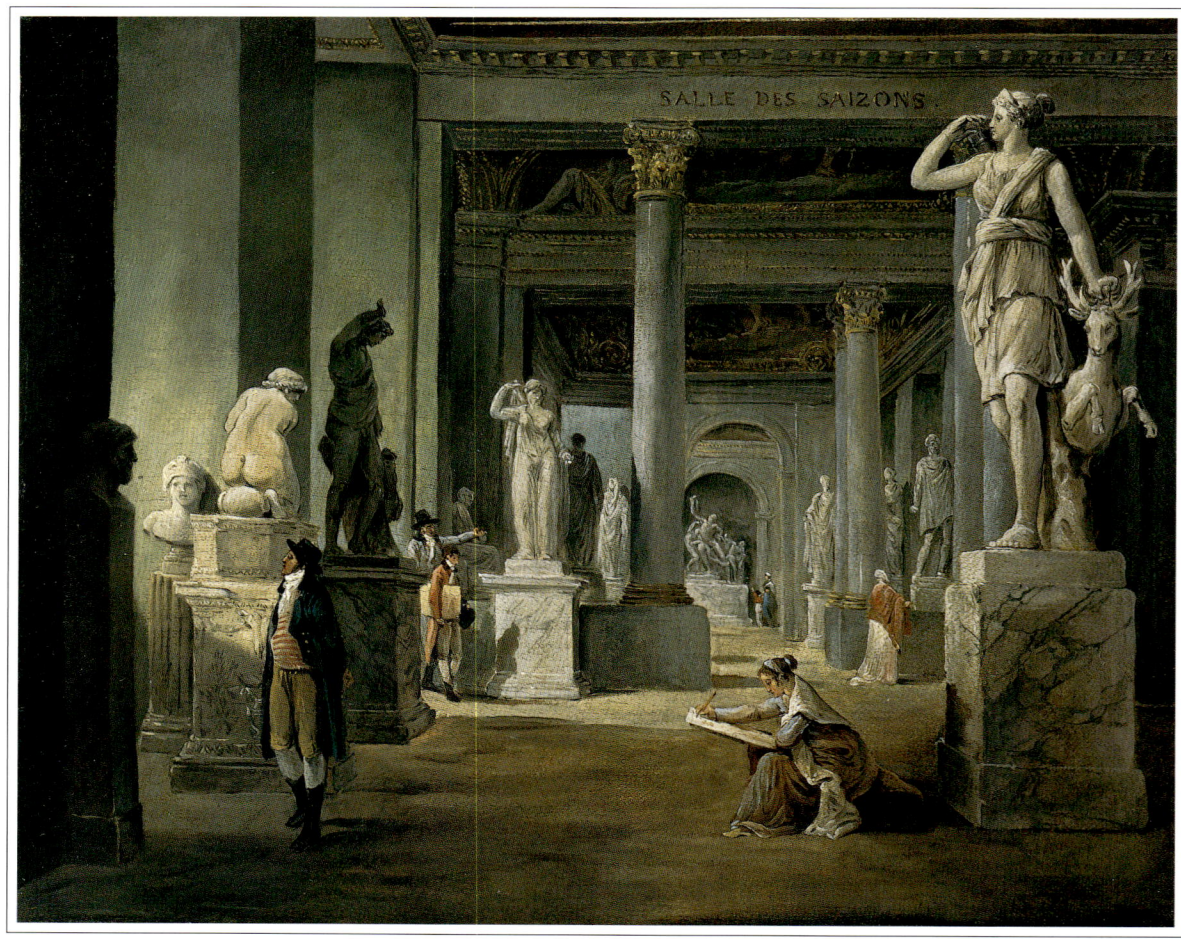

them. In 1807 the sculpture galleries were further glorified by the arrival of 523 pieces from the Villa Borghese in Rome,[4] so Napoléon—in an effort to persuade Canova to move to Paris—could justifiably call his city "the capital of the arts."[5]

Joséphine was the subject of several busts by major French sculptors, including Antoine-Denis Chaudet (1763–1810) and Jean-Antoine Houdon (1741–1828), but it's curious that she never asked her favorite sculptor, Canova, for a portrait. Among the earliest busts of the empress was a realistic, dignified 1805 marble {FIGURE 28} by Joseph Chinard (1756–1813),[6] considered the most refined portraitist of his time. Executed with his accustomed linear precision, the bust must have served official purposes, for Joséphine had just been crowned empress of France at the end of 1804, and in late spring 1805 she became queen of Italy. Chinard emphasizes her exalted position by portraying her in full court dress—a jeweled diadem with rosettes on her head, classical palmettes embroidered on her sleeves, the imperial eagle spreading his wings across the bodice of her gown, and drapery sown with King Childeric's bees, a symbol of the Empire adopted by Napoléon. If this formal image of the empress satisfied imperial decorum, Chinard's heroic bronze bust

FIGURE 27.

Hubert Robert (French, 1733–1808),
The Salle des Saisons at the Louvre, 1802.
Oil on canvas, 37 × 46 cm (14⅝ × 18⅛ in.).
Paris, Musée du Louvre.

• • •

The great *Laocoön* may be seen in its specially designed niche at the end of the gallery, and the *Diana Huntress*, a piece already in France, on the right. All the sculpture brought from Italy had been meticulously packed, and pieces in need of restoration were expertly restored, for the French led the world in this field. While in Italy, Vivant Denon claimed that the Italians did not display their art to best advantage, nor did they provide it with proper care. He intended, therefore, that the Grande Galerie for paintings and the sculpture galleries represented here be models for all of Europe.

FIGURE 28.

Joseph Chinard (French, 1756–1813),
The Empress Joséphine, 1805.
Marble, H: 65 cm (25⅝ in.).
Rueil-Malmaison, Musée national des Châteaux
de Rueil-Malmaison et Bois-Préau.

• • •

Joséphine's portrait demonstrates Chinard's unusual gifts as a portraitist, with his crisp detailing of the features and hair, and scrupulous attention to costume. Although this admired image antedates Bosio's, the empress appears here to be much more mature, perhaps referring to the traditional role of the ruler's consort as "mother of the people." This was borne out in Joséphine's case, for at her death in May 1814, as the country went into mourning, journalists lamented that France had lost her mother. This bust differs dramatically from Chinard's coquettish sculpture of Joséphine's friend Juliette Recamier.

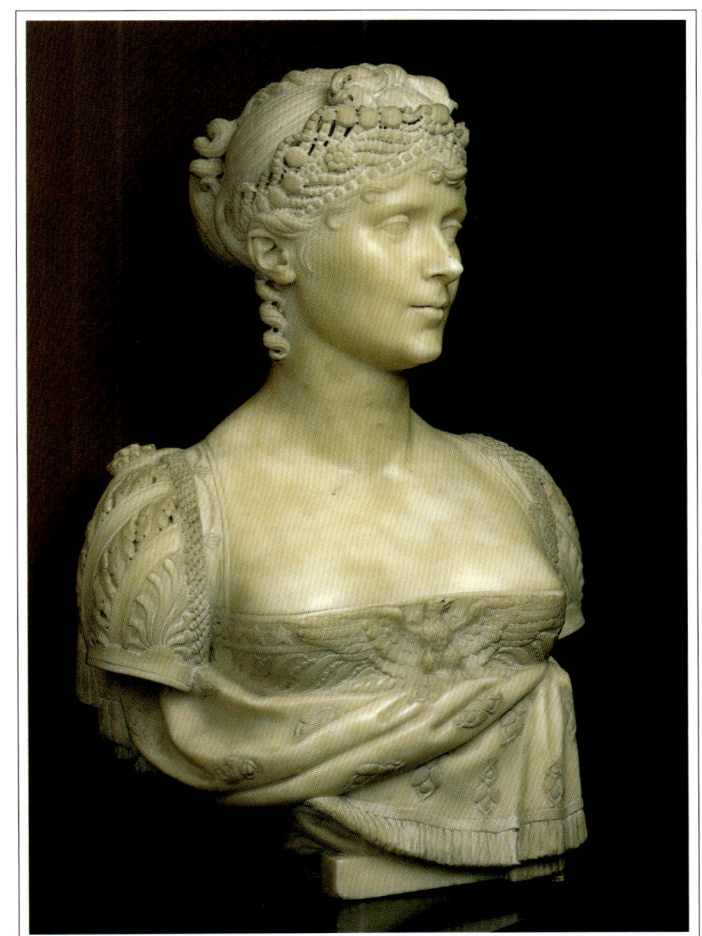

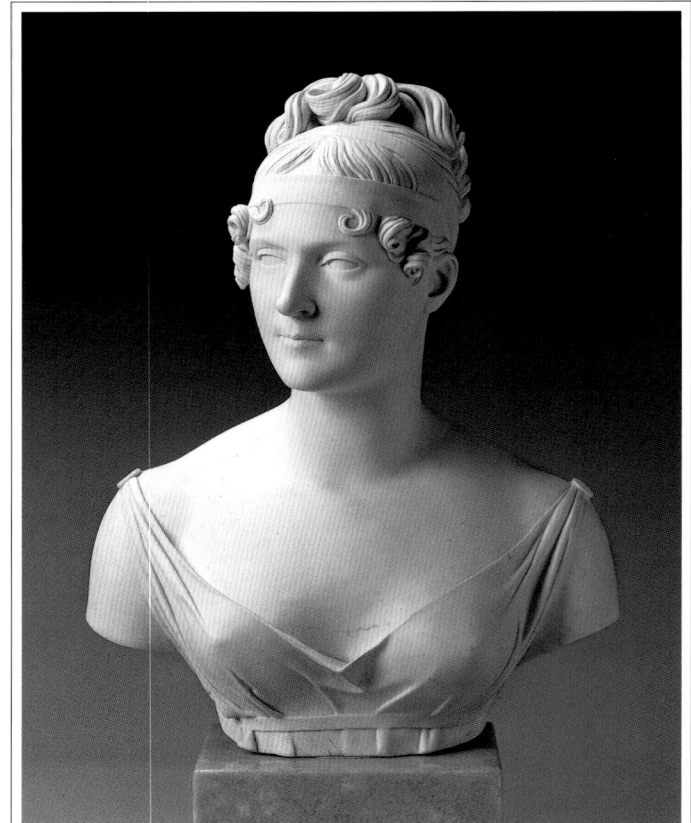

FIGURE 29.

François-Joseph Bosio (French, 1768–1845),
The Empress Joséphine, ca. 1809.
Plaster, H: 72 cm (28⅜ in.).
Rueil-Malmaison, Musée national des Châteaux
de Malmaison et Bois-Préau.

· · ·

This beautifully crafted, sympathetic likeness is the most appealing of the Joséphine busts, conveying the unusual charm, tact, and savoir faire that so endeared her to Napoléon and her contemporaries. Although the empress was forty-six at the time, Bosio presents her as a younger woman, perhaps intending to flatter her, for he was greatly indebted to her for inaugurating his long, productive career. Bosio's bust (like Chaudet's) was reproduced in Sèvres porcelain, one example of which exists at the Marmatton Library. The one at Malmaison rests on the curator Bernard Chevallier's desk.

of Bonaparte (1798) in the Louvre was equally majestic, and it later became the emperor's official portrait.

A more intimate likeness of Joséphine is by François-Joseph Bosio (1768–1845) from Monaco, whose brother, Jean-François, a pupil of David's, was well known for his amusing vignettes of Paris society.[7] After François-Joseph's return from Rome in 1807—where he had been studying with Canova—Joséphine sponsored his Paris debut, encouraged by her influential friend and adviser, Vivant Denon, director of the Musée Napoléon. Joséphine was obviously so impressed by this gifted young artist that, through Denon, she granted Bosio permission to execute her portrait {FIGURE 29}, which presents his patroness as an alluring young woman in a simple Grecian gown with no jewelry. This charming, seductive work became the most popular representation of the empress.

Bosio's delicate, sensitively modeled bust so pleased Napoléon that he asked the sculptor to execute his own, a singular honor that had been granted previously only to Canova. Bosio was the Italian master's most important disciple, and Alison West considers him, along with Chinard and Chaudet, to be one of the triumvirate she calls "the Canovians."[8] Joséphine's bust was so compelling that it brought the artist additional princely and imperial commissions, and under the Restoration he was named baron.

Between 1808 and 1812 Bosio produced *Cupid Loosing His Arrows and Flying Away*. Joséphine had paid an evening visit to the renowned Salon of 1808, where the plaster model of this sculpture so attracted her attention that she commissioned it in marble and then generously lent it to the Salon of 1812.[9] She set this example of Bosio's refined sensuality at the center of a spacious salon in her huge garden conservatory where it could be appreciated from every angle and its classicism would resonate with the Attic ceiling paintings {FIGURE 30}.

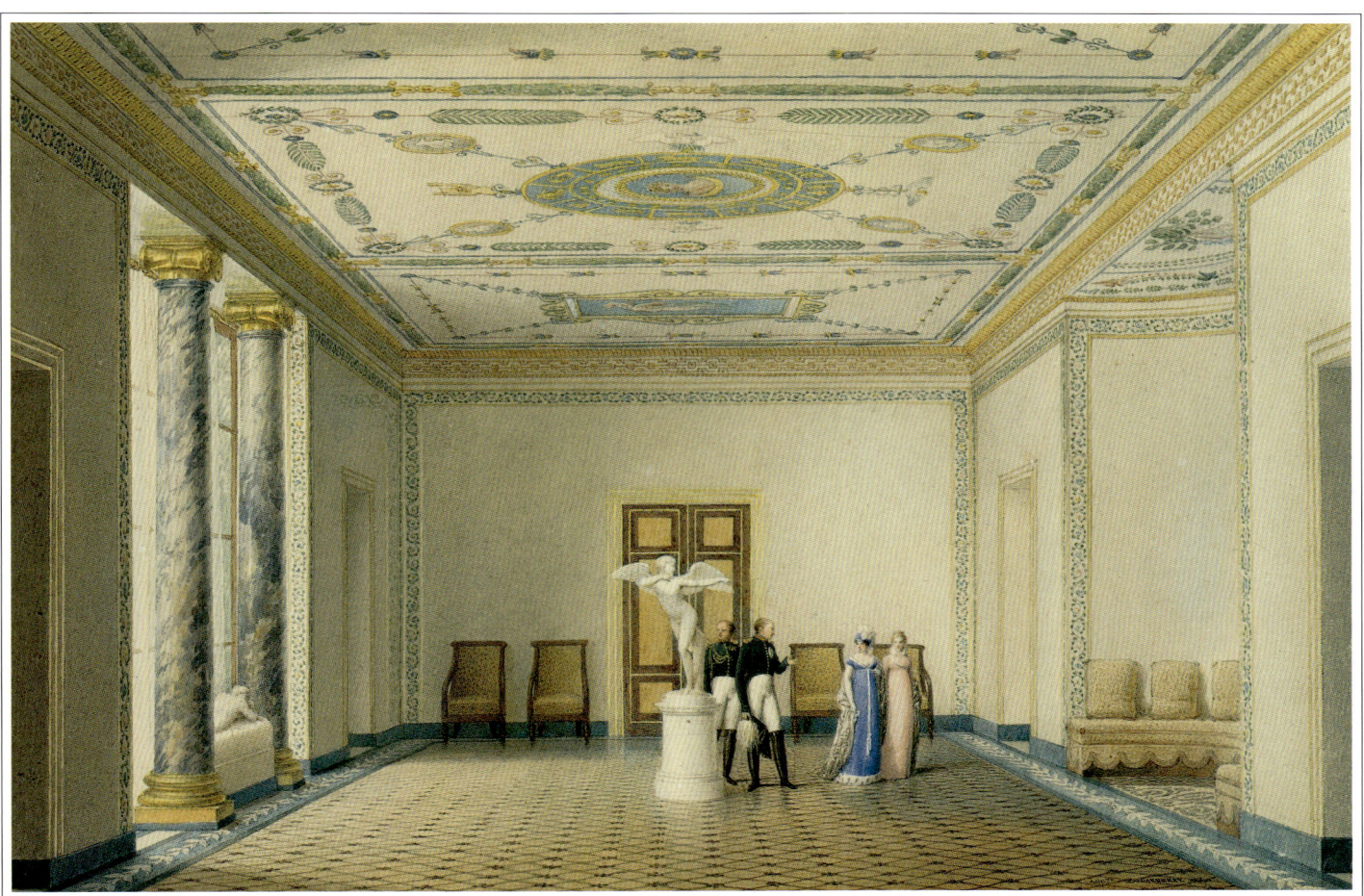

The same is true of the classical *Sleeping Hermaphrodite* {see FIGURE 30} owned by Joséphine.[10] This figure was transformed into the dreaming shepherd in Anne-Louis Girodet-Trioson's *Sleep of Endymion*, Bosio's supine *Hyacinth*, and Canova's interpretation of *Endymion* at Chatsworth.

One sculptor whose work was ever before Joséphine's eyes was the fine classicist Pierre Cartellier (1757–1831), who participated in the sculptural decor of most of the capital monuments. Like Joséphine, Cartellier was a product of the ancien régime. His career was promoted by both Denon and Antoine Chrysosthôme Quatremère de Quincy (1755–1849),[11] a close friend of Canova's and an influential connoisseur and critic who designed many public programs and was also trained as a sculptor. Cartellier's statues of the statesmen Aristides and Verniaud stood in the senate; his bas-reliefs decorated the Diana Salon of the Tuileries; and his *Glory Distributing Crowns* (1807) surmounted the eastern entrance of the museum at the doorstep of the Tuileries. For Joséphine, the latter relief was not merely an abstraction but a tangible tribute to her illustrious husband's victorious campaigns of 1805–6, when Joséphine represented Europe's foremost court in the key cities of Strasbourg, France, and Mainz, Germany. In his masterful *Glory Distributing Crowns*, Cartellier forged a "vigorous new language"[12] with the winged figure of Glory

FIGURE 30.

Auguste Garnerey (French, 1785–1824), *Salon of the Conservatory at Malmaison*, ca. 1814. Watercolor, 16.3 × 24.3 cm (6⅜ × 9⅝ in.). Rueil-Malmaison, Musée national des Châteaux de Malmaison et Bois-Préau.

• • •

In this painting, Czar Alexander and his brother, Nicholas I, are being received in the conservatory by Joséphine and her daughter, Hortense, just days before Joséphine's death. They stand beside Jean-François Bosio's *Cupid Loosing His Arrows and Flying Away*, one of the sculptures that Alexander took to Saint Petersburg after Joséphine died. Between the marble Ionic columns on the left is a partial view of *Sleeping Hermaphrodite*, representing a subject common to sculpture and painting.

distributing laurel leaves and standing in a Roman chariot drawn by symmetrical teams of lively war horses that spread out above the arch.

Yet it was an example of Cartellier's more intimate classicism that Joséphine chose for her gallery—the delicate yet noble statue *Modesty* {FIGURE 31}. Whereas his *Glory* relief was based on the ancient *Carpegna Cameo*, which depicted a *Triumph of Bacchus* recently acquired by the Musée Napoléon, his *Modesty* owed its pensive elegance to the Capitoline *Venus*, which was in Paris at the time. *Modesty* was one of several statues from Joséphine's gallery that she lent to the acclaimed Salon of 1808, as seen in the painting by Louis-Léopold Boilly {see FIGURE 4} that records Joséphine and her daughter, Queen Hortense of Holland, looking on as Napoléon decorates Cartellier for his achievements. The Salon of 1808 was an especially gratifying occasion for Joséphine, for also shown there was the sculptor's full-length marble statue of Hortense's husband, Louis Bonaparte, King of Holland, which Denon considered to be a remarkable likeness and the most beautiful of all the statues that had been ordered. Cartellier executed a bust of Louis as well, and Joséphine commissioned from the sculptor—probably through Denon—a bust (now lost) of her adorable grandchild, Napoléon-Charles.[13] Hortense and Louis' son had tragically died in March 1807, before his fifth birthday. Had he lived, Napoléon would doubtless have adopted this child he so loved.[14]

Like Joséphine's favorite painter, Prud'hon, the versatile Cartellier also turned his hand to decorative projects. He modeled the torchères for the empress's coronation, the cupids for her monumental jewel cabinet—a masterpiece of *ébénisterie* (cabinetwork) by François-Honoré-Georges Jacob (1770–1841), known as Jacob-Desmalter—and the Three Graces for the spectacular silver-gilt centerpiece designed by Prud'hon and made by Pierre-Philippe Thomire (1751–1843) for Joséphine's brother-in-law, the discriminating collector Lucien Bonaparte.

Since Joséphine held the sculptor Cartellier in high regard, it is fitting that her children, Eugène and Hortense, chose him to execute their mother's funerary monument for her tomb in the church of Rueil-Malmaison. Cartellier appropriately invokes the pose that David made famous in his monumental canvas recording her coronation—Joséphine genuflecting as her husband, the Emperor Napoléon, steps forward, about to bestow the crown upon her head. But in Cartellier's moving image, Joséphine kneels to receive her heavenly crown from the unseen hand of her Lord and Creator.

FIGURE 31.

Pierre Cartellier (French, 1757–1831),
Modesty, 1808.
Plaster, marble, H: 163.5 cm (64⅜ in.);
W: 48 cm (18⅞ in.); D: 38.5 cm (15⅛ in.).
Amsterdam Historical Museum.

· · ·

Vivant Denon probably prompted Joséphine to commission this marble personifying the virtue of modesty after a plaster version of it was exhibited at the Salon of 1801. It is modeled with subtle nuances and graceful lines, conveying the sculptor's personal interpretation of a quality considered admirable in women. Cartellier was equally adept at creating public works. Even during the Revolution, through Quatremère de Quincy, Cartellier was commissioned to execute a pendentive of the Pantheon and later the reliefs of War and Vigilance for the Luxembourg Palace, seat of government during the Directoire period.

FIGURE 32.

Antoine-Denis Chaudet (French, 1763–1810),
Young Oedipus Brought Back to Life by the Shepherd Phorbas, 1802–10.
Marble, H: 196 cm (77⅛ in.);
W: 75 cm (29½ in.); D: 82 cm (32¼ in.).
Paris, Musée du Louvre.

· · ·

This important piece was left unfinished at Chaudet's death in 1810 and was completed by Cartellier and Charles Dupaty (1771–1825) between 1815 and 1818. Its suave finish should no doubt be credited to Cartellier. At the Salon of 1801 Chaudet had received a prize for his plaster of this sculpture based upon an antique. The vigorous modeling of the dog's fur, Phorbas's carefully stylized ringlets, and the baby's soft, petal-smooth skin are typical of Chaudet's delight in textural contrasts.

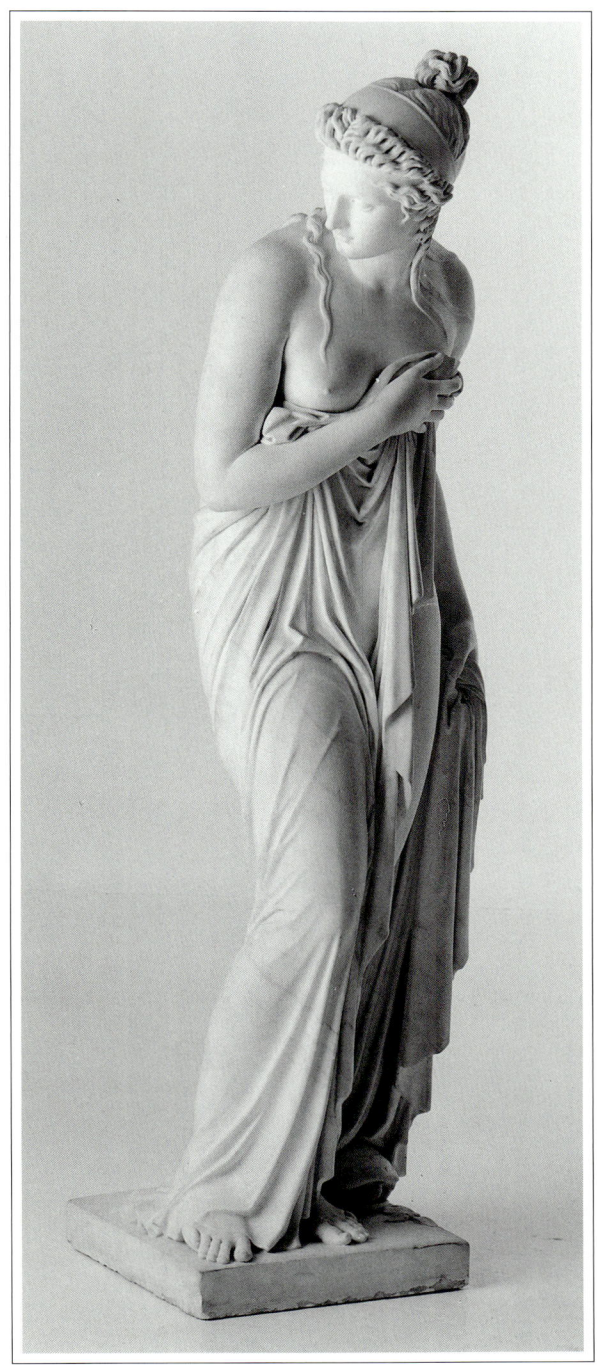 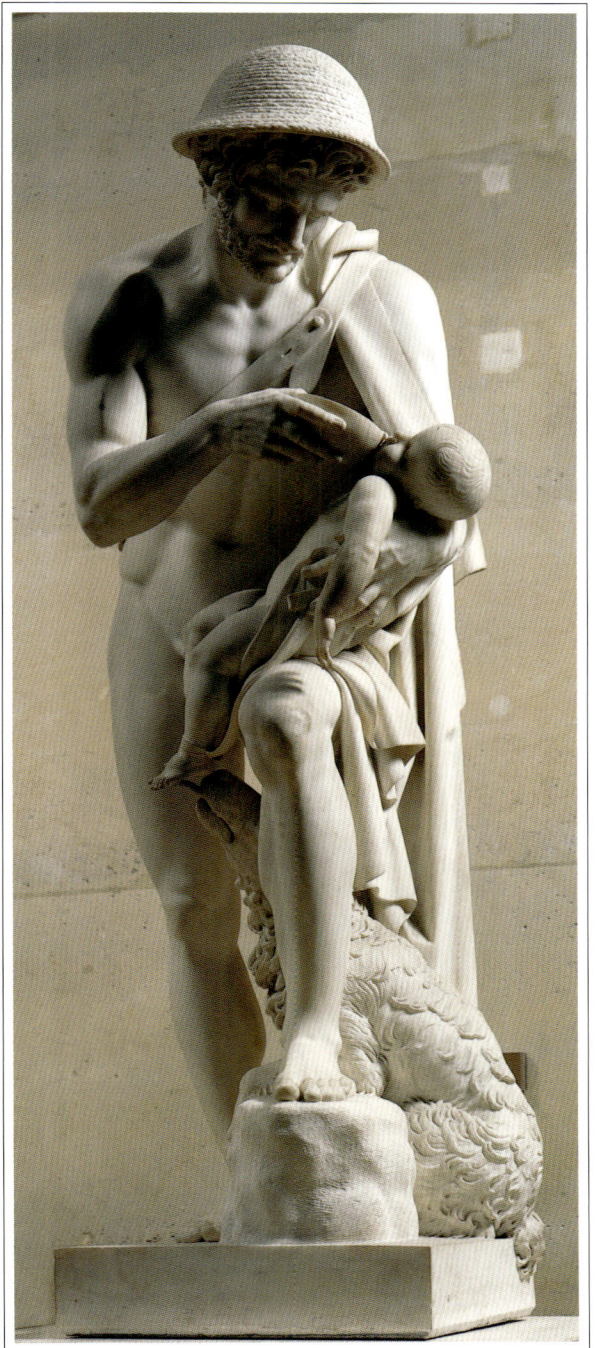

The enormously gifted Antoine-Denis Chaudet (1763–1810), a close friend of Cartellier's, died at the apex of a brilliant career. Like his contemporaries, Chaudet valued the hallowed classical tradition, but his was a classicism based on a gracious antiquity rather than the tragic, virile antiquity embraced by David. It was no doubt for this reason that Chaudet's beautifully executed work particularly appealed to Joséphine. His heroic official portrait of Bonaparte (1798) and his charmingly discreet bust of Joséphine in plaster, marble, and Sèvres porcelain established his reputation.[15] Chaudet thus became the emperor's principal portraitist. Joséphine also owned Chaudet's *Blind Belisarius*, a bronze portrayal of the hapless Byzantine general, who is represented seated, staff in hand, with his young companion asleep at his feet. Like the motif surrounding the *Sleeping*

Hermaphrodite {see FIGURE 30; and chapter 1}, the Belisarius theme also pervaded various arts, including literature, music, painting, and ceramics.

Chaudet's fame had already been virtually ensured after he completed his plaster model of the anecdotal *Cyparissus Mourning His Fawn* in 1798. The artist's tender treatment of this sentimental subject from classical mythology, with its undulating lines, Praxitelean grace, and polished skin, obviously appealed to Joséphine, so she acquired it for her Malmaison gallery. It took its place beside the empress's paintings by the sculptor's wife, Elisabeth Chaudet,[16] among them *Young Girl Feeding Her Chickens*, which, despite its bucolic subject, reveals a graceful female figure that might have descended from one of Joséphine's Attic vases. More attuned to the elegiac note running through the painting and sculpture of the Consulate and Empire periods was Elisabeth's *Young Girl Mourning the Death of Her Pigeon*, closely related in sentiment to her husband's sculpted *Cyparissus*.

A more sanguine subject that Chaudet undertook around the same time was the complex *Young Oedipus Brought Back to Life by the Shepherd Phorbas* {FIGURE 32}. The strong yet compassionate figure of Phorbas supports the limp body of the baby Oedipus, whom Phorbas has untied from a tree and is nursing back to life. Chaudet also introduces a note of gentle humor in the figure of the curly-haired dog, who is helping his master revive the baby by licking the sole of his tiny foot.

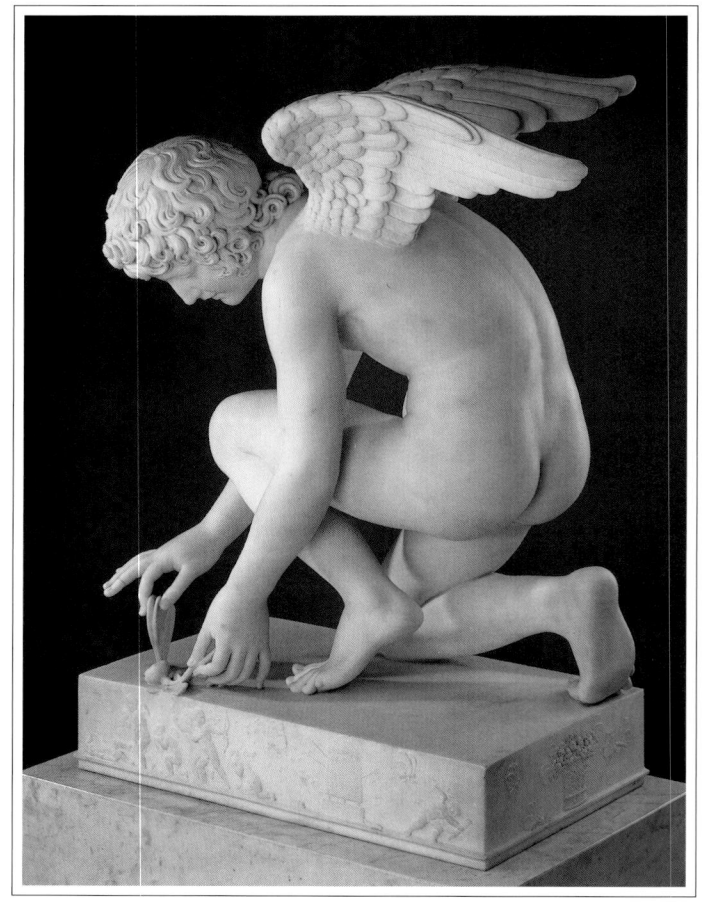

FIGURE 33.

Antoine-Denis Chaudet (French, 1763–1810), *Cupid Playing with a Butterfly*, 1802–17.
Marble, H: 77.5 cm (30½ in.);
L: 64 cm (25¼ in.); D: 44 cm (17⅜ in.).
Paris, Musée du Louvre.

• • •

Like the *Young Oedipus* (see FIGURE 32), this engaging marble was also left unfinished by its author; and, at the request of Chaudet's widow, it too was completed by their longtime friend Pierre Cartellier. The iconography was readily understood by Chaudet's contemporaries, since the theme of love beguiling the soul—symbolized by the butterfly—was exploited in numerous works of art. One was François Gérard's exquisite painting of 1798, *Cupid and Psyche*, in which Cupid leans protectively over Psyche as the butterfly hovers overhead.

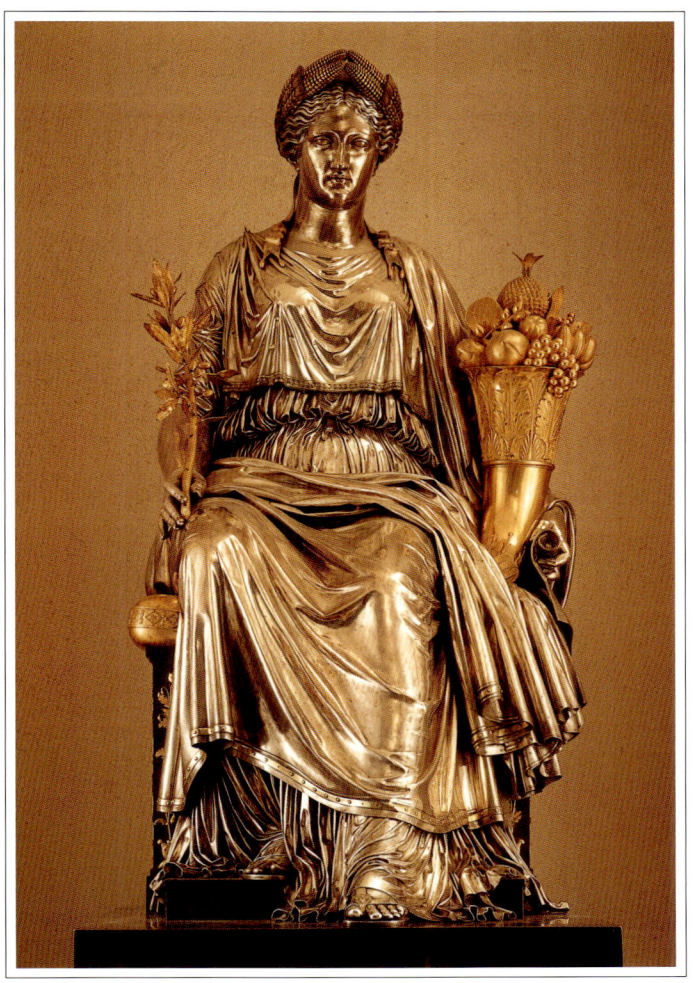

Figure 34.

Antoine-Denis Chaudet (French, 1763–1810),
Peace, 1803–5, cast in 1806.
Silver statue with gold chasing, H: 167 cm (65¾ in.);
w: 108 cm (42½ in.); D: 84 cm (33⅛ in.).
Paris, Musée du Louvre.

• • •

The opulence of the Empire is manifested in this noble figure of Peace, made from silver irreverently melted down from silver angels that had adorned the reliquaries for the hearts of the Bourbon kings, Louis XIV and his father, from the church of Saint Paul du Marais. Nevertheless, the transformation wrought by Chaudet and cast by Cherest is appropriate to the abundance implied by the subject. This stunning achievement typifies—in another medium—Chaudet's precision of detail, from the wheatears in her hair to the rippling drapery flowing about her feet, a superb passage of sculpture.

At the Salon of 1802 Joséphine's taste for Graeco-Roman subjects drew her to Chaudet's delightful plaster model for *Cupid Playing with a Butterfly* {FIGURE 33}, although she never owned it.[17] In this "most typically Neoclassical work in French sculpture,"[18] Cupid kneels to offer a rose to a butterfly, a symbol of the soul. In its purity of line and delicate modeling, the completed marble recalls the Canovian charm of the Italian master whose work Joséphine so passionately collected. One of her Canova pieces, the standing *Cupid and Psyche* (discussed in detail later), depicts the two figures contemplating a butterfly held in the palm of Psyche's hand.

Chaudet's was such a flexible talent that he lent his hand in 1803 to one of the most precious pieces created during the Empire period, both in the subtle nuances of its execution and costly material—a large silver statue of Peace {FIGURE 34} in the Louvre. In 1800 a provisional forty-foot statue of this figure had been erected on the Pont Neuf with the usual celebrations and fireworks, but at the end of the year Counselor Chaptal ordered its removal and replacement with a life-size sculpture. Ultimately, it was made not of marble but of silver with gold chasing, and Chaudet was commissioned to execute it.

When a viewer first encounters *Peace* in the Louvre, the visual impact is unforgettable. The sculptor conceived this authoritative, hieratic image as an ancient Ceres, with an overflowing cornucopia in her left hand symbolizing the blessings of peace, the traditional olive branch in her right hand, and a diadem of wheatears crowning her stylized hair.[19]

The formation of Chaudet's style owed much to his years in Rome (1784–88), where he had been privileged to meet Canova. According to Gérard Hubert, Chaudet became "the best representative of Neoclassical idealism in France in the style of Canova."[20] In 1802 Canova was called to Paris to carve the heroic bust of the first consul, and Quatremère de Quincy, the sculptor's intimate friend and advocate, took this occasion to emphasize to French sculptors the preeminent authority of the Italian master. Not that the illustrious artist came willingly, but since it was the master of Europe who had summoned him, and because Paris was now the acknowledged center of Western civilization, Canova could hardly refuse. As it turned out, his pleasurable association with Joséphine helped compensate for having to leave his Roman atelier, as did his flattering appointment to the prestigious Institut de France. In fact, Canova's period of association with the Bonapartes marked the summit of his career.

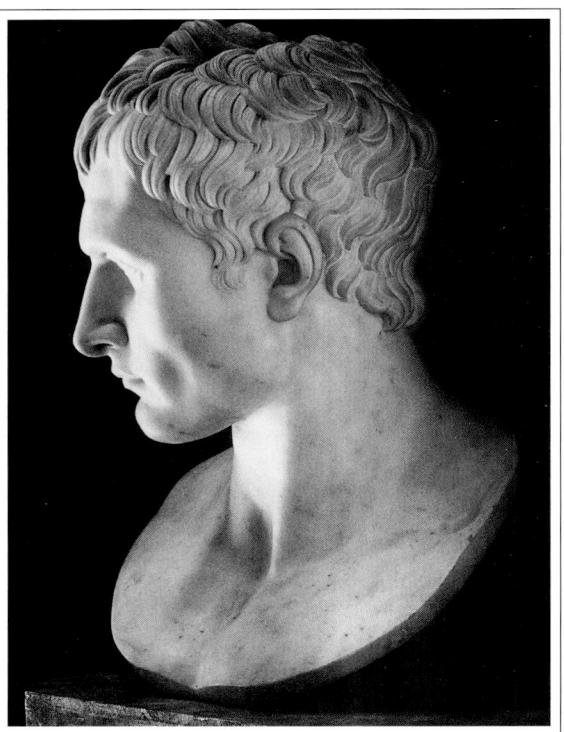

Joséphine would first have seen his early *Daedalus and Icarus* in 1797 while staying at the Palazzo Pisani Moretto in Venice, when she visited Bonaparte during his Italian campaigns. Her husband provided Canova a pension, and her brother-in-law, the famed cavalryman Joaquim Murat (who married Napoléon's sister, Caroline Bonaparte), protected Canova's atelier and became the first in the Bonaparte family to own a work by Canova—the reclining and standing groups of *Cupid and Psyche*.[21]

During the summer of 1802, with all France celebrating the Peace of Amiens, Caroline and Joaquim Murat gave a lavish party to honor the first consul and Joséphine at their château Villiers-la-Garenne near Paris.[22] The two Canova groups had just arrived, and Joséphine was so overwhelmed that she became, from that moment on, an impassioned collector of his work. By September 28 of that year—through the scholar Ennio Visconti, then working at the museum—Canova had agreed to sculpt for Joséphine a second group of the Murats' standing *Cupid and Psyche*[23] and a second version of *Hébé* that was commissioned by the Venetian patrician Giuseppe Albrizzi.[24]

That fall Joséphine and Bonaparte were living at Saint-Cloud, where she must have been eagerly supervising the preparations of a temporary atelier for Canova to work on his monumental portrait of Bonaparte {FIGURE 35}.[25] When the sculptor arrived in late October, his initial impression of Joséphine's husband was similar to that experienced by Jacques-Louis David, who found Bonaparte "as beautiful as the antique." When Canova, accompanied by Quatremère de Quincy, was presented to Bonaparte, the sculptor, too, was "pleased to say that he had found, in the features and physiognomy of his model, forms most favorable to sculpture, and most applicable to the heroic style of the figure that he was envisioning."[26]

FIGURE 35.

Antonio Canova (Italian, 1757–1822),
Napoléon as First Consul, ca. 1803.
Marble, H: 72.4 cm (28½ in.);
W: 50.8 cm (20 in.); D: 33 cm (13 in.).
New York, Collection of Roger Prigent.

• • •

Canova's brooding, canonical head of Napoléon evokes his restless intelligence, becoming the "portrait of a mind," as Baudelaire would say. It also suggests the mysterious power Napoléon's superhuman life exerted over his contemporaries, for Etiènne Léon Langon (1786–1864) noted that, although Napoléon was of medium height (approx. 168 cm [5 ft. 6 in.], like Alexander the Great—and sufficient in both cases), by optical effect he dominated all others with the majesty of his gestures, his irresistible eyes, and seductive smile.

FIGURE 36.

Antonio Canova (Italian, 1757–1822),
Cupid and Psyche, ca. 1804.
Marble, H: 150 cm (59 in.).
Saint Petersburg, Hermitage Museum.

• • •

This piece was entirely consistent with Joséphine's taste, so it was fortuitous that she was able to acquire it. Canova used the same plaster model, but there are slight differences in the rendering of the hair and drapery. He said he took the subject from Apuleius's story of Cupid and Psyche as lovers, but this version portrays them in an affectionate pose more suggestive of brother and sister. Both the reclining and standing versions were widely praised and celebrated by poets; Keats's "Ode to Psyche" could be considered a transcription of Canova's marble into verse.

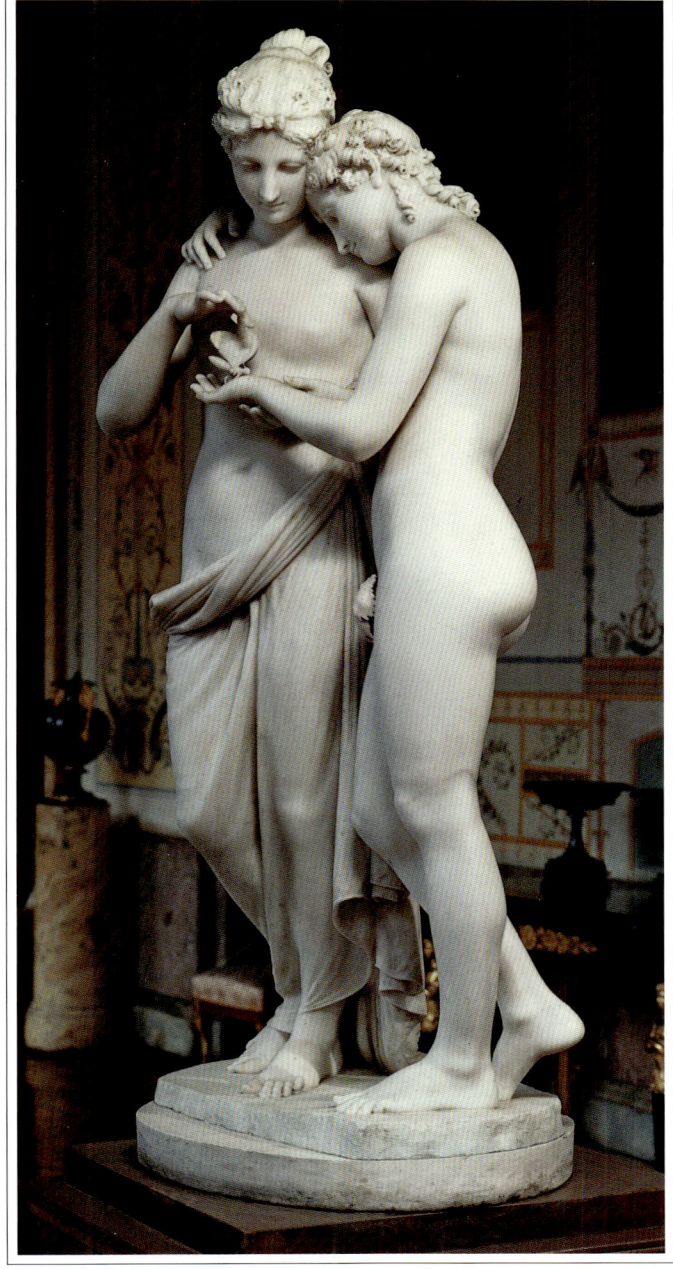

Canova was also anxious to visit the Murats at Villiers, probably to show his friend Quatremère de Quincy the two *Cupid and Psyche* groups, which the French critic had never seen. Quatramère considered the standing pair {FIGURE 36} even more accomplished than the reclining couple, although the latter is considered a major work in art history. He recorded his impression as follows: "I could not refrain from complimenting him [Canova] on the visible progress that I saw in the second group, not for its elegance, voluptuousness, or the picturesque composition; but on the contrary, for its simplicity, purity, nobility of style and design, the truth of the nude, the ingenuity of the antique manner, which I saw with pleasure he had so frankly embraced."[27]

Fortunately, Canova had begun to carve another version of it for Colonel John Campbell (later First Baron Cawder), who had lost his own Canova sculpture to Murat, but this one, too, went amiss. So the standing *Cupid and Psyche* became the first work by the great Italian to enter Joséphine's collection at Malmaison.[28]

Her next acquisition, Canova's ethereal *Hébé* {FIGURE 37}, is one of the most extravagantly admired statues in the world. He used his original *modello*, so Joséphine's *Hébé* is

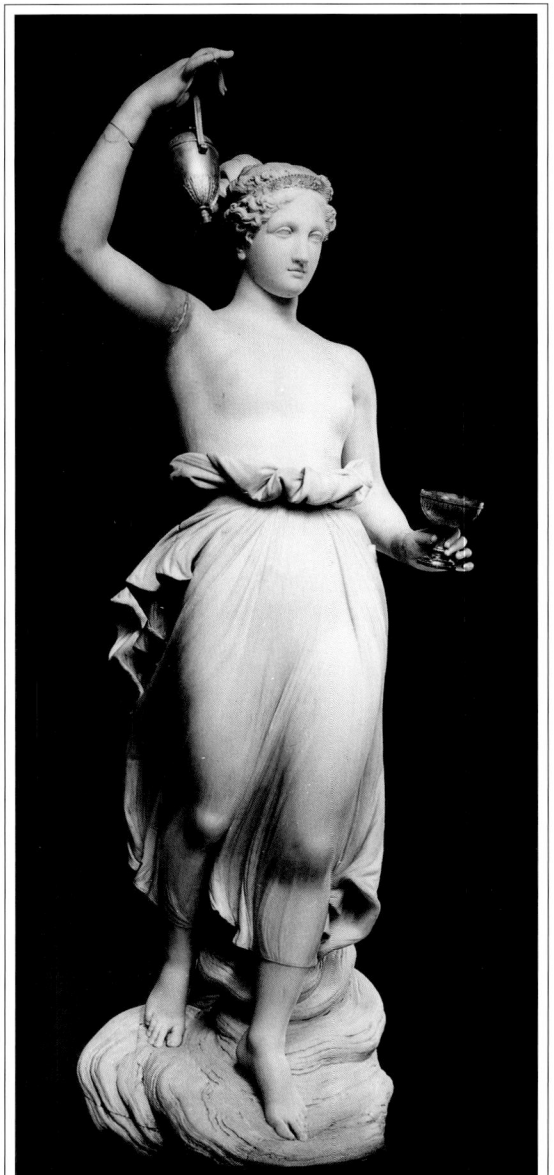 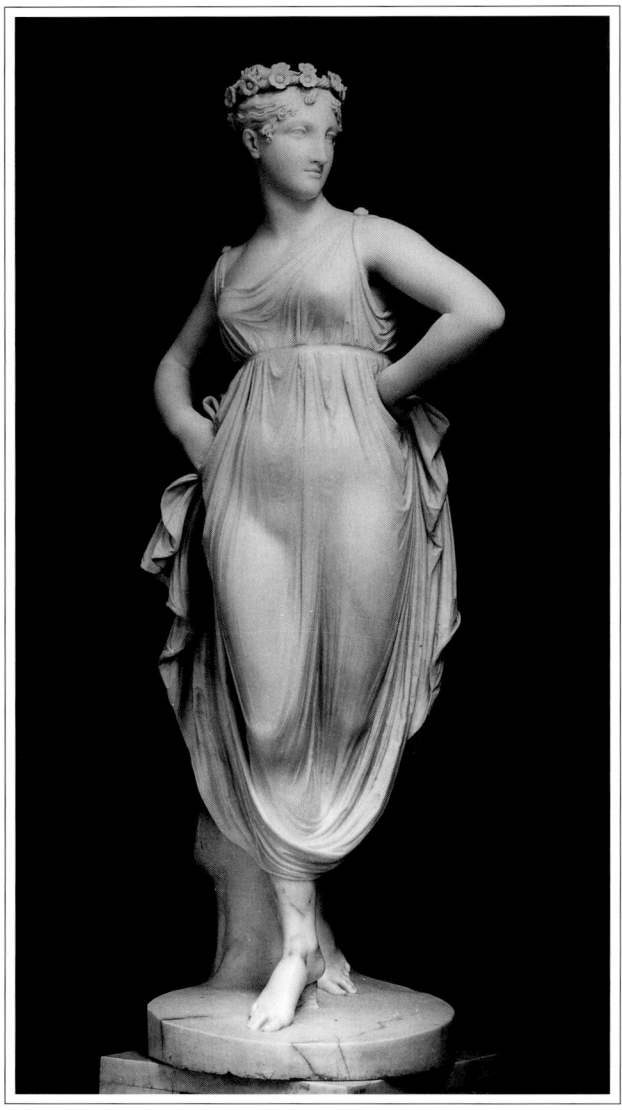

FIGURE 37.

Antonio Canova (Italian, 1757–1822),
Hébé, 1801–5.
Marble and gilt bronze, H: 158 cm (62¼ in.).
Saint Petersburg, Hermitage Museum.

• • •

Fred Licht claims that *Hébé* is "the last figure in Western art to levitate as if flight were a perfectly natural attribute of humanity," and is one of Canova's works that meets his own exacting ideal of beauty. The counterpoise of the silhouette is exquisite from every angle and shows a touch of genius in the poetic line running from the uplifted hand through the billowing, filmy material covering the leg, terminating in one foot emerging from a vaporous cloud. Another is the glorious passage of cascading drapery flowing from the material knotted at the figure's waist in the back.

quite similar to the first in its details, employing the unusual combination of white marble for the figure and gilt bronze for the cup and ewer.[29] As cupbearer to the gods, Hébé descends from Mount Olympus, borne on an insubstantial cloud, her transparent, fluttering drapery blown by the wind, her hair arranged in a fashionable coiffure *à la grecque*. The sculpture was praised by critics and poets alike. In Canova's image the Italian poet Ippolito Pindemonte saw "stone and movement in one conjoined."[30]

The poet's observation might well apply to the next piece to enter Joséphine's gallery which, like the lyrical *Hébé*, reflects Canova's educated interest in choreography. This was an original work, the *Dancer with Her Hands on Her Hips* {FIGURE 38}. Quatramère thought it "une composition tellement naïve et tellement simple" (a composition so naive and simple), and notes that she is about to execute a dance, indicated by the position of her arms and feet. Although, according to Quatramère, no

FIGURE 38.

Antonio Canova (Italian, 1757–1822),
Dancer with Her Hands on Her Hips, 1806–12.
Marble, H: 179 cm (70½ in.); W: 76 cm (29⅞ in.);
D: 67 cm (26⅜ in.).
Saint Petersburg, Hermitage Museum.

• • •

Particularly alluring are the profile view of the insouciant dancer's upswept coiffure crowned with flowers and her hands lifting the transparent drapery, which falls in intriguing patterns at each side. This subject obviously appealed to Joséphine because of her abiding patronage of the theater. In fact, the dancer might even represent her talented daughter, Queen Hortense, who wrote music, painted, and participated in private theatricals at Malmaison with professionals from Paris.

FIGURE 39.

Antonio Canova (Italian, 1757–1822),
Paris, 1807–12.
Marble, H: 203 cm (79⅞ in.); W: 85 cm (33½ in.);
D: 54 cm (21¼ in.).
Saint Petersburg, Hermitage Museum.

• • •

Canova was pleased with his bust of Paris, and critics such as Quatremère de Quincy, Stendahl, and Leopoldo Cicognara raved about the statue, which exemplifies the two salient qualities Quatremère considered invariable in Canova's work: life and grace. *Paris* is a singularly compact, stable composition. The figure, in elegant *contrapposto*, is supported by a tree trunk draped with a chlamys, the garment's vertical folds contributing a rich decorative note. The arm positions create two triangular voids, and the diagonal extending from the left elbow to the head draws attention to Paris's contemplation of his fateful decision.

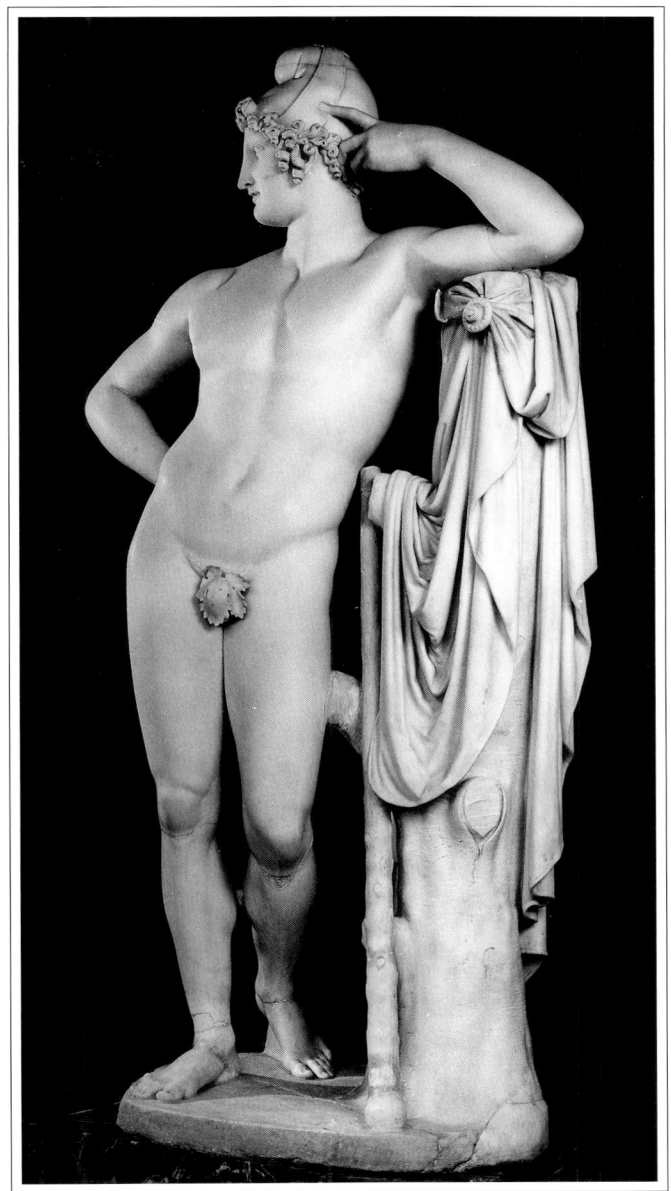

ancient example of the subject in the round exists, he considered Canova's to be closest to the antique (except for his *Perseus*) and a new invention in sculpture.

Around 1806, as Canova was working on the *modello* for Joséphine's commission of the *Dancer*, she requested another original—a large statue of Paris {FIGURE 39}. The sculptor began this new work in 1807.[31] In the ineffable beauty of its form, in its emphatic evocation of antiquity sought by the artists of this period, the completed statue created a sensation among the critics. At this time, Canova was also modeling several busts, including one of Paris, an example of which he gave to Quatremère as a token of friendship. During one of the poet's many visits to Malmaison, Joséphine coquettishly jested with him, "Can't we put your head on my statue?" To which the critic sagely replied, "No, then we would lose both."[32] Quatremère was right, for clearly Canova's *Paris* left nothing to be desired, and this penultimate masterpiece was sent to her from Rome, along with *Dancer*, in the summer of 1812.

Even before these two pieces arrived, Joséphine had asked her secretary, Jean-Marie Deschamps,[33] to write to Canova proposing an ambitious idea for a large group—*The Three*

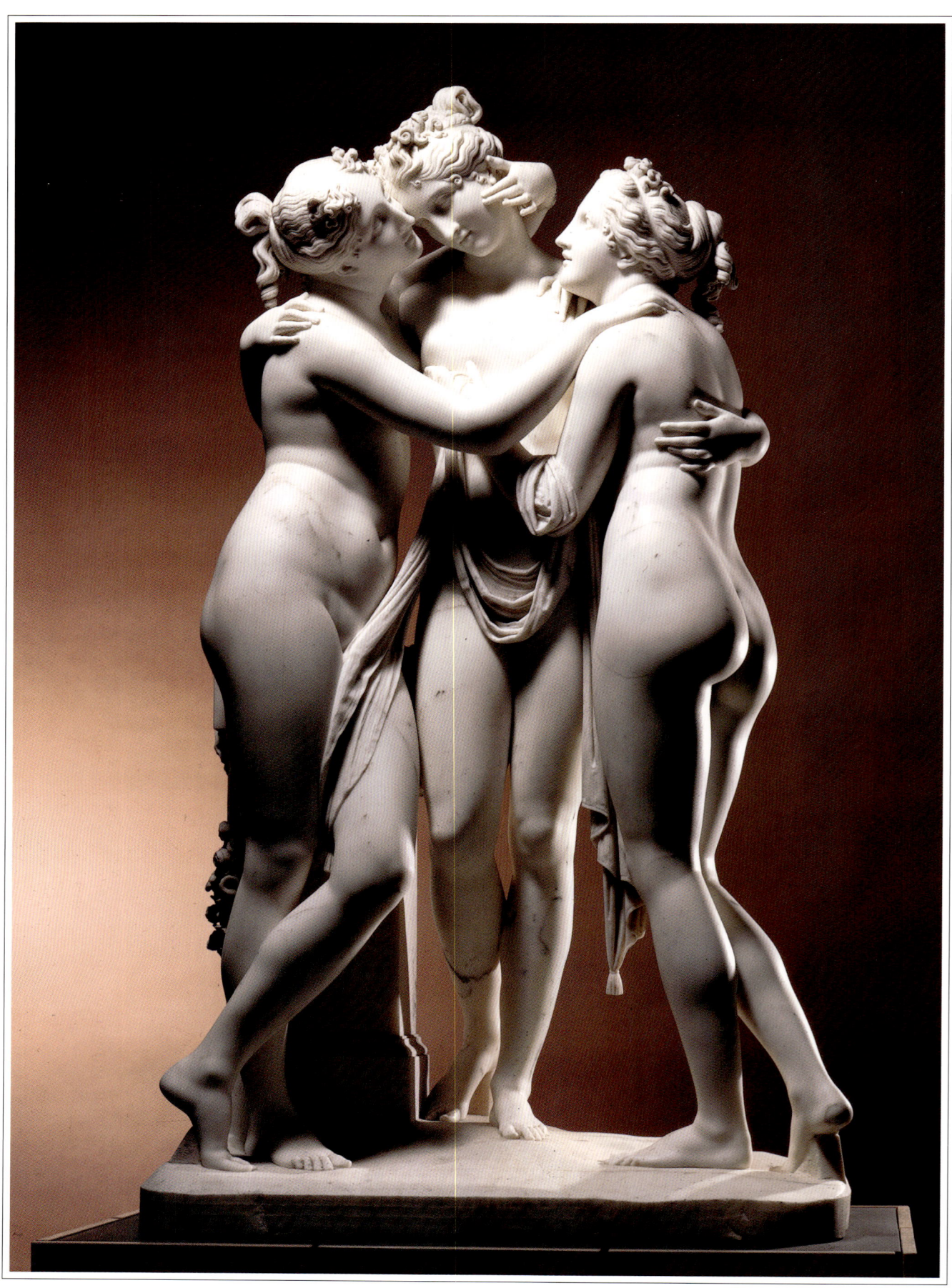

Notes

1. Eleanor P. DeLorme, *Garden Pavilions at the Eighteenth-Century French Court* (Woodbridge, England, 1996), 285–92. Pierre Julien's *Ganymede* was also in Joséphine's collection.
2. These were given to the first consul, but Joséphine confiscated them immediately, and today they are in the Louvre.
3. She acquired an additional 180 antique vases from Joaquim and Caroline Murat in 1809.
4. Napoléon bought these from Prince Camille Borghese, his sister Pauline's husband.
5. Antoine Chrysosthôme Quatremère de Quincy, *Canova et ses ouvrages, ou mémoires historiques sur la vie et les travaux de ce célèbre artiste* (Paris, 1834), 195.
6. Chinard sculpted several busts and medallions, both in terracotta and in marble, of Joséphine and her son Eugène, as well as a full-length portrait of Joséphine.
7. The Bosios were Corsicans who settled in Monaco.
8. Alison West, *From Pigalle to Préault: Neoclassicsm and the Sublime in French Sculpture, 1760–1840* (Cambridge, 1998), 103.
9. Vivant Denon decided that Salons should occur biannually, as during the ancien régime. The first one he directed was the Salon of 1802.
10. The one admired by sculpture students was a Roman copy after a Greek original (ca. 150 B.C.).
11. Vivant introduced Cartellier to Louis Bonaparte in 1805.
12. West, *From Pigalle to Préault* (see note 8), 202.
13. Although this plastic image of Napoléon-Charles has disappeared, his likeness may be seen in Gérard's painting (see FIGURE 18).
14. Napoléon was obliged to divorce Joséphine because she did not produce an heir. Although Gérard had painted the boy with his mother, Hortense (see FIGURE 18), this bust by Cartellier would have been a particularly valued plastic record of the child's appearance.
15. For more on the Sèvres busts of Joséphine, see chapter 8. Chaudet was given lodgings in the Louvre and regularly showed sculpture, paintings, and drawings at the Salon. Joséphine collected paintings by Chaudet's wife, Elisabeth Chaudet.
16. Elisabeth Chaudet was a pupil of Elisabeth Vigée-Lebrun.
17. The plaster has disappeared, but the marble — completed by Cartellier — was shown at the Salon of 1817 and bought by the state.
18. Gérard Hubert in *The Age of Neo-Classicism*, exh. cat. (London, The Royal Academy and the Victoria & Albert Museum, 1972), 221–22.
19. Joséphine sometimes wore tiaras made of diamond wheatears.
20. Hubert in *The Age of Neo-Classicism*, 219.
21. Murat did not obtain them directly from the sculptor, as they were intended for Colonel John Campbell. But when neither could be delivered due to the colonel's death, Murat acquired them. See Christopher M. S. Johns, *Antonio Canova and the Politics of Patronage in Revolutionary and Napoléonic Europe* (Berkeley, Calif., 1998), 116.
22. Caroline was treated almost as a daughter by Joséphine, who reared her with Hortense. Both attended Mme Campan's school, where Jean-Baptiste Isabey was their drawing teacher. Later Caroline would commission one of the most celebrated works in art history, Ingres' *Grande Odalisque* (1814), which recalls Canova's famous reclining sculpture of Caroline's sister Pauline, *Paolina Borghese as Venus Victorious* (1804–8).
23. The two groups arrived only in 1808, in time to be exhibited at the salon.
24. Hugh Honour, "The Three Graces," in *The Three Graces: Antonio Canova*, exh. cat., ed. Timothy Clifford, et al. (Edinburgh, National Gallery of Scotland, 1995), 19.
25. Canova finished the portrait head early in 1803, but he mistakenly used it as a model for the head of his problematic standing statue of the unclothed emperor, *Napoléon as Mars the Peacemaker* (1803–6), which Napoléon disliked so much that he relegated it to a closet. Its bronze replica met a happier fate, for in 1805 Joséphine's son, Prince Eugène, became viceroy of Italy, with his capital in Milan. So the bronze replica of Canova's marble original was erected in the courtyard of Milan's Brera Museum, which Eugène — an art lover like his mother — further embellished during his residence, preparing through his excellent administration the future unification and independence of the peninsula.
26. Quatremère de Quincy, *Canova et ses ouvrages*, 121.
27. Quatremère de Quincy, *Canova et ses ouvrages*, 119.
28. Fred Licht, *Canova* (New York, 1983), 172.
29. A reproduction in gilt bronze of Joséphine's *Hébé* was made about 1815–20 by the Milanese bronzeworking firm of Strazza and Thomas.
30. Nina K. Kosareva, "Hébé," in *Canova*, exh. cat. (Venice, 1992), 264.
31. Canova made a copy for the prince of Bavaria, probably Ludwig, Eugène's brother-in-law.
32. Quatremère de Quincy, *Canova et ses ouvrages*, 176.
33. Deschamps was also a poet who wrote couplets appropriate to Joséphine's seasonal parties.
34. Licht, *Canova*, 203, 211.
35. The group did go to her son, Prince Eugène, in Munich, before being sent to the Hermitage, along with her other sculpture.
36. See Eleanor P. DeLorme, *Joséphine: Napoléon's Incomparable Empress* (New York, 2002), 220–24.
37. Johns, *Antonio Canova and the Politics of Patronage*, 117.

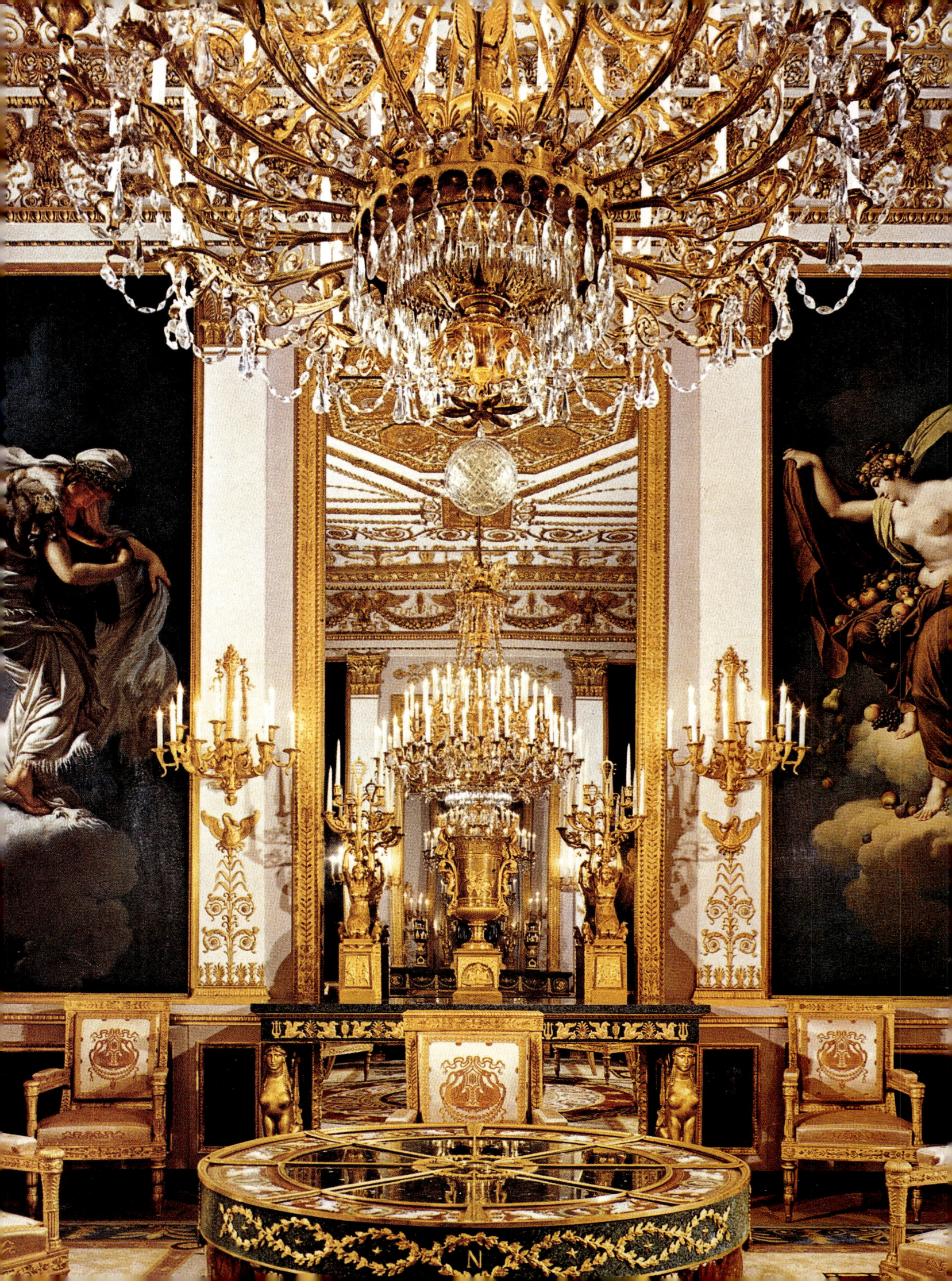

CHAPTER 3

ELEANOR P. DELORME

Innovative Interiors: The Settings for Joséphine's Life

DURING THE FINAL DAYS OF THE MONARCHY, IN THE decade of the 1780s, Joséphine was truly introduced into the world of courtly living. With her first husband, the vicomte Alexandre de Beauharnais, an aristocrat and prominent political figure, she frequented the finest *hôtels particuliers* (town houses) in Paris. Then in 1800, as consort of First Consul Napoléon Bonaparte, Joséphine and her daughter, Hortense, were welcomed as the preeminent guests into such grand establishments as that of Mme de Montesson, who resumed her famous soirées after the Revolution.[1]

These eighteenth-century town houses built for the nobility, aristocracy, and notables are still considered the consummate models of domestic architecture, and Joséphine's familiarity with their exemplary decor was a key factor in the formation of her taste. When these buildings were taken over by the new ruling class, their decoration reflected the aspirations of this ascendant society. In France it is tacitly understood that decor is a reliable index of one's taste—and certainly social status. All the Bonapartes found select lodgings in or near Paris, such as the famed Hôtel de Thélusson, and then later the Elysée Palace, for Caroline Bonaparte Murat. The Hôtel de Brissac suited the magnificent lifestyle of the connoisseur Lucien Bonaparte; and for Louis and Hortense (who were married in 1802), the first consul purchased the celebrated landmark that the illustrious architect Alexandre Brongniart had built for the actress Mlle Dervieux.[2] It stood in the rue de la Victoire (formerly rue Chantereine) near Joséphine's own house. The great François-

Joseph Bélanger had provided the interiors for Mlle Dervieux in the polished, restrained Marie-Antoinette style, and Hortense entertained in this elegant room that opened onto the garden {FIGURE 42}.

The ascension of Napoléon and Joséphine gave French artists and artisans fresh hope. With numerous commissions following the economic upswing, life returned to the ateliers of cabinetmakers, bronze workers, wallpaper firms, and Lyon silk-weavers. Among the emblematic motifs were imperial eagles, laurel leaves, griffins, stars, and bees, which were set into gilt-bronze furniture mounts, woven into silks, carved to surmount canopies, painted on Sèvres services, or used to embellish silverware. These products aesthetically evoked the Empire and manifested the political utility of the arts.

The new interiors came to fruition through the architects Joséphine sponsored—Charles Percier and Pierre-François-Léonard Fontaine, who aimed for archaeological exactitude even as they adapted ancient models to a contemporary clientele. Like Joséphine, they were children of the eighteenth century, when an architect designed not only the building but also its interior and furnishings, which accounts for the rhythmic harmony that produces a true style. Percier so faithfully followed this tradition that he omitted nothing essential to the decoration of a room, even providing models for textile manufacturers and makers of passementerie (special trim) for furniture and hangings.

Typical of their spare, linear style is the *Bed Made in Paris for M. O.*, in which meticulous attention is paid to each detail {FIGURE 43}. Its theatricality reflects the fact that this team of architects designed sets for the opera, for the room is conceived as a stage upon which the life of the owner is to be played out.

Joséphine was entirely conversant with the time-honored principles of noblesse oblige, one of which required that a gentleman reside in an impressive town house to fulfill the duties of his rank. So after her son-in-law, Louis Bonaparte, became grand constable in 1804, Joséphine would have encouraged him to move Hortense into the princely Hôtel de Lannoy, built about 1798, on rue Cerutti.[3] This hotel's recently completed decor had been carried out by Joséphine's favorite artist, Pierre-Paul Prud'hon, who executed a remarkable suite of allegorical wall paintings for its resplendent Salon de la Richesse (1798–1801).[4] During her official receptions, Hortense received her guests in these exquisite surroundings,

FIGURE 42.

Francois-Joseph Bélanger (French, 1744–1818), *Dining Room in the House of Mlle Dervieux.* Drawing by Michel Gallet (destroyed).

• • •

In Bélanger's vaunted decoration, the walls are articulated by pilasters with arabesques and grotesques in low relief from the classical repertoire, standing on shallow plinths of *faux marbre* (imitation marble). The free-standing gilt-bronze imitations of ancient candelabra between the pilasters flanking the door are by the famous Pierre-Philippe Thomire (1751–1843), whose work Joséphine highly favored. These ornamental bronzes surprisingly reappeared on the Paris market in 1988. This room is an outstanding example of late Marie-Antoinette style, in marked contrast to the music salon and Napoléon's study at Malmaison, where the pilasters become columns in the round, raised on deep plinths—a trademark of the Percier and Fontaine manner.

FIGURE 43.

Charles Percier (French, 1764–1838) and Pierre-François-Léonard Fontaine (French, 1762–1853), *Bed Made in Paris for M. O.* Engraving, 22 × 29.5 cm (8⅝ × 11⅝ in.), from Percier and Fontaine, *Receuil de décorations intérioreures* (Paris, 1827 ed.), plate 25.

• • •

A synthesis of antiquity and Renaissance styles, the decor of this imposing bedroom revolves around the bed itself, raised on a platform like an ancient altar. It is conceived as a small temple of Diana, goddess of the night, who, in the frieze behind the bed, is being conducted by Cupid into the arms of the shepherd Endymion, the object of Diana's love. The stag motif in the wall hangings and crowning the pediment refers to her role as huntress, as do the hunting horns, bow, and quiver of arrows. The herms flanking the bed represent Silence and Night. This ensemble for an important Paris town house may well have been designed for the banker Gabriel-Julien Ouvrard, one of the most affluent financiers of his day.

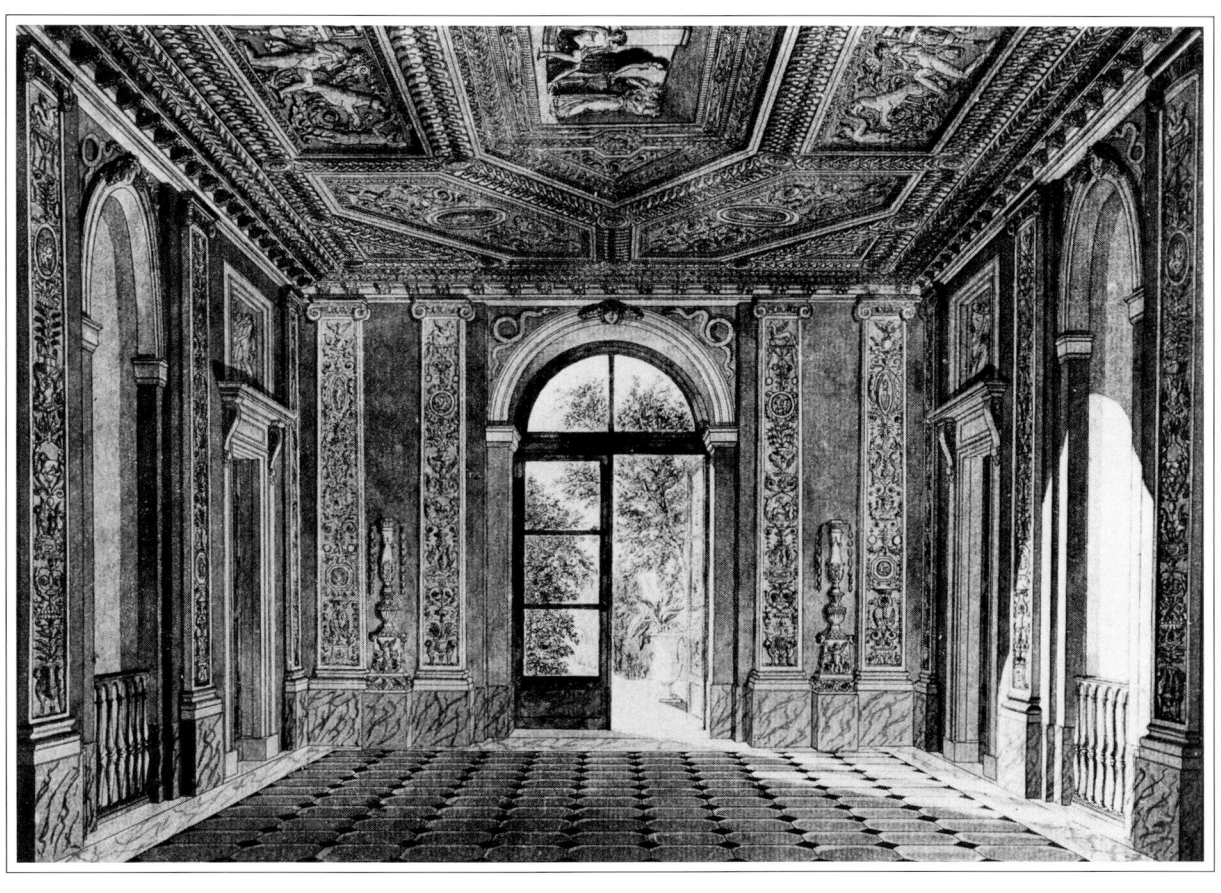

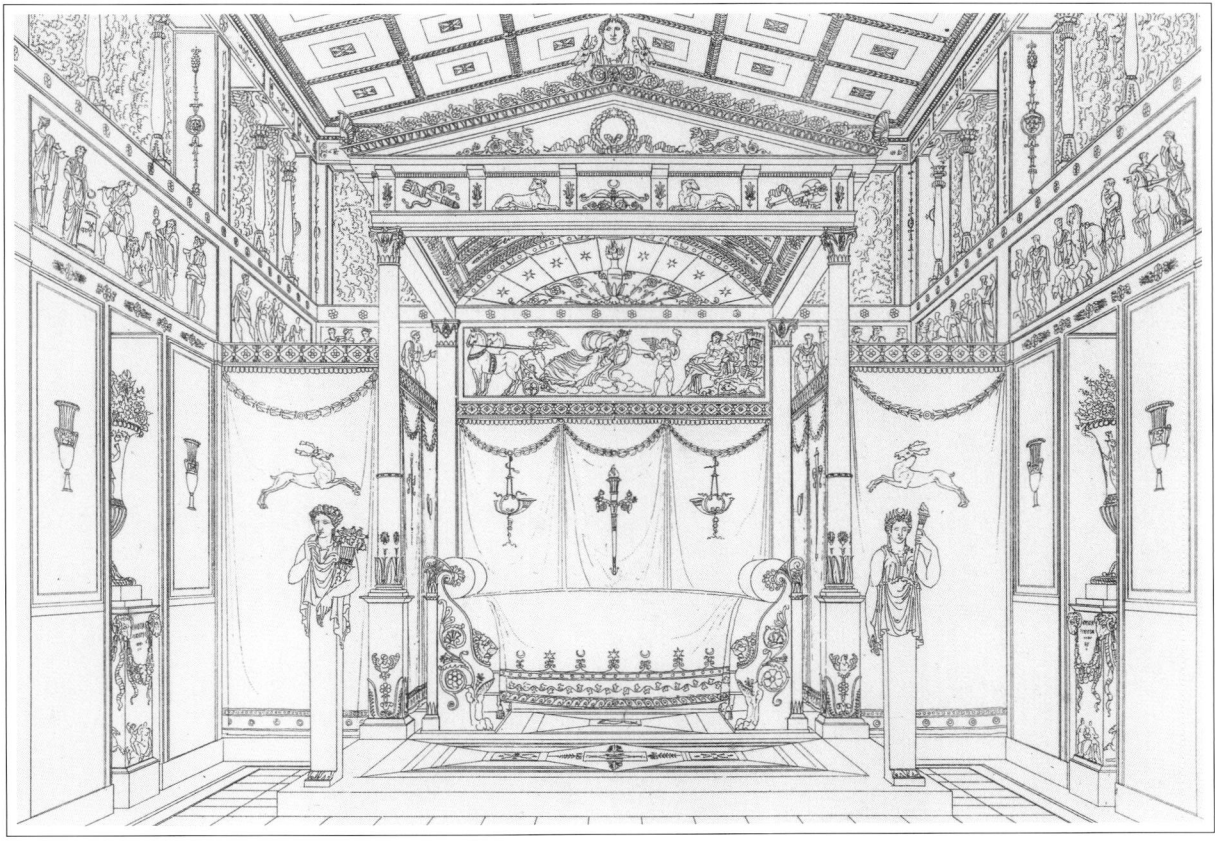

but she was most at home on the evenings when her salon was filled with (other) musicians, writers, and artists who would be sketching, playing instruments, or discussing the most provocative offerings at the current Salon.

Hortense's capacious Salon de la Richesse, like the Hall of Mirrors at Versailles, received light from French windows opening onto the garden, reflected by mirrors on the opposite wall. Flanking the mirrors that were centered on each side wall were panels depicting four women wearing gowns that derive from the high lineage of antiquity. On one side were personifications of Wealth {FIGURE 44} and the Arts; and on the other, Pleasures and Philosophy, each holding her attribute.[5] By posture and gesture, they acknowledge each other across the room and are visually bound together through reciprocal coloration — the reverberation of golds, sage greens, and rusty reds. Seated against Wealth's pedestal is a smiling putto reveling in the effulgence of glittering golden coins cascading from two cornucopias {FIGURE 45}. The Hellenistic theme of cupids had been rediscovered in the Herculaneum excavations and delightedly exploited

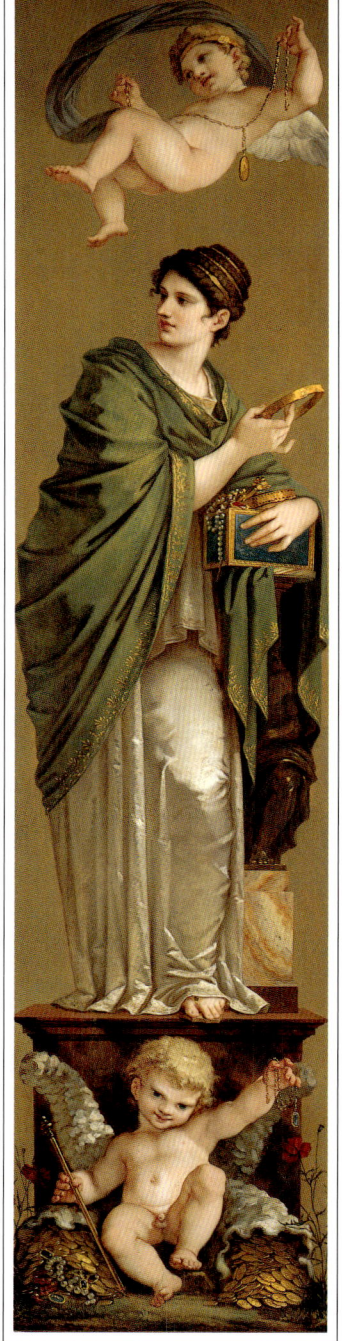

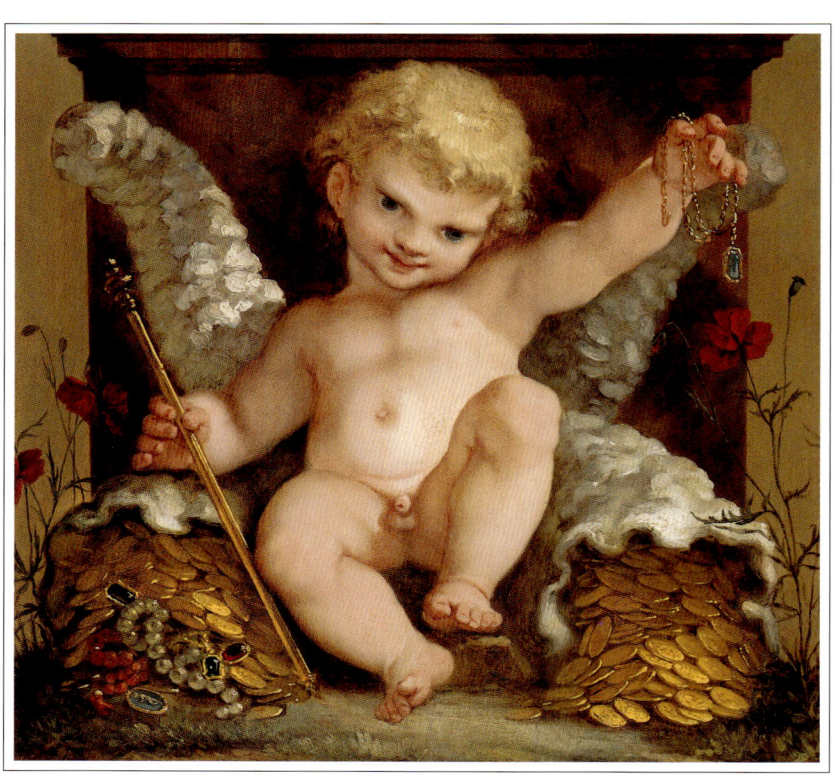

FIGURE 44.

Pierre-Paul Prud'hon (French, 1758–1823), *La Richesse (Wealth)*, 1798–1801. Oil on panel, 305 × 76 cm (121⅝ × 29⅞ in.). Private collection.

• • •

The figure of Wealth leans against a statue of Plutus, who represents agricultural prosperity and abundance in general. She is enveloped in a shimmering white-satin gown and sage-green mantle bordered with gold palmettes. One putto hovers above holding a necklace with another seated below. Wealth turns to offer a gold band from her jewel casket to the adjoining figure of the Arts, who wears a complementary russet mantle and strums a lyre. Exceptional in his own right, Prud'hon was not David's student but developed his own style and excelled in allegory.

FIGURE 45.

Pierre-Paul Prud'hon (French, 1758–1823), Detail of *Wealth* (FIGURE 44).

• • •

In one hand, this impish putto, symbolizing the spirit of Wealth, holds a scepter as an emblem of his power and, in the other hand, dangles a necklace before the eyes of Pleasure. The poppies at the cupid's side are probably intended as symbols of the ennui that often accompanies a superfluity of possessions.

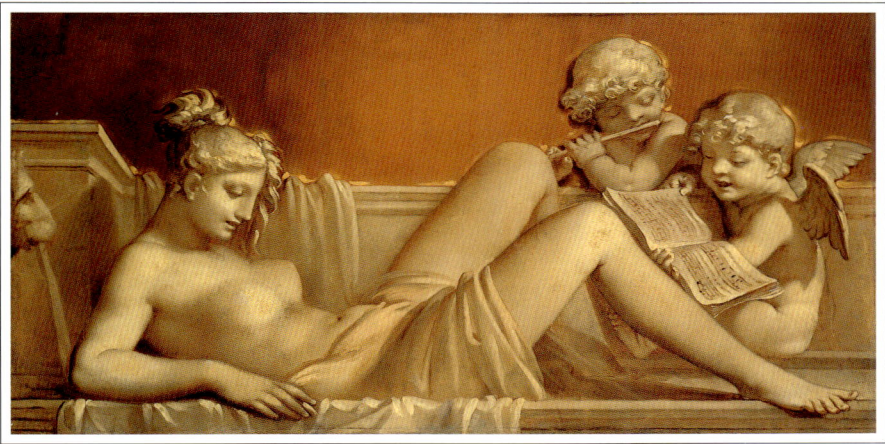

FIGURE 46.

Pierre-Paul Prud'hon (French, 1758–1823),
Noon, 1798–1801.
Oil on canvas, brown *camaieu* heightened with gold,
72.3 × 141 cm (28½ × 55½ in.).
Private collection.

• • •

Originally, Prud'hon had intended to place the two winged infants with a book and flute at the bottom of his figure of the Arts. Later, he changed his mind and arranged them here to serenade Noon at her bath. They reappear in the overdoor, *Afternoon*, again in *Night*, and in Prud'hon's drawing of Morning, for which the overdoor was apparently not completed.

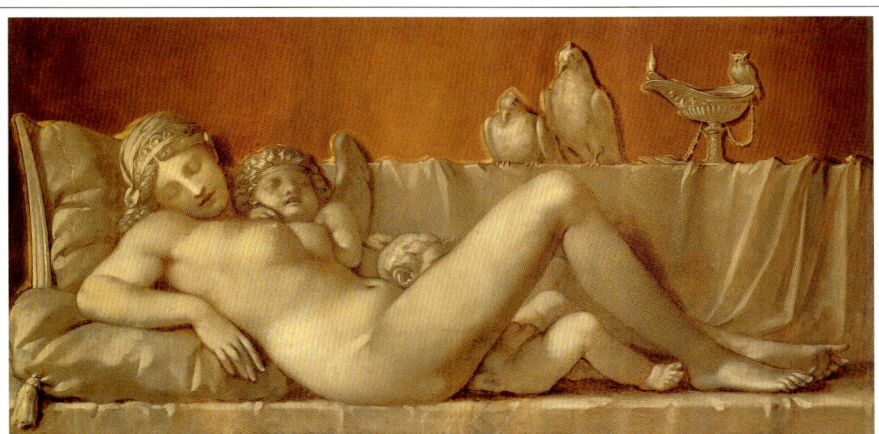

FIGURE 47.

Pierre-Paul Prud'hon (French 1758–1823),
Night, 1798–1801.
Oil on canvas, brown *camaieu* heightened with gold,
72.3 × 141 cm (28½ × 55½ in.).
Private collection.

• • •

Whereas the figure of Noon appears to be illuminated by the noonday sun, Night reposes in a penumbral light. The actively engaged putti with Noon have now fallen asleep with Night and are watched over by winged creatures of darkness, feebly lit by a Roman lamp. Similar imagery had been used by the Versailles school of sculptors in the Sun King's gardens: Noon is a smiling Venus with Cupid at her side, and Night holds a torch.

in all the arts. These little winged babies aim arrows or compose music on the walls of Hortense's salon; they carry flowers or torches on the panels of the bedroom doors at Eugène's Hôtel de Beauharnais; and chubby Amours attend the toilette of Venus in the gilt-bronze mounts of Joséphine's monumental jewel cabinet, designed by Percier.

As foil for the principal figures and to amplify the theme of Prud'hon's ensemble, titled *The Alliance of Wealth and the Arts*, he painted four overdoors of reclining females, the *Times of Day*, also attended by putti. *Noon* shows a woman at her bath, with water pouring from the lion's masque of the fountain behind her, attended by two winged Amours, one of whom plays a flute to accompany his cherubic friend singing from a handheld score {FIGURE 46}.

Like its complement in *Noon*, the sculptural female form in *Night* is presented within an architectural framework, although her bath has now become a couch {FIGURE 47}. Both figures assume similar postures, and the delineation of these lyrical forms recalls Prud'hon's *académies* (academic studies) that reveal his prowess as a draftsman. This richly figural decoration, which Sylvain Laveissière considers "a veritable poem in painting,"[6] was highly influential for its time and is considered to be "one of the finest, if not the finest of this period."[7] In fact, Anita Brookner calls Prud'hon "the greatest decorator *manqué* of the Empire period,"[8] equally talented as both a painter and decorator.

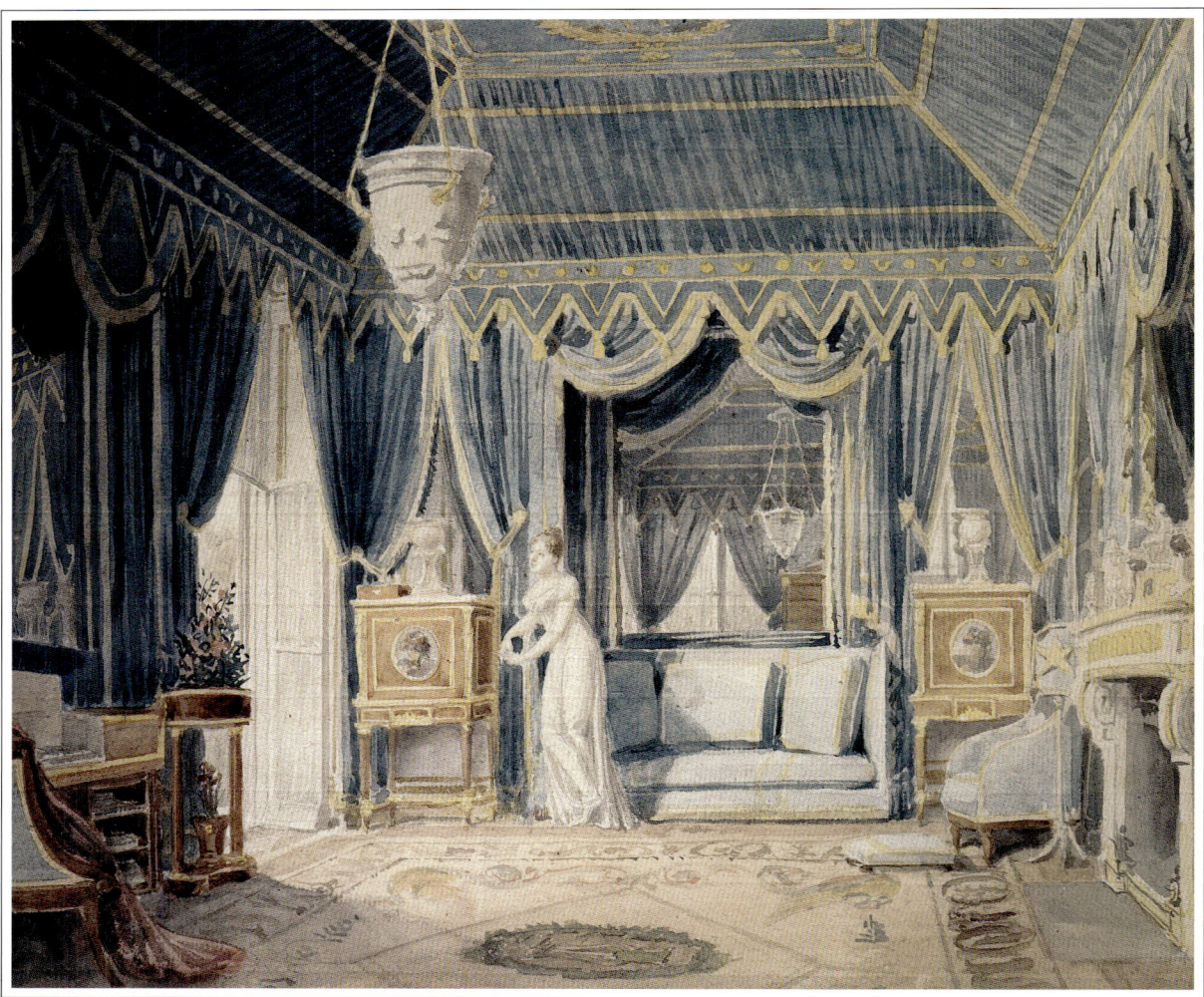

FIGURE 48.

Auguste Garnerey (French, 1785–1824),
The Boudoir of Queen Hortense, rue Cerutti, 1811.
Watercolor, 29 × 33.5 cm (11 3/8 × 13 1/4 in.).
Paris, Olivier Lefuel Collection.

• • •

Queen Hortense was the very incarnation of Empire sensibilities. Her romances set to music were among the most popular of the day. Her most famous battle song, *Partant pour la Syrie*, was played throughout Napoléon's Wagram campaign and became virtually the national anthem of the Second Empire of Hortense's son, Napoléon III. The watercolors with which she illustrated her romances heralded the taste for the medieval, reflected in her decor and in her sponsorship, with Joséphine, of the *style troubadour*. The alabaster lamp was perhaps a gift from Hortense's brother, Eugène, viceroy of Italy, and the oval jardiniere is now at Malmaison.

Although Hortense's Hôtel de Lannoy has been destroyed, an image of one interior remains: *The Boudoir of Queen Hortense, rue Cerutti* {FIGURE 48}. Like Joséphine's private salon at the Tuileries, the walls of Hortense's boudoir are mirrored, with the fabric parted to reveal the mirror over the mantel, the mirrored niche with a divan, and the wall behind the cabinets. The fabric is lavishly gathered at the ceiling, and the pointed valance suggests the incipient *style troubadour*. Like her mother, Hortense also favored eighteenth-century furniture, and the two cabinets (probably *bureaux à abbatant*) are by the excellent *ébéniste* (cabinetmaker) Adam Weisweiler (1744–1820), who had worked for Marie-Antoinette.

With Hortense palatially ensconced in the capital, it was obligatory that Joséphine's son, Prince Eugène, reside in a regal establishment as well. A venerable eighteenth-century town house in the rue de Lille was chosen and transformed into the Hôtel de Beauharnais.[9] Since Eugène, viceroy of Italy, was rarely in Paris, its refurbishing was doubtless carried out by his doting sister and mother. Her lawyer, Etiènne Calmelet, supervised the renovation (1804–6), and the artists involved are closely associated with the empress as well.

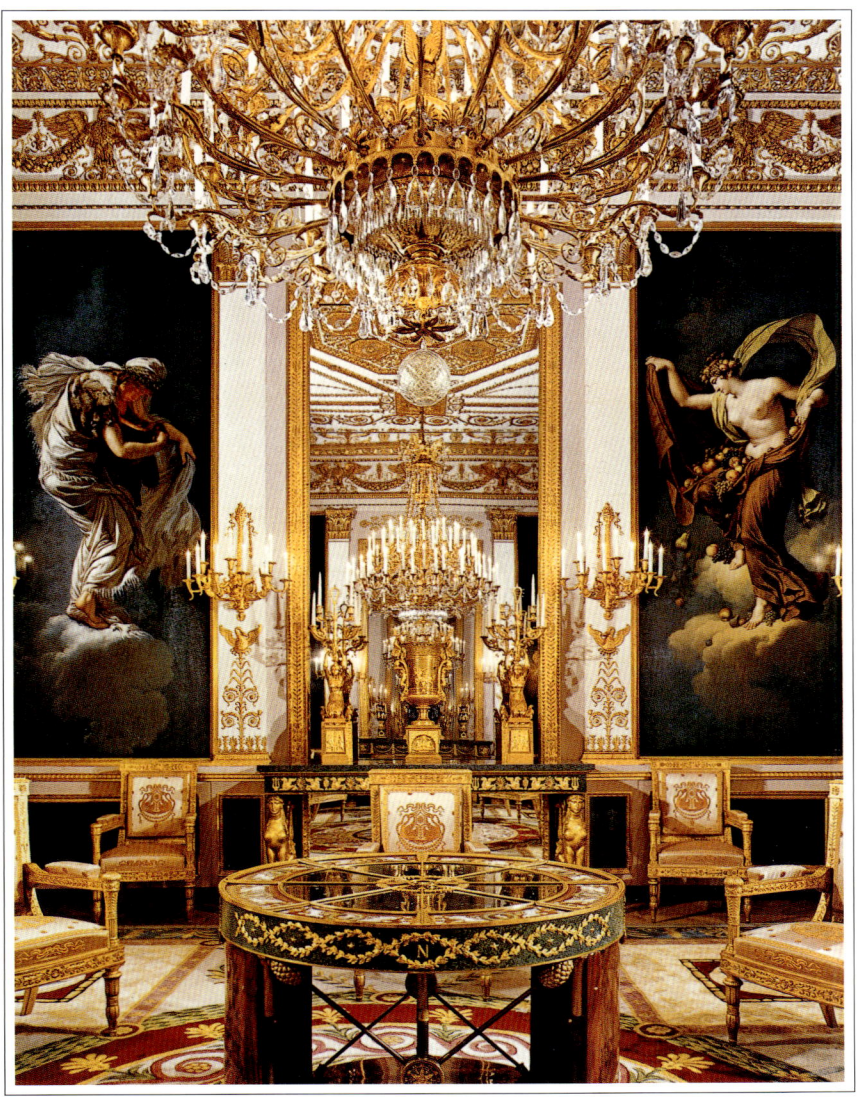

FIGURE 49.

View of the Salon des Saisons, Hôtel de Beauharnais, rue de Lille, Paris, ca. 1968.

· · ·

This impressive reception room now receives guests of the German ambassador, for the house has become the German Embassy. There is a compartmented stucco ceiling of dancing winged goddesses, a border of *rinceaux* scrolls, and a deep frieze of imperial eagles joined by festoons. Joséphine's favored swan motif adorns the pilasters, and the console garniture is a prime example of the Egyptomania commemorating the campaign in which Eugène participated. A gueridon is properly placed under the splendid chandelier of gilt bronze and crystal on the central medallion of the Savonnerie carpet, rewoven after the original.

Clearly, Joséphine's hand is in evidence throughout: palmettes, flowers, and swans embellish Hortense's bedroom as well as the formal state room, the Salon des Saisons, probably the best example of its type {FIGURE 49}. The crescendo of this symphony in gold and white is the series of four large wall paintings personifying the seasons, once erroneously attributed to Anne-Louis Girodet-Trioson, whom Joséphine favored for his canvases as well as his decoration.

On February 19, 1800, Bonaparte and Joséphine moved into the Tuileries Palace, formerly royal and soon to be imperial. The revolutionists had left it in frightful condition, but the architect Felix Lecomte (1737–1817) freshened it up, and by 1808 the Tuileries had regained much of its formal grandeur, with most of the remaining furnishings those that had been seized from recently executed royalty or émigrés.[10] For Joséphine it was unsettling, haunted as it was by the memory of Marie-Antoinette, who lived there shortly before her execution. "I feel," Joséphine said, "as if the shadow of the queen were asking what I am doing in her bed. There is an air of monarchy about this palace that one cannot breathe with impunity, and I am still disturbed by it."[11]

Yet she was somewhat compensated by the collection of old masters and some paintings by Jacques-Louis David. Bonaparte, who was attracted to sculpture, created a gallery

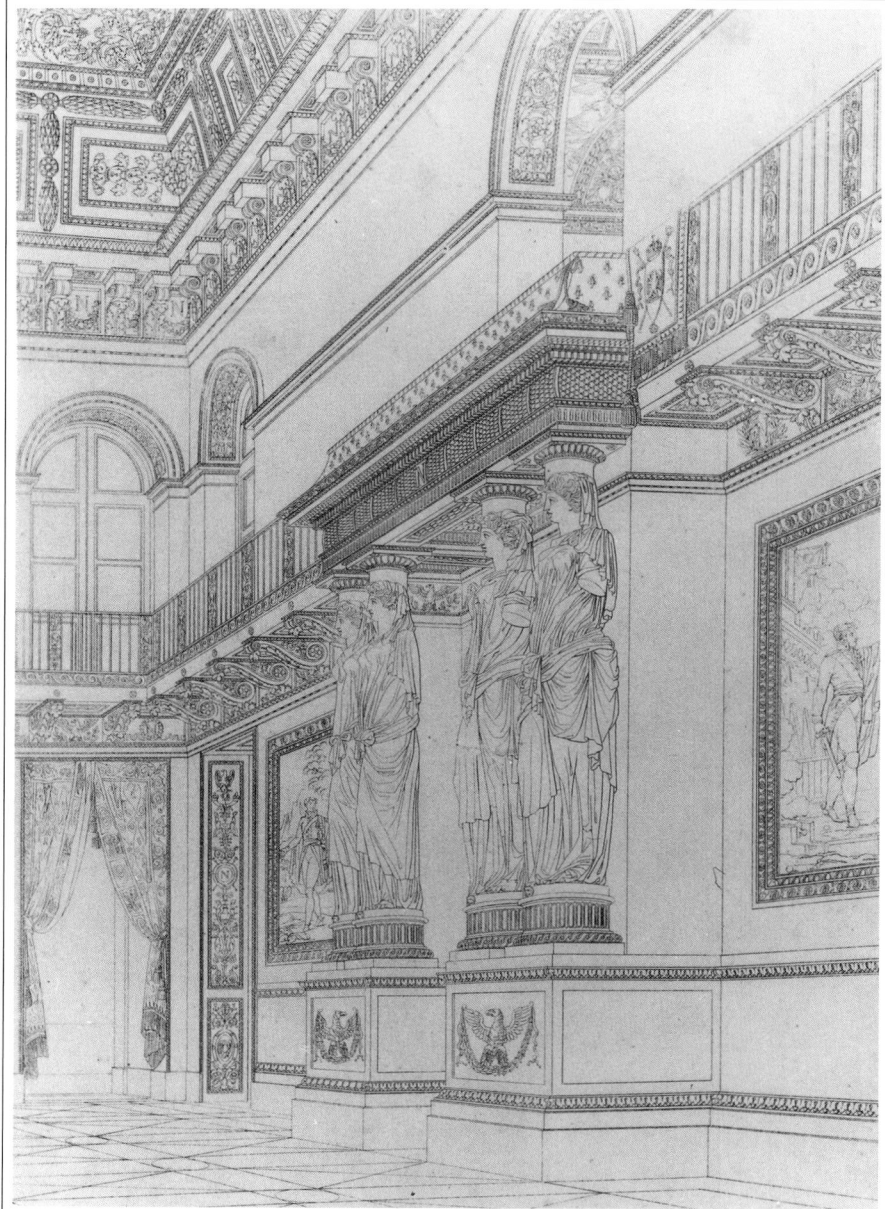

FIGURE 50.

Charles Percier (French, 1764–1838) and
Pierre-François-Léonard Fontaine
(French, 1762–1853),
The Marshals' Salon.
Engraving, 37.7 × 27 cm (15 × 10½ in.),
from Percier and Fontaine,
Receuil de décorations intérieures
(Paris, 1812 ed.), plate 49.

• • •

To undergird the loge for the imperial couple, Percier and Fontaine constructed a tribune with replications of Jean Goujon's well-known caryatids for Henri II's Guard Room in the old Musée du Louvre. In 1794 the Salle des Caryatides had been restored by the sculptor François Lemot (1772–1827), with Claude Michallon's help, and in 1806 Lemot created these caryatids for the Marshals' Salon, adding imperial eagles to the plinths. The official box is hung with red velvet embroidered with gilt bees. It is here that Napoléon and Joséphine sat in state after the coronation and on other grand occasions.

featuring busts of the ancients and famous generals, including George Washington, in whose honor he had declared ten days of mourning when America's leader died in 1799.[12]

The state rooms were the backdrop for Joséphine's public life, with the old Guard Room being transformed into the Marshals' Salon, the largest in Paris and the setting for important fetes {FIGURE 50}. Dedicated to the terrible art of war, Charles Lebrun's battle paintings for Louis XIV were displayed there by Napoléon's order,[13] a reminder that the Sun King's valiant troops were forerunners of the *beaux sabreurs*, the dashing cavalrymen honored in this capacious gallery. Illuminated with immense crystal chandeliers, its ceiling was decorated with trophies. Across its walls paraded portraits of Napoléon's marshals, and extolling fallen Napoleonic heroes were twenty-two busts of generals and admirals killed in battle. It was against this impressive backdrop that Napoléon and Joséphine presided in state. The Marshals' Salon complemented the Diana Salon, setting for official banquets. The grand finales of these gastronomic tours de force were the intricate, many-tiered architectural confections of meringue and almond paste towering over the dessert table, the ingenious invention of the renowned pastry chef Antonin Carême.

Since Joséphine's orders for more furniture were curtailed, she brightened her private apartments at the Tuileries with colorful textiles. Her first salon was done in mauve taffeta embroidered with antique honeysuckle motifs in a rich chestnut color, trimmed in fringes of lilac and amaranth, like the suite of Jacob chairs, and console tables held porphyry vases.

Her larger salon—dignified by the Mars and Minerva vases from Versailles—featured yellow-and-brown satin fringed with rusty red. The walls were first mirrored and then hung with drapery attached to a ceiling rod around the perimeter, the drapery parted at strategic points to reveal the chimney piece and consoles. Although no other images of her rooms survive, Jean-Baptiste Isabey's watercolor shows Joséphine's formal bedroom as it looked two years after her departure {FIGURE 51}.

Contemporaries were uniformly impressed with her Tuileries apartments. In the opinion of Louis Bourrienne, "Mme Bonaparte's suite...is decorated with exquisite taste, yet with no display—a few beautiful bronzes I distinctly remember seeing at Versailles, a small number of old masters...marbles and mosaics made at Florence and some fine Sèvres vases."[14] Coming from a distinguished diplomat and former habitué of Versailles, this is high praise indeed.[15] Mme de la Tour du Pin thought "the apartments had been entirely refurbished as if by enchantment."[16] The haughty Laure d'Abrantès, of the "noble faubourg" Saint-Germain (and therefore given to understatement), conceded that Mme Bonaparte's rooms "were furnished with taste, but without ostentation. The...reception salon was hung with [yellow] silk...furniture standing against walls covered with Indian silk.[17]...The other rooms [were] new and elegant."[18]

With the Tuileries now sparkling and the imperial châteaux freshly restored, Joséphine and Napoléon demonstrated to all Europe that France had not lost her hegemony in the *art de vivre* (art of living). Mme Divoff was so moved by the ambience of the capital that she launched into an apostrophe: "Paris, Paris, after having seen you, I am not surprised that the French have no desire to travel, for where could they find a city like you? Unfortunate is he who...is forced to leave you and alas, has no hope of returning!"[19]

In 1802 the imperial couple took over the previously royal château of Saint-Cloud for their official summer residence.[20] Its gardens and breathtaking view of the Seine were perfect, but the interior needed to be refurnished in record time.[21] The decor of the late sovereigns was retained, and Joséphine's touch is perhaps most evident in the Princes' Salon hung with Marie-Antoinette's renowned Lyon silk embroidered with lilacs and peacock feathers from her Versailles bedchamber.

Joséphine also chose many vases and other royal objets d'art for her rooms at Saint-Cloud, and in her salon with its extant Louis XVI decor, she virtually reconstituted an eighteenth-century interior. At Fontainebleau—their second country residence where the court hunted in the fall—Joséphine's apartments were almost invariably adorned with sumptuous Sèvres porcelain, that remarkable decorative art that lends both color and character to interiors.[22]

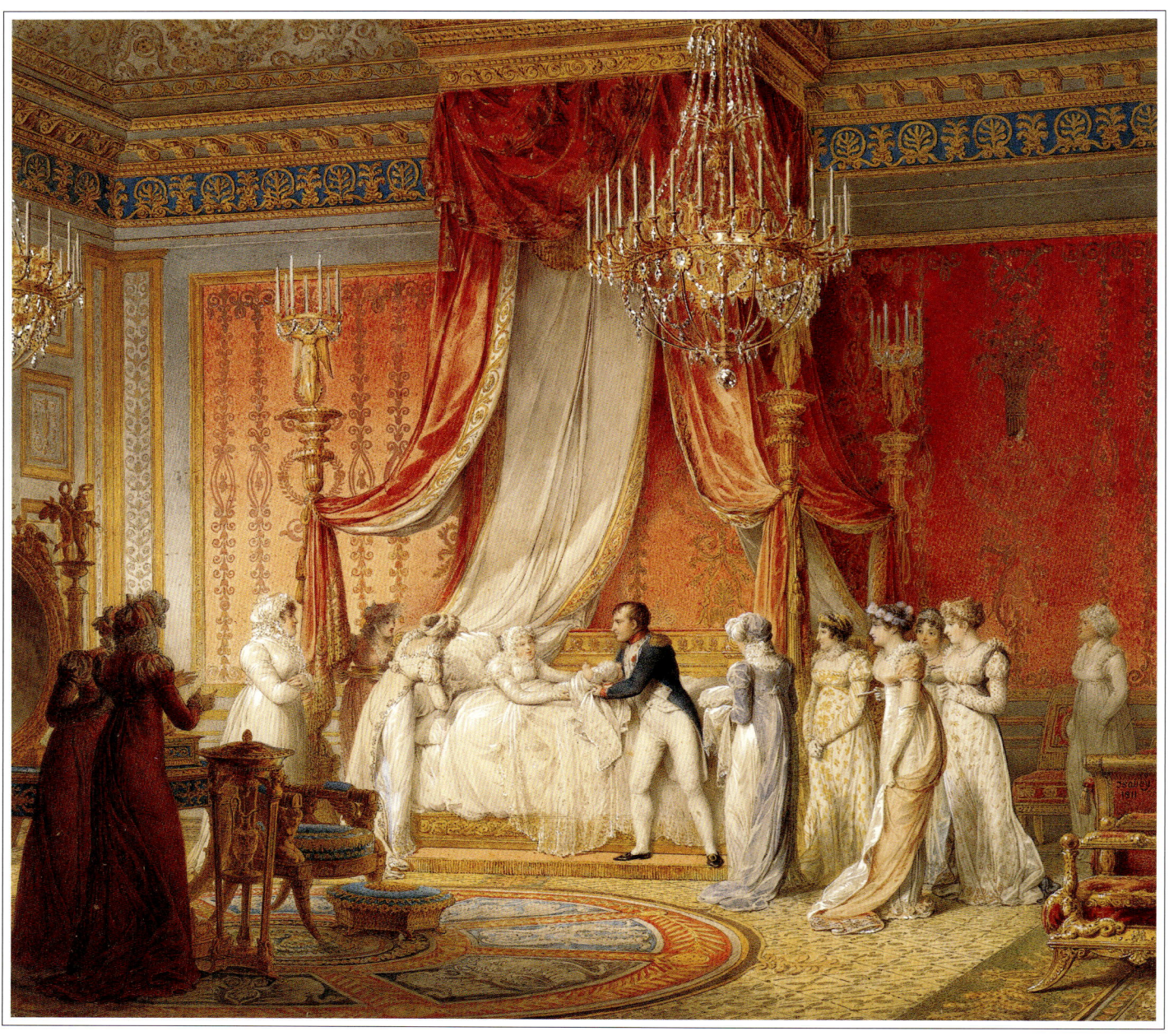

The home most closely identified with Joséphine and that most faithfully reflects her personality is Malmaison, which still seems to be inhabited by her radiant presence.[23] The architects chosen for its restoration were naturally Percier and Fontaine,[24] whose significant publication, *Receuil de décorations intérieures: Comprenant tout ce qui a rapport à l'ameublement comme vases, trépieds, candélabres, cassolettes...miroirs, ecrans, &c.&c.&c.* (1801–12), ultimately codified Neoclassical decor. They worked first for Joséphine at Malmaison and then for the court. While her husband was occupied with state affairs or on campaign, Joséphine supervised the conversion of the seventeenth-century château into a dwelling that would be—in Fontaine's words—"worthy of the great man [they] were serving."[25] It is obvious that Joséphine worked closely with the two architects, for Fontaine noted in his journal, "Mme Bonaparte takes a very active interest in our work...she regards Malmaison as her property."[26]

It remained her favorite residence and provided refuge from the demanding protocol of the Tuileries for, as she told Hortense, "I was not made for such grandeur." At the Tuileries Palace she had to preside at interminable banquets, sit in state in the imperial loge, accept homage from the official bodies, and receive royalty and foreign ambassadors, always remembering their titles, ranks, and genealogies with uncanny accuracy.

At Malmaison, though, she and Bonaparte (as she always called him) could relax with family and friends. Despite her knowledge of the courtly tradition, she boldly took liberties. The entrance was pure Joséphine—a small military tent of blue-and-white striped ticking with red fringe[27]—a flagrant breach of convention, of course, for châteaux were not entered through striped tents.[28] The vestibule recalls a large Roman atrium—its coffered ceiling painted to imitate granite, supported by four massive polished free-standing scagliola columns, and pale-yellow stuccoed walls ornamented with antique trophies. Joséphine properly furnished it with sculpture: four white marble busts copied after antiques in the Salle des Antiquités of the Musée Napoléon, and two bronze heads of philosophers salvaged by her consultant for antiquities, Alexandre Lenoir, all evoking the quiet grandeur of the classical legacy. But the serenity of the sedate vestibule was shattered by the raucous cacophony that erupted from the ornamental aviaries housing brilliant tropical birds, reminiscent of Joséphine's luxuriant native island, Martinique.

To the right is the billiard room, a requisite for all proper châteaux, and especially at Versailles. Joséphine often played after dinner, and there were chairs for the ladies and officers.[29] Upholding tradition, she also offered games of quadrille and *bouillotte*, from which the famous desk lamp of the period received its name. Here a decorous antique note was introduced as well—a pair of white alabaster vases depicting the Sacrifice of Iphigenia and a bacchanale.[30]

In the principal salon (Salon Doré), Bonaparte's taste reigned supreme. In July 1800 he ordered somber mahogany wainscoting and pilasters, with dark green velvet as backdrop for the principal feature of the room—the two large paintings on the subject of Ossian, one by Anne-Louis Girodet-Trioson, the other by François Gérard. These works flanked the precious white-marble fireplace encrusted with agate, jasper, carnelian, and lapis in the Florentine manner, a gift from Pope Pius VII. After the divorce, Joséphine immediately redecorated the room in a more intimate style and sent the Ossian canvases to Prince Eugène.[31]

A distinctly personal flavor is introduced in Joséphine's music salon, originally used for the amateur theatricals in which Hortense, Isabey, Eugène, and the other young officers performed.[32] A watercolor of the room {FIGURE 52} by Auguste Garnerey (1785–1824) is so meticulously painted that we can identify some of the pieces in Joséphine's collection of contemporary works that hung there.[33] One is *The Torch of Venus* by Constance Mayer (ca. 1775–1821), Prud'hon's close collaborator. On the right wall are canvases in the Troubadour

FIGURE 51.

Jean-Baptiste Isabey (French, 1767–1855), *Napoléon Presenting the Newborn King of Rome to His Mother, the Empress Marie-Louise*, ca. 1812. Watercolor, 14.5 × 22 cm (5¾ × 8⅝ in.). Private collection.

• • •

Even though the silk has been changed from blue to crimson, Joséphine's state bed remains the same. The finials are four gilt-bronze colonnettes surmounted by winged Victories holding candles, similar to the candelabra in her rooms at Saint-Cloud and Fontainebleau. If the bed represents Joséphine's taste, so does the carpet with its central medallion adorned with swans and a peacock. It was made in 1808 by the factory of Jean Sallandrouze at Aubusson, and the central medallion is conserved at Malmaison.

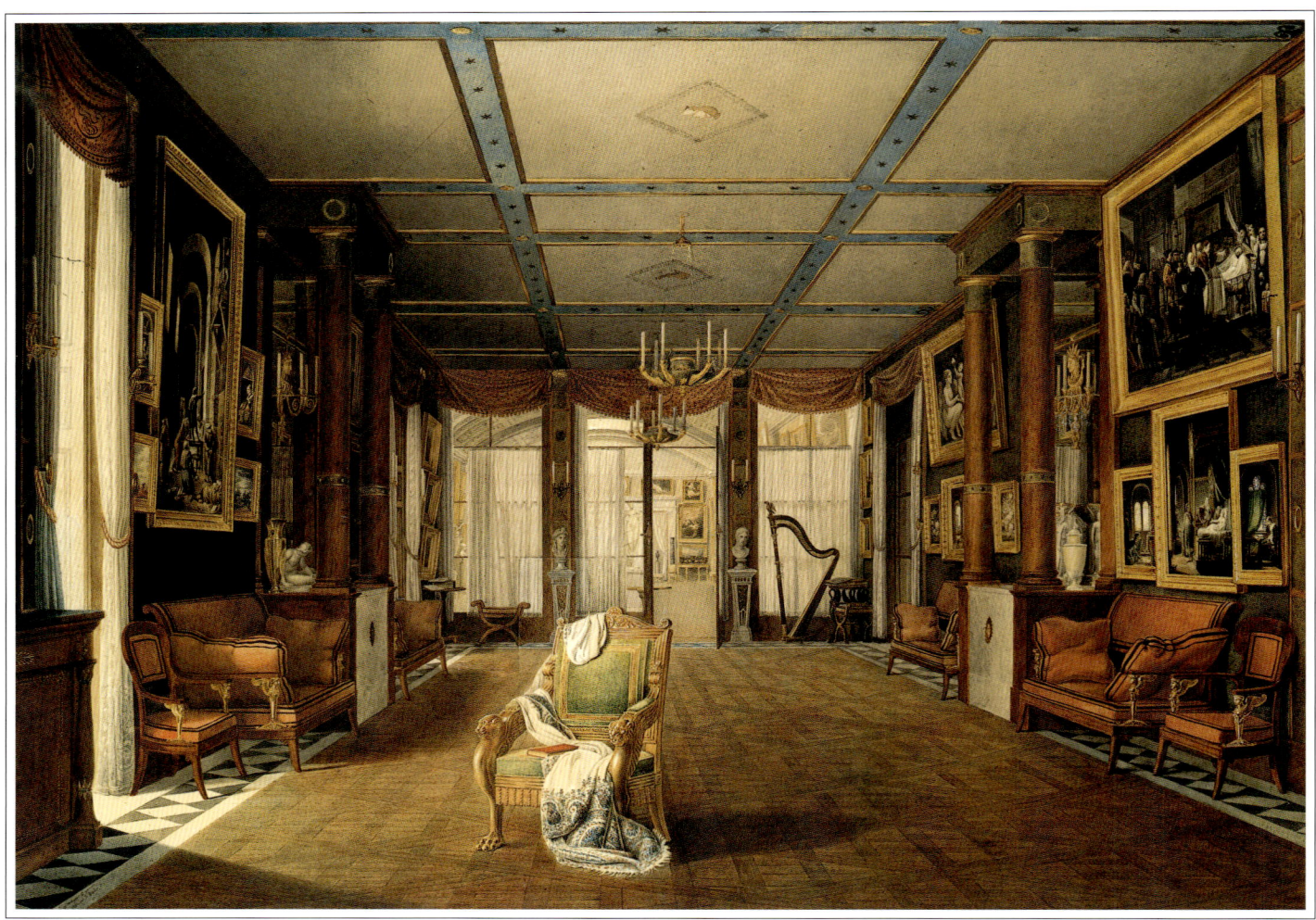

FIGURE 52.
Auguste Garnerey, (French, 1785–1824),
The Music Salon at Malmaison, 1812.
Watercolor, 66.5 × 91 cm (26⅛ × 35⅞ in.).
Rueil-Malmaison, Musée national des Châteaux
de Malmaison et Bois-Préau.

• • •

The north wing is terminated by the music salon and the south wing by Napoléon's study. By repeating this theme of coupled columns in the study, the architects achieved a pleasing symmetry. The same device was used in 1830 by Charles Percier's pupil, Auguste Richard de Montferrand, in the Malachite Room of the Winter Palace, Saint Petersburg, except the columns were of malachite. To make the study appear wider, the architects placed mirrors behind the columns, which reflect white marble copies of antique sculpture and a large Atlas clock.

manner, harbingers of Delacroix's dramas a generation later. Joséphine was the foremost patron of this avant-garde style that nostalgically honored France's illustrious past.

In Garnerey's painting, the furniture is shown covered in a deep red material with black passementerie, the same color scheme as the studio furniture that Georges Jacob made for Jacques-Louis David just before 1789. They are of red wool with black palmettes copied from "Etruscan" vases, some of which can be glimpsed in Joséphine's art gallery just beyond.[34] The room is illuminated by three black *lustres* (chandeliers), two of which are visible in the painting. These evoke the antique manner with gilt-bronze mounts by Martin-Eloi Lignereux (1752–1809). Four half-lights hang against the mirrors, and eight *appliques* (wall lights) are attached to pilasters framing the doors. Both doors and windows are hung with festoons harmonizing with the seats and embellished with the monogram "J.B." In the foreground stands the empress's significant fauteuil in gilt wood with lion's-paw feet and heads inspired by Egypt or Assyria.[35] The cashmere shawl draped over it implies that the owner has just stepped out of the room.[36]

Beyond the salon and through the door at the back is a partial view of Joséphine's art gallery in which her outstanding, comprehensive collection was displayed, much of which

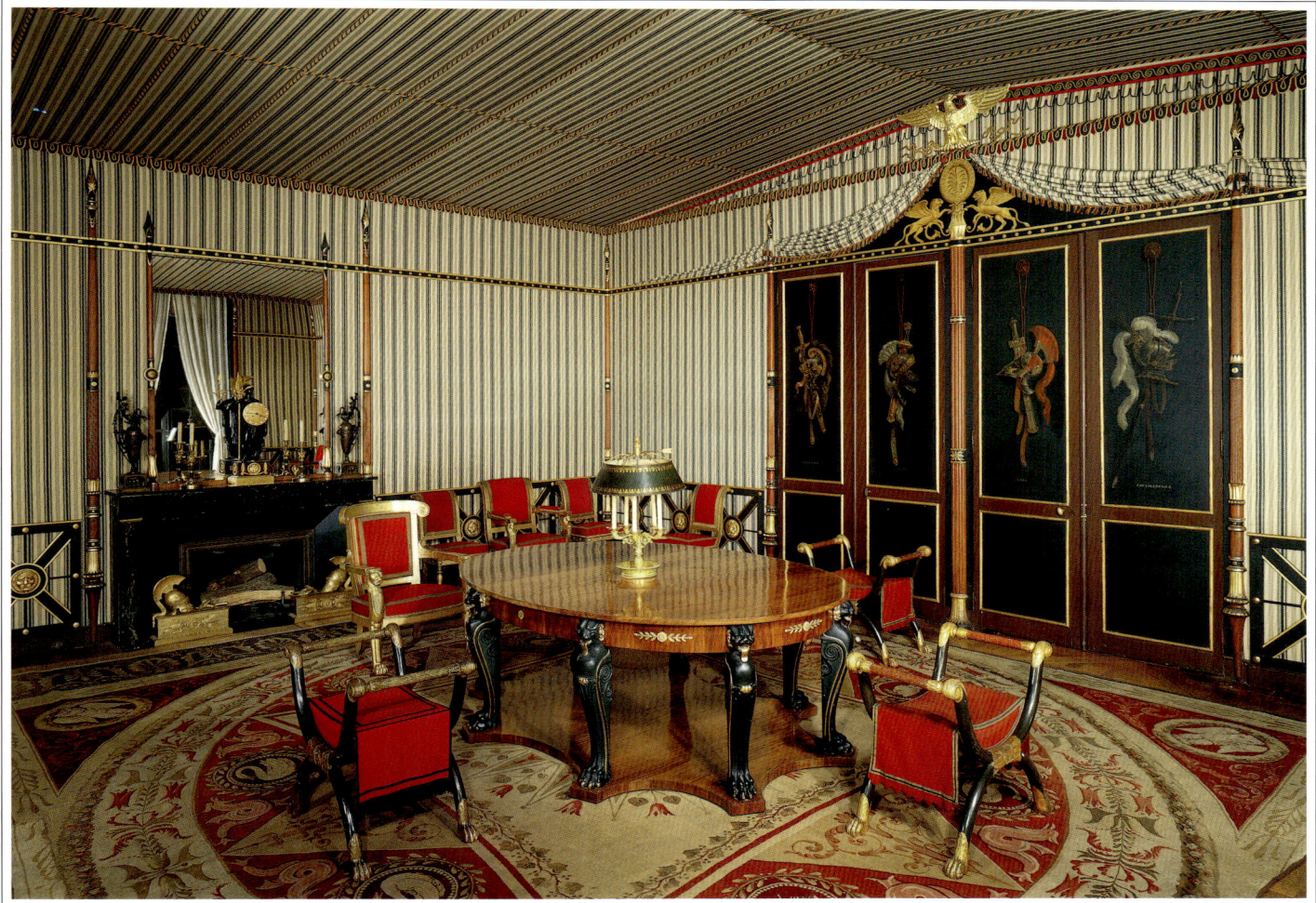

FIGURE 53.

View of the Council Chamber at Malmaison. Photograph, Réunion des Musées de la France.

• • •

The council chamber, a metaphor for the emperor's campaign tents, was an immense success. At Charlottenhof, Potsdam, the German architect, Karl Friedrich Schinkel—who worked for Eugène de Beauharnais in Munich and was in Paris in 1826—designed a version of it for a German prince. At her château of Arenenberg near Lake Constance in Switzerland, Queen Hortense created a still-extant striped tent room, hung with paintings of the First Empire. As late as 1835, Eugène Delacroix recorded the elegant tent room of the comte de Morny.

today glorifies the Hermitage Museum. This gallery featured the foremost Renaissance painters; Dutch, Flemish, and French masterpieces; as well as ivories; Greek ceramics; choice antique busts, statues, bronzes, and frescoes; and the best contemporary sculpture. A skylight provided ideal conditions for viewing the art by day, permitting an ever-changing illumination from above and more wall space for paintings by eliminating the need for windows.[37] This up-to-date feature was most likely suggested by her sophisticated friend and adviser Vivant Denon, whose own collection closely resembled Joséphine's.

Consoles with alabaster or marble tops displayed her priceless vases, two state armchairs were appointed in green velvet with gold trim for the emperor and empress, and other chairs and tabourets (stools) were placed against the wall. The walls were covered in a deep green material (the color of Napoléon's favorite uniform), a matte background for the colorful paintings and dazzling white marble sculpture.

Joséphine entertained an international roster of guests in her gallery, and even if they could not always communicate verbally, they could at least share the international language of the arts.

Returning to the vestibule and turning left into the south wing, today's visitor encounters the dining room paved in black-and-white marble, its almost monochromatic decoration the perfect environment for Joséphine's sumptuous collection of dinnerware.[38] The grisaille and *terre d'Egypte* (pale rust-colored) panels of tripods and eight Pompeian dancers on the walls were painted by Louis Lafitte (1770–1828) as early as 1799,[39] when Prud'hon was executing the panels for Hortense's Hôtel de Lannoy. Against one wall stood a fountain in the form of an antique female term (a pillar adorned with a figure at the top), pouring water into a basin from two urns. Distinguised visitors would join the family for dinner, but it is doubtful that Joséphine's orangutan, clad in redingote, dined with them when crowned heads were present. The dining room represents the understated Consular style at its best and was a relatively new idea, for the concept of a room set apart for dining had not appeared until the latter part of the eighteenth century.

From the dining room, one passes into Percier and Fontaine's famous council chamber in the form of a striped military tent where Bonaparte convened his ministers for government business {FIGURE 53}. Although considered a dramatic innovation, it was no novelty to Joséphine, who must have conceived the idea, given her penchant for tents. She knew her husband's headquarters usually consisted of five marquees of blue-and-white ticking, so why not provide him one at Malmaison? Joséphine's first Paris bedroom had been in tent form, and besides, a room hung with fabric could be realized within the ten days Bonaparte allotted. So the architects covered the walls with striped blue-and-white cotton trimmed with red-and-yellow wool fringe, supported the ceiling with lances and fasces, and had the doors painted with ancient helmets and swords, for Percier and Fontiane were perennially seduced by the lure of antiquity.

The passementerie for the council chamber, like Joséphine's beds, was very costly, and Napoléon often exploded when he saw the bills. So Joséphine confided to her upholsterer, Michel-Jacques Boulard, that she was willing to pay him 10,000 francs more if he would only keep the passementerie of her bedroom "simple!" The architect Mies van der Rohe was not the first to insist on simplicity no matter what the cost—the empress had anticipated him by at least a century.

The appointments and furniture of the council chamber also carried out the military theme. The tabourets (made to resemble folding campaign seats) were uniformly covered with red material trimmed with black-and-gold velvet, and the important armchair is now in the New York Historical Society.[40] After the fall of the Empire, an appropriate portrait was added—*Frederick the Great* by the cavalry officer Jean-Baptiste-François Carteaux (1751–1813).[41] The council chamber was so precious to Joséphine that she would permit no changes to the room after her sad divorce of 1809.

Terminating the south wing is the emperor's library, an ingenious nineteenth-century evocation of the Italian Renaissance {FIGURE 54}. The arches of the vaulted ceilings are supported by two architectural elements with coupled mahogany columns breaking forward from the walls, echoing Joséphine's music room. The vaulting of the two arches,

FIGURE 54.

View of Napoléon's Library at Malmaison. Photograph, Réunion des Musées de la France.

• • •

Displayed in the library, or study, in 1814 was a silver reproduction of the temple in Strasbourg that had been given to Joséphine while she was holding court there in 1805, along with a bronze model of the temple of Dendera in Egypt, a marble obelisk ornamented with bronze, the white marble bust of Joséphine by François-Joseph Bosio (between the columns at right), and Bosio's bust of Queen Hortense. Napoléon liked the location of his library, for he could go from his work directly into the gardens.

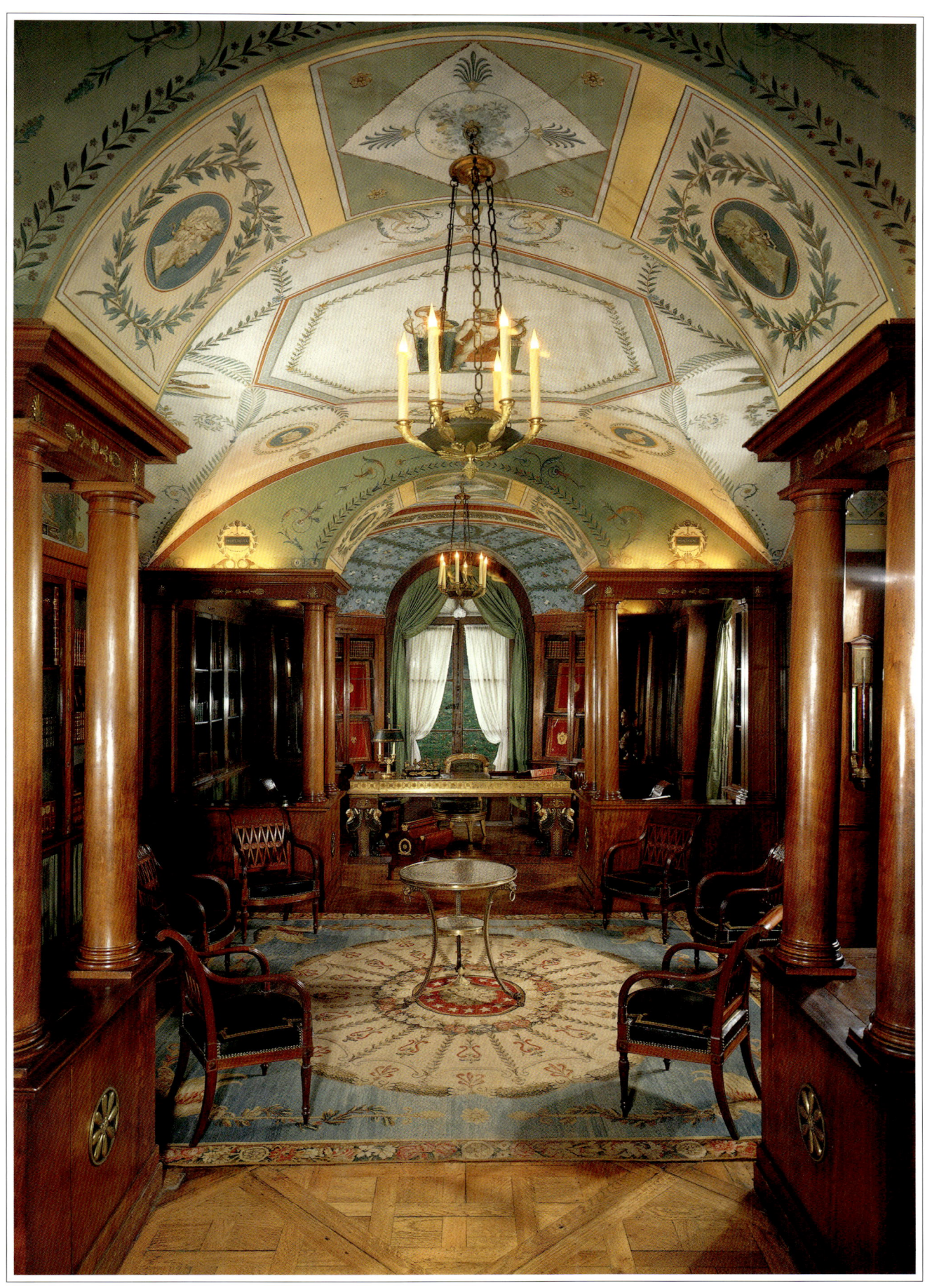

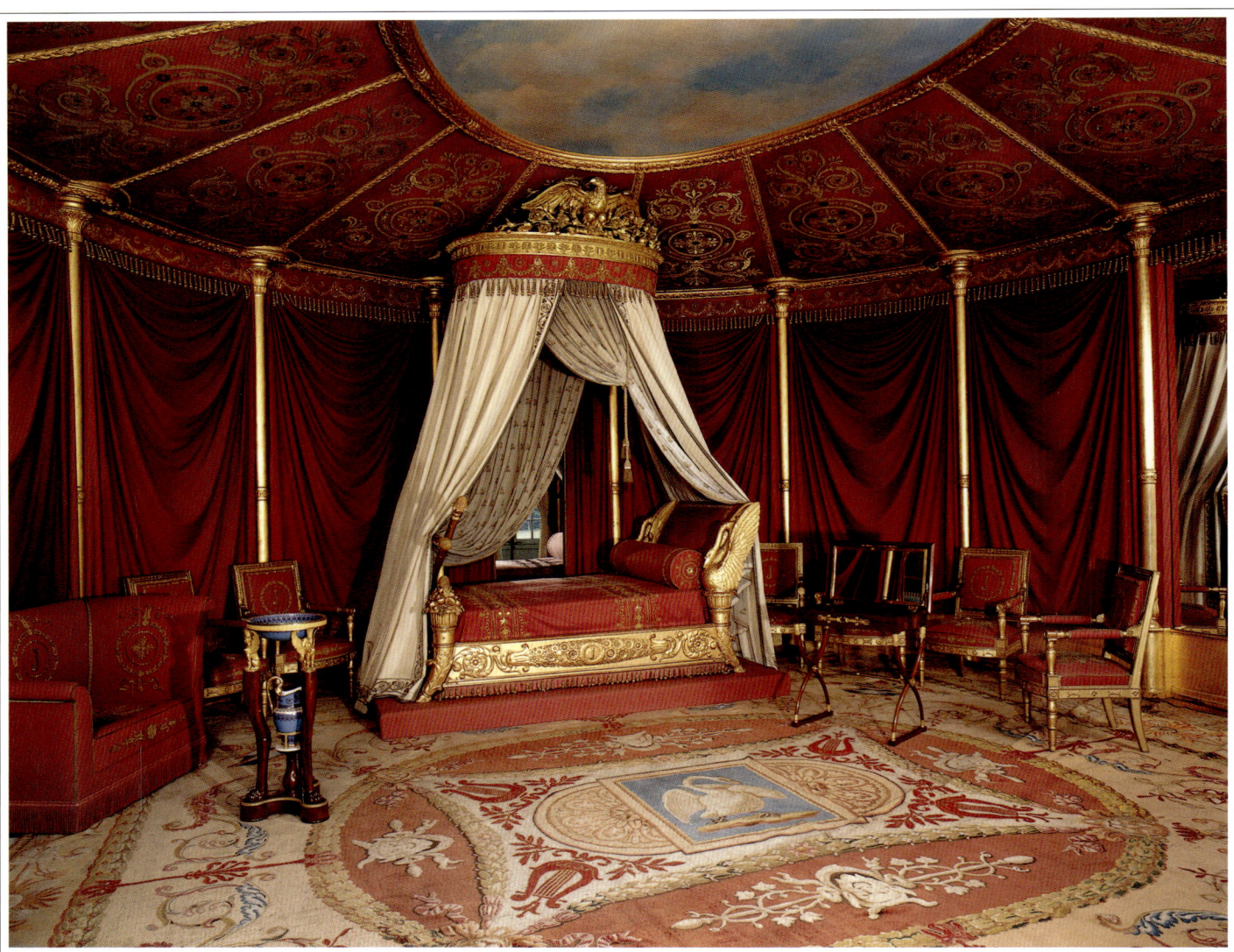

FIGURE 55.

View of Joséphine's Formal Bedroom at Malmaison. Photograph, Réunion des Musées de la France.

• • •

recesses, and half domes—reminiscent of the Raphael Loggia in the Vatican—was painted by Frederic Moench (1784–1867) from Percier's designs. They contained figures of Apollo and Minerva and medallions of philosophers and poets enframed with laurel.

Since the architects intended that their rooms express the interests of the occupant, they lined the walls with bookcases, for Napoléon was an omnivorous reader. Whether at Malmaison or the Tuileries, the lamp burned late in his study, and during his brilliant Consulate period the first truly modern code of laws came into being. He worked closely with its formulators, and the Napoleonic Code "so impressed [other] governments...that the nineteenth century became the greatest century of legal codification."[42]

Joséphine did not usually sleep here, but in her *chambre ordinaire* on the floor above. The only item that remains in place today is the gilt-wood bed made by Jacob-Desmalter in 1812. The classical emblem of cornucopias, usually held by the corn goddess Ceres, was probably designed by Louis-Martin Berthault, who updated the room after the divorce. It was in this bed that Joséphine died on May 29, 1814. Pierre-Joseph Redouté's precious watercolors of the flowers in Joséphine's garden, which were hanging in this room, apparently went to Eugène in Munich and to Hortense in Augsburg at their mother's death. These gems of botanical illustration have reappeared in such far-flung places as Calcutta and Monaco, and today command astronomical prices.

Joséphine's formal bedroom was redesigned by Louis-Martin Berthault after the divorce, and it epitomizes her taste—a canopied bed within a tent {FIGURE 55}. The nearly circular tent was made of *casimir* (thin wool) in sixteen sections, separated by gilt columns, with the material folded in godets within each section. Originally each ceiling division enclosed sixteen circular, gold, embroidered medallions enframed with palmettes. At the center, a trompe l'oeil oculus appeared to be open to the sky, although it was in fact a ceiling painting of a mythical heaven—*Juno in Her Chariot Pulled by White Horses* by Merry-Joseph Blondel,[43] one of the many young artists Joséphine patronized.

To make the room seem larger, Berthault installed facing pairs of mirrors: one on the wall between the windows overlooking the garden to echo the mirror behind the state bed, another over the chimney piece that faced the mirrored doors on the opposite side. All upholstery was in the same material as the walls, and the curtains were muslin laminated with gold. On a table between the windows rested Joséphine's magnificent silver-gilt toilet service by Odiot and Biennais, presented to her by the City of Paris for the coronation and covered with a piece of English lace sprinkled with bees. A series of Pierre-Joseph Redouté's exquisite watercolors of Joséphine's choicest flowers were displayed on the walls of rich, cockscomb red, known as amaranth. Symbolizing immortality, amaranth is always identified with the Bonaparte family, so it was a fitting choice for the canopied room where Joséphine passed the last hours of her life.

Among the numerous visitors to Malmaison after her death was General Alexander Mercer, commander of the Ninth Royal Artillery Brigade, who paid his respects after Waterloo on July 14, 1815, and left the following impression of her bedroom: "I never saw any room so remarkable for its decoration and so interesting from every point of view." The officer then described it in detail and concluded, "The walls, instead of being hung with paper, were covered in [rich material], with lace used as a border around the panels. There, I truly appreciated the taste of Joséphine."[44]

In spite of her impressive art collection and her conservatory renowned throughout Europe, Joséphine never allowed Malmaison to be pretentious, and she always considered it a family haven. Yet it was counted a singular honor to be invited to Joséphine's small château, which occupied a special place among the imperial residences and where countless eminent guests were entertained. In February 1805 the pope asked if she would receive him, and in 1809 the allied sovereigns inquired if they might come again, so that even as a deposed empress supposedly in retirement, Joséphine once again played hostess to the crowned heads of Europe.

"It [Malmaison] owed its celebrity to Napoléon, but its charm to Joséphine," wrote Gérard Hubert. "In spite of the two centuries that have gone by, the light and shadow of the Empress always hovers about this much-loved domain . . . the fascinating Créole has imparted to it a part of her own gracious mystery."[45] Nowhere is this more apparent than in Malmaison's decor—a manifesto of good design. But above all, the empress intended it to evoke the personalities and history of its inhabitants and be attuned to the diapason of its time.

Notes

1. The marquise was deeply indebted to Joséphine for the restitution of almost all of her fortune. She, Mme Renaudin, and Mme Campan instructed the empress in "the grand manner" of the old court.
2. Bonaparte bought it from Mlle Lange, whose scandalous portrait by Girodet was a sensation at the Salon of 1799.
3. It was originally known as the Hôtel de Saint-Julien, but it was bought in 1797 by Marie-Antoine de Lannoy. The street had been called rue Cerutti since 1792. Louis-Martin Berthault, whom Joséphine employed at Malmaison, modernized the house. Hortense's son, the future Napoléon III, was born there.
4. It measured 9.75 × 11.28 m (32 × 37 ft.). Vivant Denon, who shared Joséphine's admiration for Prud'hon, owned four oil studies for the four vertical panels and commissioned numerous works from Prud'hon.
5. The wainscoting below was embellished with pairs of *mascarons* (masks) relating to the principal allegories: Time and Old Age, Mercury and Bacchus, Plutus and Fortune, Mnemosyne and Apollo, Love and Folly, Pan and Minerva.
6. Sylvain Laveissière, *Pierre-Paul Prud'hon* (New York, 1998), 138.
7. Laveissière, *Pierre-Paul Prud'hon*, 137.
8. Anita Brookner, "Prud'hon: Master Decorator of the Empire," *Apollo*, September 1964, 192. It was, however, carried out during the Consulate period. That Prud'hon intended to execute a decorative program for Joséphine herself seems almost certain in light of his paintings of *The Four Seasons* (private collection) for which a drawing exists in the Musée Bertrand, Chateauroux. *The Four Seasons* series was executed at the same time Prud'hon was at work on the allegories for the Hôtel de Lannoy, so it is most likely that the latter was so demanding that the *Seasons* project for Joséphine's room was never completed. She was immersed at that time in refurbishing Malmaison, so she may have ordered these four panels for the dining room of her château, but when Prud'hon became too busy, she and her architects turned to Louis Lafitte (1770–1828). Her posthumous inventory lists "Les Quatre Saisons" (Item 314).
9. It was the former Hôtel de Torcy, built in 1713. The architect Laurent-Edmé Bataille (1758–1819) was involved in the restoration, but the extent of his work is unknown. The state apartments, with windows looking down on the Seine, are typical of Joséphine's eclectic taste. Bronzes adorning the grand Salle des Saisons ranged from a Louis XVI clock from Gouthiére's workshop and another from the atelier of Thomire, whose work spanned the ages of Marie-Antoinette and Joséphine, to sumptuous candelabra with Nubian slaves by the Feuchéres, inspired by the Egyptian campaign. The wall paintings in this salon, as well as those in the Salon de Musique, were possibly executed by pupils of Prud'hon, Joséphine's favorite painter, and the vertical panels of birds in natural colors in the Salon de Musique were taken from the renowned publication *l'Histoire Naturelle* by the naturalist Georges-Louis Buffon (1707–1788).
10. These were aristocracy and nobility who had fled the Revolution.
11. G. Lenôtre, *Les Tuileries* (Paris, 1933), 156–57.
12. Washington had always been considered a legendary figure by the French and was especially honored by the French army under General Rochambeau, who went to fight for the colonists in the American Revolution.
13. Fontaine's journal states that Napoléon ordered Lebrun paintings for the Diana Gallery, but Ledoux-Lebard claims that the Diana Gallery was hung with Gobelins tapestries representing the battles of Constantine, interspersed with marble statues of France's military heroes—Condé, Turenne, Bayard, and so on, although the source of her quotation is not given. See Denise Ledoux-Lebard, "The Furnishing of the Tuileries under the Consulate," *Apollo*, September 1964, 200.
14. Louis Bourriènne, quoted in Ledoux-Lebard, "The Furnishing of the Tuileries," 200.
15. Bourrienne's Paris hotel was regarded as a model of the Directoire style, and still stands.
16. La marquise de la Tour du Pin (Henriette-Lucie Dillon), *Recollections of the Revolution and the Empire*, trans. and ed. Walter Geer (New York, 1920), 311.
17. Ancien régime rules required that chairs remain against the walls.
18. Denise Ledoux-Lebard, "Joséphine and Interior Decoration," *Apollo*, July–September, 1977, 19.
19. Bernard Chevallier, *L'Art de vivre au temps de Joséphine* (Paris, 1999), 7.
20. Louis XVI had purchased it for Marie-Antoinette from the duc d'Orléans in 1785 and ordered extensive decorative work. Saint-Cloud became a public dance hall after the Revolution.
21. Also in Marie-Antoinette's apartments at Saint-Cloud were the magnificent commode and secretary by J.-H. Riesener in the Wrightsman Collection, The Metropolitan Museum of Art, New York.
22. Probably thanks to Joséphine, Etiènne Calmelet (1763–ca. 1820) was made director of the Imperial Warehouse, and in charge of furnishing the imperial residences. It was probably through Calmelet that Joséphine acquired the splendid mauve, fuchsia, and deep blue Sèvres vases by Leriche and Lagrenée depicting themes of love.
23. She bought it on April 21, 1799, and it became her personal property on December 16, 1809, at the time of the divorce.

24. By February 20, 1800, the vestibule was almost finished. The work can be followed month by month in Fontaine's journal. See Pierre-François-Léonard Fontaine, *Journal, 1799–1853*, 2 vols. (Paris, 1987).
25. Fontaine, *Journal*, vol. 1, 11. Hortense said that people in her stepfather's presence felt a special awe. Only one marshal "tutoyed" him, and none sat in his presence. See Jean Hanoteau, *Mémoires de la Reine Hortense*, vol. 1 (Paris, 1927), 85.
26. Fontaine, *Journal*, vol. 1, 14. In November 1799, they began the demolition of the old interior walls to create new, rational spaces and replace the parts beyond redemption.
27. In its original state, the tent appeared to be supported by fasces from which two lances sprang, supporting a globe and a crescent, which either alluded to the recent Egyptian campaign or were perhaps symbols of the sun and moon. Napoléon did not like it, claiming that it looked like a cage for animals.
28. The frailest excuse would suffice to satisfy Joséphine's passion for tents, and one was the celebration following the victory at Marengo in 1800, for which she asked Pierre Fontaine to provide canopies to shelter the tables, no doubt made of the striped cotton material she bought in such large quantities. Another opportunity came with a theatrical performance in May 1802, when Joséphine ordered a fabric-covered gallery for the refreshments to be put up beside the theater. One of the baths in Malmaison looked like a white cotton tent, and next to the canopied entrance to the vestibule, a blue-and-white awning protected the garden exit, as did a canvas suspended over the door leading from Napoléon's library into the garden.
29. Originally hung here was a memento of the Egyptian campaign—six portraits of sheiks by the Italian artist Michel Rigo.
30. They stood on two tripods of wood treated to look like bronze, mounted with gilt bronze. In the adjoining antechamber were *tric-trac* tables in lemonwood and mahogany that Joséphine had brought from Martinique.
31. The ceiling and doors (still extant) were painted with delicate, antique-gilt motifs on a light ground, but the medallions (probably by Redouté) have disappeared. For one suite of furniture (1811), Joséphine and her ladies made tapestry upholstery in petit point on a white ground centered by the letter "J" surmounted by a crown of roses. In Etiènne-Pierre Ventenat's dedication to his two folio volumes, *Le Jardin de la Malmaison* (1803–4), he speaks of the empress's "studious leisure."
32. It soon proved to be too small, however, and a separate theater pavilion was put up outside the château.
33. After 1811 she added a sketch of David's *The Lictors Bringing Brutus the Bodies of His Sons* (National Museum, Stockholm).
34. Juliette Recamier's salon furniture in the Abbaye-aux-Bois in 1826, as seen in a painting by François-Louis Dejuinne (1784–1844), is also covered in red material edged in black, like Joséphine's. If the mauve material and bed with gilt-bronze swans, which Louis Berthault had used in 1798 for Juliette's famous bedroom in the Hôtel Recamier, influenced Joséphine's preference for lilac (and especially swans), possibly the black-and-red seats in Joséphine's music room in turn inspired Juliette's upholstery. Yet both may well have looked to the ultimate source—Georges Jacob's furniture designed for Jacques-Louis David's studio.
35. Under the monarchy only sovereigns, certain members of the royal family, and visiting royalty were allowed to sit in armchairs. The custom was perpetuated under the Empire, and Joséphine sat in a specially designed fauteuil at formal sessions or receptions.
36. For more on Joséphine's love of shawls, see chapter 10.
37. The skylight had more recently appeared in Hubert Robert's renovations in 1803 at the Musée du Louvre, which became the Musée Napoléon.
38. It included royal Berlin, Sèvres, and the Paris factory of Dihl et Guérhard.
39. Clare Crick, "Wallpapers by Dufour et Cie.," *Connoisseur*, December 1976, 312.
40. It had been brought to America by Joseph Bonaparte.
41. Carteaux was a cavalry officer under whom Bonaparte served during the siege of Toulon and must have painted this portrait after he moved to Germany. It was placed there at the end of the Empire, replacing portraits of Mme Joseph Bonaparte and one of Queen Hortense and her sons by Marie-Eléonore Godefroid.
42. Robert B. Holtman, *The Napoleonic Revolution* (Philadelphia, 1967), 97
43. An excellent portrait of an unknown man by Blondel was acquired by Mount Holyoke College (ca. 1997). Blondel worked at the Dihl et Guérhard factory, where he learned to draw, then went to Italy in 1809, from which he had just returned in 1812 when he received the Malmaison commission.
44. Bernard Chevallier, *Malmaison: Château et Domaines des Origines à 1904* (Paris, 1989), 133–34.
45. Gérard Hubert, "Une journée de Joséphine à Malmaison," *Le Souvenir Napoleonien*, January–February, 1994.

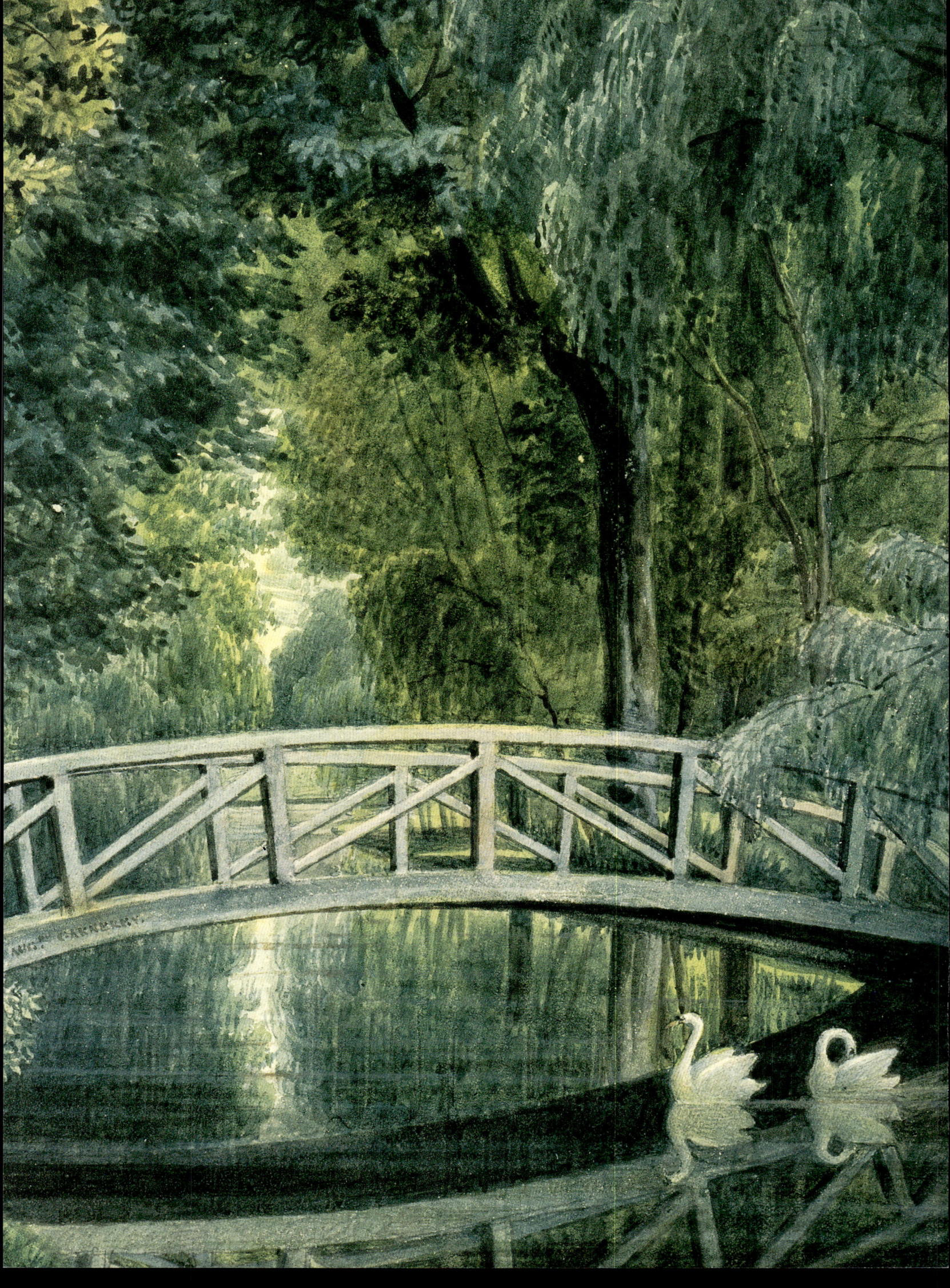

CHAPTER 4

Eleanor P. DeLorme

Her Magical World: Joséphine's Gardens and Conservatory

Although Joséphine's art collection was constantly being augmented by purchases and gifts, her true passion was the natural sciences, as Bernard Chevallier has pointed out (see chapter 7). In fact, the empress's commitment to botany and zoology was such that her garden at Malmaison rivaled the Jardin des Plantes in Paris. Behind that former royal enclave lay three centuries of history, whereas Joséphine created hers in just over a decade. What made these two gardens significant was their dynamic, persevering collaboration in discoveries "characterized...by connoisseurship, acclimatization...of a quantity of trees and plants [imported] from other continents, [and] by a scientific approach to the possibilities of differentiating and improving them, especially the flowers."[1]

Exploration of exotic climes was exploding in the early nineteenth century, and, as symbol of their status, trendsetters were amassing collections of botanical and zoological specimens that others did not have. Because of her virtually unlimited resources and her husband's position, Joséphine not only had first choice in this arena but also possessed the taste and sagacity to fully implement this singular opportunity. So rigorous was her pursuit of unusual horticultural and zoological specimens that she garnered professional approval from the august professors of the Museum of Natural History, who extended their appreciation for her interest in and contributions to the natural sciences. This tribute was followed by a letter to the professors from comte Jean-Antoine Chaptal (1756–1832), who, as an eminent chemist and minister of the interior, occupied a commanding position in the Napoleonic pantheon. He was so impressed by Joséphine's promotion of the sciences that he urged these scholars to collaborate with her in every possible way, pointing out the empress's great success in the cultivation of plants and nurturing of rare animals and asking them to support her fully in the interests of science and to the glory of France.

Joséphine's achievements were so spectacular and unsurpassed for their time that her gardens and conservatory attracted preeminent naturalists and botanists from far and wide, including the Prussian ambassador Baron Alexander von Humboldt (1769–1859), who had embarked in 1799 on an exploratory voyage to America with the accomplished botanist Aimé Goufau, called "Bonpland" (1773–1858). They were even received by President Thomas Jefferson and returned to France on August 3, 1804, after a five-year voyage. Baron von Humboldt kept in close touch with Joséphine until she died; and Bonpland, her devoted naturalist, stood at her deathbed.

In addition to the scientific merits of her gardens, its aesthetic qualities were valued by leading garden historians. One was Alexandre de Laborde (1773–1842), youngest son of the marquis de Laborde, who had created at his vast estate, Méréville, the most comprehensive landscape garden in France,[2] which Joséphine would have visited. Alexandre was also a good friend of Joséphine's daughter, Hortense de Beauharnais, contributing lyrics for her popular song, "Partant pour la Syrie," and he often visited Malmaison. Laborde so greatly admired "the abundance and beauty of the most precious and exotic plants" that he termed the empress's garden "the true Jardin des Plantes of France."[3] Given the universal prestige of the former royal garden, especially under the Empire, Alexandre de Laborde was paying Joséphine the ultimate compliment.[4]

The naturalistic landscape, or picturesque garden, had evolved from the English style beginning around the 1730s. Influenced by landscape painting, Chinese gardens, and travel literature, it had become the height of French fashion in the latter part of the eighteenth century. Ever since she left Martinique, Joséphine had wanted a country house to decorate with her own touch, and especially a terrain to embellish—not simply as a complement to the château but as a landscape garden in its own right.

After emerging from prison in August 1794, while living at Croissy on the right bank of the Seine, Joséphine noticed across the river a heavily wooded tract with natural waters and an old manor house that captured her fancy. Through Jean Chanorier,[5] the mayor of Croissy, she learned that the property had belonged to Jean-Jacques Le Couteulx du Molay, whose family "ruled…the [left] bank of the Seine between Rueil and Bougival,"[6] and that Mme du Molay had conducted a salon there, convening the literary, intellectual, and artistic elite.[7] This social history and the distinction of the estate's owners enhanced its desirability. Besides, by 1798 the small house on rue de la Victoire no longer met Joséphine's needs. What she and Bonaparte needed now was a dignified, seigniorial domain. So, shortly after Bonaparte's return from Italy early in 1798, they visited the property for the first time. Although the general found the price excessive, Joséphine was undeterred, and, after persistent bargaining, her offer was finally accepted.

During her husband's prolonged absence in Egypt, Joséphine began to refurbish this country retreat where they would spend their happiest hours as a family. Capitalizing on the social and political advantages of her acquisition, she staged two opulent dinners at Malmaison for members of the Directoire. By November 1799 she had engaged the architects Charles Percier and Pierre-François-Léonard Fontaine to completely transform the old manor house inside and out, and she began planning her extensive garden.

The property's natural resources appealed to her, with its seductive, undulating land nestled at the foot of rolling hills animated with running brooks and sheltered by verdant groves. Although it comprised only 105 acres, Joséphine kept enlarging it through exchanges and purchases so that at her death it numbered 294 acres.

The château proclaimed a novel interior landscape, while its park announced an exterior landscape that blended old and new. Moreover, part of Malmaison's charm is the intimate wedding of interior and exterior, contrived by tall casement windows, footbridges spanning the dry moat that links house and garden, awnings that shelter both the central garden

FIGURE 56.

Jean-Victor Nicolle (French, 1754–1826),
Vue de la Cour d'honneur du château de la Malmaison, ca. 1810.
Watercolor, pen and black ink, and graphite on paper,
20.5 × 32.3 cm (8 1/8 × 12 15/16 in.).
Rueil-Malmaison, Musée national des Châteaux de Malmaison et Bois-Préau.

· · ·

This view of Malmaison shows the tall roofs of the south and north wings at left and right, respectively, dating from the seventeenth century. The central corps is also from this period. The wings with triangular pediments projecting forward at either side to form the courtyard were built at the end of the eighteenth century, the one on the right housing Joséphine's art gallery. The orange trees in classic *orangers* are reminiscent of those used during the ancien régime. At center is the entrance veranda in tent form, typical of Joséphine's taste.

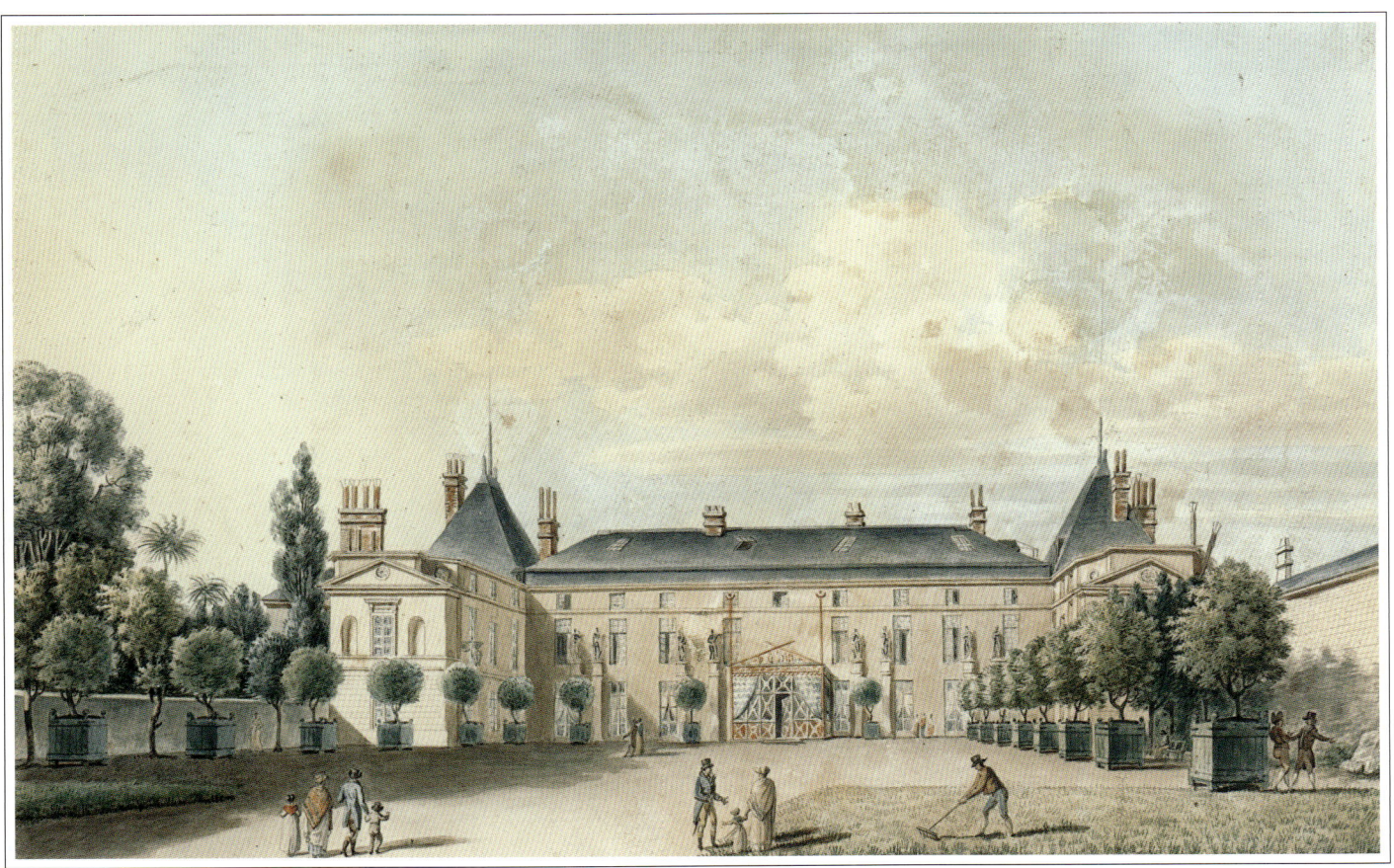

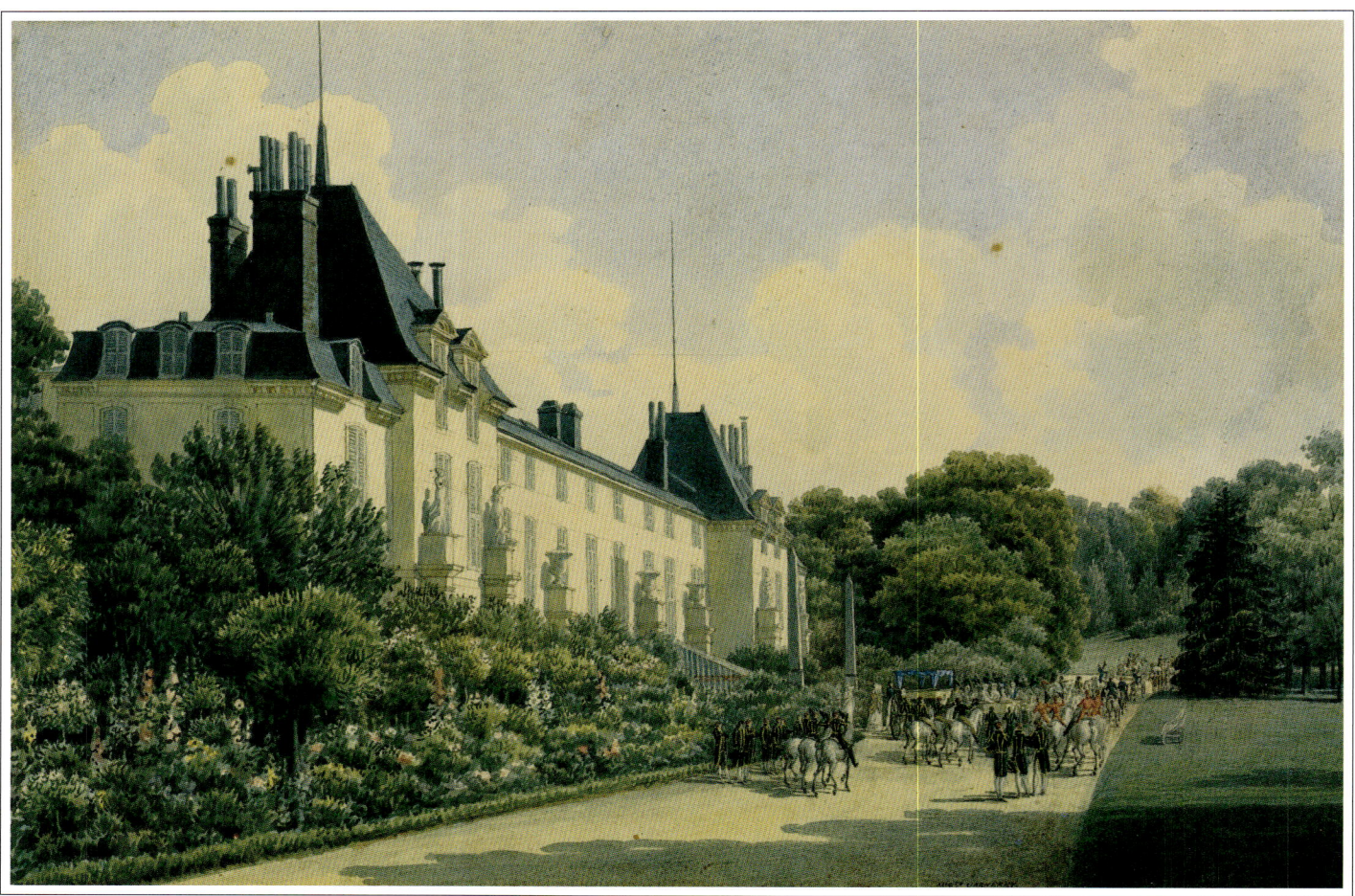

entrance and the library door that opens onto the garden behind the house, and the modified military tent at the front entrance {FIGURE 56} (see chapter 3, note 27).

One feature of Malmaison was the orange trees arranged along each side of the courtyard in straight rows like sentinels. In winter these fragile plants were protected in a heated orangery built in 1800, which housed frames for three hundred pineapples. This attractive tropical fruit was the subject of a ravishing watercolor by Pierre-Joseph Redouté (1759–1840), and when Laure Junot (wife of Napoléon's aide-de-camp) craved a pineapple during her pregnancy, Joséphine sent her one from the Malmaison orangery.

Any hint of ceremony was dispelled when a visitor passed through the vestibule, serenaded by Joséphine's caged tropical birds, and emerged on the western side where the landscape garden spread out like a bucolic scene by the French painter and landscape designer Hubert Robert (1733–1808). His pastoral views, along with those of other landscape painters of the time, were an inspiration to many garden designers.[8] Framing Malmaison's garden entrance, protected by its blue-and-white canopy, were tall hollyhocks and other simple flowers {FIGURE 57}. The massing of plants with densely packed flora against the house was deliberate, as it softened the forbidding facade, which was dignified by statues and vases surmounting tall plinths added to stabilize the structure. These vases, executed by such eighteenth-century masters as Jean Louis Lemoyne (1665–1755) and Jacques Verberckt (1704–1771), came from for-

FIGURE 57.

Auguste Garnerey (French, 1785–1824), *View of the Facade of the Château on the Park Side*, n.d. Watercolor, 16.3 × 24.3 cm (6⅜ × 9⅝ in.). Rueil-Malmaison, Musée national des Châteaux de Malmaison et Bois-Préau.

• • •

Auguste Garnerey was born into a family of painters and studied with his own father as well as with Jean-Baptiste Isabey, an artist closely associated with Joséphine and her daughter, Hortense. The empress particularly liked Garnerey's work, and his watercolors of the gardens and interiors of Malmaison show a refinement commensurate with his patroness's taste. He often animated his views with strollers or, as in this case, cavaliers and attendants who appear to be awaiting the imperial couple.

mer royal houses and included eight from Louis XIV's fabled pavilion complex at Marly.[9] This association with the Sun King's royal estate delighted Joséphine, who would point to the Marly aqueduct crowning a distant hill and jest that it was a gallantry proferred her by Louis XIV.

Joséphine always identified herself with the former court, and Chateaubriand declared that the one desire of returning French nobles and aristocrats (whose cause Joséphine championed)[10] was a picturesque English garden. As the landscape garden was another symbol of a person's social standing, these informal gardens, where nature and fantasy were allowed free rein, expressed the aspirations of the returning émigrés whom Joséphine attracted to the court. According to Jean-Marie Morel (1728–1810), "Not only was this style à la mode…but [it was also] a sign of social and political stature."[11]

As to the design of Malmaison's garden, Bonaparte no doubt would have preferred a scaled-down version of the traditional French garden in which vegetation was coerced into geometric shapes on either side of a central allée bordered by clipped greenery; in other words, a garden conceived as an architectural element in which the human hand is unmistakable. Its regimental precision accorded with Bonaparte's orderly manner (he enjoyed walking along the straight lines of the Tuileries gardens). Even more to the point, he would have chosen the formal garden for its imagery of power and command. He was avidly seconded in this preference by Percier and Fontaine, yet even against this formidable triumvirate Joséphine held her ground.

Fortunately, the Le Couteulx family had already begun to build over the preexisting formal garden a fashionable landscape garden with numerous trees and rare plants, ornamented with pavilions such as a belvedere and a small summer house, which Bonaparte would claim as his office. This renovation also included replacing the formal parterres with a serpentine river coddling two artificial islands, so certain elements of Joséphine's vision were already in place {FIGURE 58}.

After a succession of architects and gardeners whose plans failed to please, in September 1801 Joséphine turned to the highly respected garden theorist Jean-Marie Morel.[12] This met with the obvious disapproval of Fontaine, and a skirmish broke out between Morel and Fontaine, who grumbled that the septuagenarian was "insulting nature and warring upon art."[13] But Morel had designed the original enclosed park of Malmaison for its former owners, and this magnified his worth in Joséphine's eyes. Plainly, Morel's plans were being implemented, for in the same month Fontaine censoriously remarked, "Our heresy concerning the present taste in gardens has offended Madame.… She wishes only groups, effects, oppositions, and especially sentiment."[14]

Morel worked at Malmaison until 1805, contributing both landscape design and garden pavilions,[15] including a rustic "hamlet," much like those at Chantilly and Versailles, but because of his cantankerous disposition, he was replaced in early 1805 by Jean-Thomas Thibault (1757–1826) and Barthélemy Vignon (1762–1846), who completed the vast glass conservatory and Joséphine's sheepfold. For purely emotive effect Joséphine incorporated ephemeral, decorative elements such as windmills, bridges, columns, towers, mausoleums, and ruins. Fortunately, she had the professional advice and material aid of the noted

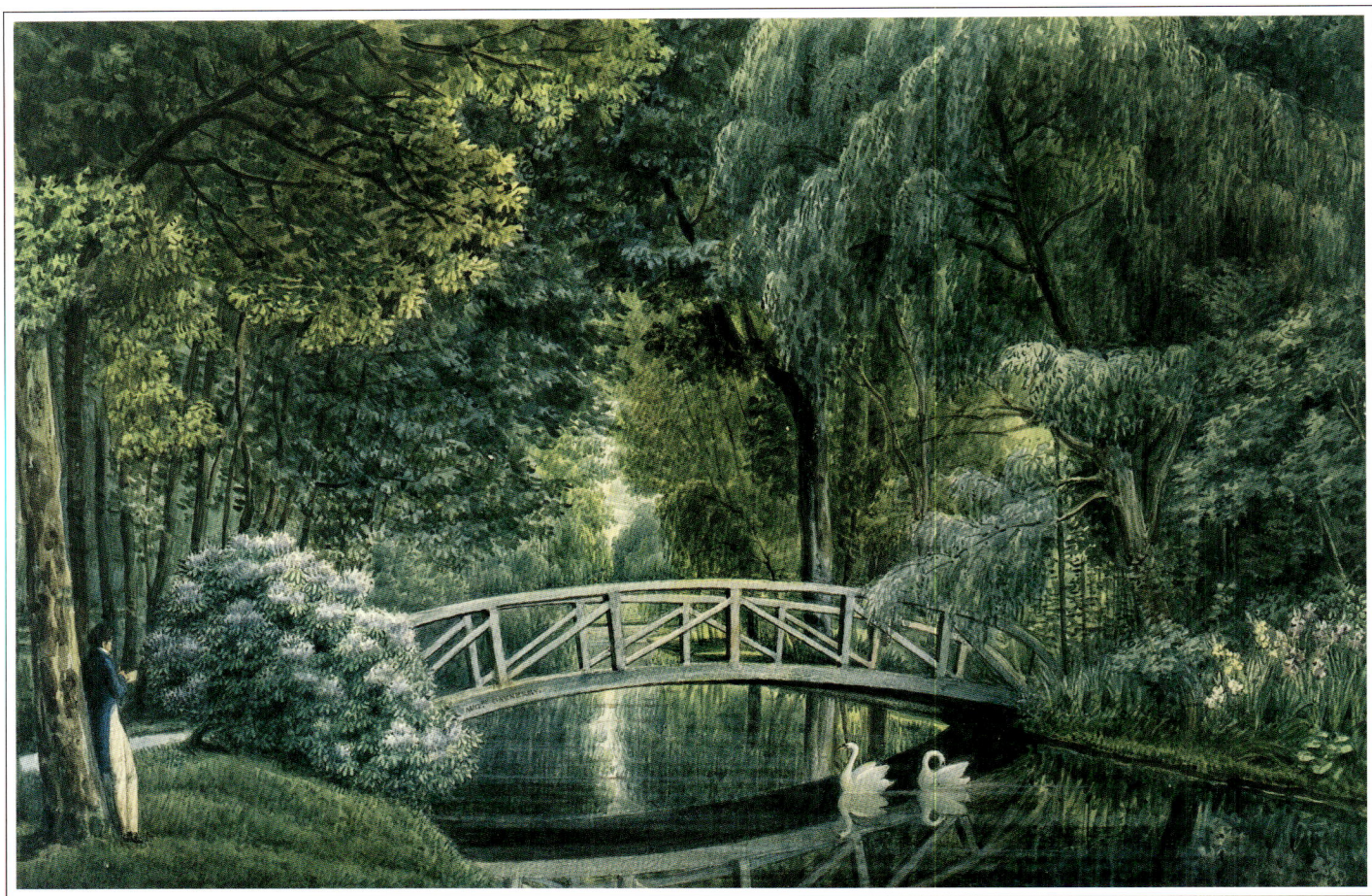

FIGURE 58.

Auguste Garnerey (French, 1785–1824),
View of the Wooden Bridge.
Watercolor, 16.3 × 24.3 cm (6⅜ × 9⅝ in.).
Rueil-Malmaison, Musée national des Châteaux
de Malmaison et Bois-Préau.

• • •

Picturesque bridges were a feature of the eighteenth-century landscape garden, providing a decorative and practical link between shores. The wooden bridge spanning the river at Malmaison is still present today, but the setting is less idyllic than it was during Joséphine's lifetime. Malmaison was Joséphine's private world, where she offered performances in the little theater, cold collations under the trees, drives through the park to visit her hamlet, and boating parties on the river.

archaeologist Alexandre Lenoir (1761–1839), curator of the Museum of French Monuments, who sent her rare objects from his museum and purchased vases, pieces of statuary, and fragments of ancient sculpture for Malmaison.

In September 1805 Joséphine summoned Louis-Martin Berthault (1767–1823), the highly fashionable architect who had decorated Juliette Recamier's renowned town house and whom Laure Junot had praised for his exquisite taste. His plans pleased the empress,[16] for both envisioned a garden with breathing room. So Berthault, under Joséphine's constant surveillance, limited architecture to a few choice pavilions, each of which contributed to the overall effect they both sought. To expand the view from the château, as was typical of the Anglo-Chinois eighteenth-century garden,[17] Berthault created a vast lawn punctuated by groups of trees. It was so harmoniously assembled that the trees appeared to be veritable bouquets, "with a great diversity of forms, varying nuances of foliage, obviating any monotony."[18] Many of the trees and shrubs were small, allowing Berthault to integrate into the landscape a view of the Seine, the church steeple at Croissy, the massive château of Saint-Germain looming on the horizon, and the famous aqueduct of Marly to close the

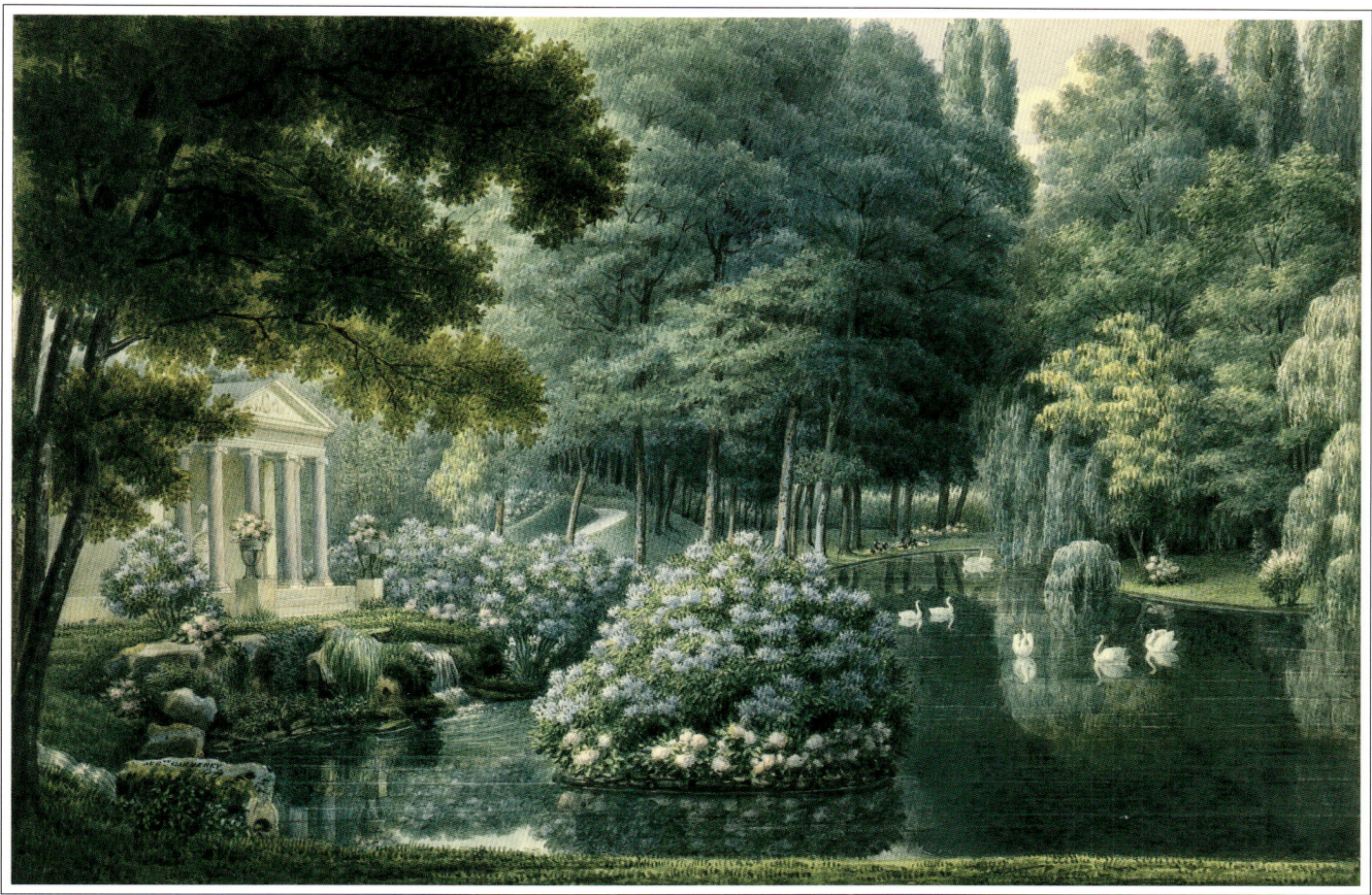

FIGURE 59.

Auguste Garnerey (French, 1785–1824),
Temple of Love.
Watercolor, 16.3 × 24.3 cm (6⅜ × 9⅝ in.).
Rueil-Malmaison, Musée national des Châteaux
de Malmaison et Bois-Préau.

• • •

Joséphine's Temple of Love exists, but no longer within the Malmaison property. Originally it was decorated with the Rococo marble *Cupid Preparing to Shoot an Arrow* by Pierre-Antoine Tassaert (1728–1788), acquired for Joséphine by Alexandre Lenoir. Garnerey's watercolor is one of his most inspired, with the delicate mauve of rhododendrons reflected in the water, a sparkling cascade pouring over the rocks. A rock formation surmounted by a temple was another eighteenth-century feature that also appeared at Hortense's château of Saint-Leu. The classical tripods flanking the portico of six red-marble Ionic pillars are distinctively Joséphine.

perspective, like an antique ruin in one of the paintings by Claude Lorrain (1604–1682) in Joséphine's galleries. The aqueduct played the same role in her garden as had the Bastille in Caron de Beaumarchais' Paris estate, where this ancient tower could be glimpsed as a backdrop through willow branches.

A unifying feature of the Malmaison grounds was the circuitous river that meandered through the landscape, now disappearing behind shrubbery, later reappearing as a rushing waterfall below the Temple of Love, and finally widening to form a lake on which a bouquet of rhododendrons floated {FIGURE 59}. For her boating parties, Joséphine ordered a fanciful flotilla of ten boats of varied shapes, some decorated with fish heads; and Vivant Denon came out for the launching.

Along the banks, flowering shrubs were set against a textured backdrop of weeping willows, maples, Indian chestnuts, and cypresses imported from Louisiana. This diversity immeasurably enriched the garden's beauty and horticultural import. In 1804 Humboldt and Bonpland brought back mimosas, heliotropes, lobelias, and cassias. Other voyages yielded Chinese peonies, the rose-scented Honan peony, and the white peony of Siberia.

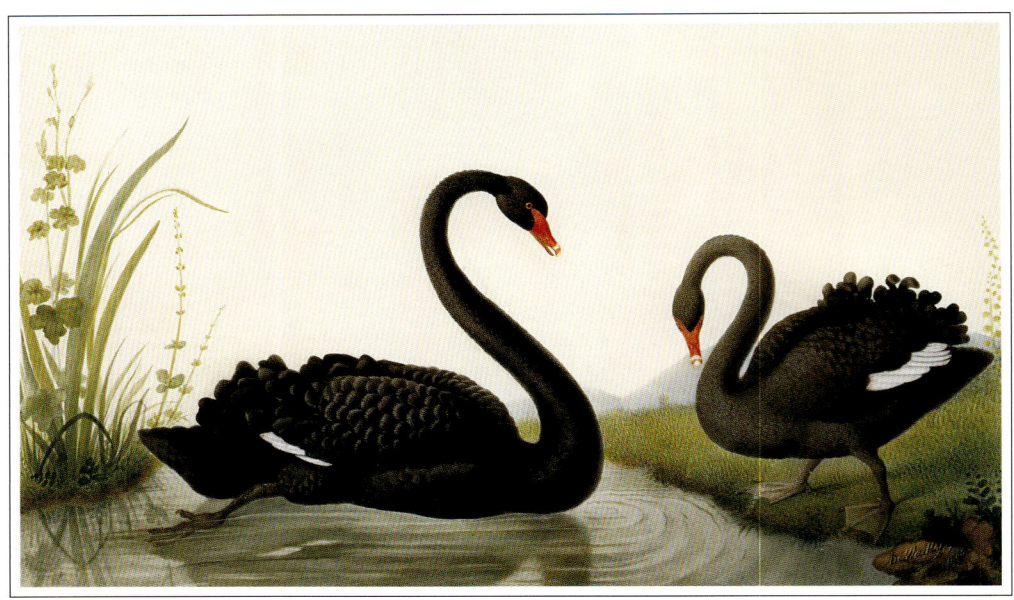

FIGURE 60.

Léon De Wailly (French, act. 1801–24),
Black Swans, 1806.
Watercolor on vellum, 31.2 × 46.2 cm (12¼ × 18⅛ in.).
Paris, Musée National d'Histoire Naturelle.

• • •

Joséphine's black swans were a constant attraction to visitors. When the Allies were approaching Paris in 1814 and Joséphine was compelled to leave Malmaison, she was greatly concerned because the swans had just given birth to cygnets, and she was fearful for their safety. These singularly graceful birds from Australia, with their wave-shaped wings, ebony plumage, and startling coral beaks were woven into the legend of Joséphine's Malmaison, thanks to Chateaubriand's haunting description in his *Mémoires d'outre-tombe*.

One most extraordinary tree was a rare species of magnolia (*Magnolia macrophylla*), found along the west bank of the Catawba River in Gaston County, North Carolina, during the American explorations by the celebrated botanist André Michaux (1746–1802/3).[19] His son, François-André, transported it to Malmaison, where its huge glossy leaves and fragrant blossoms, measuring up to 45.7 cm (18 in.) in diameter, created a sensation among European botanists.

Joséphine's collection of roses was so extraordinary that she is credited with popularizing the rose in France. More than 250 varieties were cultivated at Malmaison, and many of today's finest roses can be traced back to this garden.

Botanists and plant taxonomists paid tribute to her by naming new species in her honor, such as the *Josephinia imperatricis*, the *Lapageria rosea* (after her maiden name, Tascher de la Pagerie)—the deep pink national flower of Chile—and *Brunsvigia josephinoe*, a coral amaryllis from South Africa featured in a spectacular Redouté watercolor. So extensive were her experiments that Joséphine was responsible for introducing at least eighty-four new plant species, and her goal was to provide every department in France with horticultural material from Malmaison.

Visitors to Malmaison discovered a new world, one that seemed far removed from the majestic authority emanating from the official residence, the Tuileries Palace in Paris. This was precisely the owner's intent. To heighten the illusion, she brought into her botanical wonderland birds and animals that appeared to be living in their natural habitats. These included the coral-beaked, black swan {FIGURE 60} native to Australia; Joséphine became the first, at least in France, to successfully raise these dramatic birds in captivity.

The waterfowl were meant to impart an air of untamed nature, as were the placid animals that wandered amid the lush foliage and flowers that bloomed in a symphony of brilliant colors reminiscent of Joséphine's native Martinique. The habitat was peaceful but alien to many, for there were extrinsic species—gazelles, zebras, llamas, Malbrouk monkeys, antelopes, chamois, and kangaroos. One spectacle was the trained elephant Joséphine had brought to Malmaison to entertain her two grandsons (Hortense's sons), but—like the czar's horses—the pachyderm regrettably trampled her lawn. The bey of Tunis offered her some lions, a gift she politely and prudently declined, so they were dispatched to the Jardin des Plantes. Like other botanical gardens of its time, but greatly magnified, Joséphine's park was intended to transcend the usual picturesque garden and to suggest a "utopian reduction of Paradise Lost," according to Chevallier (see chapter 7).[20]

Most of the animals were acquired through military campaigns and special expeditions, or as gifts from foreign sovereigns and friends. Some fell into English hands en route, but even those that didn't barely survived. Bonaparte sent Captain Nicolas Baudin (1754–1803) on a voyage to Timor in 1800, and he reported from the Bay of Compan, "My kangaroos are in good shape, for I still have six, [but] I have lost more than a hundred birds."[21] To preserve his remaining kangaroos (the others having presumably died from humidity), Baudin had two of his ship's officers sacrifice their cabins to provide the surviving kangaroos with drier quarters.

A truly remarkable creature at Malmaison had been found on King Island between Australia and Tasmania—a rare, dwarf form of emu (*Dromaius demenianus*). Baudin's crew managed to capture several and transport them on his ship, *Le Géographe*. Two survived the voyage and were sent to Malmaison, where they reputedly lived until 1822. Today the remains of these two emus—the only ones known in the world—are preserved in the Museum of Natural History in Paris.[22]

It was equally challenging to gather the flora and bring it safely home, for the rolling of the ship, frequent touching by inquisitive sailors, and even the spite of malcontents resulted in the loss of precious plants. Captain Baudin warned his subordinate, Captain Hamelin, whom he was sending out in 1803, "Water them with the same amount each time, once every ten days in temperate zones, twice in tropical... and those to whom you are entrusting this work must merit your confidence.... What happened to me on my last voyage could also happen to you. Among the disgruntled... there are some who are quite capable of substituting salt water for fresh. Watch carefully and taste the water yourself." Despite the vicissitudes of the voyages, Baudin nevertheless persisted, and he ended his instructions to Hamelin with this admirable conclusion, to which Joséphine would have heartily concurred, "Everything is honorable in agriculture."[23]

So anxious was she to obtain seeds from the New World that in 1803 Joséphine dispatched a note to the French subcommissioner at Portsmouth, New Hampshire, that said, "Please send me a collection of American seeds... for I want to convert part of the land at Malmaison into a nursery... of exotic trees and shrubs which could be grown in our climate. The First Consul takes the greatest interest in this project.... [I]t is a new source of prosperity for France.... I count on your enlightened help and patriotic zeal."[24]

The young man on whom Joséphine was depending was only twenty-nine and needed all the encouragement he could get, for he could hardly wait to return home, having languished—as he said—for eight dreary years in Portsmouth.

However tedious a sojourn in New Hampshire may have been for a Frenchman, it paled by comparison to the tribulations suffered by those on collecting voyages. To the nineteenth-century European, the South Pacific was an utterly remote region, and many sailors contracted deadly fevers. Joseph Martin, director of tree cultivation at Cayenne, reported that an entire cargo of animals and seeds had been captured by the British, and he was taken prisoner. The courageous Captain Baudin, who explored the western coast of Australia and retrieved many exotic marvels for Joséphine, reached the Ile-de-France on August 27, 1803, in a state of extreme exhaustion, only to die five days later.

In theory, Baudin's collections were to have been divided between Malmaison and the Museum of Natural History in the Jardin des Plantes—only in theory, though, for even the official minister, Claude Chaptal, favored Joséphine, instructing museum officials to allow Mme Bonaparte first choice and to set aside any material she desired.

Naturally, her collecting was facilitated by her husband's position. The botanists who accompanied Bonaparte to Egypt brought her the blue lily of the Nile (*Agapanthus umbellatus*), along with other specimens. After his campaigns in Germany, Bonpland obtained valuable plants for Malmaison, thanks to doors opened by his traveling companion Baron von Humboldt. From the greenhouses at Schönnbrunn in Vienna, Bonpland made off with another cache of unusual plants for the beloved domain.

Even the English contributed, although the two countries were at war. James Lee, an English nurseryman near London, supplied Joséphine with amaryllis, tulips, magnolias, eucalyptus, hibiscus, hortensias, and jasmines from Martinique. Another Englishman, the botanist John Kennedy of Hammersmith Gardens, was even provided a special passport, which allowed him to pass through the blockade so that, despite Napoléon's efforts to enforce his embargo, rare seeds and plants destined for Joséphine went through. So, "surrounded by the best botanists, horticulturists, and artists...[she] made of Malmaison an example for all Europe."[25]

Merging her connoisseurship with her love of botany, Joséphine went beyond mere collecting by engaging the paramount botanical illustrators, most notably the immortal Pierre-Joseph Redouté, to record her specimens. Furthering the European tradition of watercolor depictions of botanical subjects that would flourish throughout the nineteenth century,[26] Redouté spent his most productive years under Joséphine's auspices. With a salaried appointment as her painter, he worked among her extraordinary plants, producing his finest work. The watercolors were bound into three volumes titled *Jardin de la Malmaison* (1803–5), *Les Liliacées* (1802–16), and *Description des plantes rares cultivées à Malmaison* (1812–17).[27] Scholars regard these superlative visual records of Joséphine's collections to be among the most significant milestones of botanical illustration ever published (see chapter 5). *Les Liliacées* so delighted Joséphine that she commissioned a Sèvres porcelain dessert service based on Redouté's watercolors {FIGURE 61}.

For her fragile plant material, Joséphine ordered the construction of her most impressive garden building—the huge conservatory looming over the eastern end of the park, set off by trees on either side {FIGURE 62}. It contained nearly two hundred species that were grown for the first time in France. According to d'Arneville, "The great conservatory

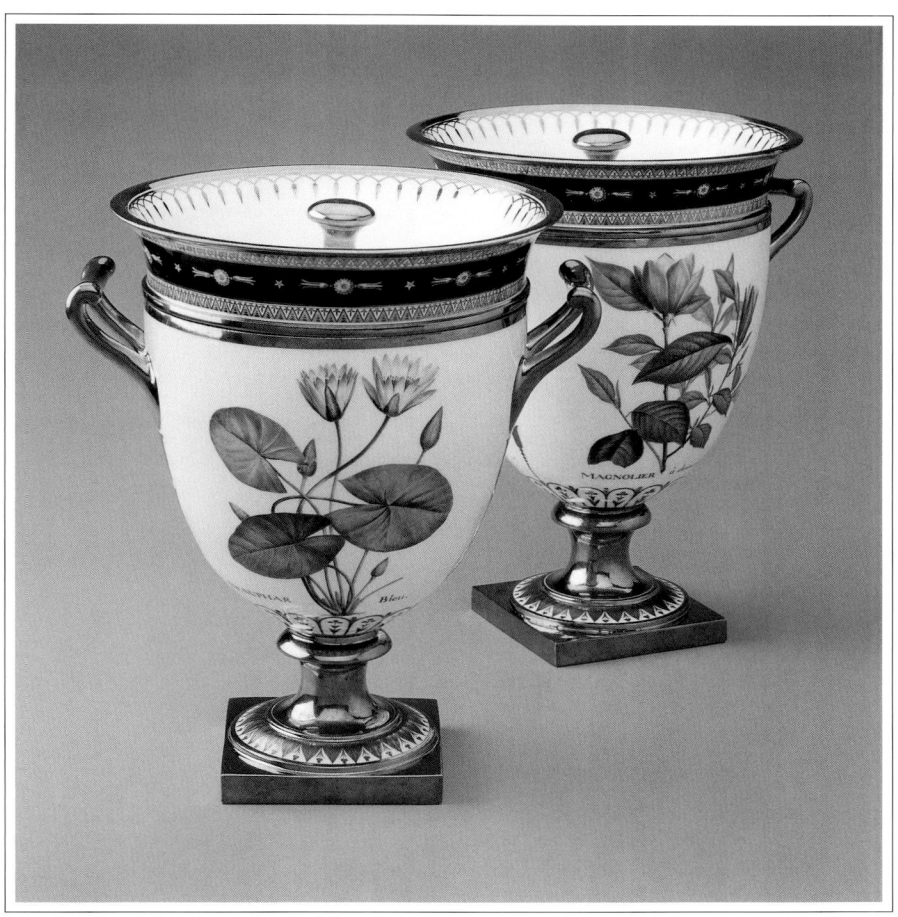

Figure 61.

Pair of Ice Cream Coolers (or "Servers")
French, Manufactory of Sèvres. 1802/5.
From the Liliacée service. Decoration after paintings
of lilies from *Les Liliacées* by Pierre-Joseph Redouté
(Belgian, 1759–1840).
Hard-paste porcelain.
Museum of Fine Arts, Boston.

• • •

These pieces are an eloquent tribute to Joséphine's rare botanical collection. Pierre-Joseph Redouté's bound volume of watercolors, *Les Liliacées* (1802–16), inspired the 108-piece dessert service that Joséphine commissioned from the Sèvres factory. The painters at Sèvres followed Redouté's watercolors on vellum for these imposing pieces in Neoclassical krater form. The service has been lost to view since 1805, but now fourteen pieces have happily been acquired by an American museum.

[was] the model of a new type."[28] Joséphine never tired of conducting visitors through it, relating the botanical names of her plants. Some privileged guests even received specimens. René de Chateaubriand was accorded a rare reddish purple magnolia, the only one in France other than Joséphine's.

The warm, fragrant greenhouse with its singular collection of flowers, parasol palms, orange trees, and tropical birds was — for Joséphine — like reliving her childhood, for she claimed that the jasmines from the islands recalled her early youth and the sound of her mother's voice. It was Martinique under glass. In fact, the very first plants to flower were grown from seeds sent from the Antilles by Joséphine's mother, Mme de la Pagerie. To the delight of Joséphine's grandsons, there was also sugarcane, which they cut to suck out the sweet juices, just as their grandmother had done on Martinique.

Every distinguished visitor to France wanted to see the conservatory. Baron E. T. von Uklanski left this description after visiting it in 1809: "Inside the hothouse I discovered, to my surprise, an entry of greenery, surrounded by mimosas in flower, fragrant lilacs, tulips, narcissi, hibiscus, anemones.... At right and left were two green tunnels which revealed at each extremity two magnificent marble statues copied after the antique: the Medici Venus and the Callipygean Venus."[29]

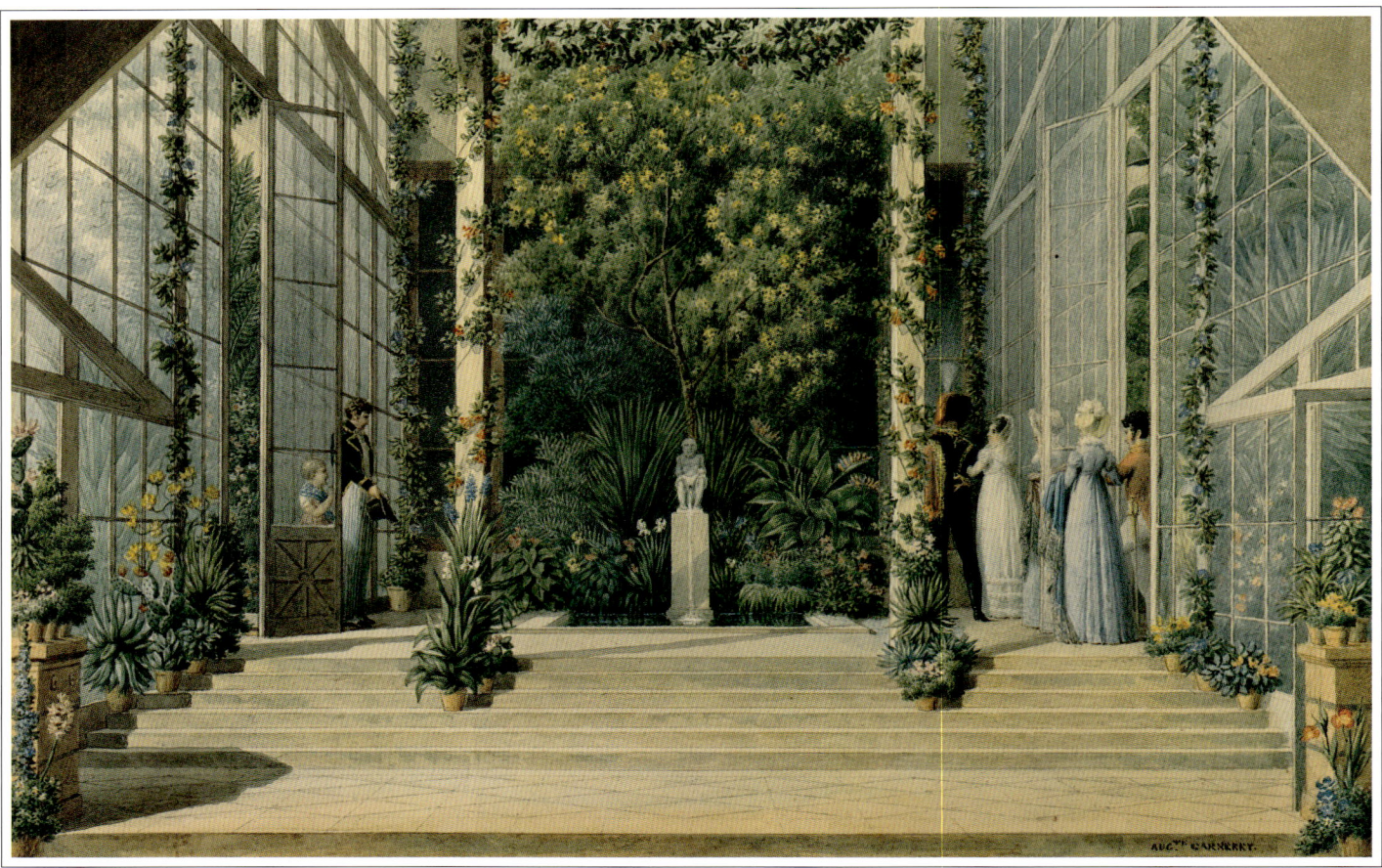

FIGURE 62.

Auguste Garnerey (French, 1785–1824),
The Conservatory, n.d.
Watercolor, 16.3 × 24.3 cm (6⅜ × 9⅝ in.).
Rueil-Malmaison, Musée national des Châteaux
de Malmaison et Bois-Préau.

• • •

Joséphine, on the arm of a hussar, is about to show guests through the conservatory, watched by a young man at left, who has respectfully removed his hat. The satyr fountain at center was added by the architect Louis-Martin Berthault (1767–1823). At the time the conservatory was built (1805), it was doubtless the largest structure in Europe that was surfaced entirely in glass. At the rear, the roof was raised to accommodate tall trees. In 1807 Berthault installed a fountain in front of it, with a circular basin supporting four bronze griffins shooting jets of water, and at the center stood an antique granite column crowned by an ancient porphyry vase.

Although such arbors, or green tunnels (*berceaux de verdure*) through which people strolled, had been a feature of gardens for thousands of years, what is unusual here is that Joséphine should have chosen this clipped, geometrical greenery not for her park but for the confines of her conservatory.[30]

Joséphine's garden complex at Malmaison was of such originality and distinction that it ranked with "the most spectacular designs of the end of the eighteenth century, and the beginning of the nineteenth."[31] Yet nothing is so ephemeral as a garden, and a visitor today could not possibly imagine the enchanted fairyland that it was during Joséphine's lifetime. She was its creator and animating spirit, and after her untimely death in May 1814, it would never be the same.

Certainly, Napoléon never forgot it. In his lonely exile on the miserably humid atoll of Saint Helena, he remembered Malmaison; so, with trowel in hand and enlisting the help of his household, he set about planting a little touch of Joséphine. Two specimens he introduced into this obdurate climate were Sydney golden wattle (*Acacia longifolia*) and Australian golden everlasting (*Bracteantha bracteata*), both of which still bloom on that inhospitable island.

Just after Napoléon's banishment following the battle of Waterloo in June 1815, a dispirited René de Chateaubriand (1768–1848) came over from La-Vallée-aux-Loups to Malmaison. As he wandered through Joséphine's gardens, the writer remembered her evening salons where, in the empress's drawing room, he would read passages aloud from his books and leisurely promenade with Joséphine through her perfumed greenhouse. With her wondrous Eden lying in ruins about him, he recorded his melancholia in *Mémoires d'outre tombe*: "Malmaison, where the Emperor was accustomed to take his ease, is empty. Joséphine is dead.... In these gardens, where formerly the feet of numerous visitors trod the sandy paths, grass and weeds are growing ... the exotic trees are perishing, and the swans from Oceania no longer float upon the water."[32]

NOTES

1. Marie-Blanche d'Arneville, *Parcs et jardins sous le Premier Empire* (Paris, 1981), 139.
2. Eleanor P. DeLorme, *Garden Pavilions and the Eighteenth-Century French Court* (Woodbridge, England, 1996), 293.
3. Alexandre de Laborde, *Nouveaux jardins de la France et ses anciens châteaux* (Paris, 1808), 65.
4. The remarkable collection of plant material in the Jardin des Plantes, its distinguished Museum of Natural History, and its innovative re-creation of natural habitats for the various species contributed to its renown.
5. Chanorier, following the physiocrats of the eighteenth century, also took a practical interest in agriculture, acquiring from the Berry region a flock of Spanish sheep, and planting an apple orchard with seeds given to him by Benjamin Franklin.
6. Christophe Pincemaille, *Il y a 200 ans: Joséphine achetait Malmaison* (Paris, 1999), 11.
7. Pincemaille, *Il y a 200 ans*, 37.
8. Hubert Robert designed the gardens for Louis XVI and Marie-Antoinette as well as Méréveille for the Laborde family. See DeLorme, *Garden Pavilions*, 293.
9. Dora Wiebenson, *The Picturesque Garden in France* (Princeton, N.J., 1978), 83; see also DeLorme, *Garden Pavilions*, 54.
10. These were people forced to leave France for political reasons, often having to forfeit large estates.
11. Jean-Marie Morel, quoted in Joseph Disponzio, "Jean-Marie Morel," *Studies in the History of Gardens and Designed Landscapes* 21, nos. 3, 4 (Autumn–Winter 2001): 151.
12. In 1777 Morel had published his famous *Théorie des Jardins*, the second edition of which (1802) he would dedicate to Joséphine. Under the ancien régime he had created famous gardens for the prince de Conti and the marquis de Girardin at Ermenonville.
13. Pierre-François-Léonard Fontaine, quoted in Bernard Chevallier, *Malmaison: Château et domaines des origines à 1904* (Paris, 1989), 109.
14. Chevallier, *Malmaison*, 106.
15. None of Morel's drawings survive, but the gardens and pavilions are depicted in Auguste Garnerey's watercolors.
16. Joséphine played an active role herself, so it is not always easy to distinguish her own ideas from those of her garden architect.
17. See DeLorme, *Garden Pavilions*, 167.
18. D'Arneville, *Parcs et jardins*, 164.
19. Michaux was one of the world's great botanists, and his voyages were treacherous. He nearly lost his life and possessions returning to Paris in 1796. During a trip to Madagascar he died of fever.
20. See also John Prest, *The Garden of Eden: The Botanic Garden and the Re-Creation of Paradise* (New Haven, N.J., and London, 1981).
21. D'Arneville, *Parcs et jardins*, 182.
22. Christian Jouanin, "Josephine and the Natural Sciences," *Apollo* (July–September, 1977): 57.
23. Nicholas Baudin, quoted in d'Arneville, *Parcs et jardins*, 182.
24. D'Arneville, *Parcs et jardins*, 183.
25. Anne-Marie Bogaert-Damin, *Images de jardins du XVIe au XX siècle* (Namur, Belgium, 1996), 235.
26. Peter Mitchell, preface to Claudia Salvi, *Pierre-Joseph Redouté, le Prince des Fleurs* (Tournai, Belgium, 1999), 6.
27. Etienne-Pierre Ventenat (1757–1808) wrote the text for the first volume; and Joséphine's devoted botanist, Aimé Goufau, called "Bonpland" (1773–1858), provided the text for the third. The unsigned text for *Les Liliacées* is by botanists A. P. de Candolle, F. de la Roche, and A. Raffeneu-Delille.
28. D'Arneville, *Parcs et jardins*, 172.
29. Chevallier, *Malmaison*, 114. See DeLorme, *Garden Pavilions*, 122.
30. Its vast size (more than 48.8 m [160 ft.] long and about 6.4 m [21 ft.] wide) made it possible. One section was tall enough to accommodate tall shrubs.
31. Chevallier, *Malmaison*, 114.
32. François-Auguste-René de Chateaubriand, quoted in d'Arneville, *Parcs et jardins*, 179.

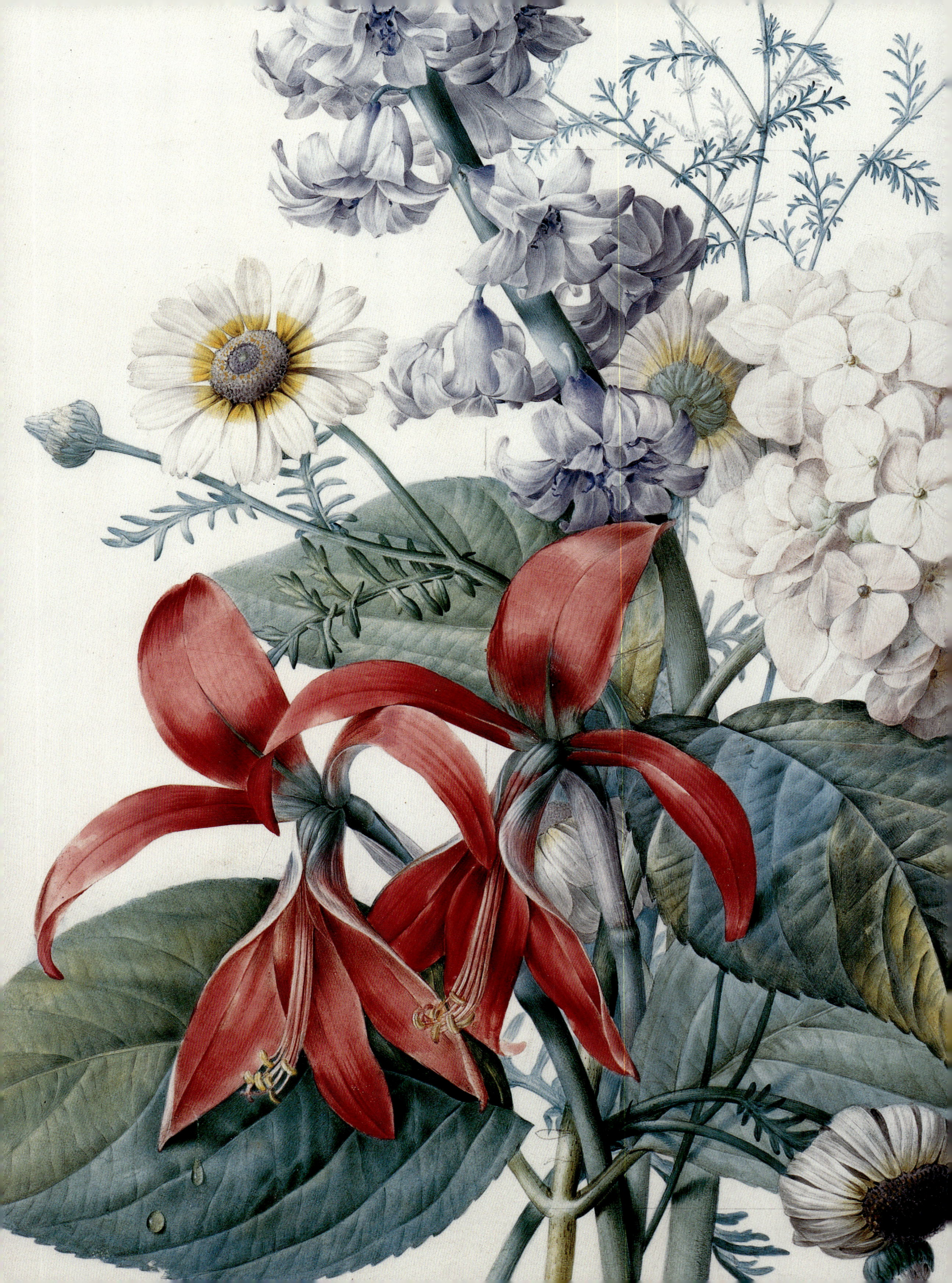

CHAPTER 5

PETER MITCHELL

Redouté: Joséphine's Watercolor Garden

For enthusiasts of Pierre-Joseph Redouté (1759–1840), the year 1985 was a memorable one. In June a group of seven of the most innovative watercolors by the artist were sold at Sotheby's, Monte Carlo. They were unusually large and all the same size, all in a superb state of preservation, all of the same dates, 1803 and 1804. Their content was carefully varied as if part of a set or series, an aspect that was even more apparent when they were hung together in a group at the viewing. The catalogue provenance went back to Francois Gérard,[1] a member of Joséphine's close circle of artists. It seemed highly unlikely that Gérard could have obtained them from his friend Redouté, as he could not have afforded them, and even more unlikely that Gérard acquired them from the empress or her heirs. Their original owner was therefore unknown, as was their original purpose, if they had one. No engravings or reproductions of these works existed, so clearly they were not intended as book illustrations.

I was successful in acquiring five of these remarkable works {FIGURES 63–67} and later, having transported the vellums safely back to London, I spent many hours studying them, unframed, with a magnifying glass in different lights, catching sight of the very slight traces of the artist's underdrawing. Standing back, I gained the overall impression of sophistication, elegance, and of being in the presence of something awe-inspiring. I did not then know why this was so.

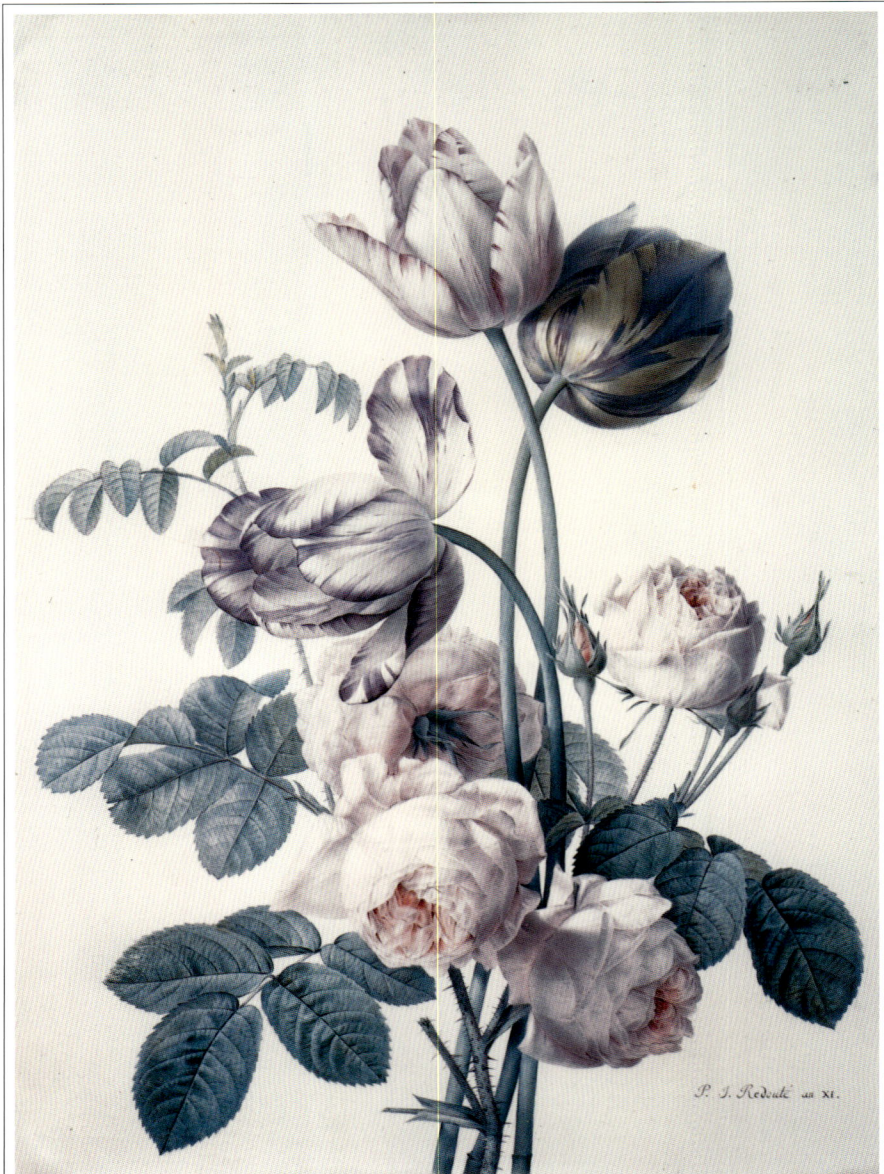

Figure 63.

Pierre-Joseph Redouté (Belgian, 1759–1840),
Tulips and Roses, 1804.
Watercolor on vellum, 48.6 × 35.7 cm
(19 1/8 × 14 in.).
Signed and dated "P. J. Redouté an XI."
Private collection.

· · ·

With meticulous exactitude, Pierre-Joseph Redouté, the "Raphael of Flowers," contrasts the enameled texture of the striated mauve tulips with the soft yielding petals of the full-blown roses in this bouquet typical of his later career. The rounded corolla of the rose is composed of many petals of a soft pink tint that deepens toward the center, one of the many varieties of roses that Joséphine cultivated in her botanical garden, which was recognized as the most prestigious in Europe.

In November of the same year, Sotheby's of New York offered for sale one of the rarest works of any kind ever to appear on the market—Empress Joséphine's bound volumes of the original watercolors for the illustrated book *Les Lilacées* (1802–16). A fine printed copy of the work was at hand, so the originals could be compared to the plates. Redouté always intended that reproductions of his work match his originals as closely as possible. Through stipple engraving of unprecedented complexity and subtlety, the engraved, color illustrations did closely replicate the luminosity, sheen, and above all, the three-dimensional quality of Redouté's original works. In leafing through the eight superbly bound volumes from the library at Malmaison, with the 486 watercolor originals of what is arguably among the greatest of printed, color-plate books, I felt as close to the empress as one could ever be.

Les Lilacées includes not only plants that belong to the lily family {FIGURE 68} but also many other species—orchids and bromeliads, for example—which seemed only to add to the book's appeal both artistically and scientifically. Although it must have taken great skill and resilience for Redouté to complete this monumental work over the fourteen years

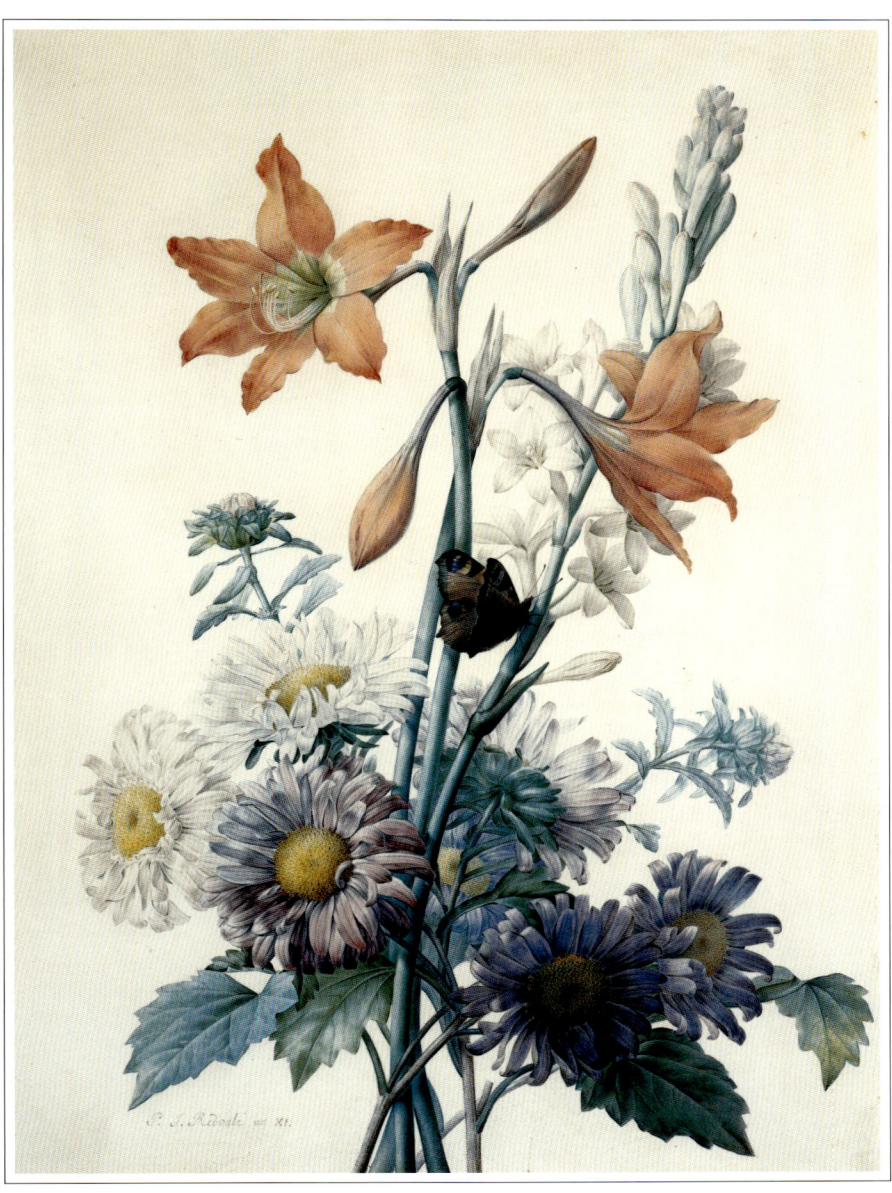

Figure 64.

Pierre-Joseph Redouté (Belgian, 1759–1840), *Amaryllis, Tuberoses, Reines Marguerites*, 1804. Watercolor on vellum, 48.6 × 35.7 cm (19 1/8 × 14 in.). Signed and dated "P. J. Redouté an XI." Private collection.

· · ·

In Redouté's day, the amaryllis was still called the "lis St. Jacques"—Saint Jacques lily—and was known in Europe from 1593. The tuberose was introduced into Europe in 1594 and most likely came from Mexico. The white and deep violet marguerites—often called "reine marguerite"—belong to the aster family, which came from China. Both the scarlet lilies and purple marguerites—being colors traditionally associated with rulers—were appropriate for a bouquet composed for the Empress Joséphine.

it required, the success of the original printed books was the result of teamwork as well. The quality of the engraving and color printing by the most advanced methods known then or now matched the artist's expertise. The level of scholarship of the accompanying text, in turn, paralleled the achievements of the artist and craftsmen. The aim was for supreme excellence throughout this great work of art and science.

Without the seemingly limitless patronage of Napoléon and Joséphine, the original copies of *Les Lilacées* would not have been possible. About 220 original copies were produced and distributed to rulers, scholars, and dignitaries throughout Europe. The message of the gift was clear. Napoléon wanted to demonstrate that the military prowess of France under his empire was equaled by the country's intellectual, scientific, and artistic accomplishments. Regrettably, this precious volume—Redouté's greatest achievement under Joséphine's patronage and support—was ultimately broken up and dispersed after the sale.

The often-used description of the right man in the right place at the right time might have been coined for Pierre-Joseph Redouté. He lived in a period rich in outstanding

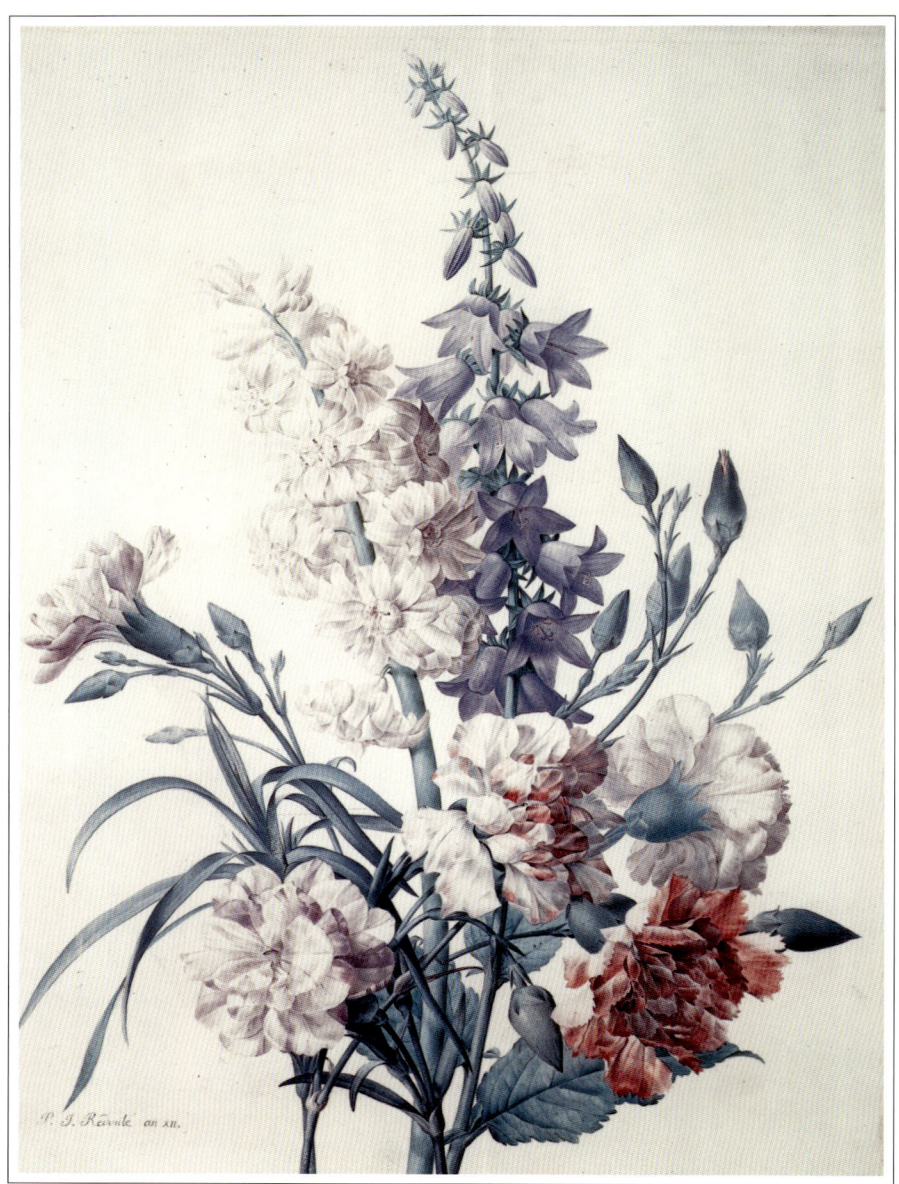

Figure 65.

Pierre-Joseph Redouté (Belgian, 1759–1840), *Pinks, Hyacinth, and Campanula*, 1805. Watercolor on vellum, 48.6 × 35.7 cm (19⅛ × 14 in.). Signed and dated "P. J. Redouté an XII." Private collection.

• • •

The fragrant hyacinth was greatly appreciated in Redouté's day and much prized by the Turks. It came into central and western Europe about 1560, most likely through the scholar Ogier de Busbecq (1522–1592), ambassador of the Holy Roman Empire to Suleiman the Magnificent at Constantinople. The delicately scented pinks derive from the clove pink found in the Mediterranean area. At the center of the bouquet projects a tall spire of campanula, distinguished by its vivid blue bell.

Figure 66.

Pierre-Joseph Redouté (Belgian, 1759–1840), *Lilac, Capucines, and Fushia*, 1805. Watercolor on vellum, 48.6 × 35.7 cm (19⅛ × 14 in.). Signed and dated "P. J. Redouté an XII." Private collection.

• • •

Forming the nucleus of this arrangement are heavily scented mauve lilacs, and soaring above them are nodding, bell-shaped red fuchsia flowers, named for the Bavarian physician, Leonhart Fuchs (1501–1566), author of one of the first books of woodcuts of plants grown in Germany. The peltate leaves of the cheerful yellow and rusty red nasturtiums are sometimes used in salads.

botanical painters, among them Gerard van Spaendonck (1746–1822) and James Sowerby (ca. 1740–1803). Yet Redouté's work—a blend of scientific exactitude and aesthetic representation—came to stand above that of his predecessors and to achieve an everlasting fame.

Redouté was born at Saint Hubert in the Belgian Ardennes, where he came to love the woodland wildflowers he found there. At age thirteen he went to Liège to study painting and, as a teenager in Holland, became so infatuated with flowers that this interest became a lifelong obsession. During the years he spent in Luxembourg, Holland, and Flanders, he furthered his skill by studying the works of such famous seventeenth-century flower painters as J. D. de Heem (1606–1684) and Jan van Huysum (1682–1749). In this way Redouté, who painted a much wider range of flowers than the seventeenth-century masters, became a worthy successor to the renowned tradition of Dutch flower painting. Furthermore, as William T. Stearn has noted, the painters of Dutch flower pieces portrayed no more than sixty species whereas Redouté depicted at least eighteen hundred. Nor are these grouped together but are shown as individual flowers.

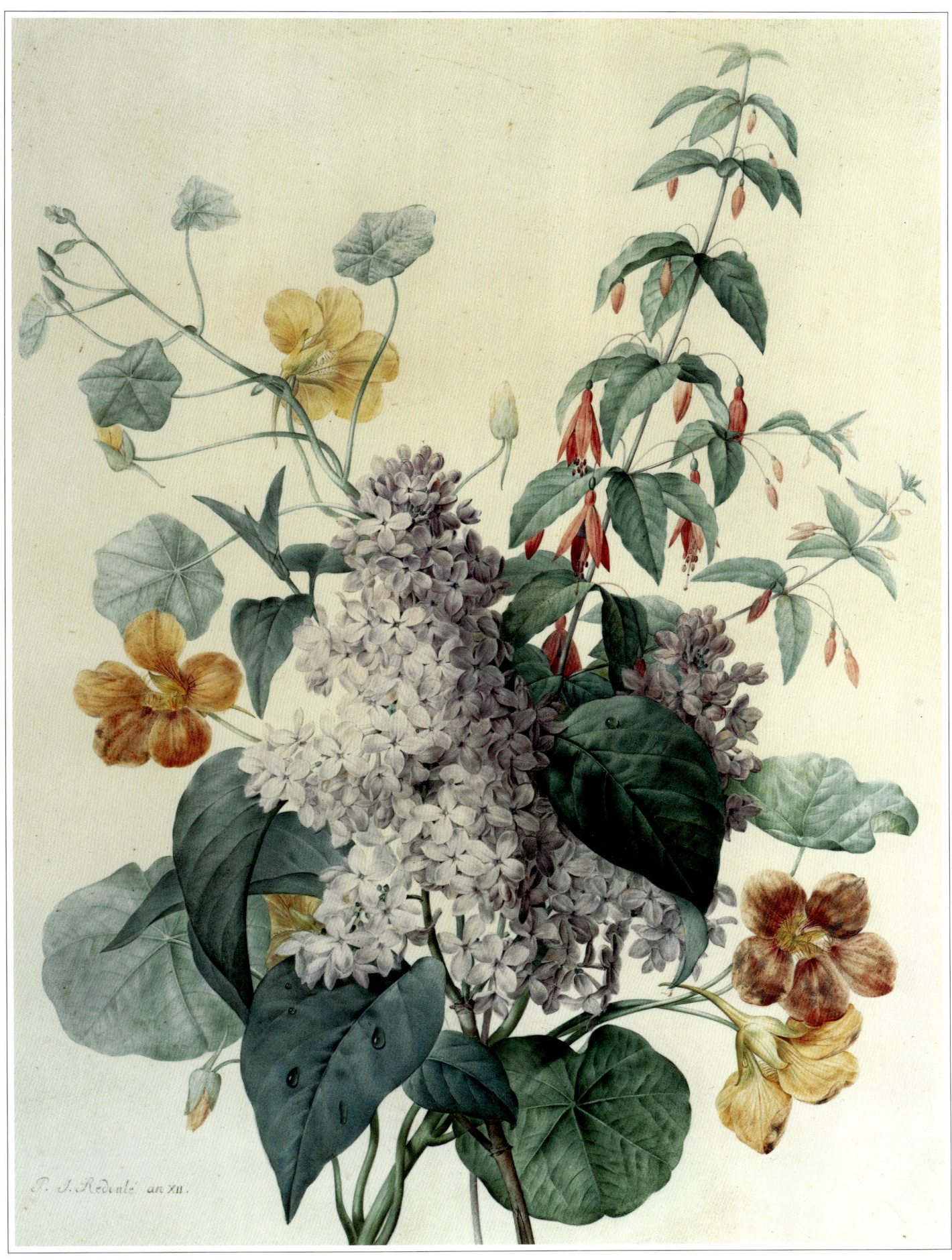

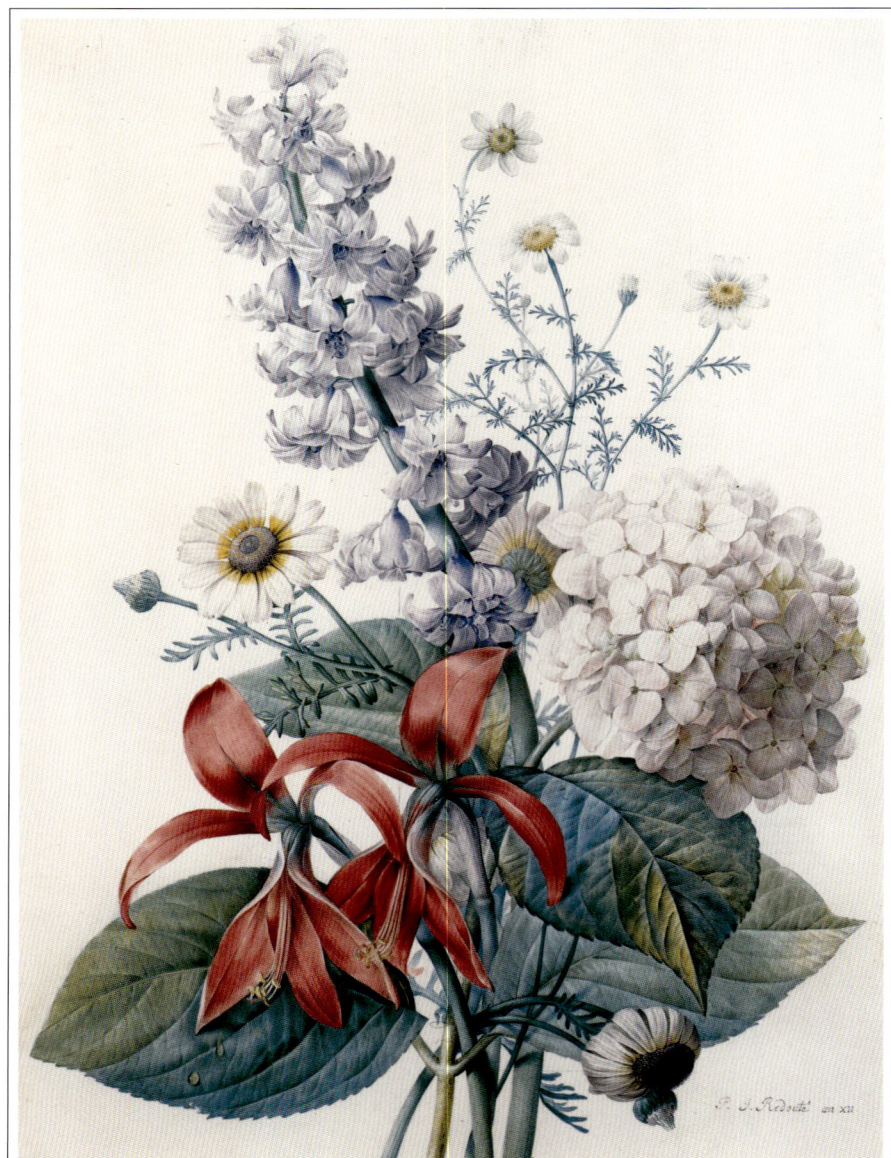

Figure 67.

Pierre-Joseph Redouté (Belgian, 1759–1840), *Hortensia, Jacinthe, Lis Saint Jacques, Chrysanthemum*, 1805. Watercolor on vellum, 48.6 × 35.7 cm (19⅛ × 14 in.). Signed and dated "P. J. Redouté an XII." Private collection.

• • •

Here Redouté's fluent brush describes a pinkish mauve sphere of closely packed hortensia, erroneously thought to have been named for Queen Hortense. Marking the apex of the composition are the airy foliage and white flowers of chrysanthemums native to North Africa and a towering soft mauve hyacinth. This subdued color scheme is ignited by the vibrant red Saint Jacques lily at the center of Redouté's delightful composition.

The story goes back to 1766 when Redouté was only seven years old, hidden away in the Ardennes. In that year Gerard van Spaendonck, then age twenty, left his native Holland for Paris. Many foreign artists were drawn to the prestige and patronage of Paris at this period, but none rose to greater significance in their chosen field than van Spaendonck. His success as a painter, draftsman, and engraver of flowers on every scale from snuffbox lid to large-scale oil, in every medium and on every support (including marble), was matched by his role as a teacher and inspiration to others. Apart from his direct pupils, not least Redouté, his immense influence was felt throughout the nineteenth century. When van Spaendonck came to Paris, the vanguard of flower painting left its traditional home in the Low Countries for the first time. The genre's status, once humble in painting's hierarchy was inevitably enhanced by van Spaendonck's very public success, culminating in the emperor's naming him a count in 1805.

No one could have foreseen that the great Dutchman's lofty reputation would, in modern times, be surpassed worldwide by the celebrity of the singular artist who was his best pupil and heir. This is all the more surprising because Redouté chose to work almost exclusively in watercolor, "le parent pauvre de la peinture a' l'huile" (the poor relation of oil painting).[2] Because of conservation problems, watercolors do not lend themselves to being displayed on museum walls. Few museums across the world own his original work, and Redouté's originals are only occasionally seen at dealers and auctioneers.

In 1782 Redouté traveled to Paris to join his brother Antoine-Ferdinand (1756–1809), and shortly thereafter Pierre-Joseph began to draw the plants in the royal greenhouses of the Jardin des Plantes. Here he met the botanist Louis L'Héritier de Brutelle (1746–1800), who taught Redouté how to dissect flowers and represent them scientifically. As a founding member of the Linnean Society, Redouté was appointed painter to Marie-Antoinette's cabinet, thereby gaining access to the queen's Trianon gardens, as he would later become an habitué of Joséphine's park at Malmaison.

Around 1785 an unusual opportunity came to Redouté: van Spaendonck asked him to contribute a number of vellums to the renowned *Vélins du Roi*, a series of botanical studies that had been started by the Sun King's uncle Gaston d'Orléans (1608–1660) and that was being continued not in gouache as before but in watercolor. From van Spaendonck and the engraver Francesco Bartolozzi, Redouté learned the art of stipple engraving, a method of color printing that he used in his publications, touching up certain copies by hand. Van Spaendonck's finest pupil in watercolor, Redouté always remained grateful to his teacher, whose best student in oils was the Flemish painter Jan Frans van Dael (1764–1840). Van Dael's masterpiece, *The Tomb of Julie*, was among five of his canvases in Joséphine's collection.

Fortunately, Redouté was blessed with phenomenal stamina and appetite for work, so the more he drew and painted, the better and faster he worked. From 1793 he was charged with continuing the *Vélins du Roi* collection at the Muséum, a national archive to which he would eventually be the greatest contributor. This was a discipline and public examination of the most rigorous kind. The task had started in 1788 under van Spaendonck, a measure of the latter's regard for his pupil and, potentially, his rival.

The years 1797 and 1798 are good examples of this extraordinary workload, but the burden would later become even more onerous. In 1797 Augustin-Pyramus de Candolle (1778–1841) looked to Redouté for all the illustrations for his *Histoire des plantes grasses* (History of Succulents), the first work wholly illustrated by Redouté, including the engravings of his own originals, and his first use of color painting from stipple-engraved plates. At the same time, René Desfontaines (1750–1833) wanted eighty-seven watercolors to record the plants found during the botanist's exploration of Tunisia and Algeria, published as *Flora Atlantica*. Routine work for learned journals and the *Vélins* continued at the same time. No doubt Redouté also found time for his son, born in May, and it is known that he sat for Louis-Léopold Boilly, to be included in the latter's group portrait entitled *Reunion of Artists in Isabey's Studio* {see FIGURE 2}, seated next to van Dael.

Redouté needed to say good-bye to his younger brother, Henri-Joseph Redouté (1766–1852), a skilled zoological draftsman who was selected to join the large team of artists and savants on Napoléon's 1798 expedition to Egypt. At the same time, an event took place of the greatest portent for Pierre-Joseph: Joséphine acquired Malmaison. Pierre-Joseph Redouté was soon to be a regular visitor to the property and to become a close friend of the owner. The charm and discretion of Redouté, the man, are well attested by contemporaries and especially his legions of female pupils,[3] both persons of royal lineage and the bourgeoisie. These personal qualities were an integral part of his success throughout decades of changing regimes. Without these attributes we could not conclude that Pierre-Joseph Redouté was, indeed, the right man in the right place.

Certainly Redouté's prime years were those spent at Malmaison under the patronage of Joséphine, in whose entourage were noted horticulturists and botanists. Named "painter of flowers" to Empress Joséphine in 1805, he produced three exquisite publications for her depicting the flowers in her gardens (see chapter 4), and he was patronized by her daughter, Queen Hortense, as well. Joséphine prized her Redouté watercolors so highly that she kept some of them in her bedroom at Malmaison.

Anyone who has seen an exhibition of Redouté's watercolors on vellum, such as the memorable 2002 exhibit at the Bruce Museum of Arts and Science in Greenwich, Connecticut, would agree with Vivant Denon, director of the Musée Napoléon and Joséphine's trusted adviser, when he wrote that Redouté's drawings "are miracles through which the naturalist as well as the most discerning colorist can profit."[4]

Joséphine was a devoted, passionate, and increasingly knowledgeable enthusiast of flowers and the natural world. If her husband may be described as a dominant personality, Malmaison was Joséphine's affair—a place where she was in charge and where she could create a paradise. By the time of her death in 1814, the property was nearly three times larger than at the time of her purchase. The mighty greenhouse she built astonished all who saw it and cannot be adequately judged from the paintings and drawings of it that survive. Even Napoléon balked at the expenditure of 140,000 francs on the project, and Charles-François Brisseau de Mirbel (1776–1854), administrator of the gardens, was unjustly blamed and dismissed.

The empress's desire to include rare or unknown plants in her garden was taken very seriously. Even at the height of Napoléon's continental blockade, Joséphine's plant orders from Lee and Kennedy in London were shipped and delivered without hindrance. Her black swans—the first in Europe—were cared for all the way from Australia but in a less spectacular manner than the botanical specimens. So many Australian plants were imported to Malmaison that one-third of the plants depicted in *Le Jardin de la Malmaison* are Australian.[5] This book, with 120 plates by Redouté to accompany Ventenat's text, appeared between 1803 and 1805. The creation and cultivation of gardens by the rulers of France had a long tradition. Yet at a period when the globe and the natural world were being explored, investigated, and recorded as never before, the introduction of

FIGURE 68.

Pierre-Joseph Redouté (Belgian, 1759–1840), *Day-Lily*, from *Les Liliacées*, 1802–16. Watercolor on vellum, 48.2 × 34.3 cm (19 × 13½ in.). Private collection.

• • •

In a dramatic arrangement of two blossoms, buds, and leaves, Redouté presents the ubiquitous daylily with his usual keen eye for color, design, and placement on the page. His pictorial brilliance is particularly apparent in this ravishing specimen, with the smooth, deep green leaves serving as foil for the dazzling red flowers. In monastic gardens white lilies were grown for beauty as well as medicinal use, being heated and then beaten into an ointment used as a dressing.

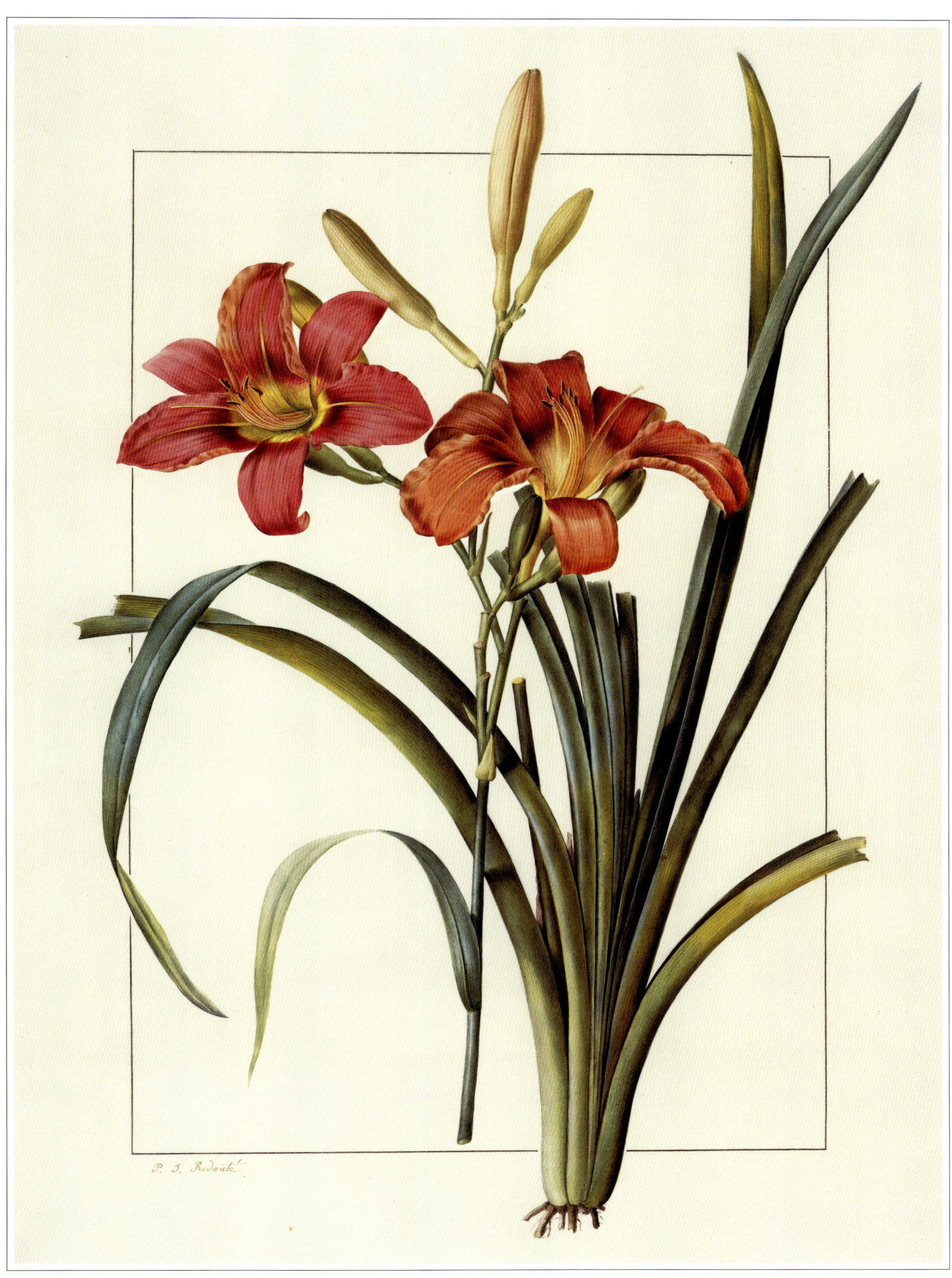

newly discovered plants and animals might be expected. With Joséphine it was carried to extraordinary lengths, and her knowledge was applauded by the directors of the museum who exchanged specimens with her. They were, however, occasionally obliged to give way to her as well. In 1803, on the return from Australia of the Baudin expedition frigates—the aptly named *La Géographe* and *La Naturaliste*—the minister of the interior's instructions to the museum's officials were clear: "You are to receive, citizens, a collection of seeds and exotic plants for the enrichment of the Museum made by Captain Baudin during his voyage. I direct all those items selected by Madame Bonaparte to be set aside. Citizen Mirbel, her representative, will call on you and inform you of her choice. I request and authorize you to respect her wishes."

Joséphine's collecting of rare and exotic animals, suitable to roam free at Malmaison, closely parallels the story of her plants, her cabinet of "curiosities," her stuffed birds and animals, her ethnographic objects, her mineral collection, and so forth. On a visit to Malmaison, some months after Joséphine's death, Napoléon summed up the situation in a remark to her first gentleman-in-waiting, "She wanted everything!"[6] It's possible to imagine the poignancy of such a visit. There is no doubt that the happiest times of the emperor's private life were spent at Malmaison with Joséphine.

One more happy chance was in Redouté's favor. Alain Pougetoux's recent, definitive catalogue of Joséphine's substantial and important collection of paintings confirms what might have been anticipated: Joséphine was an enthusiast of contemporary art and artists.[7] Two-thirds of her collection were old masters, but the remaining third (125 pieces) were contemporary works mostly chosen by her and clearly reflecting her personal taste. Some of the artists were well known—Gérard, Antoine-Jean Gros, and Anne-Louis Girodet-Trioson—but she liked to discover artists for herself and to encourage them. Jacques Barraband (1767/8–1809), who was to birds what Redouté was to flowers, Léon de Wailly (act. 1801–24), and Jean-Baptiste Huet (1745–1811) painted the inmates of the Malmaison menagerie. Her preference for Anne-Claude Thiénon's (1772–1846) Italian landscapes, which seem to foreshadow Jean-Baptiste-Camille Corot (1796–1875), may have been due to her penchant for natural English gardens. The Swiss landscape painter Adam Töpffer (1766–1847) gave her five of his landscapes as well as drawing lessons. She was also helped by the great Vivant Denon,[8] who advised and acted for her in the buying of paintings.

Joséphine was a presence in the art world due to her visits to museums, exhibitions, and auction rooms. She visited the Salons to show her support for art and artists, especially those she knew and collected. At six Salons between 1804 and 1814 (her last) she bought more than sixty paintings. At several others she exhibited paintings that already belonged to her. For example, exhibit no. 241 in the Salon of 1804 was *Six tableaux de fleurs à l'aquarelle* (Six flower paintings in watercolor). Until recently, all writers (including the present one) wrote of an important commission to Redouté for six flower bouquets to hang in her bedroom at Malmaison. They were not described or noted as untraced or lost. In 2000 it finally occurred to me that they were exhibited at the Salon of 1804. This has been accepted by art historians Claudia Salvi, Marianne Roland Michel, and Alain

Pougetoux. At the height of his powers, in the heyday of the Empire, Redouté responded magnificently to a commission that would be seen by Joséphine every day she was at Malmaison.

Redouté's modern popularity has come through countless reproductions of his work, especially *Les Roses*, whether as prints on hotel walls, table mats, or greeting cards, and, to a lesser extent, facsimile editions of the great printed books. All these reproductions vary substantially in quality. At present no catalogue raisonné of Redouté's astonishing output of more than six thousand watercolors exists, and original examples in good condition are becoming ever more rare and costly.

The fact that his reproductions are so popular conveys a fundamental truth about all of Redouté's work. His technical ability, his botanical training, and his profound knowledge of the character of a flower may have been equaled by other artists, such as Ferdinand Bauer (1760–1826), but where Redouté's gift lay, to a greater degree than any other flower painter, was in what he did before he picked up pencil or brush. He examined his subject—flowers and foliage of whatever size, color, or degree of complexity—turning them again and again in his hands. He then instinctively arranged them to best advantage on a background of white paper—a distinctive style that can be recognized from across the room. In arranging his compositions with bouquets and even single specimens, he clearly trod the perilous tightrope of botany across the chasms of fancy flower arranging, the quest for mannered effects, the pretty, and artificiality—anathemas of the true flower painter and botanical draftsman. He succeeded in the seemingly impossible task of fidelity, detail, and naturalness combined with flawless taste and elegance.

After the renowned bird painter John James Audubon had visited Redouté in his studio in Paris in 1828 and had been given some of his work, Audubon wrote to his wife, "Now my Lucy, this will be a great treat for thee, fond of flowers as thou art, when thou seest these, thine eyes will feast on the finest you can imagine!"

Notes
1. Gérard painted the best portrait of Redouté.
2. An exception is the magnificent oil painting of 1796 with French and Company, New York.
3. Elisabeth Hardouin-Fugier, *The Pupils of Redouté*, 1981.
4. Vivant Denon, quoted in Marianne Roland Michel, Peter C. Sutton, et al., *The Floral Art of Pierre-Joseph Redouté*, exh. cat. (London, 2002), 13.
5. Jill, Duchess of Hamilton, *Napoléon, the Empress and the Artist: The Story of Napoléon and Josephine's Garden at Malmaison* (London, 1999).
6. Christian Jouanin, "Josephine and the Natural Sciences," *Apollo*, July 1977, 50–59; an excellent and enduring article.
7. Alain Pougetoux, *La Collection de peintures de l'Impératrice Joséphine* (Paris, 2003).
8. Alain Pougetoux, *Les vies Dominique-Vivant Denon: La Documentation* (Paris, 2001).

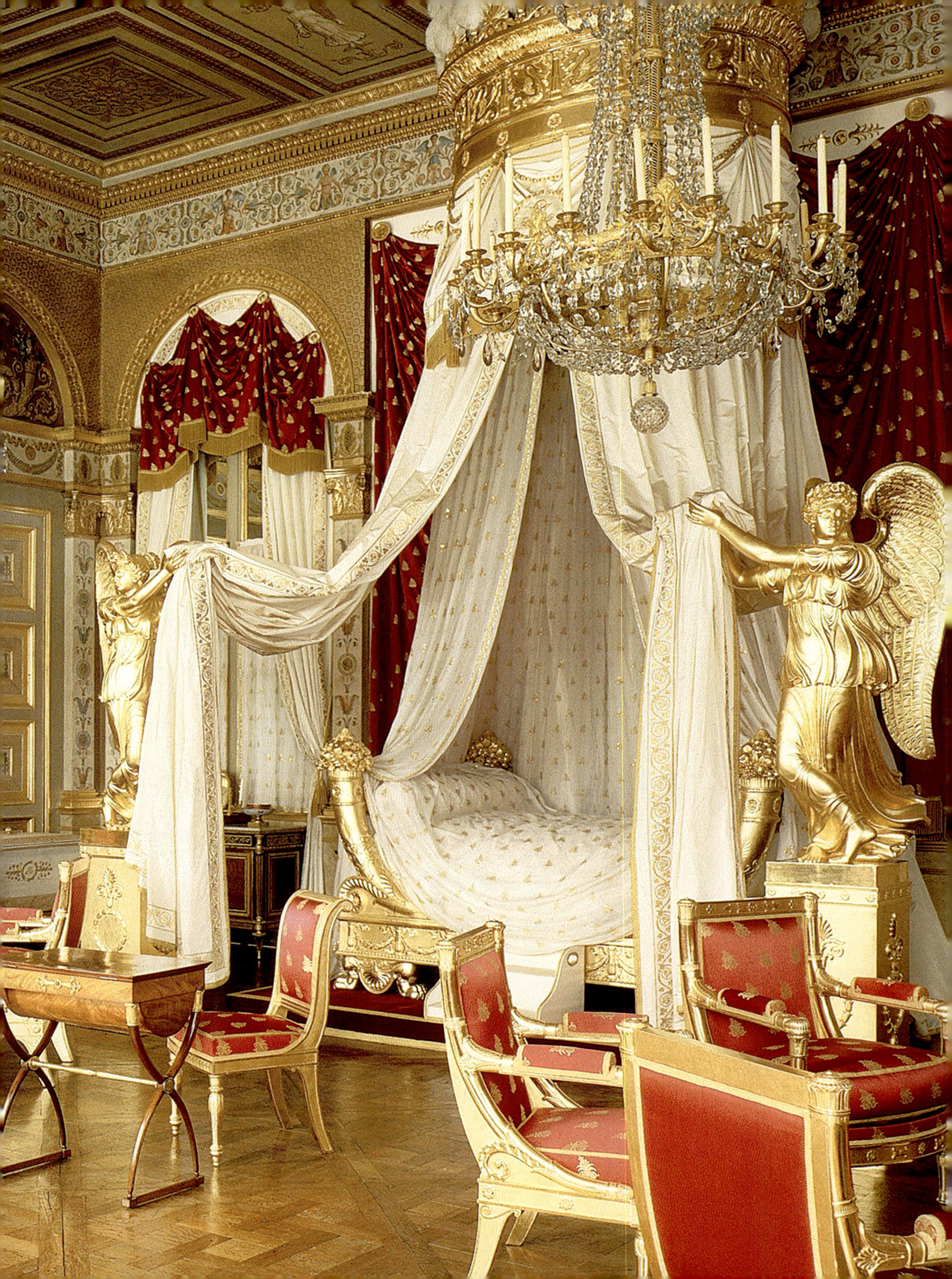

CHAPTER 6

JOHN D. WARD

From Mahogany to Gilt: Joséphine's Choices in Furniture

THE SUBJECT OF EMPRESS JOSÉPHINE'S FURNITURE immediately conjures up her swan armchair; this association of a personality and a furniture form is as compelling as any in the field. However, her influence and taste extend far beyond this icon of the Empire period, for in her furniture, as in so many other areas, Joséphine combined the grace of the ancien régime with the restraint of the Directoire and the majesty of the Empire. Each piece is the result of a triumphant collaboration between designers, cabinetmakers, carvers, gilders, silk weavers, and upholsterers who, under this perceptive patron, turned out ensembles of legendary elegance.

Joséphine's patronage spanned less than twenty years, but years as exciting and innovative for the arts as for politics. Although opinion varies as to an advancement or a decline in the decorative arts, this shift in taste produced some singularly beautiful and impressive creations, many of them designed for or owned by Joséphine. Although the shapes and ornament evolved, a continuity is evident in the originality, quality, and consistent taste of the furniture created for this aristocratic widow, commander's lady, and ultimately empress.

THE AGE OF MAHOGANY

Joséphine's first opportunity to exert her influence as a major patron of furniture came in the summer of 1797, when, while in Italy, she ordered the refurnishing of the pavilion she shared with Bonaparte on rue Chantereine. Having been fêted and housed in a princely

Italian manner, Mme Bonaparte deemed her Paris residence unworthy of her new position. She thus sent a commission to the prominent firm of Jacob Frères, asking for "tout ce qu'il avait de meiux" (all the best), as Napoléon recalled even two decades later, still furious over the cost.[1]

Like many an ambitious socialite before and since, Joséphine called upon the most sought-after decorators of the day to make her splash. The house of Jacob had been established under the ancien régime by Georges Jacob (1739–1814), *menuisier*, or chairmaker, to a royal and aristocratic clientele that included Marie-Antoinette, the comte d'Artois, and the comte de Vaudreuil. In the late 1780s and early 1790s, Jacob executed designs in the new "antique" style, first for the painter Jacques-Louis David, then for progressive aristocrats such as the prince de Salm, in whose sumptuous town house Joséphine saw Jacob's work. The craftsman's association with David stood him in good stead when the Revolution broke out and many of his former clients either emigrated or were guillotined. Defended by David through several denunciations, Jacob not only survived but was summoned as one of the suppliers to the Revolutionary government, working to David's designs and those of Charles Percier and Pierre-François-Léonard Fontaine.

In 1796 Georges Jacob retired and ceded the business to his two sons, Georges Jacob II and François-Honoré-Georges Jacob, the latter known as Jacob-Desmalter. The firm of Jacob Frères, held in high esteem by the avant-garde and supported by the government, was the obvious and almost only choice in Paris for new luxury furnishings. Since she was traveling in Italy at the time, Joséphine placed literally a blind faith in her decorators; she was not disappointed.

Joséphine's 1797 commission for rue Chantereine {FIGURE 69} is of an extraordinarily early date for what has become known as the Consular style. The Directoire was still living in heterogeneous grandeur at the Luxembourg palace, with furniture assembled largely from former royal interiors, and Juliette Recamier's famous apartment would not be unveiled until the following year. At Joséphine's pavilion, though, "everything...was of a new model, specially ordered."[2] In their influential publication, *Receuil de décorations intérieures*, which helped codify the Empire style, Percier and Fontaine would illustrate a two-tier gueridon (a small, portable table) "faite pour Mme. B. à Paris" (made for Mme B[onaparte] in Paris).[3] The architects would not in fact work directly for Joséphine until Malmaison, so the design of this table, known to have been at rue Chantereine, must have been ordered from them by Jacob Frères. Another piece from the house, the famous "arc de triomphe" desk (Grand Trianon), suggests the work of the sculptor and designer Jean-Guillaume Moitte (1747–1810). Several of the pieces, however, are refined versions of models that the Jacob workshops had been producing since the late 1780s and that Joséphine would have seen in avant-garde interiors during the early years of the Revolution.

The keynote, as it had been for antique-style interiors since the late 1780s, was the use of mahogany. This expensive wood, imported from Cuba and Santo Domingo, first became popular in sheets of large, decoratively grained or spotted veneer, mounted on Louis XVI cabinets in much the same way as were sheets of imported lacquer or panels of Sèvres porcelain. The popularity of mahogany rode the tide of Anglomania; furniture makers, led

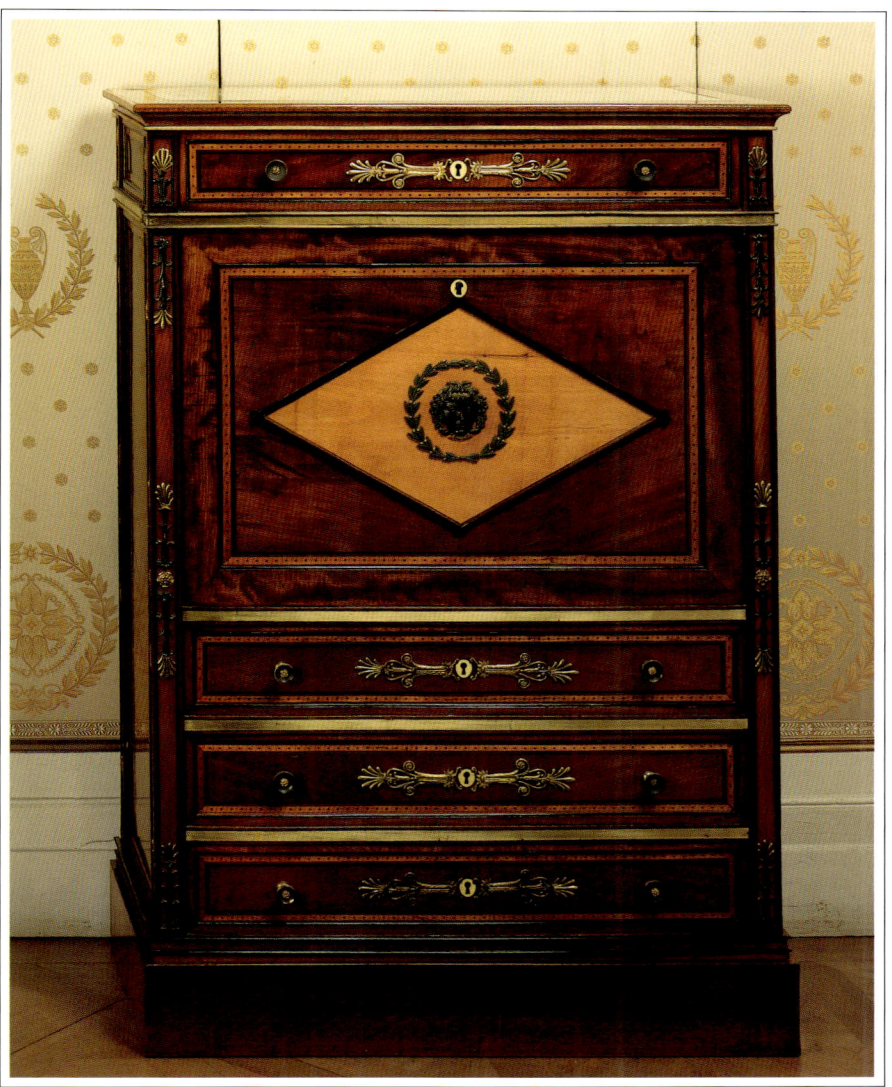

FIGURE 69.

Secrétaire, French (Paris), ca. 1797.
From the rue Chantereine.
Jacob Frères.
Mahogany, satinwood, gilt bronze,
and patinated wood, H: approx. 140 cm (4 ft. 7⅛ in.).
Munich, Wittelsbacher Ausgleichsfonds.

• • •

One of the pieces delivered by Jacob Frères for Joséphine and Bonaparte's pavilion as part of the redecoration she ordered from Italy in the summer of 1797. While the form of the piece is strictly Louis XVI, the polychromy, lozenge motifs, mask of Apollo, and central mounts to the drawers all partake of the new style. Joséphine continued to keep pieces from this first decor nearby for the rest of her life; after giving up the rue Chantereine, this secrétaire and its companion armoire were placed in the tented council chamber at Malmaison (see FIGURE 53) in 1800. After her death, it was taken by Prince Eugène to Bavaria.

by Georges Jacob, exploited its strength for chairs and its fine grain for precise carving, qualities English artisans had appreciated for decades. So ubiquitous was its use, whether solid or veneered, that 1785–1805 can truly be called the "Age of Mahogany" in French furniture.

Alongside the taste for expanses of mahogany ran one for polychromy: flat ornamental designs, usually adapted from Greek vases, were executed in ebony, brass, pale inlays such as holly or bone, and even mother-of-pearl. These were often used in place of the carved wood or gilt-bronze accents that might have been used in the previous style. The severe geometric designs of the new style were echoed by borders on upholstery, wallpaper, and even women's dresses.

On her return from Italy, Joséphine was obviously pleased with her house and with the reaction it provoked, for she retained the firm of Jacob Frères. Long after she left the pavilion on rue Chantereine, Joséphine kept its original furnishings for her private rooms in other residences. Yet this early decor had been only a start. Beginning with the acquisition of Malmaison in September 1799, the ever-ascendant Joséphine embarked on the first step of what became a huge decorative campaign. Continuing with the Tuileries from February 1800 and Saint-Cloud from October 1801, these projects would provide ample scope for her taste, impetus for the luxury trades, and would codify the Consular style in decoration.

The first interiors, and those always dearest to Joséphine, were at Malmaison. Percier and Fontaine began work there in January 1800, with Percier noting that "Mme Bonaparte takes a very active interest in our work."[4] This contrasts with her orders for the rue Chantereine furnishings sight unseen; the renovation of Malmaison—in the capable hands of Percier, Fontaine, and Jacob Frères—was probably her proving ground in the creation of elegant interiors. Elements and forms supplied for her here would be repeated in Joséphine's residences until her death.

The furniture was entirely in the new taste, a triumph of mahogany with touches of gilt and ebony, upholstered in clear colors with contrasting passementerie. Credit for the rooms and furnishings at Malmaison should be split between the architects and the cabinetmakers; while Percier and Fontaine drafted the main lines of the scheme, they relied on Jacob Frères for the execution of much of the paneling and furniture. The younger partner, Jacob-Desmalter, an accomplished draftsman, was certainly capable of matching the architects' style on lesser pieces for which they did not provide designs. Once a model had been established—whether to the designs of Percier and Fontaine or of Jacob-Desmalter—the furniture firm could then go on to supply it for their other patrons on unrelated commissions. While this undoubtedly helped spread the Empire style and contributed to the uniformity of the imperial residences, it does make it almost impossible to assign credit for a particular model without a design on paper in a recognizable hand.

An example of this is the well-known *curule* stool {FIGURE 70}, based on Roman models. The form had been introduced by the painter Jacques-Louis David in his classical-

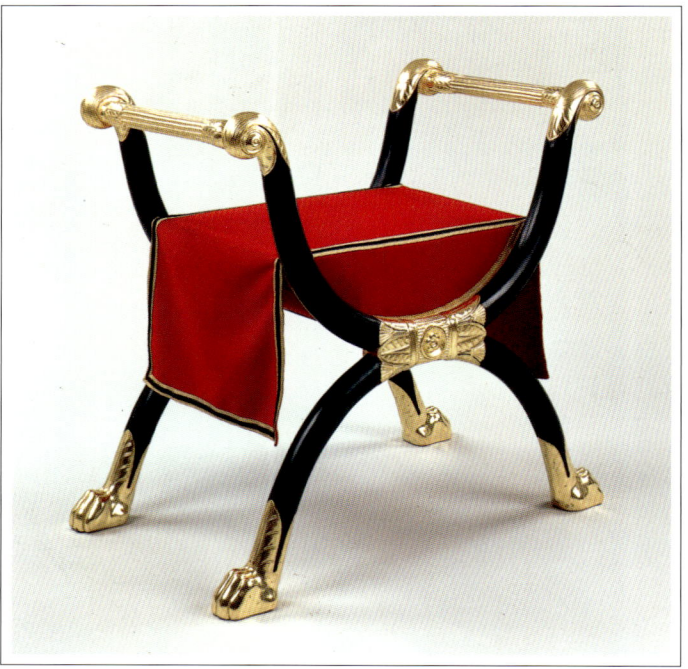

FIGURE 70.

Curule Stool, French (Paris), ca. 1800.
From the Council Chamber at Malmaison.
Jacob Frères (French, 1796–1803).
Patinated and gilt wood, restored upholstery,
H: approx. 70 cm (2 ft. 3½ in.).
Rueil-Malmaison, Musée national des Châteaux
de Malmaison et Bois-Préau.

· · ·

One of the first examples of a form that Joséphine would favor until the end of her life. Adapted from an antique model, these stools would be delivered not just for this martial-themed room but also for Joséphine's boudoir, for Napoléon's bedroom at Saint-Cloud, for salons at the Tuileries, and for other patrons such as the Murats at the Elysée and Mme Moreau. Banished by imperial etiquette after 1805 in favor of formal *pliants* (formal folding stools), this graceful form would be reintroduced by Joséphine when she redecorated the salon at Malmaison following her divorce.

style furniture made by Georges Jacob before the Revolution. At Malmaison, Jacob Frères supplied these stools for the famous tented Council Chamber {see FIGURE 53} — an interior that was such a milestone for Percier and Fontaine that they illustrated it in the *Receuil*. The architects also included an illustration of the *curule* stools, although in this case it is clear that they did not originate the form. While this is the first instance of the stools being supplied for the Bonapartes, they would reappear in Joséphine's boudoir at Malmaison, her boudoir and Napoléon's bedchamber at Saint-Cloud, and at the Tuileries. Other examples would be delivered to the Murats at the Elysée palace, for General Moreau's salon in Paris, and for other patrons such as Maréchal Mortier.

After the coup d'état of 18 *brumaire* (November 10), 1799, Napoléon and Joséphine were installed for a short time at the Luxembourg Palace, and even during this brief span Joséphine created surroundings to her taste. The wife of the minister for foreign affairs noted,

> Mme Bonaparte's receptions are very popular; we attended the other evening. She occupies at the Luxembourg the former apartment of Moulin…the rooms had not been altered on my first visit, but this time everything was changed; nothing recalled the austerity of Moulin. The furnishings were of a refined elegance, and in the last salon a tea table was particularly admired; it was placed in the middle of the room, and twenty people could take their places around it. A column of gilt wood rose from the center of the marble top and supported a vase of rare flowers. Needless to say, Mme Bonaparte makes a far better hostess than Mme Moulin, and aesthetics were certainly the winner on the 18 *brumaire*.[5]

On February 19, 1800, the first consul and his wife moved into the Tuileries Palace. The sheer size of the Tuileries and its dependencies, plus the fact that it was being furnished — at least hypothetically — from the private funds of the first consul, produced a heterogeneous mélange composed of former royal furnishings, pieces seized from émigrés, and items drawn from existing government offices. The firm of Jacob Frères, which had proved its abilities to both the government and the Bonapartes, delivered what new furniture was required, while the textiles were purchased from various Parisian merchants.[6] Many of the new pieces were destined for Joséphine's rooms, including "a bed in mahogany of antique form, with two ends with plain panels; the front richly sculpted and gilded."[7]

Following closely on the restoration and refurnishing of the Tuileries was that of Saint-Cloud, for which the architectural work began in January 1801; most of the furnishings were delivered in 1802–3. As with the Tuileries, the decoration was supposed to be personally funded by Napoléon. The first consul had begun to organize his household on a larger scale, recalling more and more that of the former kings. This entailed an increasing bureaucracy through which Joséphine would have to make her taste and wishes known. Irritated by excessive expenditure at the Tuileries, Napoléon ordered Fontaine to "employ for the furnishings as much as possible objects coming from the national warehouses," and he warned that any expenditure over the allotted budget would be at the architect's own cost.[8] The actual orders for furnishings were placed not through Joséphine nor even the architects but by an intendant appointed for this purpose. Still, for 1802–3, deliveries amounted to more than one million francs.[9]

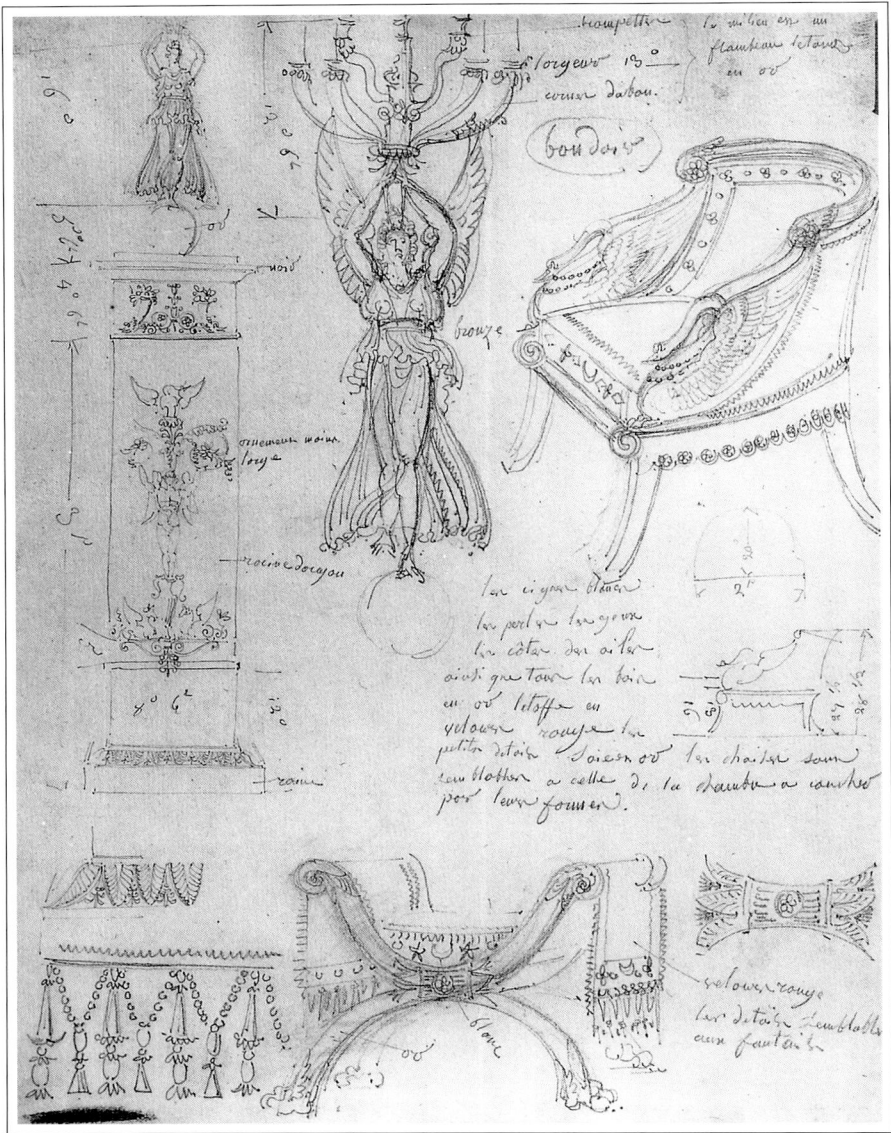

FIGURE 71.

Charles Percier (French, 1764–1838).
Furniture designs for Joséphine's boudoir
at Saint-Cloud, ca. 1801 (detail).
Graphite on paper, 36.7 × 24.4 cm (14½ × 9⅝ in.).
New York, The Metropolitan Museum of Art,
Whittelsey Fund, 1963.

· · ·

The *curule* stool shown on this well-known sheet had appeared the previous year at Malmaison in the Council Chamber and Joséphine's boudoir; Percier carefully delineates the upholstery, but the form is understood and would be repeated separately for the Murats, the Moreaus, and other clients of both Percier and Jacob Frères. The candelabrum and pedestal, more precisely drawn, are probably new for this room, but would be used again, as in the Moreaus' salon. As for the swan armchair, the sketchiness again suggests a known form; the basic *gondole* armchair was delivered in 1800 for Joséphine's boudoir at Malmaison and in 1802 for Mme Moreau, while the swan version was later duplicated exactly for Caroline Bonaparte Murat at the Elysée.

FIGURE 72.

Console, French (Paris), ca. 1802.
From Joséphine's Grand Salon at Saint-Cloud.
Adam Weisweiler and Pierre-Philippe Thomire
for Martin-Eloi Lignereux.
Carved, gilt, and patinated mahogany,
gilt bronze, marble top, w: 162 cm (5 ft. 3¾ in.).
Grand Trianon, Musée national des Châteaux
et de Trianon.

· · ·

One of four impressive new consoles supplied for Joséphine's grand salon at Saint-Cloud, formerly the bedroom of Louis XVI. Conforming to Napoléon's dictates for economy, the seats in this room were the important suite by Georges Jacob delivered in 1787 for the games room of this same palace, still covered in a blue floral brocade. However, amid the Louis XVI-style paneling and furniture, the mahogany and *verd antique* of these consoles in the latest style would have indicated that the occupant (Joséphine) was entirely cognizant of current taste.

While Napoléon's rooms at Saint-Cloud displayed Louis XVI consoles and commodes, Joséphine's quarters received fashionable new furniture. For her boudoir, Charles Percier drew classical pedestals, bronze candelabra supported by winged goddesses, and the famous swan armchairs {FIGURE 71}. The basic form of the armchairs was a *gondole* (gondola) model that Jacob Frères had already supplied for Joséphine at Malmaison; the contribution of the architect was to apply winged swans to the incurved arm supports. The chairs in Joséphine's salon had been delivered to Saint-Cloud almost fifteen years before for Louis XVI's games room, but the interior was updated by four impressive new consoles with lion-pawed, Egyptian-headed supports and elaborate, bronze, chimera-form mounts {FIGURE 72}. These were probably delivered by Martin-Eloi Lignereux, former associate of the *marchand-mercier* Dominique Daguerre, father-in-law of Jacob-Desmalter and owner of a workshop in close competition with Jacob Frères. The *ébéniste* and *bronzier* most closely associated with Lignereux at this period, and probably responsible for these consoles, were

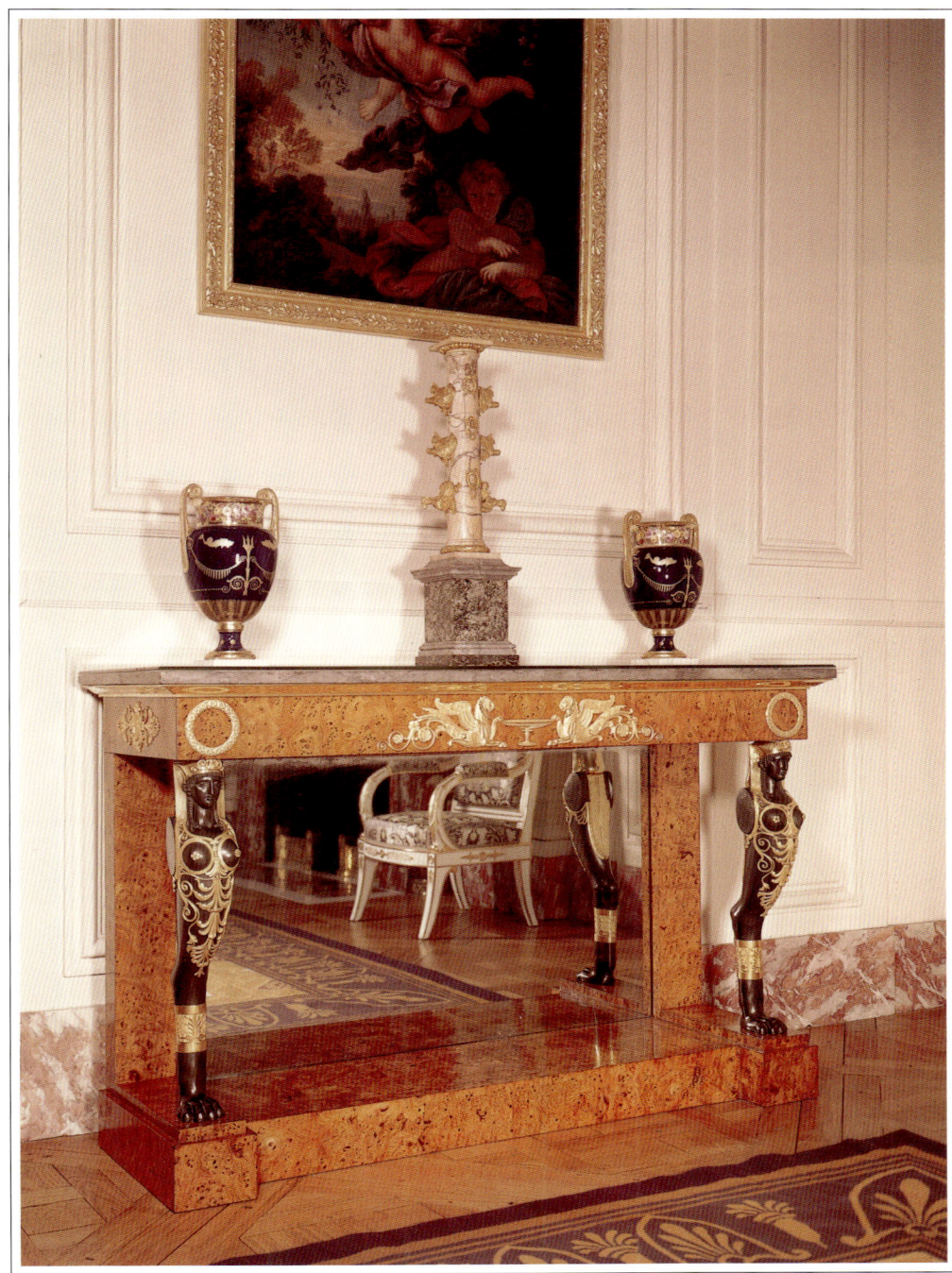

Adam Weisweiler (1744–1820) and Pierre-Philippe Thomire (1751–1843), respectively. The presence of pieces by makers other than Jacob Frères suggests that the campaign to furnish two rich palaces and a château in two years had outstripped the production of their workshop, and that furniture was now being purchased on the regular Parisian furniture market, albeit from makers of the highest quality and reputation.

With the installation of Napoléon and Joséphine at Saint-Cloud, the consular palaces were completed. With a laudable parallelism, the death of Georges Jacob II in October 1803 brought an end to the association of Jacob Frères. Jacob-Desmalter was rejoined by his father to form the firm of Jacob-Desmalter et Cie.; they would be the preeminent suppliers of furniture for the entire imperial period, and largely responsible for "Empire" taste

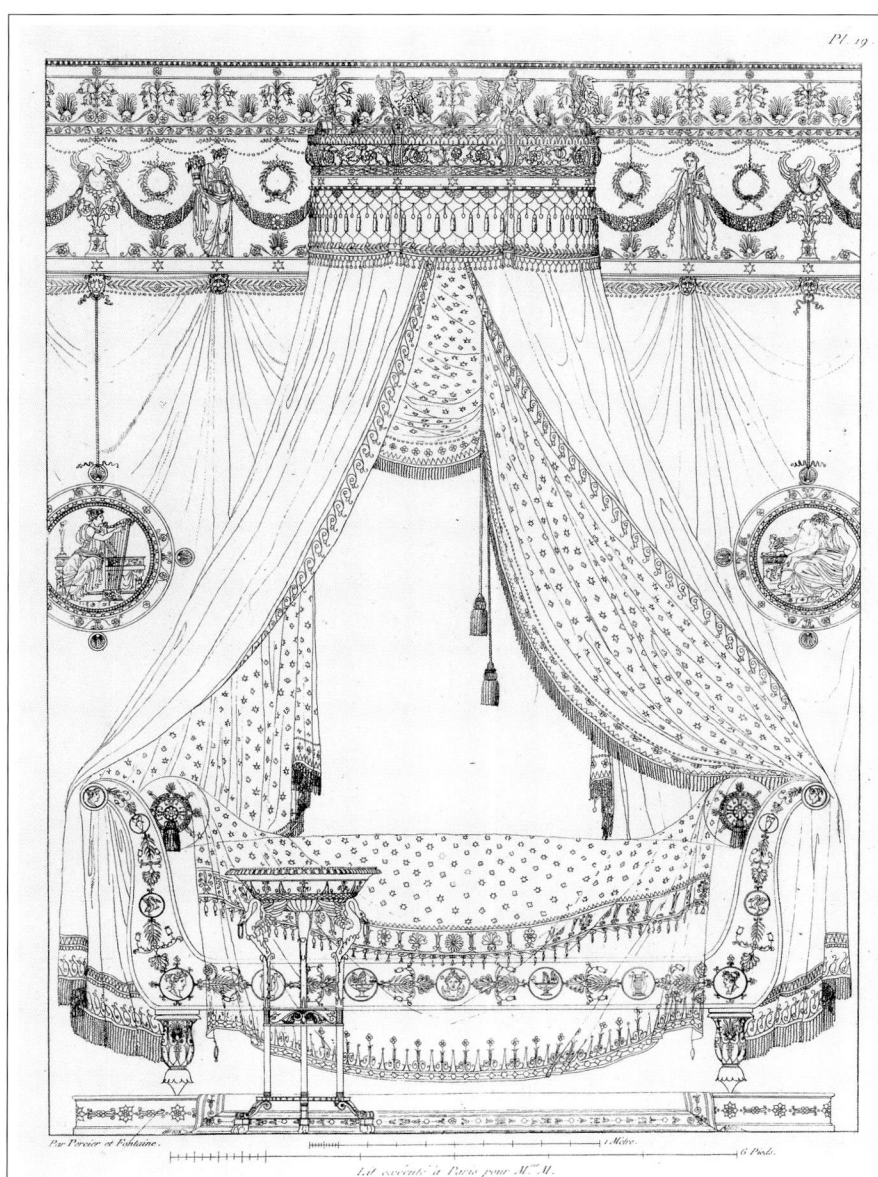

Figure 74.

Charles Percier (French, 1764–1838) and
Pierre-François-Léonard Fontaine
(French, 1762–1853),
Bed executed for Mme Moreau (1802).
Engraving, 30 × 22 cm (11¾ × 8½ in.),
from Percier and Fontaine,
Receuil de décorations intérieures (Paris, 1827 ed.),
plate 19.

• • •

This ensemble was originally designed by Percier and Fonaine for the wife of General Moreau. However, after the general's conviction for conspiracy, the furniture was purchased by the government and installed at Fontainebleau, where Mme Moreau's bed became Joséphine's, in the bedroom formerly occupied by Marie-Antoinette. The elegant Consular-style bed, with its mahogany frame, classical roundels with blue-enameled grounds, and diaphanous draperies would have been very much to Joséphine's taste, and the blue roundels would have echoed those on the Neoclassical doors installed in 1787. Within six months, though, Napoléon would demand a more regal interior for his empress.

as it is understood today. Subsequent events, however, brought one last great ensemble by Jacob Frères into the palaces. After the confirmation of Napoléon as emperor in May 1804, the impending arrival of Pope Pius VII at Fontainebleau in November required that neglected palace to be put in order in nineteen days. Much of the furniture for this hasty installation was to be taken from "the château de Grosbois and the house on the rue d'Anjou that belonged to General Moreau and which, after his trial, are now at the disposition of the Government."[10]

Jean-Victor-Marie Moreau (b. 1763) had been the primary rival to the popularity of General Bonaparte before the establishment of the Consulate, and his wife had been pointedly rude to her fellow Creole but social rival, Joséphine. The luxury of the Moreaus' Parisian *hôtel*, decorated in 1801–2 by Percier and Fontaine, must have seemed an affront; certainly the Moreaus were the last major private clients of the team that thereafter became Napoléon's personal architects. In 1804 Moreau was found guilty of conspiracy, and the government purchased his two residences, along with their contents. Designed by Percier and Fontaine, executed by Jacob Frères, and often identical to pieces already supplied for Malmaison, the Tuileries, or Saint-Cloud, the furniture transported from the Moreaus' Paris

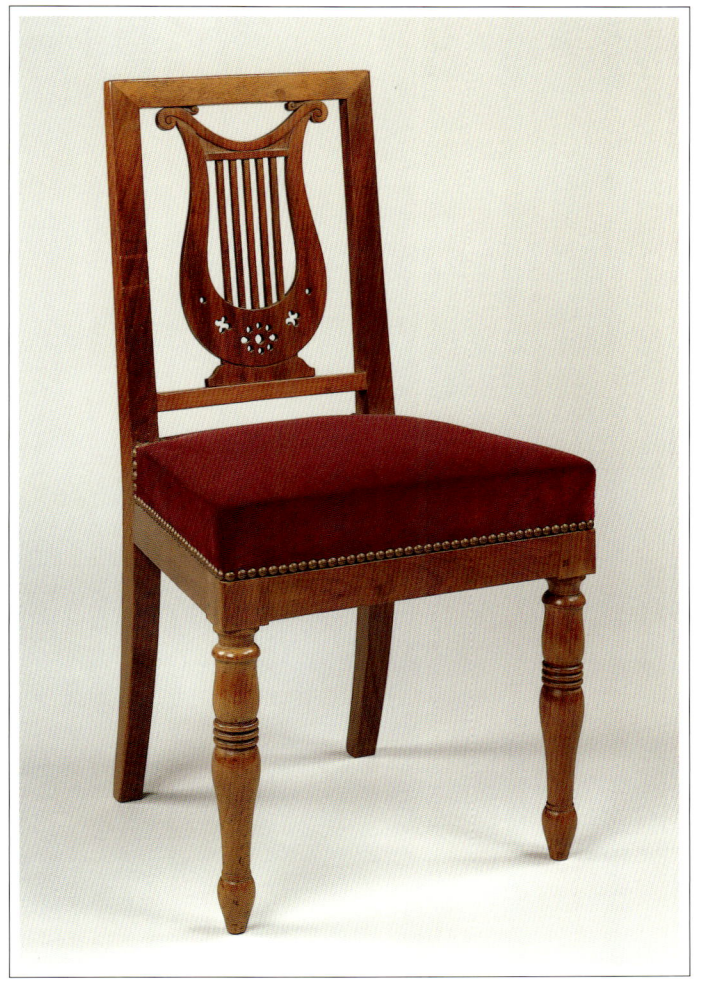

FIGURE 75.

Side Chair, French (Paris), 1805/6.
From Joséphine's music room at the Tuileries.
François-Honoré-Georges Jacob-Desmalter et Cie.
Carved mahogany, upholstery restored,
H: 96 cm (3 ft. 1¾ in.).
Paris, Musée du Louvre.

• • •

This chair stands at the junction of the Consular and Empire styles. Lyre-back mahogany chairs had appeared as salon furnishings as early as the mid 1780s, and accompanied mahogany or gilt suites in most Consulate drawing rooms. The late date of this example, delivered 1805/6, is evident in its heavy frame and baluster-turned front legs. Even before the full suite of sixty was delivered, the Garde-Meuble was noting that the chairs "were made before the etiquette of the *pliants* was instituted." Henceforth, such chairs would be suitable only for dining rooms; indeed, this model was furnished as such for both Joséphine and Napoléon at Compiègne.

residence to Fontainebleau was completely to Joséphine's liking. Mme Moreau's bed {FIGURE 74}, mahogany with classical roundels in gilt bronze and gold-embroidered transparent hangings, was installed amid the Renaissance mantel, Baroque ceiling, and Neoclassical paneling of the bedroom last inhabited by Marie-Antoinette. However, these elegant and refined mahogany forms so representative of Joséphine's personal taste were not to remain long in the former queen's apartment. With the proclamation of the Empire, Napoléon would demand a style more commensurate with his visions of imperial grandeur.

THE AGE OF GILT

After the coronation on December 2, 1804, each château became an imperial residence. In July of that year Napoléon's reorganization of his household had sown the seeds of the Garde-Meuble Impériale, a government department specifically charged with the ordering and upkeep of the imperial furnishings. The nomination in 1805 of Pierre Daru (1767–1829) to the position of *intendant général de la Maison de l'Empereur*, and in 1806 of Alexandre Desmazis (1768–1833) to that of *administeur du Mobilier*, with thirty people under him, established a new bureaucracy of furniture, replicating in many ways the former Garde-Meuble de la Couronne (which formerly oversaw the furniture of the kings). The new organization was responsible solely to the emperor—his taste, his pretentions,

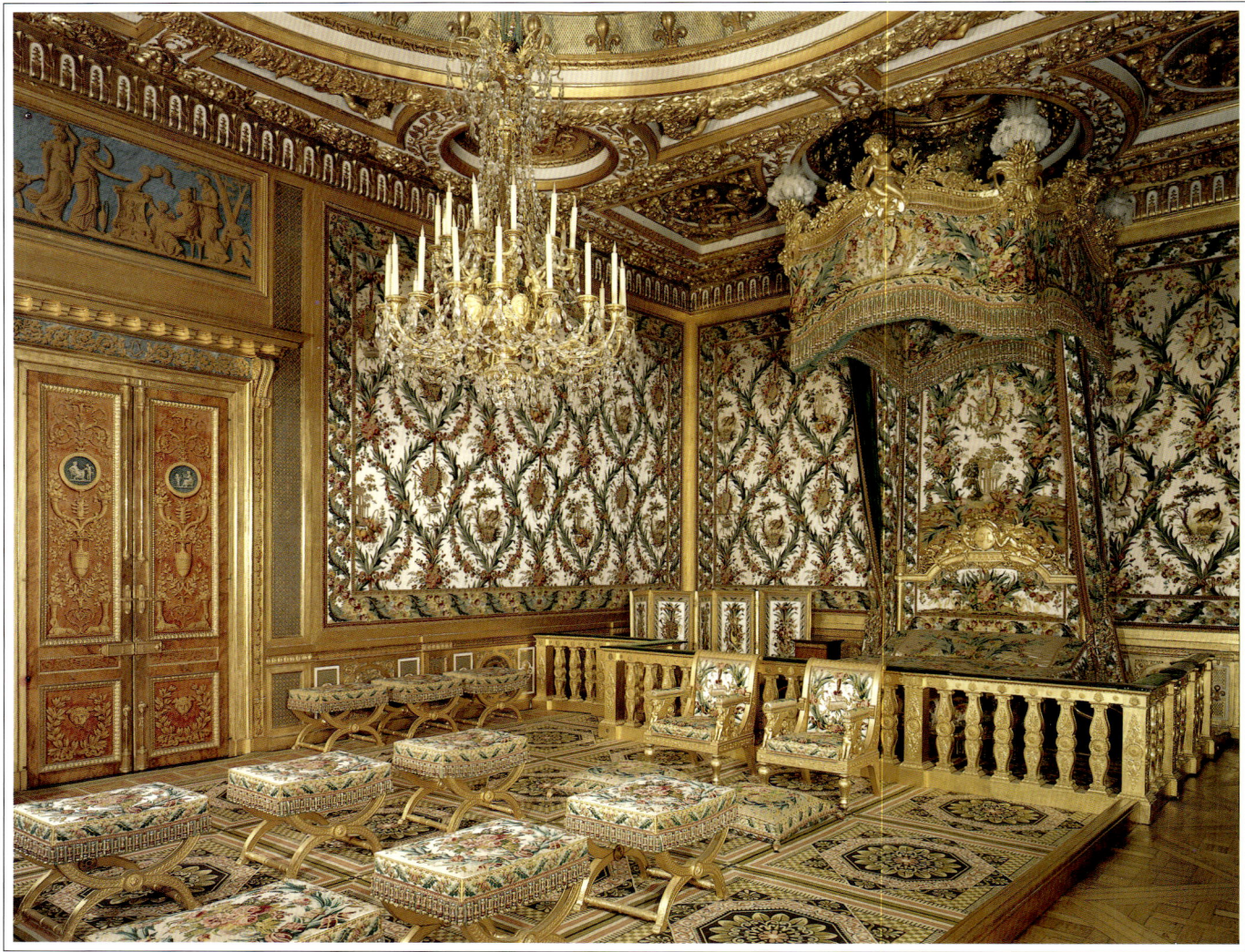

Figure 76.

View of Joséphine's State Bedchamber at Fontainebleau, as installed in 1805. Bed by Sené and Laurent, 1787, textiles restored. Carved and gilt wood, silk upholstery. Musée national du Château de Fontainebleau.

• • •

Joséphine's bedroom was one of ancien régime grandeur, as dictated by the new emperor. The bed is that delivered by Sené for Marie-Antoinette in 1787; Joséphine may even have seen it in place originally, as she was then living in the town of Fontainebleau. The hangings by Gaudin and Savournin were purchased by the Garde-Meuble de la Couronne in 1790 and remained in storage until used here fifteen years later. In a manner that would do Louis XIV proud, the bed has been enclosed by a formal balustrade originally designed for Napoléon's throne at the Tuileries. Even Mme Moreau's armchairs, mahogany with gilt Egyptian heads, after a Jacob Frères model similar to those in Joséphine's salon at Malmaison, have been replaced by the eternal *pliants* and two stately Jacob Frères gilt armchairs.

his architects, his budgets. Joséphine, formerly the primary arbiter of elegance, was now a secondary patron; her strong personal tastes and complete disregard for cost would bring her increasingly into conflict with the new department.

In 1805 Joséphine was able to arrange her new music room at the Tuileries with forty-eight mahogany chairs for the spectators {FIGURE 75}. In 1806 Napoléon, ever more obsessed with the formalities of the ancien régime, had published the *Etiquette des Palais Impériaux*, a sixty-page volume on the correct ceremony to be used at his court. The provision of necessary antechambers, graduated salons, and *pliants* (formal folding stools) would sweep away both Napoléon's economical but heterogeneous furnishings and Joséphine's elegant Consular-style installations in favor of the official splendor of the Garde-Meuble.

In a telling maneuver, the graceful *curule* stools of Joséphine's game room at Fontainebleau, originally from the Moreaus' salon, were crudely lopped off just above the seat to transform them into the *pliants* prescribed by etiquette; the stumps of their arms were hidden by upholstery, but the proportions were destroyed. Even

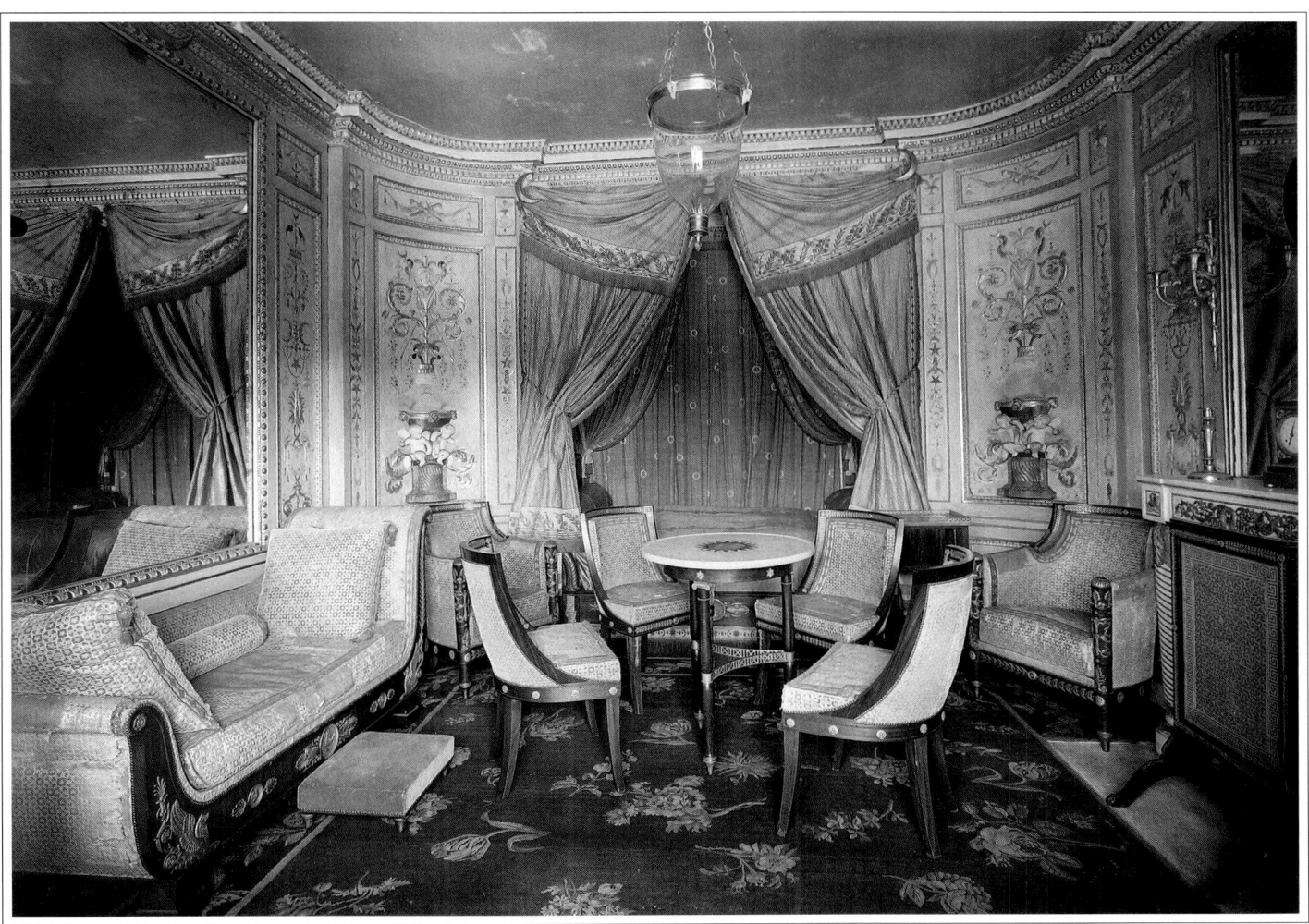

FIGURE 77.

View of Joséphine's Private Bedchamber at Fontainebleau, as installed in 1806. Furniture attributed to François-Honoré-Georges Jacob-Desmalter et Cie. Fabrics delivered by Vacher and applied by the upholsterer Susse. Musée national du Château de Fontainebleau.

• • •

After the state bedroom was formalized, Joséphine created this retreat in Marie-Antoinette's former *cabinet turc*. Located on the entresol, here she could still surround herself with mahogany furniture decorated with exquisite bronze mounts, *curule* chairs, and white-and-gold upholstery, all to her personal taste. The whole, still retaining the upholstery applied in 1806, is a rare, unrestored example of a private interior created for Joséphine.

the vocabulary used for a similar operation at Rambouillet reveals the change in attitude: after the emperor noted that *curule* stools "did not conform to the model [demanded by etiquette]," the "partie vicieuse de ces tabourets"—the curving armrests—was "suppressed."[11] The whole has the aspect of a campaign against domestic unrest. At Fontainebleau, Mme Moreau's elegant Grecian bed—praised by contemporaries in 1802 and proudly published by Percier and Fontaine—was judged inappropriate for its situation. The emperor himself insisted it be replaced with "a very beautiful state bed of a decoration commensurate with the rest of the apartment... employ in its making the Lyon fabrics."[12] The result was the reinstatement of Marie-Antoinette's bed of 1787, now hung with a palm-frond silk brocade of 1790 that had remained in the storerooms since the fall of the monarchy. The new bedchamber {FIGURE 76} was a deliberate re-creation of ancien régime pomp and magnificence.

The response of the woman who was to sleep in the new room, though, is telling: the following year Joséphine created a small bedchamber in the former *cabinet turc* on the entresol. Approached only by a narrow staircase, her retreat {FIGURE 77} was a harmony of the white, yellow, and gold fabrics that she favored and was furnished in mahogany with the *bergères en gondole* (gondola armchairs) and *chaises curules* (fixed stools in the antique mode) of which she was so fond but that etiquette had banished from her public rooms in favor of *pliants*.

By 1808 relations between the empress and the officers of the Garde-Meuble, appointed by her husband, were becoming somewhat strained, as indeed was Joséphine's position at court. Despite the pressures on her marriage and disagreements with the architects and agents of the Garde-Meuble, there were three new decors to be worked out, an activity that Joséphine approached with her usual attention. The redecoration of the empress's state apartment on the ground floor of the Tuileries had been planned since 1805, when the new, more formal etiquette had demanded it be augmented by an antechamber and two salons. The Garde-Meuble, trying to increase the opulence of the rooms, applied bronzes to the existing mahogany consoles or added more gilt chairs to the salons.[13] Fontaine noted in his *Journal* that Joséphine herself wanted a new decor. "For a long time, she had been asking for changes and embellishments to her apartments . . . desiring above all that we create a beautiful bedroom."[14]

A sum of eighty thousand francs was allotted, and by July 1808 the Garde-Meuble was working with the empress on her furnishings. Joséphine asked specifically that the Garde-Meuble use the upholsterer Michel-Jacques Boulard, son of Jean-Baptiste Boulard (1725–1789), the *menuisier* who had supplied the Garde-Meuble de la Couronne in the 1780s. The younger Boulard was the most fashionable upholsterer, and therefore interior decorator, of the later imperial period; he had worked for Joséphine's daughter, Hortense, at the Hôtel de Lannoy, for the Murats at the Elysée, and possibly for Joséphine herself as early as the Consulate period. The Garde-Meuble noted, "She finds he has much taste, and she prefers him of all those who could be employed."[15]

It seems probable that Joséphine was not just following fashion but also wanted to be represented by her own man against the bureaucracy of the Garde-Meuble imposed upon her. The extent to which she relied on Boulard can be judged from notes in the archives. When the empress protested that "the fabric chosen for the First Salon does not seem to have a good effect; for the rest it must be viewed before making a decision," the administrator of the Garde-Meuble responded, "M. Boulard, in whose taste [Her Majesty] seems to have confidence, chose the fabric for this salon and designated the color. He assures that it will have a good effect."[16] This room would be Joséphine's famous yellow salon, referenced in the memoirs of Laure d'Abrantès and others of the period.[17]

The story of the Second, or Grand, Salon shows how rooms and furniture had become a battleground between the empress, Fontaine, and the Garde-Meuble—in other words, between Joséphine's ideas and her husband's concept of imperial grandeur tempered by economy. The fabric had been chosen in 1805—a blue, silver, and gold brocade originally ordered in 1802 for Joséphine's Grand Salon at Saint-Cloud. So that the rest of the room would match the grandeur of the textiles, all of the paneling, cornices, and so on, needed to be more elaborate; it was partly this expense that pushed the redecoration back to 1808. However, despite this long-planned scheme, in June 1808 the empress indicated that "the Grand Salon should be paneled and painted gray-white with gilt details, thus without wall hangings." It was relayed that the hangings were to be rejected, "[Her Majesty] absolutely does not want them," and that Joséphine wished for crimson or poppy-colored upholstery. The answer came back from the Garde-Meuble that Fontaine had arranged the walls for fabric hangings, that crimson upholstery would not be appropriate because the color would be too close to that of the bedchamber, and that using a different fabric from the blue brocade that had already been prepared would cost an additional sixty thousand francs.[18] In short, the room would be installed as first planned.

Thus, in the decoration of the main salon of her apartment, Joséphine saw her wishes thwarted and had to concede defeat to the Garde-Meuble and the architect; her pique no doubt made itself felt. Fontaine records that after the whole redecoration was finished, "[the empress] thought the ornaments too heavy, the furnishings not beautiful or rich enough. I asked her pardon and implored her indulgence, thinking that it was easier to find grace in her goodness than in her reason."[19]

Joséphine was quite specific about the furnishing of this salon, and her instructions indicate the active role she took in the creation of her apartments in the imperial palaces. For this room, she asked for "three sofas under the three mirrors at the back... and... a single console under the mirror... across from the fireplace. The two sofas under the mirrors in the corners should be a little curved to follow the outline of the room, and this way the salon can hold more people."[20] Jacob-Desmalter created the seat furniture {FIGURE 78}; the rollover backs and the elaborate armrests in the form of fully carved, female-headed sphinxes are elements that appeared under the Consulate, but the heavy front legs in the form of half-balusters and the wide seat rails carved with rose leaves now gave a richer air to the suite. The cabinetmaker charged for such elaboration; including gilding, the large sofa cost seven thousand francs and the armchairs one thousand francs each.

The bedroom exhibited the great jewel cabinet {FIGURE 79}, designed by Charles Percier and supplied by Jacob-Desmalter with bronzes after models by the sculptor Antoine-Denis Chaudet. For the new piece, the seventeenth-century cabinet shape has been reinterpreted in an Empire-style antique vocabulary, with echoes of Marie-Antoinette's famous jewel cabinet of 1787 (placed under the Empire at Saint-Cloud). In the words of Jacob-Desmalter's bill, "All of the ornaments relate to the principal subject, *The birth of the Queen of the Earth to whom Cupids and goddesses hurry to present their offerings.*"[21] On a ground of mahogany the *Venus Anadyomene*, in gilt-bronze after a relief by Jean Goujon (1510–ca. 1565), is

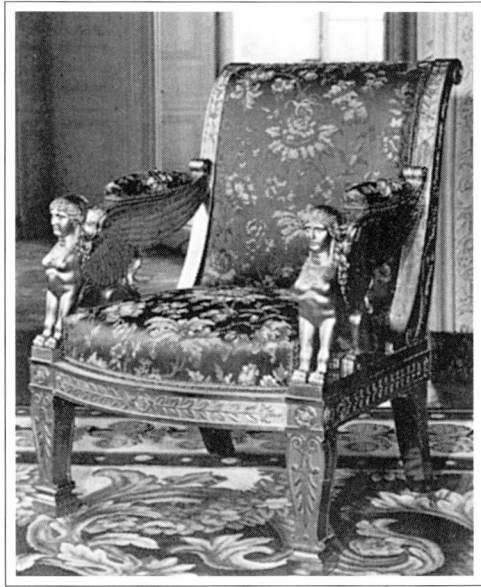

FIGURE 78.

Armchair from Joséphine's Second Salon at the Tuileries, French (Paris), 1809. François-Honoré-Georges Jacob-Desmalter et Cie. Carved and gilt wood, originally upholstered in blue-and-silver brocade, 96 cm (3 ft. 1¾ in.). Grand Trianon, Musée national des Châteaux de Versailles et de Trianon.

· · ·

This majestic seat conveys the monumentality of a throne, despite being intended as a piece of salon furniture. Fully carved sphinx supports were known in the Louis XVI and Consulate eras, and similar ones were delivered by Jacob Frères about 1800, but here they have achieved a new bulk. This armchair was one of six, covered in a blue-and-silver brocade patterned with daisies. This fabric was en suite with the sumptuous wall hangings by Camille Pernon, Lyon, ordered in 1802 for Joséphine's Grand Salon at Saint-Cloud with the express intention of encouraging French weavers.

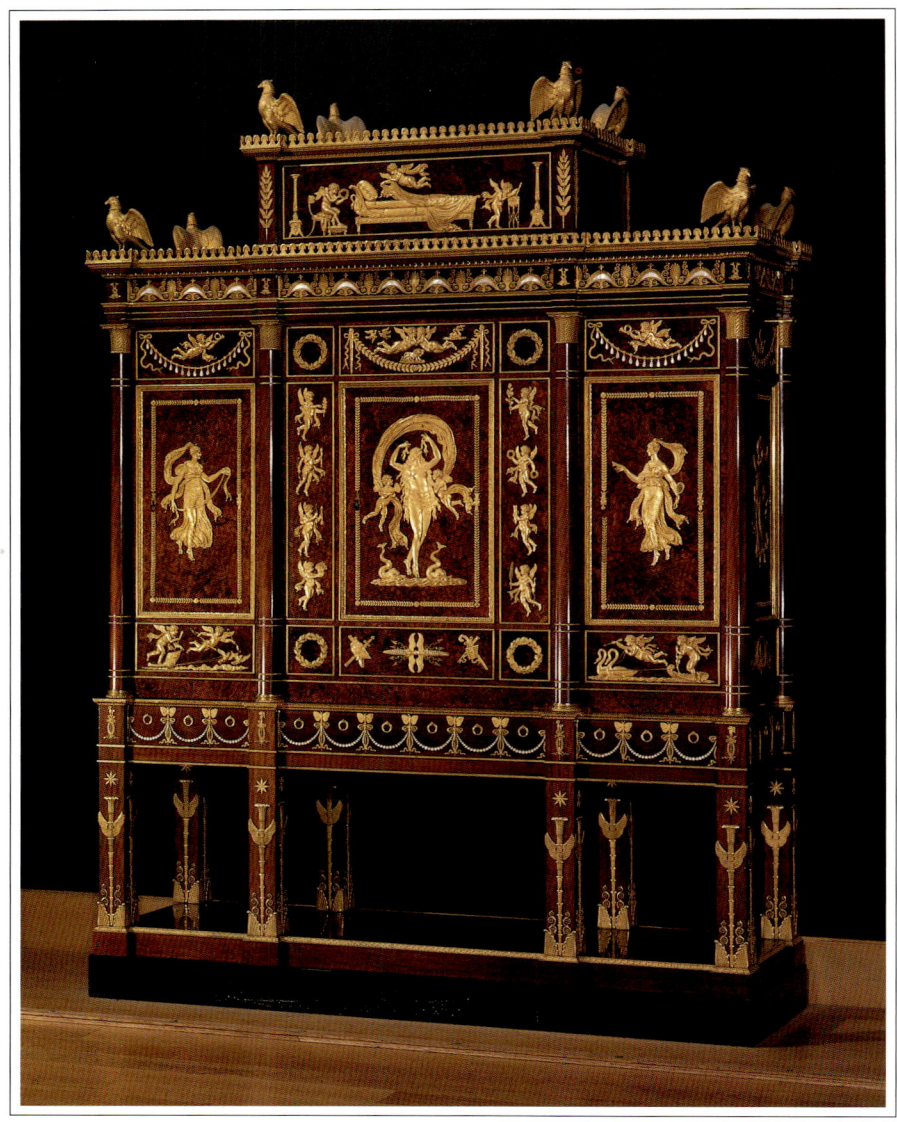

FIGURE 79.

Jewel Cabinet (*Grand écrin*), French (Paris), 1809.
From Joséphine's State Bedchamber at the Tuileries.
François-Honoré-Georges Jacob-Desmalter
et Cie, after a design by Charles Percier.
Yew burl, amaranth, mother-of-pearl,
gilt bronze, H: 272 cm (8 ft. 11⅛ in.).
Paris, Musée du Louvre.

• • •

An architectural composition that recalls both great cabinets of Louis XIV and Marie-Antoinette's jewel cabinet of 1787, this piece was the most expensive item delivered by Jacob-Desmalter to the Garde-Meuble Impériale. The mother-of-pearl inlays evoke the contents, including diadems and strands of round and pear-shaped pearls. The bronzes, on the theme of the Toilet of Venus, were modeled by the sculptor Antoine-Denis Chaudet, and the piece is topped by Venus's doves rather than the usual imperial eagles. All of the secret compartments had to be changed when Marie-Louise succeeded Joséphine just one year after the piece was delivered.

FIGURE 80.

Armchair, French (Paris), 1808.
From Joséphine's Cabinet at Fontainebleau.
Sculpture by Rode, gilding by Chatard,
upholstery by Gagnol.
Carved and gilt wood, silver-and-gold
brocade in cashmere style,
H: 98 cm (3 ft. 2⅝ in.).
Paris, Mobilier national.

• • •

In 1808 Joséphine redecorated Marie-Antoinette's silver-and-gold boudoir at Fontainebleau. For the upholstery, she presented the Garde-Meuble with panels of silver-and-gold brocade in Indian style, probably from a diplomatic gift and originally intended for her wardrobe. The frames were to be "of a richness parallel with that of the room." Ordered from the sculptor Rode, with gilding and upholstery the price reached about 906 francs for each armchair. Despite this coordination, the Garde-Meuble rendered an unfavorable verdict on the overall effect, probably influenced by its opinion of the often-demanding patron.

flanked by handmaidens in Grecian gowns and panels of cupids playing with swans or doves and making up antique beds. Amid all this fluttering classicism, the contents of the cabinet are evoked by friezes of necklaces and diadems inlaid with mother-of-pearl. Joséphine's jewel collection was legendary for its extent and value; appropriately, the cabinet to hold it was the most expensive item that Jacob-Desmalter ever delivered to the Garde-Meuble — a staggering fifty-five thousand francs — and a fitting climax to the empress's state apartment.

Joséphine was to be successful in imposing her taste with the new furnishings of her boudoir at Fontainebleau, the "silver boudoir" originally created for Marie-Antoinette. The new suite of gilt-wood furniture {FIGURE 80}, supplied through the Garde-Meuble, was covered by the upholsterer Gagnol in gold and silver brocades of Eastern origin, provided by the empress herself. The Persian patterns recall Joséphine's cashmere shawls, and it seems probable that these fabrics were originally acquired or given to her for use in her wardrobe before being employed here as upholstery. Despite the harmony of coloring with the silvered wall panels, though, the Garde-Meuble seems not to

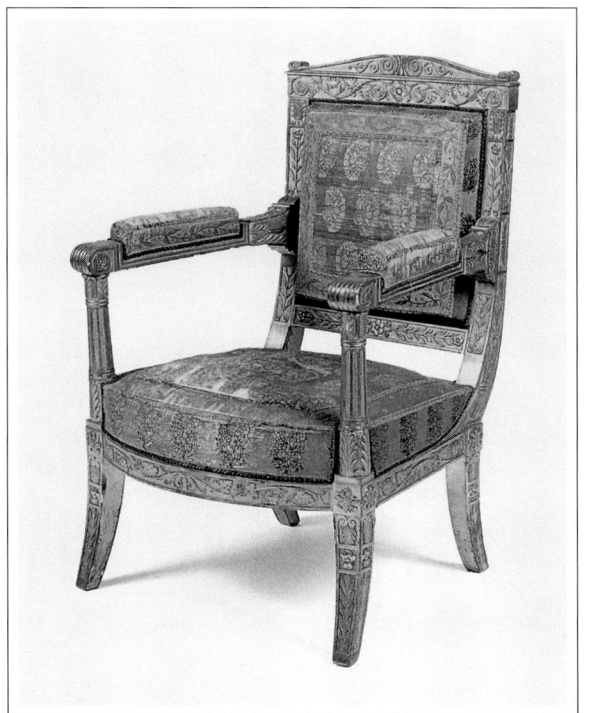
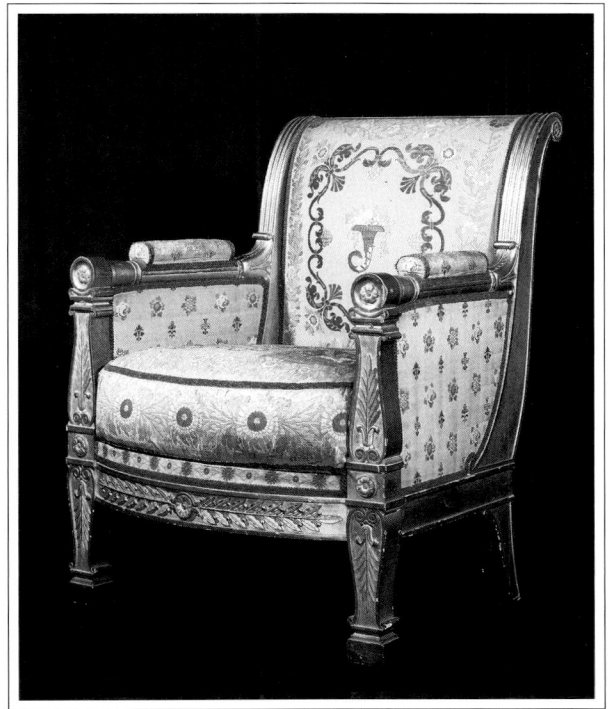

have been impressed by the final result. A note in the margin of an inventory critiques, "the upholstery of the seats is in a gold-and-silver fabric of unpleasant appearance and does not match the beauty of the room's decoration. This fabric has a distinctly cheap and tinsel-like look."[22] The waspishness of this comment seems a response to Joséphine's criticisms of her rooms at the Tuileries. Joséphine would have little time to benefit from her newly decorated rooms at Fontainebleau, though; she would stay here only during the agonizing voyage of November 1809, before the announcement of divorce on December 15.

Compiègne, the last apartment arranged for Joséphine in the imperial palaces, remains one of the best examples of her taste, although she never saw it completed and many writers erroneously state that it was decorated for her successor. Work on the palace had begun in 1807 under the architect Louis-Martin Berthault, recommended by Joséphine from his work at Malmaison. By the first months of 1809, the empress's apartment was being furnished under the supervision of a secretary of the Garde-Meuble specifically charged with this château. By this time the Garde-Meuble had established a rough hierarchy of materials for furniture in the imperial residences, beginning with painted wood for antechambers and mahogany in dining rooms. Lesser salons were furnished with painted—or painted and parcel-gilt—seats upholstered in tapestry, while only major state rooms received gilt furniture and Lyon silks. Within these dictates Joséphine followed her own taste and, with the cooperation of Jacob-Desmalter, filled her rooms with forms she knew well and had appreciated at other residences {FIGURE 81}.

The carefully planned ensembles of the empress's apartment were installed at Compiègne during the last four months of 1809, "conforming to the orders and the designs" that Joséphine must have given and approved. She was at Malmaison at the time,

FIGURE 81.

Bergère Armchair, French (Paris), 1809.
From Joséphine's Second Salon at Compiègne.
François-Honoré-Georges Jacob-Desmalter et Cie.
Carved and gilt wood,
restored woven-silk upholstery,
H: approx. 100 cm (3 ft. 3⅜ in.).
Musée national du Château de Compiègne.

• • •

The model for these seats had been developed almost a decade before by Jacob Frères and delivered for the Council Chamber at Malmaison, Joséphine's music room at Saint-Cloud, and Hortense's salon on the rue Cerutti and appears in official portraits of the first consul. Like many of Joséphine's favorites, it was reused at Compiègne almost a decade later. Here, the upholsterer uses the various-size woven borders to emphasize the carved decoration of the frame; the central motif, with a cornucopia forming the initial *J*, remained in place for the Empress Marie-Louise.

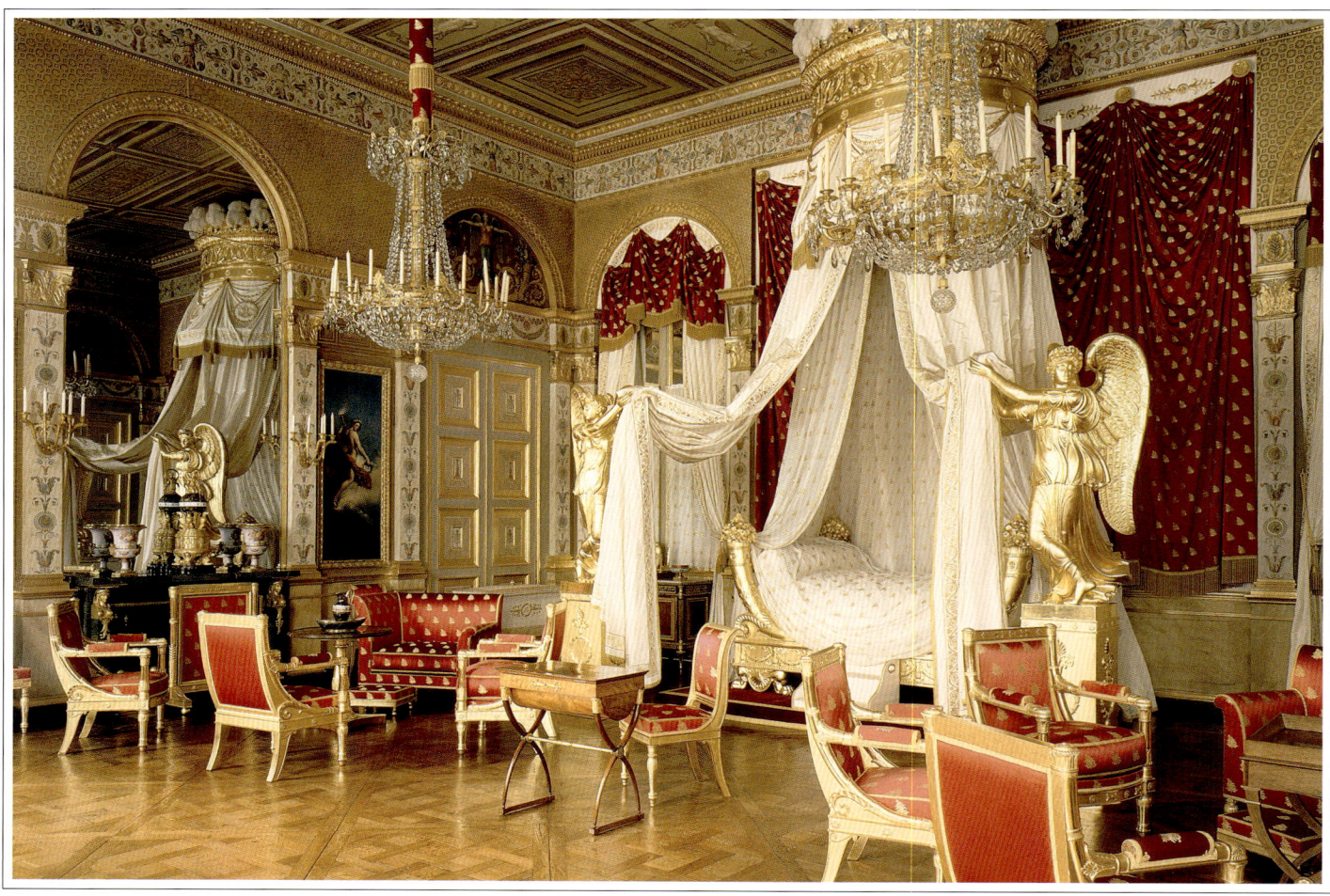

FIGURE 82.

View of Joséphine's State Bedchamber at Compiègne, as installed in 1809.
Bed and seat furniture by François-Honoré-Georges Jacob-Desmalter et Cie.
Carved and gilt wood, silk upholstery.
Musée national du Château de Compiègne.

• • •

A piece of truly imperial splendor, with the bed flanked by angels like a Baroque altar. Under the direction of the architect Berthault, whom Joséphine admired, she has come to terms with the Garde-Meuble Impériale. Stately crimon and gold are complemented by the frothy gold-embroidered muslin, similar to both Mme Moreau's bed and Joséphine's dress fabrics. Because of the divorce, Joséphine never saw the finished room; the emperor's new wife, Marie-Louise, slept in the bed, and Joséphine employed Berthault for a new state bedchamber at Malmaison instead.

however, and then at Fontainebleau, and finally in Paris in mid-December for the divorce, so she never saw the apartments finished. Instead, it was at Compiègne that Napoléon first welcomed his new empress, Marie-Louise, in March 1810. Her apartment was ready to receive its new occupant, including the bed with its symbols of fertility {FIGURE 82}, but the armchairs of Marie-Louise's salon still displayed the initial *J* of the woman who had planned the ensemble.

Although Joséphine repeatedly commissioned furniture forms that pleased her, the sheer number of pieces produced by Jacob-Desmalter for the various imperial residences led to the designs becoming repetitive. During the remainder of the Empire, the seat furniture for Trianon, Meudon, and the Elysée would show few innovations. Even the employment by the Garde-Meuble of other cabinetmakers from 1811 on—in an attempt to help the economy—would result in little variation from the models supplied for Joséphine in preceding years. Just as she remained true to certain shapes, she also continued to patronize the Jacob firm until her death—almost to the exclusion of all others.

While the form of Empire furniture remained static, its appearance changed after 1809. The Continental Blockade mounted by the British navy against French shipping halted imports of exotic timbers. The mahogany lyre chairs in Joséphine's dining room at Compiègne, a model first delivered half a decade earlier for the Tuileries {see FIGURE 75}, would be among the last of their type for the Garde-Meuble; the stocks of this Caribbean wood were shrinking and could not be replenished. Cabinetmakers were forced, initially by necessity and then by imperial decree, to look for replacement timbers and veneers. On the eve of the divorce, December 14, 1809, Anoine-Thibaut Baudouin (1759–1814) delivered an ash dressing table for the empress's bedroom at the Grand Trianon.[23] By 1812 Marie-Louise's new jewel chests to match Joséphine's great cabinet at the Tuileries would have to be made entirely in native woods; the last vestiges of the age of mahogany had vanished and the beginnings of Restoration and Charles X furniture were emerging.

After the divorce, suddenly freed of imperial duties, Joséphine partially filled her time with redecorating her beloved Malmaison. She summoned the architect Berthault from Compiègne to alter some of the older schemes and redecorate the salon and her bedroom {see FIGURE 55}. The latter introduced into still-Consular Malmaison the Empire style at its most fully developed; Joséphine may have been divorced by the emperor, but she retained imperial rank, and this setting reinforced it. Her choice of architect—and the gilt bed with its cornucopia supports and crimson, white, and gold hangings—recall the decor planned for her state bedroom at Compiègne. At the beginning of the Consulate period, the new regime had learned many of its lessons in furnishing, interior decoration, and elegance from Joséphine. For her final ensembles, she returned the compliment by adopting the style as it had evolved, for this is manifestly the bedroom of an empress.

NOTES

1. Napoléon Bonaparte, *Mémorial de Sainte-Hélène*, vol. 1, 280–81.
2. Bonaparte, *Mémorial*.
3. Charles Percier and Pierre-François-Léonard Fontaine, *Receuil de décorations intérieures: Comprenant tout ce qui a rapport à l'ameublement comme vases, trépieds, candélabres, cassolettes ... miroirs, ecrans, &c.&c.&c.* (Paris, 1801–12), pl. 39; the finished table, now without its upper tier, is at Malmaison.
4. Pierre-François-Léonard Fontaine, *Journal 1799–1853*, Paris, Ecole Nationale Supérieur des Beaux-Arts, 1987, 14.
5. Mme Reinhard, *Lettres à sa mère (1798–1815)*, 103, cited in Ferdinand Boyer, "L'Installation du Premier Consul aux Tuileries et la disgrace de l'architecte Leconte (1800–1801)," BSHAF 1941–44 (1947): 142.
6. Jean Coural, et al., *Paris, Mobilier national: Soieries Empire* (Paris, 1980), 12.
7. Hector Lefuel, *François-Honoré-Georges Jacob-Desmalter, ébéniste de Napoléon I et de Louis XVIII* (Paris, 1929), 124.
8. Coural, *Paris, Mobilier national*, 13–14.
9. Denise Ledoux-Lebard, *Le Grand Trianon: Meubles et objets d'art* (Paris, 1975), 77.
10. Fontaine's journal, cited in Jean-Pierre Samoyault and Colombe Samoyault-Verlet, *Le Mobilier du général Moreau: Un ameublement à la mode en 1802: Musée National du Château du Fontainebleau, 16 juin–14 septembre 1992*, exh. cat. (Paris, 1992), 9.
11. Lefuel, *François-Honoré-Georges Jacob-Desmalter*, 80–81.
12. Coural, *Paris, Mobilier national*, 15.
13. Lefuel, *François-Honoré-Georges Jacob-Desmalter*, 402–3.
14. Fontaine, *Journal 1799–1853*, 119.
15. Garde-Meuble Impériale, cited in Coural, *Paris, Mobilier national*, 160.
16. Garde-Meuble Impériale, cited in Coural, *Paris, Mobilier national*.
17. Laure d'Abrantès, *At the Court of Napoléon: Memoires of the Duchesse d'Abrantès* (New York, 1989), 309.
18. Garde-Meuble Impériale, cited in Coural, *Paris, Mobilier national*, 40–41.
19. Fontaine, *Journal 1799–1853*, 119.
20. Coural, *Paris, Mobilier national*, 41.
21. Lefuel, *François-Honoré-Georges Jacob-Desmalter*, 417.
22. Coural, *Paris, Mobilier national*, 59.
23. Ledoux-Lebard, *Le Grand Trianon*, 57.

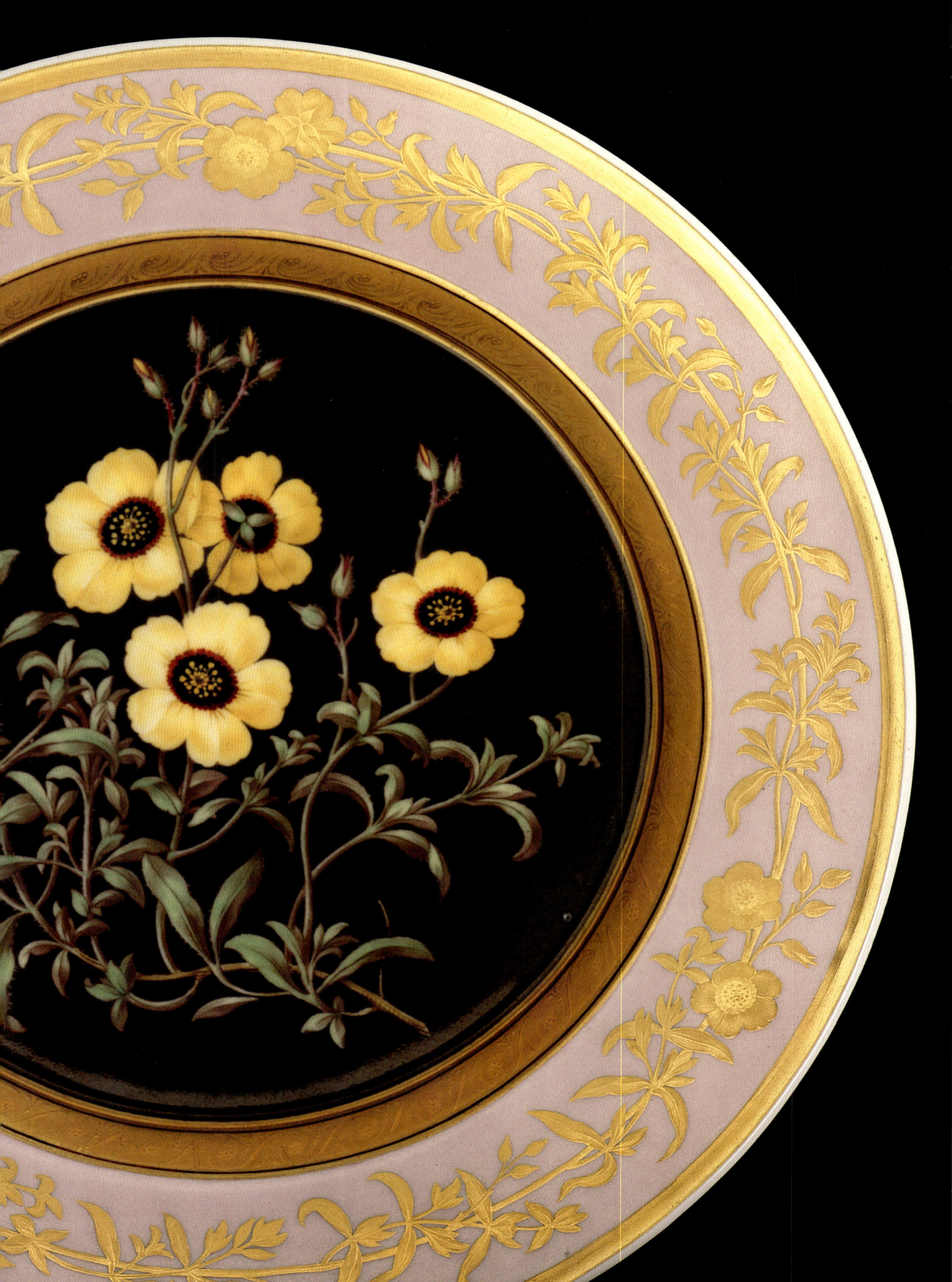

CHAPTER 7

BERNARD CHEVALLIER

The "Joséphine Taste": Porcelain for Her Table

NOTHING IN JOSÉPHINE'S BACKGROUND WOULD have predestined her to become a great connoisseur of porcelain. Little is really known of the framework of her life until the Revolution, but as the widow of Alexandre de Beaunarnais, she established herself in August 1795 in a small rented town house in rue Chantereine, then a fashionable quarter of the city. On March 7, 1796—on the very eve of signing the contract of her marriage with Napoléon Bonaparte—she ordered an inventory of Alexandre's belongings. Only at this period, when she was about to marry the greatest military leader of his time, did the first descriptions appear of objects that personally belonged to Joséphine.[1]

In the small antechamber of her town house on rue Chantereine she arranged in a cupboard a simple faience service with a *terre blanche* (white ground) surrounded by a blue border, beside which she placed an even less important service of plain white porcelain. The only somewhat refined touch was a *cabaret* (service for coffee or tea) made of white porcelain with violet and blue flowers. In the salon, crowning the chimney piece, stood three so-called Etruscan vases with a *terre noire* (black ground), one of which remains in the national collection.

Bearing the incised mark of "Wedgwood," the vase is of black basalt, or "jasperware," the name given by the Wedgwood establishment to this popular type of ware. With its handles in the form of fauns' heads and its decoration—an infant plucking a harp and seated on a lion—it is directly inspired by the decorative vocabulary of ancient Rome. Like all the furnishings of Joséphine's house, this vase was deposited in the reserves of the Garde-Meuble de la Couronne (royal warehouse). In 1851 it was sent to the Grand Trianon, where it was recently identified as Joséphine's vase, and in 1984 it appropriately joined the collections at Malmaison.

The museum of Malmaison also houses ten pieces of a table service that—according to family tradition—also belonged to the town house in rue Chantereine where the Bonaparte couple lived, and would therefore date from the years 1796–1800. The hors d'oeuvres dishes are in the form of shells, and the *chiffre* (mark), executed in trailing branches in the English manner, is entirely characteristic of ceramics made at the very end of the eighteenth century. Each piece bears the mark *JNB* {FIGURE 83}, which represents the initials of Joséphine and Napoléon Bonaparte.

According to long-standing tradition between Joséphine's family and that of Marie-Laure de Fénelon—who was born on the island of Martinique, as was the future empress—the service would have been given to de Fénelon at the time of her marriage in 1813 to the comte de Verdonnet, as the two families were very close. The remainder of the service is still retained among the possessions of the Verdonnets' descendants.[2] Made of *faience fine* (glazed earthenware), it bears no mark, but it might be attributed to any one of the numerous small manufactories that were active at the end of the eighteenth century, such as the one at Chantilly founded in 1792 by an English potter; the Montereau firm, which was likewise managed by an Englishman until 1797; or even the manufactory of Lambert at Sèvres.

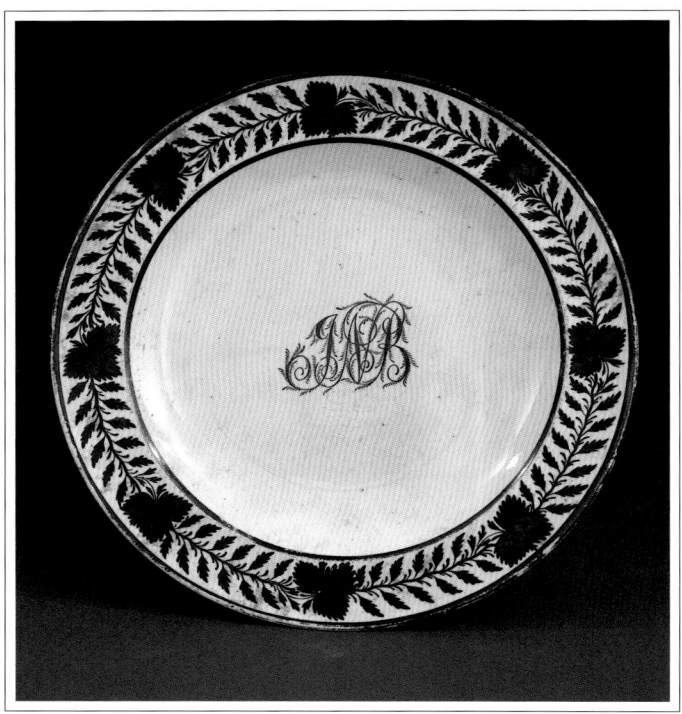

FIGURE 83.

Plate, French, manufactured by Chantilly or Montereau, 1796/1800. From an eight-piece series with the initials *JNB*.
Finely printed faience, DIAM: 24.5 cm (9⅝ in.).
Rueil-Malmaison, Musée national des Châteaux de Malmaison et Bois-Préau.

After the Empire was declared on May 18, 1804, and Joséphine was crowned empress on December 2 of the same year, she moved into the old palaces of the monarchy. Since the decorative vases and table services were furnished by the Manufactory of Sèvres, it is unknown if she personally intervened in the choice of the pieces brought to embellish her apartments or if they were simply imposed on her by the administration of the Garde-Meuble de la Couronne.

Although Joséphine did not actually see the final refurbishing of the château of Compiègne (which was terminated only at the moment of her divorce), and although the palaces

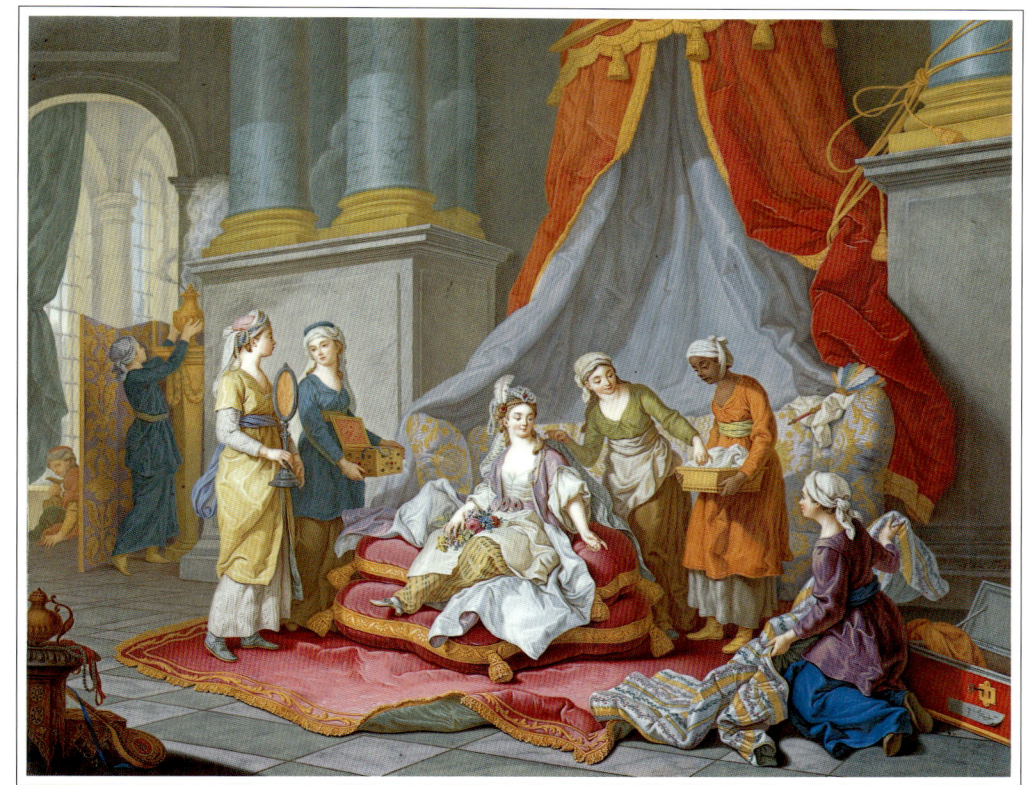

FIGURE 84.

Plaque, French, Sèvres, 1783. From the private apartments of Louis XVI at Versailles. Depicts *The Toilette of the Sultana*, painted the same year by Nicolas-Pierre Pithou the Younger (French, 1750–1818), modeled after a painting by Amédée Van Loo (French, 1719–1795) in the collection of the Chéret Museum, Nice. Hard-paste porcelain, H: 39 cm (15 3/8 in.); W: 48 cm (18 7/8 in.). Versailles, Musée national des Châteaux de Versailles et de Trianon.

of the Tuileries and Saint-Cloud disappeared in 1871, evidence of her taste remains in the furnishings of the château of Fontainebleau, where a number of vases still stand on the consoles and commodes of her apartments. According to the inventory of 1809, there were not less than forty-four of these, as well as a table of porcelain, several *vases de nuit* (chamber pots), water pitchers, basins, and clocks of *biscuit* (unglazed porcelain).[3] At least eight vases ornamented her Grand Salon and six stood in her large state bedroom, whereas in her private apartments, seven adorned her study and at least ten decorated her very small bathroom. This certainly attests to a distinct taste on the part of the empress for the productions of the Sèvres manufactory, which she intentionally accumulated to embellish her immediate environment.

It is in the château of Malmaison, however, that one can more accurately determine Joséphine's preferences in porcelain. For here no court etiquette was required and no choices were imposed on her. Here Joséphine herself chose the works she preferred. It is immediately apparent that she remained very attached to the taste of the epoch of Louis XVI, which recalled the aesthetic of her youth, and she loved to surround herself with the most beautiful porcelains that Sèvres had been able to produce at the end of the eighteenth century. Also, in the Grande Galerie at Malmaison stands the superb gueridon (round table) ordered by the comtesse du Barry, favorite of Louis XV, for her pavilion of Louveciennes, painted in 1774 by Charles-Nicholas Dodin (1734–1803) after *The Concert of the Grand Sultan* by Carle Van Loo (1705–1765).[4]

On the walls of Malmaison Joséphine also hung two plaques made of Sèvres porcelain that had decorated the private apartments of Louis XVI at Versailles: the first is *The Toilette of the Sultana*, painted in 1783 by Nicolas-Pierre Pithou the Younger (1750–1818), after a painting by Amédée Van Loo (1719–1795), which was acquired by the king in 1784 {FIGURE 84}. The second, acquired in 1787, is *The Sultana Giving Her Order to the Odalisques*, completed in 1786 by the same Pithou, again after a work of Van Loo.[5]

THE "JOSÉPHINE TASTE"

In 1803, following Marie-Antoinette's example, Joséphine ordered that a cowshed be built, accompanied by a dairy, in the woods of Saint-Cucufa near Malmaison, so she immediately reclaimed the pieces of Sèvres porcelain delivered in 1787–88 to Queen Marie-Antoinette at Rambouillet, including the famous strainer designed to drain the fresh cheese, and the no-less celebrated breast-shaped bowls resting on goats' feet.[6]

Yet one must not suppose that the empress's taste was only for old porcelain. Her name appears frequently in the Manufactory of Sèvres salesroom registers, and evidence shows that she was a great collector of hard-paste porcelain, sometimes buying isolated plates such as those representing *Paul et Virginie*, painted in 1804 by Lagrange the Younger (act. at Sèvres, 1797–99, 1801–3); *The Broken Pitcher*, a work of Martin Drolling (1752–1817) after an 1803 painting of the same name by Jean-Baptiste Greuze (1725–1805); *A View of the Champs-Elysée* and *The Hunting Party at the Pavilion of the Butard* by Jean-François Robert (1778–1832); or *The Battle of Marengo* by Jacques-François Joseph Swebach (1769–1823).[7]

Among the numerous deliveries to her was a remarkable pair of vases, now at the Museum of Malmaison, with a *beau bleu* (deep blue) ground and rich gold figure decoration. Delivered directly to Joséphine on Napoléon's order of December 10, 1807,[8] these vases were most certainly present in the apartments of Malmaison where such objects could still be seen in 1814 in the bedroom that the empress used every day, or in Queen Hortense's chamber, where "a pair of porcelain vases with blue and gold ground" is described.[9] Their shape—called *Etrusque carafe*—had been created in 1806 and repeated in every respect that of an Etruscan vase in the collection that Vivant Denon had sold to the king in 1786, still conserved in the Musée national de la Céramique at Sèvres. The figures on the two vases—a woman engaged in embroidery, another winding yarn onto a bobbin—had been designed by Alexandre-Evariste Fragonard, son of the great painter Jean-Honoré Fragonard and a decorator at the manufactory from 1806 to 1839. Although customarily inscribed strictly within the cartels, these figures are, in this case, freely painted on the rounded part of the vases, as was frequently done later, during the Second Empire. In light of Napoléon's opinion about the activities he wanted women to pursue, one may well imagine that the subject matter of these vases was not chosen by chance, but was perhaps his (playfully) malicious suggestion to Joséphine.[10]

It is not possible to list here all the isolated pieces that had belonged to the tea or coffee services that the Sèvres manufactory delivered to Joséphine. However, among her several complete ensembles, a few of the more remarkable ones may be cited: In November 1804 a beautiful *cabaret* with a gold ground, ornamented with arabesques painted by Claude-Antoine Déperais (1798–1822), was delivered, the whereabouts of which is now unknown. Then on November 20, 1809, several weeks before the divorce, two Egyptian sugar bowls by Jacques-François Micaud (1732/35–1811) arrived. Finally, two complete tea services in the Egyptian taste—one consisting of a dozen cups and six large pieces—were delivered to the empress on the emperor's order on December 29, 1808, as a New Year's gift (at a cost of 1,672 francs). The second service, eighteen cups and six large pieces (1,984 francs), entered the salesroom of the manufactory on December 5, 1810, and was not sent to

Malmaison until October 31, 1811. The order for the first of these two *cabarets* came from Joséphine herself, who had liked the one sent to Napoléon on October 2, 1808, that he later gave as a gift to Czar Alexander after the meeting of Tilsitt and today is in the Kuskowo Museum of Ceramics in Moscow. Joséphine previously had occasion to see it during the course of its fabrication while visiting the Sèvres manufactory in April 1807, when she remarked that it greatly pleased her.[11]

Joséphine's commission of this *cabaret* is documented in a letter from Alexandre Brongniart, administrator of the Manufactory of Sèvres, to Count Daru, general director of the emperor's household, as follows: "His Majesty ordered me today (August 25, 1808) to make for her [Joséphine] a breakfast service which perfectly conforms to the one which is part of the Egyptian Service. I have the honor to enclose the particulars of this breakfast service and what it will cost. We shall begin its execution this very moment, but it cannot be finished before a month or two. I ask you, Monsieur, to kindly transmit to me your orders on this subject, and also to indicate the course that I must follow in executing those for the Empress."[12]

The views of Egypt reproduced on these pieces were consigned to the painter Nicolas-Antoine Lebel. All of them were taken from *Voyage dans la Basse et la Haute Egypte pendant les campagnes du général Napoléon* (Voyage into lower and upper Egypt during the campaigns of General Napoléon, 1802), a book of engravings by Vivant Denon; the painting was carried out between June and November 1808. Although the subjects are Egyptian, there is nothing in the forms of the pieces themselves that suggest Egypt at all, for most were copied from the Greek vases that Denon himself had sold to Louis XVI in 1785 to train artists of the Manufacture of Sèvres in the antique taste.

Moreover, the names of the pieces are descriptive in themselves: a fluted Etruscan sugar bowl; an Etruscan milk jug with elongated beak; Denon Etruscan cups or a Denon teapot. Only the container for punch is called Egyptian, as is the strange Egyptian sugar bowl in vase form, mounted on a tripod of *faux bois* (imitation wood), in which the administrator of Sèvres took such pride, for it represented the manufactory's highest technical expertise. Appearing in the Sèvres salesroom on December 21, 1808, this *cabaret* was delivered to the Tuileries Palace on January 13, 1809, the bill of delivery carrying the personally inscribed consent of Joséphine herself, "approuvé Joséphine" {FIGURE 85}.[13]

Joséphine was not indifferent to this taste for Egyptian decoration, as she would amply demonstrate thereafter. On January 7, 1810, a few days after the divorce, Napoléon wrote to her from the palace of the Tuileries: "I have ordered that they make a very beautiful porcelain service for you. They will follow your orders so that it will be beautiful indeed."[14] A credit of thirty thousand francs was soon placed at Joséphine's disposal, and she had Brongniart come out to Malmaison to tell him to make another set of the so-called Egyptian service (which had recently been given to the czar), to which the empress decided to add thirty-six beautiful plates that were to be painted with various subjects.

Yet, without even allowing the time necessary for its production—which required almost a year—she was anxious to see it finished. She asked just how far the manufactory had progressed, but Brongniart felt less compelled to satisfy her demands now that she was no longer the reigning empress, so the ensemble was not actually finished until the spring of 1812. Finally, on April 1, 1812, twelve men ceremoniously transported this second Egyptian service to Malmaison. Joséphine, having reconsidered it, summoned the unhappy administrator, who—not a little discomfited—relates, "Several days afterward, Her Majesty gave me the honor of asking for me, and she told me that—after a more thorough examination—she found the service too severe, and that she would prefer to have another one, for which she would provide me the designs."[15]

The archives of the manufactory give evidence of Joséphine's desire to order a new service according to the designs of her architect Louis-Martin Berthault. It was not until December 17, 1812, that the invoice for it was entered, but since the empress did not give a formal order, it seems that the only piece that was finished was a basket decorated with swans, intended as a centerpiece, today in the Metropolitan Museum of Art, New York {FIGURE 86}. As for the Egyptian service that Joséphine refused, it was returned to the manufactory and then presented in May 1818 by Louis XVIII to the Duke of Wellington, Napoléon's conqueror, and is today in the collections of Apsley House, London.[16]

By a decree of December 16, 1809, Napoléon placed the Elysée Palace, the most splendid palace in Paris after the Tuileries, at the disposition of his divorced wife. After taking possession of it on the evening of February 3, 1810, Joséphine ordered that Sèvres deliver to her—beginning on March 9—a double dinner service, and dessert plates ornamented with bouquets of flowers as foil for the border with a *vert de chrome* (chrome green) ground. The dinner service was made up of thirty soup plates and twenty-eight large pieces

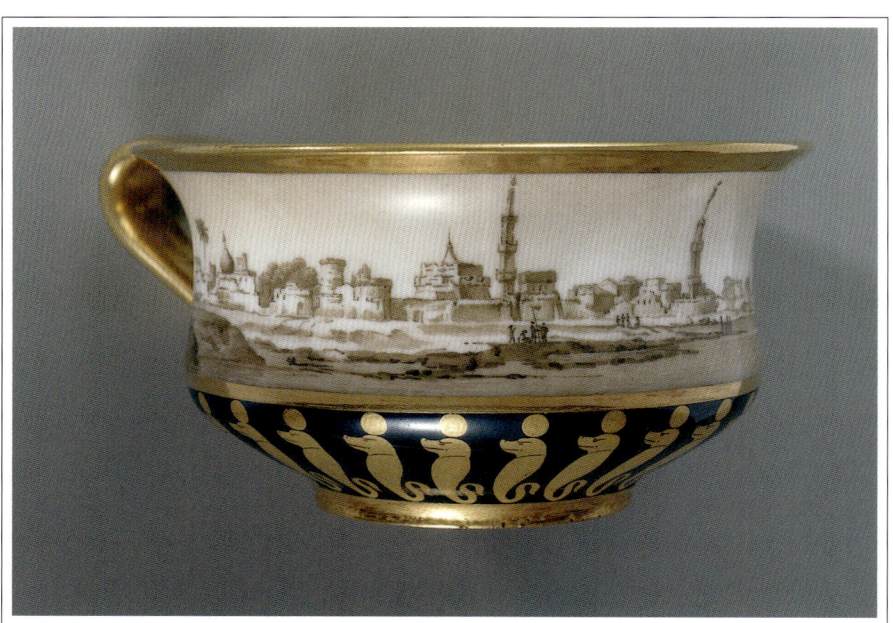

FIGURE 85.

Cup, French, Manufactory of Sèvres, 1808.
From Joséphine's Egyptian *cabaret* service.
Decoration by the painter Nicolas-Antoine Lebel
(French, act. 1804–45).
Hard-paste porcelain, H: 5 cm (2 in.);
DIAM: 9 cm (3½ in.).
Rueil-Malmaison, Musée national des Châteaux
de Malmaison et Bois-Préau.

FIGURE 86.

Flower or Fruit Basket, "Corbeille aux Cynges"
(Basket with Swans),
French, Manufactory of Sèvres, 1823.
Model by Louis-Martin Berthault
(French, 1771?–1823), 1814;
decoration by Pierre-Louis Micaud
(French, act. 1795–1834).
Hard-paste porcelain, H: 36 cm (14³⁄₁₆ in.);
DIAM: 40.6 cm (16 in.).
New York, The Metropolitan Museum of Art.

• • •

According to Tamara Préaud, when in May 1812 Joséphine rejected the *surtout* (centerpiece) for the Egyptian service as "too severe," she ordered a replacement for it. It was designed by Berthault and was made up entirely of ornamental baskets, such as this one, launching a new fashion in table decoration.

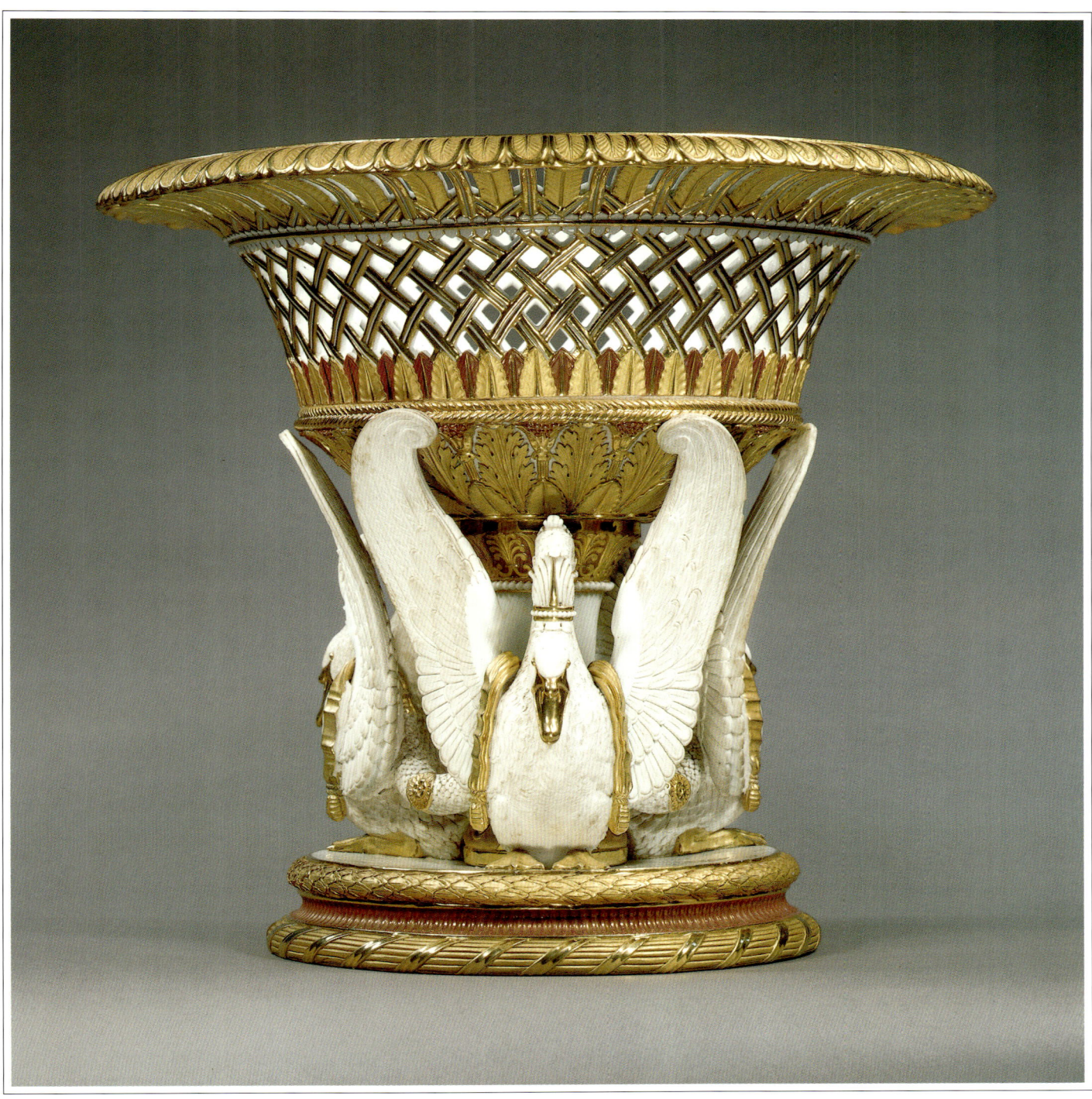

(2,560 francs), whereas the one reserved for the dessert comprised seventy-two plates and twenty large pieces (5,680 francs). They were actually services withdrawn from the salesroom of the manufactory, which they had entered on December 31, 1809, and not pieces especially ordered for the empress. It seems likely that these services decorated with bouquets of flowers were suggested to gratify her well-known taste for botany.

In 1812, when Joséphine was obliged to exchange the Elysée Palace for the one at Laeken, near Brussels, she had these two services transported to Malmaison, where they were at the time of her death in 1814, incomplete with some pieces damaged. In 1992 the Museum of Malmaison was able to acquire five of the seventy-two plates from the dessert service {FIGURE 87}.[17]

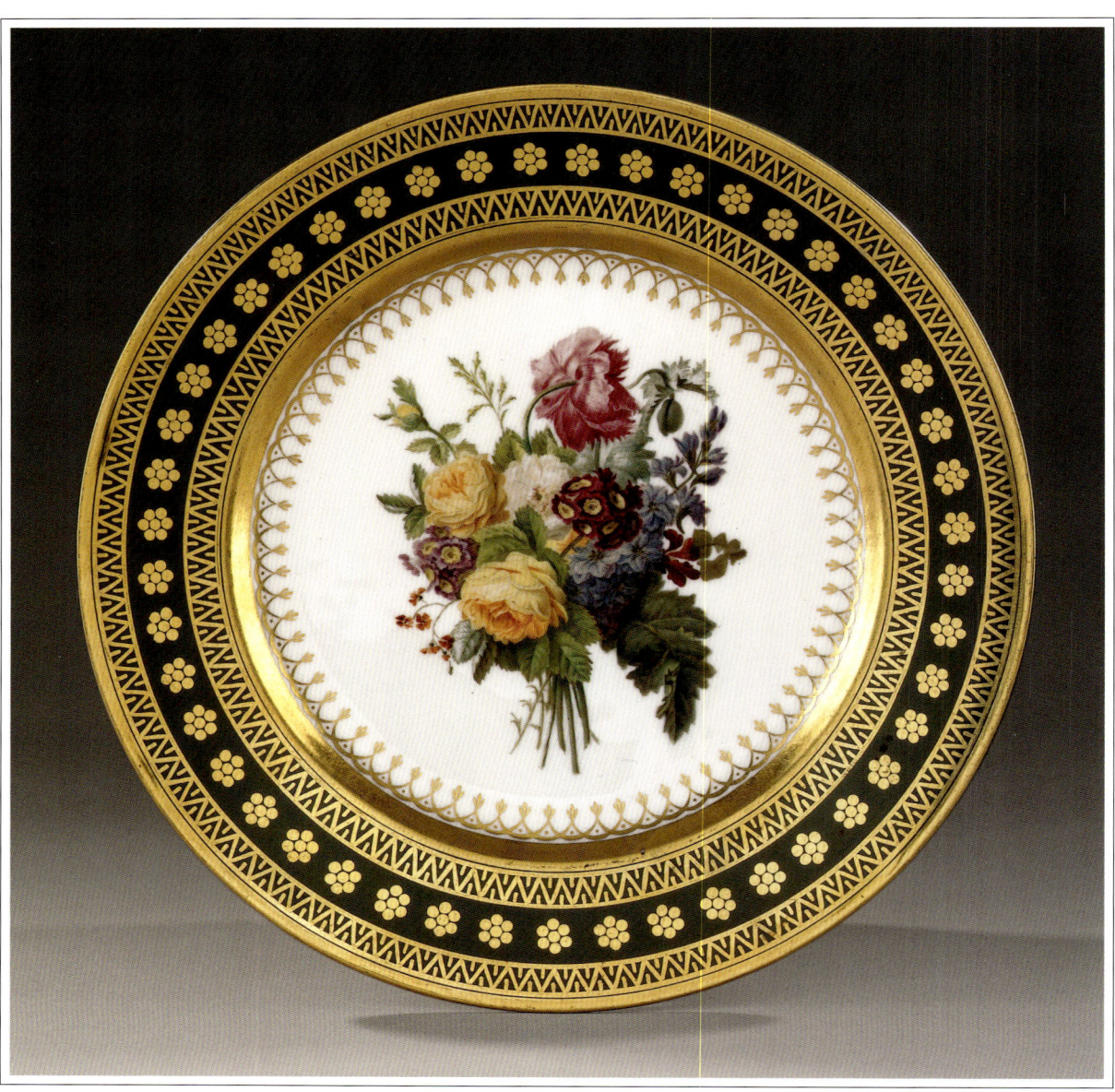

FIGURE 87.

Dessert Plate, French, Manufactory of Sèvres, 1808.
Decoration with painting of rose bouquet in center,
dark border with gold.
Hard-paste porcelain, DIAM: 23.5 cm (9¼ in.).
Rueil-Malmaison, Musée national des Châteaux
de Malmaison et Bois-Préau.
Gift of the Honorary Consul General and
Mrs. Proctor Patterson Jones, 1992.

• • •

This floral plate is from a seventy-two-piece series in
Joséphine's dessert service originally at Elysée Palace.

Thanks to diplomatic gifts to her while she still reigned as empress, Joséphine came to possess quite a large number of porcelains from the Royal Manufactory of Berlin. As early as 1805, Queen Louise of Prussia had sent her two very large vases painted with views of Malmaison (whereabouts unknown today), which the *Journal des débats* claimed "surpass everything that had already been seen of this type." They were accompanied by a handwritten letter from the sovereign, Queen Louise, dated Potsdam, September 22, 1805, that reads as follows:

> Madame my sister! My personal consultant Rosentiel is coming to Paris, with orders to present
> to Your Imperial Majesty in my name a collection of vases which she would have received some
> time ago if numerous unforeseen obstacles had not retarded its departure. It only remains for

me to hope that this product of our manufactory is worthy of Your favor, Madame, and especially that this inconsiderable token of remembrance proves to be of some value in your eyes through the sentiments of friendship which it brings to you, and with which I shall remain, Madame, the sister of Your Imperial Majesty.

The good Sister, Louise[18]

Apparently the vases met with Joséphine's favor because, beginning in July 1807, this same Rosentiel, director of the Manufactory of Berlin, sent a service to France that his company had made especially for the empress, obviously under pressure from the French authorities who—after the battle of Iena—occupied Prussia and Berlin. Nothing had been spared to please the empress Joséphine. Besides the forty-four assorted vases and ice cream pots, four supports for curtains, six groups of figurines, a statuette of the goddess Flora, and a bust of Napoléon, the service comprised 168 plates: 72 for knives, 72 dessert plates, and the remainder for soup, each plate representing an exotic plant, most of them copied from *Le Jardin de la Malmaison*, which was published under the auspices of Joséphine and painted by Pierre-Joseph Redouté. A part of the inheritance of the empress's daughter (although Queen Hortense did not keep it), this service was dismantled during the nineteenth century. Several of these plates appeared in recent public sales, and the museum of Malmaison owns four pieces, two of which represent "*Mesembryanthemum carinatum*, Cape of Good Hope" and "*Cistus algarvensis*, Portugal" {FIGURE 88}. Two of the four fruit urns are

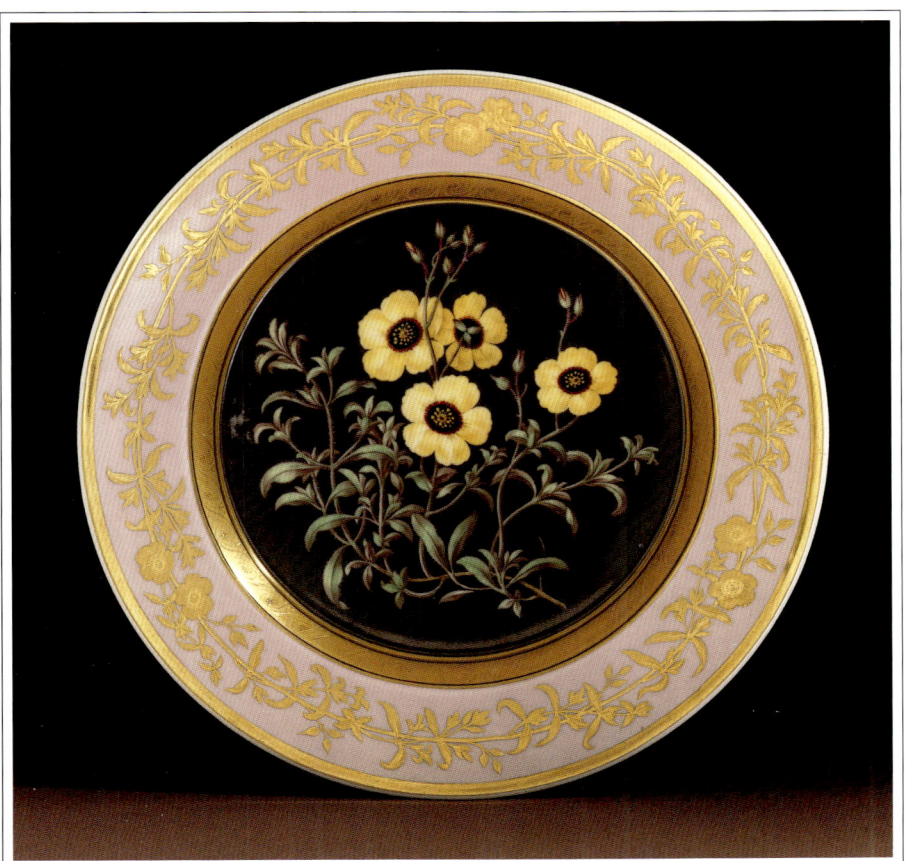

FIGURE 88.

Plate for Knives, German, manufactured by Rosentiel, Berlin, 1806/7. Decoration after the painting "*Cistus algarvensis*, Portugal" (White Flowers) by Pierre-Joseph Redouté (Belgian, 1759–1840). Hard-paste porcelain, DIAM: 24.1 cm (9½ in.). Rueil-Malmaison, Musée national des Châteaux de Malmaison et Bois-Préau. Purchased with the participation of the Society of Friends of Malmaison.

• • •

This richly decorated plate is part of a 168-plate service sent to Joséphine from Berlin in 1807, after Napoléon's successful Prussian campaign and during the French occupation of Berlin.

decorated with *Myrtus tomentosa* and the *Glycina rubicunda* {FIGURE 89}, copied from paintings by Pierre-Joseph Redouté.[19]

Joséphine did not reserve all of her commissions for the Manufactory of Sèvres. Respecting the traditions of the ancien régime, she quickly patronized, like all the sovereigns of her time, a private manufactory—that of Pierre-Louise Dagoty who, as soon as the Empire was proclaimed in May 1804, issued his invoices adorned with the arms of the empress; all the pieces of porcelain belonging to his factory carried the red mark, "Manufacture de S. M. l'Impératrice." Situated on the boulevard Poissonnière, Dagoty's establishment was one of the most elegant of the capital, and one could not even imagine a birth among those in high society that was not honored with a vase produced by Dagoty's atelier. The museum of Malmaison still owns four cups and a sumptuous inkwell marked "Dagoty," but none of these belonged to Joséphine. The disappearance of the Dagoty archives, as well as those of the empress, prevents a determination of the exact nature of the pieces made for her. It may be possible, however, to attribute to Dagoty the pair of *glacières* (ice pails) of simple white porcelain decorated with a crowned *J*, today on display at Malmaison, that would have been used on the table on days when there was no formal reception.[20]

The tableware cabinets at Malmaison contained several other services at the time of the empress's death, one of which is a very important piece in "old Japan porcelain" (of which there were still 215 pieces remaining in 1814). Another was of *terre de Naples* (Naples ware), consisting of 82 pieces, and a third in old white porcelain, to which had been added similar pieces that blended with it (256 total). Yet another was of *terre de pipe* (white clay) intended for the servants (374 pieces), and finally the most sumptuous of all—the one that was ordered from the manufactory of Dihl and Guérhard, and designated in the inventory compiled after Joséphine's death as *porcelaine riche*.[21]

However, instead of addressing herself to the manufactory of Dagoty, of which she was official patron, Joséphine gave her preference to that of Dihl and Guérhard, which had been protected before the Revolution by the Duke d'Angoulême. The excellent quality of the production attracted her attention, for the best painters worked there, including Jean-Louis Demarne (1744–1829), Drolling, Charles-Etienne Leguay (1762–1840), Piat Sauvage (1744–1818), and Swebach.

Founded in 1781, this manufactory had won a gold medal at the Exposition of Industrial Products of 1806. From the beginning of the Empire, Joséphine decorated her apartments at Saint-Cloud with Dihl flower vases that were her personal property. In the sales that followed her death some of the most sumptuous pieces from that manufactory were found. In 1819 two gueridons painted by Demarne and two large porcelain vases were sold, valued at the considerable sum of 3,600 francs, which is to say, exactly the price of the two Egyptian *cabarets* that Sèvres had delivered to her in 1808 and 1811.[22] Many of the gifts she presented to her entourage were in this category, such as the miniature by Fernando Quaglia given to Mme Bignon, widow of the librarian of Louis XV, or an inkwell with her monogram that Joséphine gave to Nicolas-Rodolphe de Watteville, magistrate of the canton of Berne, during a voyage to Switzerland.[23]

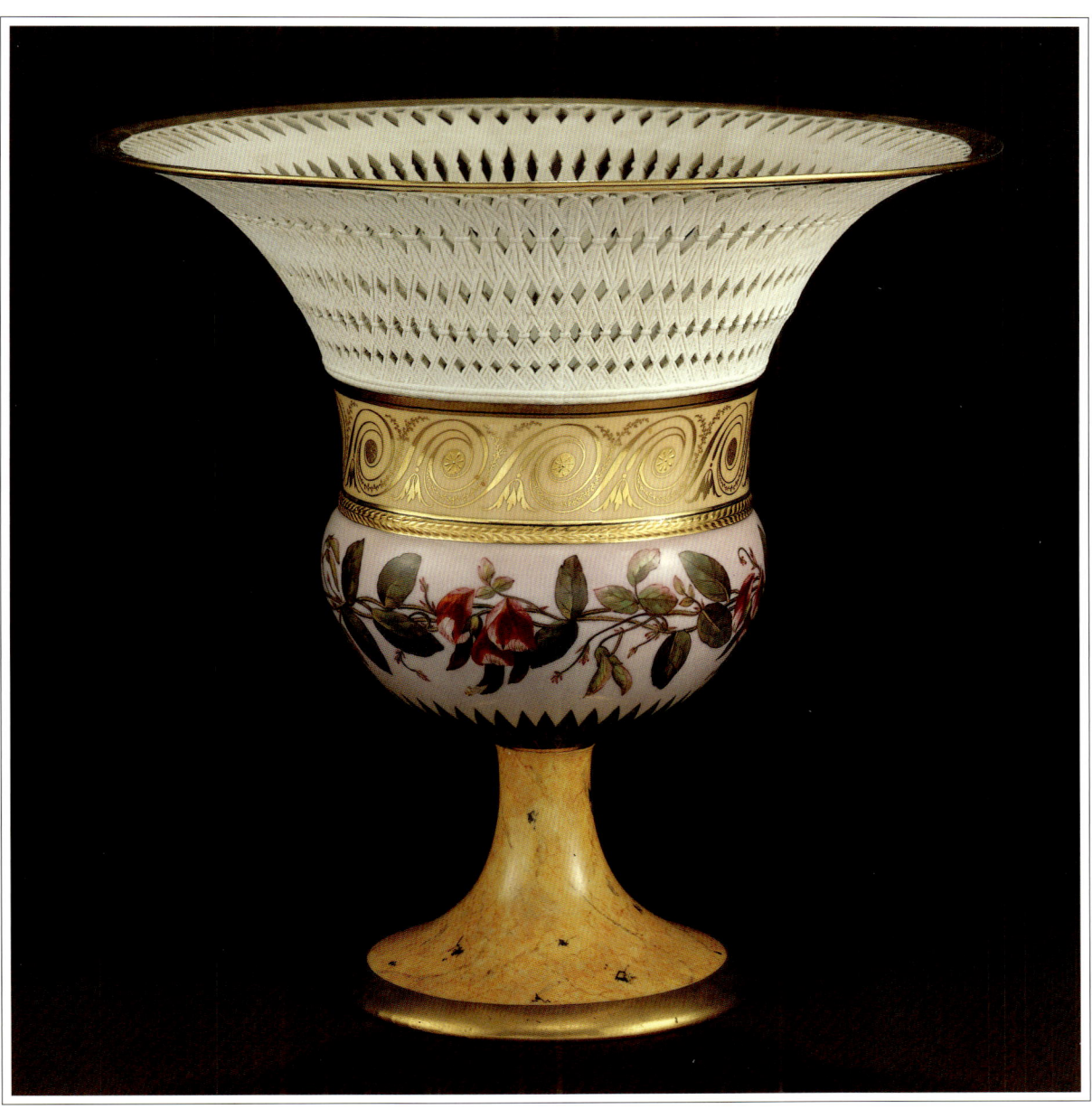

It was, therefore, perfectly natural that Joséphine should turn to Dihl to order a magnificent dessert service, most of which—accompanied by a centerpiece—was delivered to her in May 1811, with several other complementary pieces on June 4 of the same year. On October 2, 1812, there were others, and finally the last in 1813. It comprised 213 pieces and cost 46,976 francs, that is, about ten thousand francs more than the Egyptian service she had refused in 1812. It's not difficult to understand her reasons for rejecting it. Besides the severity and outmoded nature of the Egyptian pieces, Joséphine did not wish to be encumbered with another rich service at the very moment when she had just received the new one from Dihl. Its paintings, which were of unusually high quality, and the extraordinary burnished gold, which gave the effect of vermeil in the most surprising manner, explain the cost. Besides the numerous pieces entirely gilded and marked with her arms, the service contained two ice pails {FIGURE 90}.

FIGURE 89.

Fruit Urn, German, manufactured by Rosentiel, Berlin, 1806/7.
From the "exotic plants" service delivered to Joséphine in 1807.
Decoration after the painting *Glycina rubicunda* (Pink Flowers) by Pierre-Joseph Redouté (Belgian, 1759–1840).
Hard-paste porcelain, H: 28.5 cm (11¼ in.); W: 29 cm (11⅜ in.).
Rueil-Malmaison, Musée national des Châteaux de Malmaison et Bois-Préau.

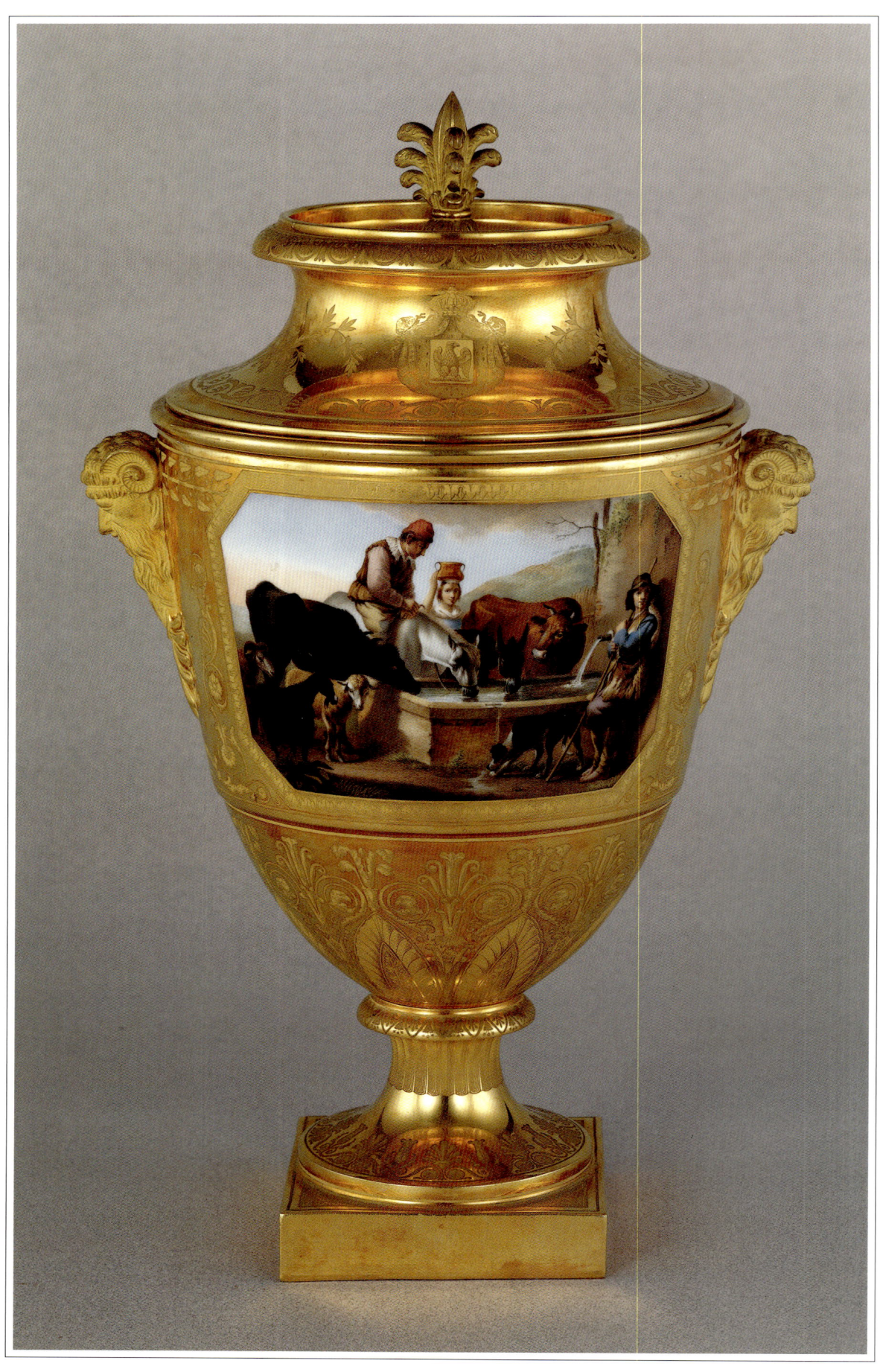

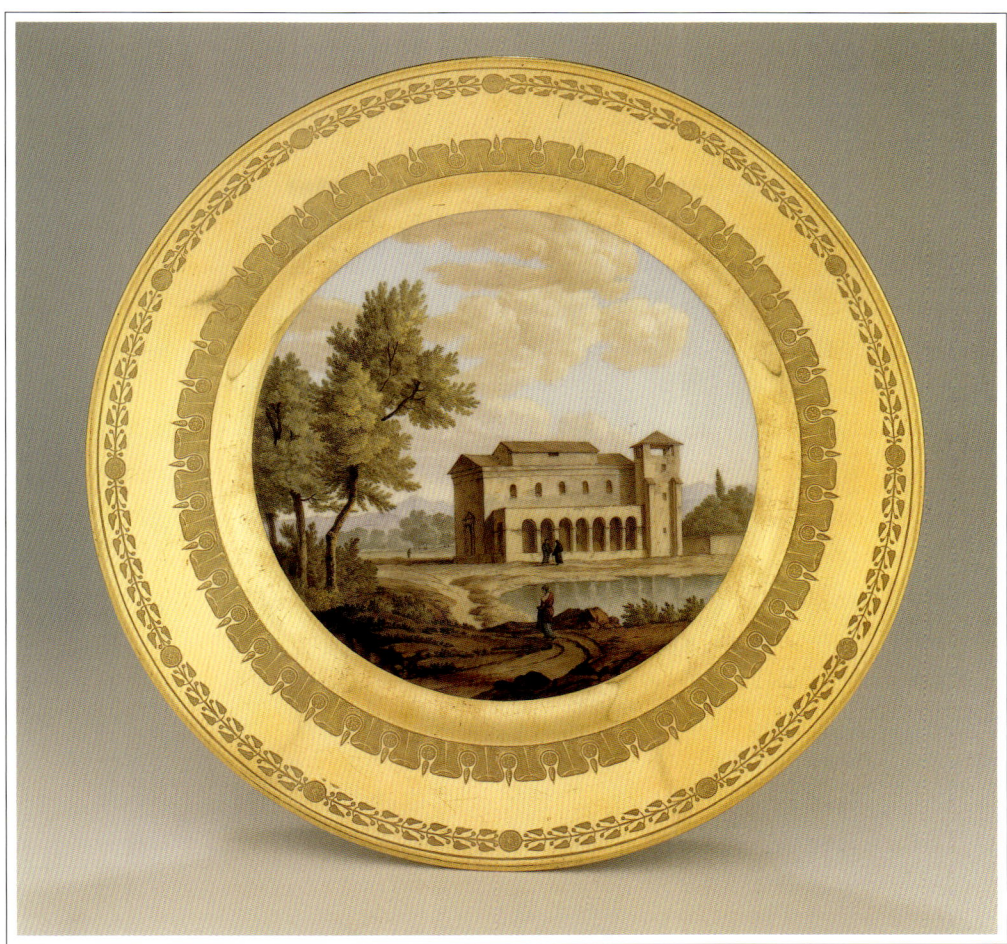

FIGURE 90.

One of a Pair of Ice Pails,
French, manufactured by Dihl and Guérhard, 1811.
From Joséphine's dessert service.
Decoration after the painting *Figures and Water Animals* by Jan Miel (Flemish, 1599–1664).
Hard-paste porcelain, H: 40 cm (15¾ in.);
W: 25 cm (9⅞ in.).
Rueil-Malmaison, Musée national des Châteaux de Malmaison et Bois-Préau.

FIGURE 91.

Plate, French, manufactured by
Dihl and Guérhard, 1811.
From Joséphine's dessert service.
Decorated with painted view,
"At Pisa in Tuscany," unsigned.
Hard-paste porcelain, DIAM: 24 cm (9½ in.).
Rueil-Malmaison, Musée national des Châteaux de Malmaison et Bois-Préau.

There were also eighty plates *à tableau* (with landcape scenes), representing the Dutch and Flemish paintings in her own collection, portraits of her grandchildren, and several landscapes of France but principally many sites in Italy. The last were copied by the painters at Dihl after engravings taken from two books, *A Description of the Kingdoms of Naples and Sicily* by the Abbé de Saint-Non and *A Collection of Views and Picturesque Garden Buildings of Italy Sketched after Nature* by Constant Bourgeois. This service was accompanied by a centerpiece made up of a large basket and four smaller ones, to which eight figures of putti and eight vases were added. Her son, Prince Eugène, viceroy of Italy, had ordered a similar service from Dihl and Guérhard, but a less extravagant one, for it consisted of only 93 pieces, of which only 48 plates were decorated with paintings. The gilt pieces carried only a simple *E* for Eugène, and there was no centerpiece.[24]

Reunited at the death of the empress, the two services—comprising 307 pieces—were sent in 1816 to Munich, where Eugène resided after the fall of the Empire as the duke of Leuchtenberg. When his son, Maximilien de Leuchtenberg, married the daughter of Czar Nicolas I in 1839, the young couple left for Saint Petersburg to live in the Marie Palace, where the double service was used by their descendants until the beginning of the twentieth century. At the time of the October Revolution, the service was confiscated, and a third of it—some 93 pieces—entered the museum of the Hermitage in 1920, where it is still conserved. It consists principally of the centerpiece in its entirety and thirty-four plates *à tableau*. The other part of the service passed to the West at the time of the sale of objets d'art organized by the Soviet Union between the two world wars, and it reappears sporadically on the art market.

Today there are forty-eight pieces—of which thirty-one are plates *à tableau*—on view at Malmaison {FIGURE 91}. Rarely had a richer service been delivered by a French company under the Empire. Even though not signed, the paintings and the views reproduced on the vases and plates are clearly the work of painters who worked for the Dihl factory, such as Demarne, Drolling, Leguay, or Sauvage.

A better appreciation of the work represented by the empress's service may be gained by comparing the price of one of the pieces with those made at the same time by Sèvres. Each plate *à tableau* was billed to her for 288 francs, or 432 francs, according to the richness of the decoration, whereas the plates of the Egyptian service cost only 200 francs, and those of the very sumptuous personal service of the emperor cost 425 francs. If the Egyptian *cabaret* that belonged to Joséphine is used as an example, each cup decorated with a view of Egypt was valued at only 72 francs, as opposed to 132 francs for one cup from Dihl. The pitcher, which cost only 150 francs at Sèvres, was billed by the Parisian manufactory at 300 francs.

In the taste that she displayed for porcelain—both ancient and modern—one discovers in Joséphine a mania for collecting, a determination to possess, that constituted a vital necessity for her. As in her love for botany, paintings, and antiquities, her pleasure was not found in possession itself but rather in the process of acquiring, and that veritable passion did not really appear until after Bonaparte's coup d'état, which allowed her the limitless resources whereby she might satisfy this intense desire. The education she had received under the ancien régime had informed her eye for beauty, but when she became empress, her aesthetic choices became so sure and authentic that, just as one often speaks of the "Marie-Antoinette style," one must also acknowledge the "Joséphine taste."

NOTES

Translated from the French by Eleanor P. DeLorme and Charles P. DeLorme.

1. The following is from an inventory compiled after the death of Alexandre de Beauharnais, March 7, 1796: "In a room where fruits were conserved, located on the second floor with a view of the garden: three Etruscan vases in black terracotta, which were used to ornament the mantelpiece" (old copy, Bibliothèque Thiers, Fonds Masson). Momentarily placed in the store room on the second floor of the hotel in the rue Chantereine (or the rue de la Victoire), these vases must have decorated the mantelpiece of the salon, and one of them reappeared in the "List of Furniture of the rue de la Victoire returned to the Depot the sixth, seventh, and eighth of May 1806, the objects which were either in storage or in the workshop of the cabinetmaker: A vase in English jasper ware (*terre noire*) with handles in the form of fauns' heads, on the front a child plucking a harp and mounted upon a Lion" (Archives Nationales, o^2 721 and o^2 502, dossier 13, document 44). Remaining in storage until 1851, it was sent at that time to decorate the great gallery of the Trianon palace, and was deposited in the Museum of Malmaison by a decree of January 17, 1984 (inv. GT 215 C and MMD 35).

2. On exhibit at the Museum of Malmaison are four large plates, four small ones, and two hors d'oeuvres dishes (inv. MM 40-47-1962 to 1971);

Gift of Mme Philippe de Vilmorin (née Mélanie de Gaufridy de Dortan, 1876–1937), the great granddaughter of Marie-Laure de Fénelon.

3. Paris, Archives nationales, O² 654.
4. Purchased in 1978 for the Department of Art Objects at the Musée du Louvre (inv. OA 10.658); see S. Grandjean, "Le guéridon de Madame Du Barry provenant de Louveciènnes," *La Revue du Louvre et des Musées de France*, no. 1 (1978): 44–49; Marie Laure de Rochebrune, *Le Guéridon de madame du Barry* (Paris, 2002).
5. The two plaques were bought by the Museum of Versailles in 1978. See C. Baulez, "Notes sur quelques meubles et objets d'art des appartements interieurs de Louis XVI et Marie-Antoinette," *La Revue du Louvre et des Musées de France*, no. 5/6 (1978): 359–73.
6. Archives des Musées nationaux, v³ 1812.
7. In 1963 the Museum of Malmaison purchased the plate with *The Hunting Party at the Pavilion of the Butard* (MM 63-8-1). Painted in 1808 by Jean-François Robert, this plate with gold ground was placed in the salesroom of the manufactory on June 20, 1808, and cost 330 francs. It was given by Napoléon to the empress on August 20 of the same year following her visit to the manufactory (Archives de la Manufacture nationale de Sèvres, Vbb² f⁰ 86; Vy¹⁸ f⁰ 52 r⁰). Thanks to a deposit from the National Ceramics Museum of Sèvres, since 1992 the Museum of Malmaison has displayed the plate depicting *The Battle of Marengo*, painted in 1803 by Jacques-François Joseph Swebach and delivered to the empress by order of the emperor on May 18, 1804, for a price of 600 francs. After having been taken from the palace of Saint-Cloud, this plate was restored to Napoléon III by Alfred Windus, lieutenant of a British Navy ship; the plate had been received from Lt. Windus's father. The emperor made a gift of it afterward to the Museum of Sèvres (inv. MNC 4793); Archives de la Manufacture nationale de Sèvres, Vy¹⁵ f⁰ 19 v⁰; Vj¹⁵).
8. Archives de la Manufacture nationale de Sèvres, Vu¹.
9. Archives de la Manufacture nationale de Sèvres, Vu¹, Vu¹⁴.
10. In the twentieth century, these vases adorned the palace of the princes de Thurn und Taxis at Ratisbonne; they figured in the sale of some of the furnishings of that property in October 1993 (inv. MM 95-1-1 and 2, purchase; Archives de la Manufacture nationale de Sèvres, Vbb² f⁰ ⁷⁷ v⁰; Vy¹⁸ f⁰ 29 v⁰; Pb 1, 1807).
11. Alexandre Brongniart, letter to Count Daru, April 10, 1807, Archives de la Manufacture nationale de Sèvres, T 3 l. 1 d. 5.
12. Brongniart, letter to Count Daru, August 25, 1808, Paris, Archives nationales, O²922.
13. In 1983 the Museum of Malmaison acquired the first of these *cabarets*, delivered in 1808 (Sale Monte-Carlo, Sporting d'Hiver, Sotheby Parke Bernet, June 26, 1983, no. 219); see S. Grandjean, "Musée de Malmaison, le cabaret egyptien de l'Impératrice Joséphine," *La Revue du Louvre et des Musées de France*, no. 2 (1985): 123–28 (inv. MM 83-9-1 to 30, purchase). The second *cabaret* has now been located, in part: The Fondation Napoléon in Paris already had one cup in its collection; in 2003 it acquired eight more cups and the teapot. Some other pieces are still missing.
14. Paris, Archives nationales, 400 AP 6, vol. 3, no. 200.
15. Brongniart, letter to Count Daru, January 10, 1810, Archives de la Manufacture nationale de Sèvres, Vc 4.
16. For the second Egyptian service, see P. Arizzoli-Clementel, "Les Surtouts impériaux en porcelaine de Sèvres 1804–14," *Keramik-Freunde der Schweiz, Mitteilungsblatt* 88 (May 1976). C. Truman, *The Sèvres Egyptian Service 1810–12* (London, 1982).
17. Archives de la Manufacture nationale de Sèvres, Vy¹⁹ f⁰ 2 v⁰ et 3 r⁰ (inv. MM 92-16-1 to 5; Gift of the Honorary Consul General and Mrs. Proctor Patterson Jones, 1992).
18. *Bulletin de la Société des Amis de Malmaison*, no. 31 (1997): 37–39. The letter entered into the collection of the Museum of Malmaison in 1996 (inv. MM 96-20-1; Gift of the Chamber of Commerce and Industry, Paris).
19. *Pflanzen auf Porzellan*, exh. cat., Berlin, Schloss Charlottenburg, 1979; *L'Impératrice Joséphine et les sciences naturelles*, exh. cat., Malmaison, Musée national des Châteaux, 1997, 180–81, 184–88. Two fruit dishes (inv. MM 40-47-7243 and 7244; Gift of Mlle René du Minil); one dessert plate, *Mesembryanthemum carinatum* (inv. MM 73-5-1; Gift of Dr. Erich Kollmann), and one plate for knives, *Cistus algarvensis* (inv. MM 86-6-1, purchase, with the participation of the Society of Friends of Malmaison).
20. Two ice pails (inv. MM 40-47-184; Gift of Her Majesty the Empress Eugénie, 1906).
21. S. Grandjean, *Inventaire après decès de l'impératrice Joséphine à Malmaison* (Paris, 1964), 84–89.
22. "Notice d'une très belle collection...le tout provenant du château et de la galerie de la M....," sale in Paris, rue Louis-le-Grand no. 16, March 24, 1819, and days following. Not included in catalogue.
23. Oval miniature on porcelain, signed at the bottom right "Dihl/at Paris" (inv. MM 70-12-1, Gift of the Society of the Friends of Malmaison): inkwell with monogram *J* (inv. MM 76-4-1, Gift of the Society of the Friends of Malmaison).
24. B. Chevallier, "Les services de Dihl et Guérhard de l'impératrice Joséphine et du prince Eugène," *Sèvres, Revue de la Socété des Amis du Musée national de Céramique*, no. 3 (1994): 25–29 and 74–75. *Bulletin de la Société des Amis de Malmaison* (1991): 42; (1992): 35; (1994): 40–42; (1995): 40; (1996): 36; (1998): 43–47.

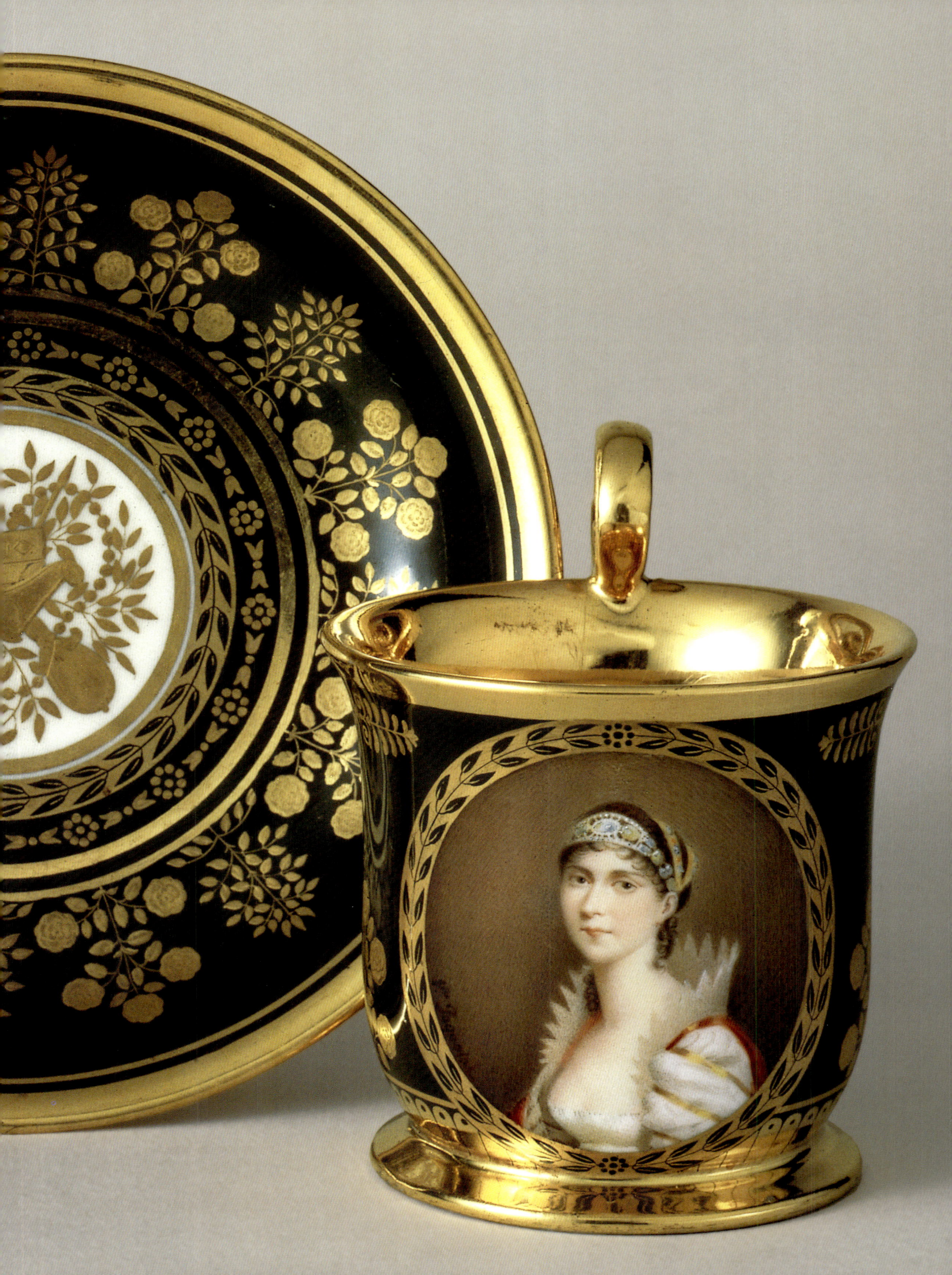

CHAPTER 8

TAMARA PRÉAUD

On Her Majesty's Order: Joséphine and Sèvres

THE PRODUCTIONS OF THE MANUFACTORY OF SÈVRES had been admired and copied throughout Europe in the eighteenth century, but the revolutionary period had practically ruined it, depriving it of its royal and noble clientele. Alexandre Brongniart, named administrator in May 1800, had to make enormous efforts to rectify a difficult situation; beginning in 1804 the manufactory was inscribed on the civil list of the emperor and finally received an annual budget, permitting it to function normally.

Joséphine certainly did not limit her purchases of porcelain to Sèvres alone. She did, however, maintain a consistent relationship with this establishment. From all evidence, the empress was a difficult client, constraining Brongniart to summon all of his diplomatic resources. He had received orders, upon Sèvres' being reinstated to the civil list of the sovereign in 1804 (and the injunction was renewed several times), to deliver nothing to members of the imperial circle or government without a written order from the *intendant général* (general administrator) of the House of the Emperor, and not to agree to a discount. Joséphine, however, insisted on several occasions that she immediately take possession of the objects she had chosen, intending to handle the administrative matters later. This is evidenced in 1807 by Brongniart's sending "a copy of the list of porcelains that Her Majesty has chosen and taken on March 11 at the time of her visit to the manufacture," asking for a formal order, even after the fact, and adding, "The Empress promised me that I would get it."[1] Then, armed with this order, he wrote to the *intendant général*, "The

Empress came to visit the manufactory last Wednesday the eleventh of the month. Her Majesty ordered me to give her several pieces, the inventory of which is herewith enclosed. She even had them put immediately into her carriage. Her Majesty was good enough, on my request, to give me this order in writing."[2]

This procedure was almost the same in December 1807, except that Brongniart, having learned on the sixth of the month that "Her Imperial Majesty wants some vases or a very elegant luncheon service" to be presented to the Tuileries Palace[3] and having been asked for proposals, immediately inquired "about how much must these objects cost since the price would guide my choice," noting a "pretty breakfast service... of elegant form... and a pair of vases with a *beau bleu* ground and gold figures by Fragonard for 1,000 francs."[4] The empress chose the vases {FIGURE 92}, and the register of deliveries specifies that they had been "delivered to Her Majesty the Empress according to her order."[5] The situation evidently became easier when it concerned orders whose fulfillment allowed Brongniart time to warn the administration and obtain the necessary orders or authorization.

Payment for the pieces bought by Joséphine was not without problems. It was not until February 1810, following a note from the secretary of Joséphine's expenditures, that Brongniart sent a bill corresponding to two purchases made in 1804; again complaining that the sum finally paid had been reduced from 3,804 to 2,000 francs, asking twice for an explanation,[6] only to get the answer that "the price reductions made on the objects delivered by the manufactory for the service of Empress Joséphine has been ordered by a superior authority; that is all I can tell you."[7] Since no such order has been preserved at Sèvres, it is not impossible that Brongniart invented it to be able to justify the price discrepancies in his accounts, inscribing in his registers, "by Imperial decree of February 3, 1810, His Majesty made a reduction of... on these porcelains."[8] The payments for these purchases until the time of the divorce were made by the imperial administration, once the administrative procedures were accomplished.

The problem of paying for them, however, reappeared after 1810, especially since Joséphine would sometimes change her mind in the middle of an order; thus in 1810 she asked first for the delivery of a complete service with a green ground; then in the end she decided to give up certain pieces and to take instead a similar *cabaret* and two small cream pots. Even though the purchase had been delivered to her on February 16, 1810, Brongniart had to ask several times before being able to register the sale in March.[9] When he had finally completed the Egyptian service and centerpiece ordered in 1810 (see chapter 7), Joséphine must have asked him for a reduction in price, since the administrator wrote on April 6, 1812, to her *intendant général*, "I am busy, Monsieur, as I had promised you, reviewing the prices of the pieces which compose the so-called Egyptian service and luncheon service delivered to H. M. the Empress Joséphine. My desire was to reduce as much as possible the

FIGURE 92.

Pair of Vases, French, Manufactory of Sèvres, 1807. "Etruscan" ornaments and figures designed, painted in gold, and burnished by Alexandre-Evariste Fragonard (act. 1805–39). Hard-paste porcelain, *beau bleu* ground, H: 42 cm (16⅓ in.) each.
Rueil-Malmaison, Musée national des Châteaux de Malmaison et Bois-Préau.

. . .

In a letter of July 21, 1808, Brongniart wrote to the *intendant général* about Fragonard, "For the moment, he only draws on the gold with the burnisher and has done in this line beautiful things for the manufactory." In fact, Fragonard had begun in Sèvres in 1805 by painting a plate in brown *camaïeu* (monochrome). Fragonard collaborated actively with Sèvres, designing shapes as well as decorations. A design for one of these vases remains in the Sèvres archives today. The vases entered the salesroom separately on September 30 and December 14, 1807, for a sales price of 500 francs, and were delivered to the empress "on her order" in December 1807.

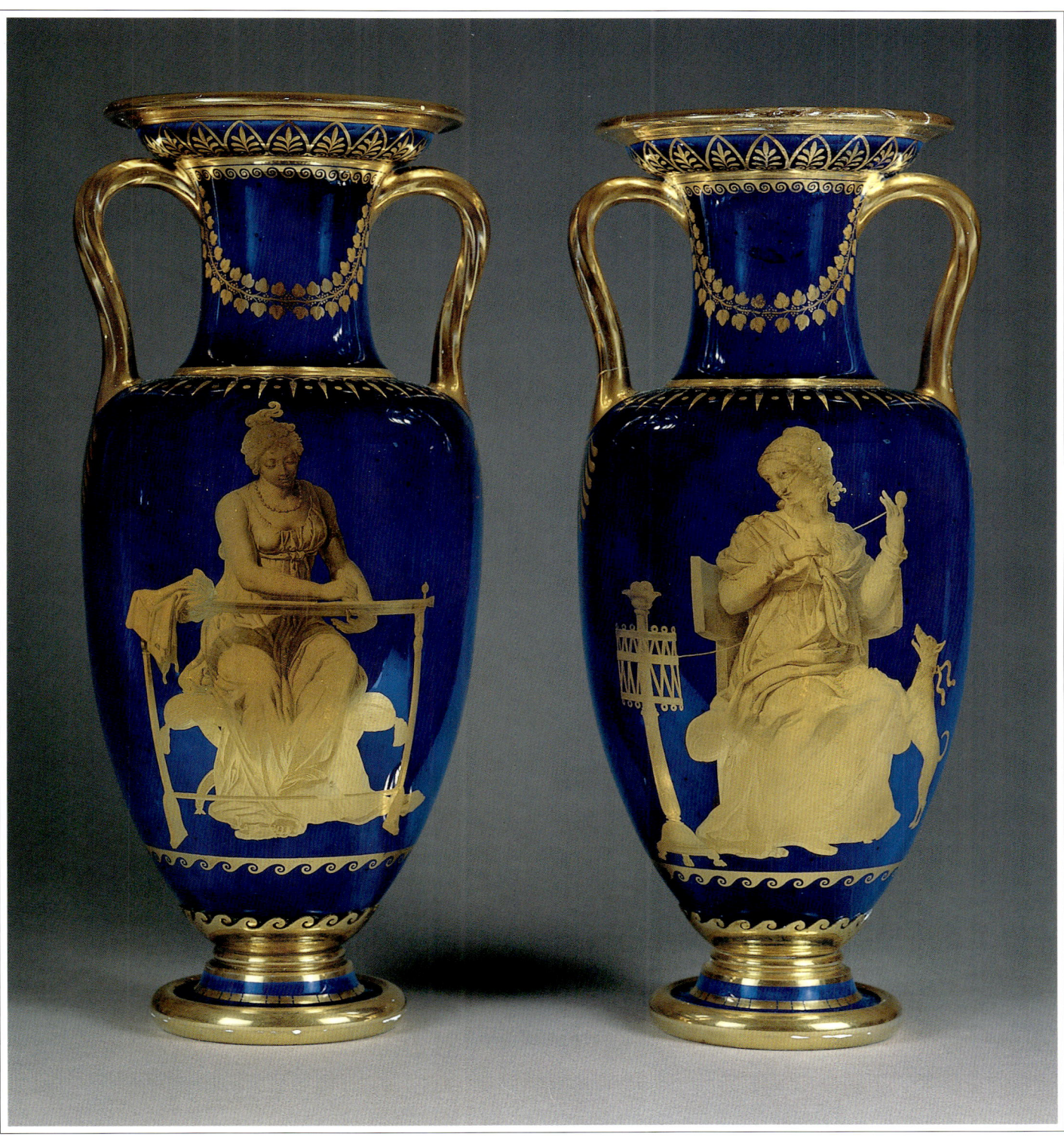

price of these pieces by not including the costs of the models, molds and [eliminating] other costs which have already been accounted for by the first service."[10] In the same letter he replied in like manner regarding the portrait vases requested in 1812, doubtless a little annoyed by these discussions about prices: "As for the portrait vases of H. M. it is possible, Monsieur, to make them for 800 francs per piece, but in order for you to decide about this price, you must envision the size and type of decoration on these vases compared with the scale and type of decoration of the vases for 1,200 fr."

In any case, it does not seem that relations between the administrator and the empress were too strained; apparently they even transcended the strict framework of orders and deliveries, since Brongniart intervened at least twice on the side of the sovereign in favor of the poor people of Sèvres.[11]

— The Empress's Image —

Joséphine paid very careful attention to her image, whether painted or sculpted. Several pieces produced between 1805 and 1807 are known, at least through documents, to contain painted portraits of Joséphine {FIGURE 93}, either alone or with Napoléon.[12] Nevertheless, as Brongniart wrote to the *intendant général* on August 26, 1807, "When the empress came to visit the factory, she found several portraits that we made for Her Majesty to be of poor likeness."[13]

Joséphine had made known her preference for François Gérard's portrait of her,[14] so Brongniart contacted this artist, who, busy with other orders, did not send anything.

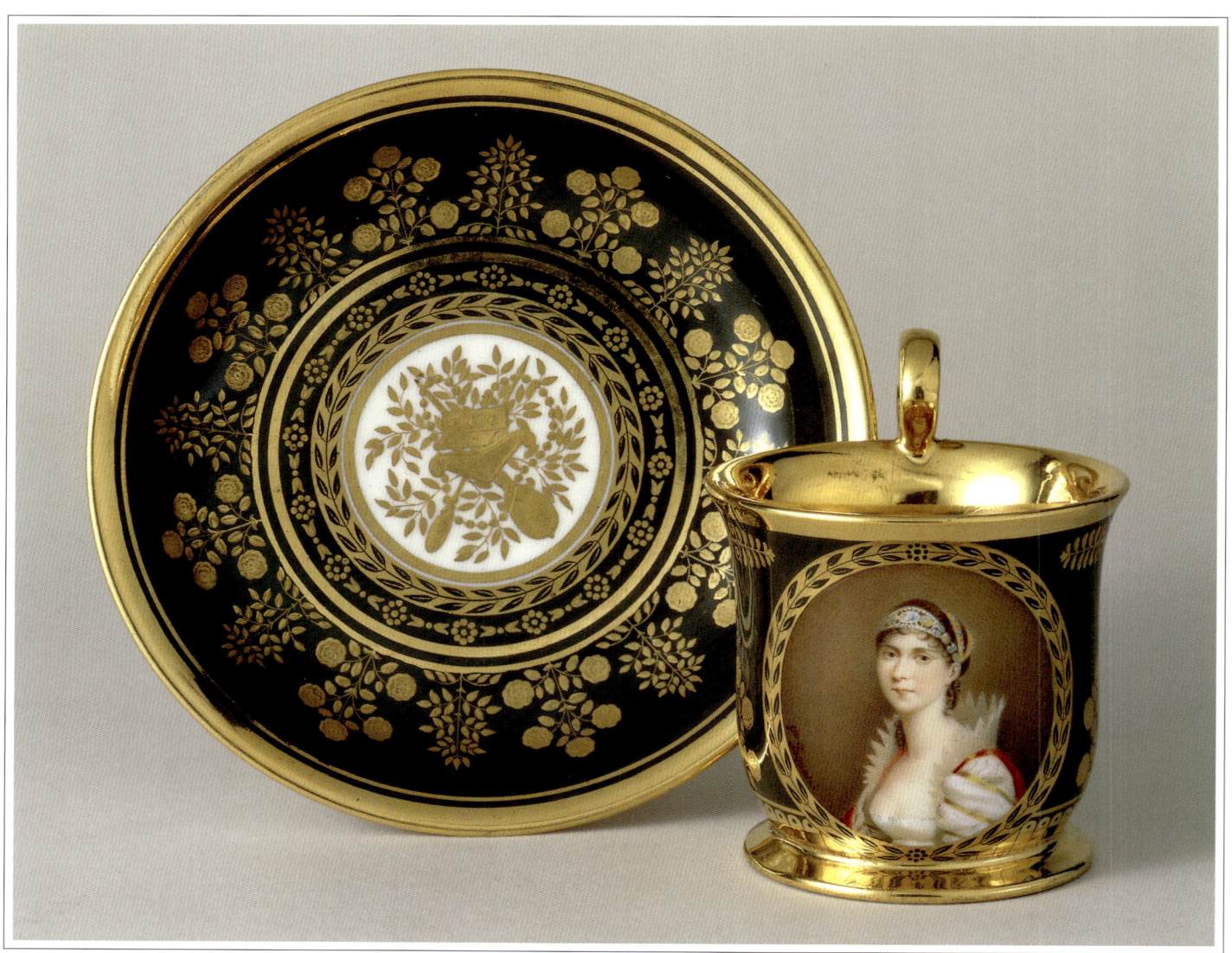

FIGURE 93.

Cup and Saucer, French, Manufactory of Sèvres, 1807.
Polychrome portrait of Joséphine painted by
Marie Victoire Jaquotot (act. 1801–42).
Hard-paste porcelain, chromium-green ground
with gold ornaments. Cup, H: 9 cm (3½ in.).
Sèvres, Musée national de Céramique.

• • •

The portrait is signed by M. V. Jaquotot, a gifted painter who began as a portraitist, was obviously much appreciated by Joséphine, and became one of the first and best of ceramic painters, copying old and contemporary masters on porcelain. This cup and its saucer entered the salesroom on January 31, 1807, for a selling price of 200 francs. Portraits of Napoléon Bonaparte had been painted on the same shape since 1803.

FIGURE 94.

Model for a Medallion Portrait of Joséphine,
French, Manufactory of Sèvres, October 1806.
After Antoine-Denis Chaudet (French).
Plaster, DIAM: 8.2 cm (3¼ in.)
Manufacture Nationale de Sèvres, Archives.

• • •

This portrait was one of several different models created at Sèvres and remains in the archives today; but the documents never specify which models were used. Two examples of this one exist: a small one (diam. 7.5 cm [3 in.]), engraved on the back *27 mars 1807 2eme gr[andeur]*; and the present one, engraved, *1ere gr[andeur] . . . chaudet rectifié en octobre 1806*; it is the only model bearing an author's name. All the medallions could be produced with the head in white on a blue ground (*médaillon camée*), in biscuit (with or without a border), or with the head only (*médaillon découpé*). The prices varied between one and seven francs.

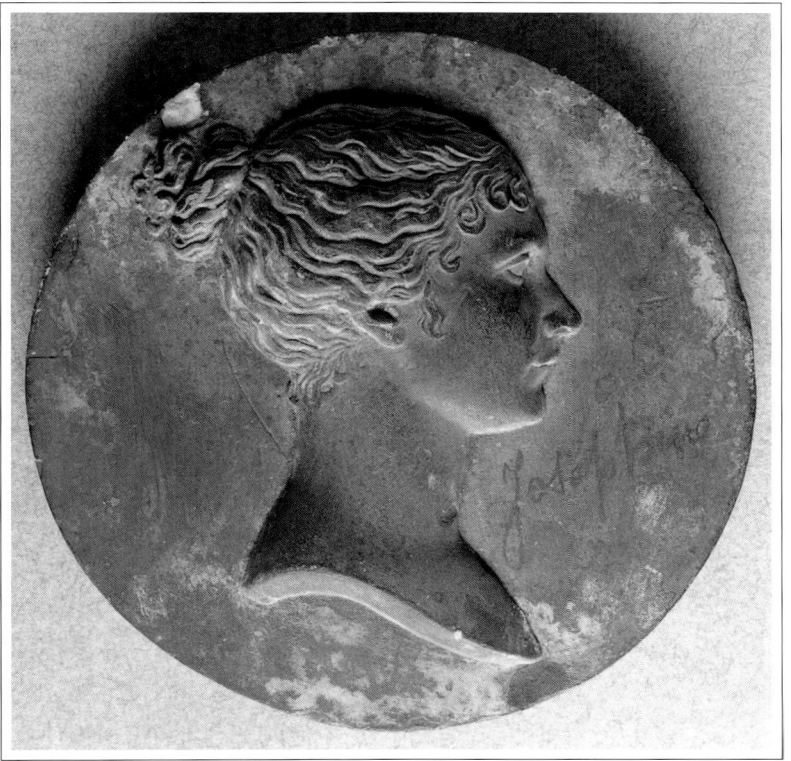

Brongniart's letter to the *intendant général* continues, "M. Isabey during this interval was kind enough to come to Sèvres and to himself execute a portrait of the empress in the center of a richly adorned plate. This portrait was a total success even though it was the first time that M. Isabey painted on porcelain."[15] It is not known if this plate actually served as the model for the several portrait pieces entered afterward.[16]

On April 12, 1812, Brongniart was summoned to Malmaison to receive a new portrait of Joséphine.[17] According to a letter from Brongniart to Baron de Vaux, we learn that it was a portrait by Daniel Saint,[18] intended for an order of three vases with portraits of the empress "according to the given model."[19] Only one was finished in time to be delivered to her on April 22, 1813.[20] Finally, she seems to have ordered some portraits of herself and Queen Hortense directly from the painter Marie Victoire Jaquotot.[21]

The manufactory also produced sculpted portraits in the form of medallions and busts. The Sèvres archives today possesses six models of different medallions {FIGURE 94}. Since the corresponding objects in porcelain (which were of little value) have been poorly conserved, and since the archival references are very vague, there is no information on how many of these models were actually produced under the Empire.[22] The first mentioned examples were fired on January 17, 1806;[23] it seems that several versions existed – in blue-and-white or plain biscuit, with enameled and gilt edges, or possibly with the head only; but nothing suggests whether it was always the same model, and the empress seems never to have intervened on this subject.

The first busts of Joséphine do not enter the shop at Sèvres until January 1808[24] and are then produced according to the model for which Chaudet was paid the same year.[25] This must not have been entirely satisfactory since, on January 30, 1809, Brongniart wrote to the *intendant général,* "Her Majesty the Empress called my attention to a bust that had been made of her by M. Bosio and which Her Majesty told me pleased her," asking that the promised plaster model be sent to him.[26] The first biscuit example of the bust after Bosio, much larger than the one by Chaudet, entered the shop in November 1809, with a marble base for 700 francs,[27] and it was immediately delivered to Joséphine.[28]

To summarize, purchases and orders from this important client remained relatively limited and, apart from the volte-face in the history of the Egyptian service, reasonable enough. This brusque change seems all the more surprising since the other deliveries reveal a predominant taste for Middle-Eastern Egypt in which one might acknowledge the influence of Dominique-Vivant Denon. Perhaps one could explain her often-mentioned relinquishing of the Egyptian service by a sudden realization that the price of this extravagant ensemble far surpassed the sum available to complete the "gift."

If the postmortem inventory correctly reflects her possessions, Joséphine seems to have given away a large number of pieces that she had either bought or received as gifts.

Notes

All quoted documents are in the Archives de la Manufacture nationale de Sèvres, unless otherwise stated.

1. Carton T 3, liasse 1, dossier 5, Brongniart to Jean-Marie Deschamps, secretary of Joséphine's orders, March 12, 1807.
2. Carton T 3, liasse 1, dossier 5, March 18, 1807.
3. Carton T 3, liasse 1, dossier 2, December 6, 1807, Dumanoir, chambellan of the empress to Brongniart.
4. Carton T 3, liasse 1, dossier 5, December 8, 1807, Brongniart to Dumanoir.
5. Registre Vbb 2, folio 77 verso, December 10, 1807. The vases had entered the salesroom on September 30 and December 7, 1807 (Registre Vu 1, n° 207.10 and 211.35).
6. Carton T 3, liasse 1, dossier 8, letters from Brongniart to Ballouhey of February 26 and March 14, 1810.
7. Carton T 3, liasse 1, dossier 8, letters from Ballouhey to Brongniart, March 21, 1810.
8. Registre Vy 15, folios 21–21 verso (28 *floréal* year XII [May 19, 1804]) and 42 (5 *messidor* year XII [June 25, 1804]).
9. Carton Pb 2, file of works for Josephine, letter from Brongniart to Richaud, officer of the table of the empress, February 21, 1810; and Registre Vz 1, folios 272 verso–273.
10. Carton Pb 2, liasse 3, dossier 2.
11. In an undated letter of year XIV [1805] (Carton T 2, liasse 2, dossier 5), Brongniart reminds Joséphine that she must "decide the amount she has been good enough to grant to the poor of the parish of Sèvres." Similarly, he writes to her on April 1, 1807 (Carton T 3, liasse 1, dossier 5), "I will be bold enough to remind Your Majesty of the petition I had the honor of giving her from a man named Brochard, a mason with a numerous family, whose house had just collapsed because of the flood of the River Seine."
12. Two "tasse et soucoupe à anse volute" with gold inside and cameo portraits of the emperor and the empress painted by J. Georget enter the salesroom on 23 *floréal* year XIII (May 12, 1805) for 150 francs each (Carton Pb 1, valuation sheet of 16 *floréal*)—one cup and saucer gilt inside with a *beau bleu* ground and a portrait of the empress enters for 180 francs on March 24, 1806 (Registre Vu 1, folio 18, n°178.9) and is offered on April 23 to M. de Cramayel (Registre Vbb 2, folio 64 verso)—a "Bouillon cup *beau bleu* ground portraits of Their Imperial and Royal Majesties by Parant" enters the salesroom on April 21, 1806 (Registre Vu 1, folio 18 verso, n°178.24) and was offered to Mme d'Alberg on April 22 (Registre Vy 17, folio 15)—two vases of the Fuseau form, with a pale blue ground, garlands of flowers, and portraits of the emperor and empress in the manner of cameos and gilt-bronze handles, entered the salesroom on June 25, 1806, for a global price of 500 francs (Registre Vu 1, folio 22 verso, n°182.11) were offered to M. de Champagny on June 30 (Registre Vy 17, folio 18 verso)—a bouillon cup and saucer with *beau bleu* ground and

portraits of the emperor and empress in the manner of cameos by Parent, supposedly entered in the salesroom on August 6, 1806 (Registre Vu 1, folio 25 verso, n°185.9) seems to have been offered to Mme de Bouillée during the visit of the emperor on April 21, 1806 (Registre Vbb 2, folio 50 verso). What happened to the cup of Jasmin shape and its saucer with a gold ground, a polychrome portrait of the empress and ornaments in grisaille, entered for 240 francs on November 30, 1806 (Registre Vu 1, folio 30 verso, n° 190.42) is unknown. The cup with a volute handle, chromium green ground, and portrait of the empress entered for 200 francs on January 31, 1807 (Registre Vu 1, folio 34 verso, n° 194.42) is probably the one painted by Marie Victoire Jaquotot that is today in the Musée national de Céramique, Sèvres.

13. Carton T 3, liasse 1, dossier 5.
14. Carton T 3, liasse 1, dossier 5, letter from Brongniart to Joséphine, April 1, 1807.
15. The plate painted by Isabey entered the salesroom for 400 francs on August 26, 1807 (Registre Vu 1, folio 45, n°205.18).
16. A cup and saucer, Jasmin shape, gold ground, gray ornaments and portrait, entered in the salesroom for 340 francs on December 28, 1807 (Registre Vu 1, folio 52, n° 212.3)—another same shape, chromium green ground, entered for 350 francs on September 13, 1809 (same register, folio 82 verso, n° 242.35)—a cup and saucer with gold band and printed portraits of the emperor and the empress entered for 7 francs on October 18, 1809 (Registre Vu 1, folio 84 verso, n° 244.19)—a cup and saucer, Jasmin form, gold ground, with portrait, entered for 350 francs on August 17, 1810 (Registre Vu 1, folio 98, n° 258.18), probably the one painted by Marie Victoire Jaquotot that is today in the Musée national de Céramique, Sèvres (inv. 2008). Two vases, Oeuf shape, with chromium green ground and standing portraits of the emperor and empress painted like cameos by Parent, entered for a global price of 7,000 francs on December 4, 1811 (Registre Vu 1, folio 121 verso, n° 281.22) were offered to Eugène de Beauharnais, viceroy of Italy, on December 31 of the same year (Registre Vbb 4, folio 4 verso).
17. Carton Pb 2, liasse 3, dossier 2, letter from Beaumont, Joséphine's *chevalier d'honneur*, to Brongniart.
18. Carton T 7, liasse 4, dossier 1, letter of July 8, 1814: "I have a miniature portrait of Empress Joséphine by Saint; since it has been trusted to me only so that I could have copies made at Sèvres, I will give it back to whomever you will designate."
19. Registre Vtt 1, folio 4 verso, May 28, 1812. The empress wanted one vase of Fuseau shape, second size and three third size, with a blue or green ground, gilt ornaments, and bronze handles.
20. Carton Pb 2, liasse 2, invoice of April 22, 1813. The vase was in a private collection; see Serge Grandjean, "Du nouveau sur les collections de Joséphine à Malmaison," *Hommage à Hubert Landais* (Paris, 1987), 176–79, fig. 8.
21. Carton T 6, liasse 2, dossier 4, letter from Marie Victoire Jaquotot to Brongniart of June 21, 1813, and dossier 5, Brongniart's reply of June 22, protesting that he cannot accept such an order without following the normal rules.
22. Only one model, known in two sizes, showing Joséphine in right profile, bears on the small size *27 mars 1807/2eme g[ran]d[eu]r*, and on the larger *Iere gdr. Chaudet rectifie en octobre 1806*.
23. Registre Vc' 6, kilns of January 17, 1806, and ff.
24. Registre Vy 20, folio 36, n°9, four busts, 72 francs each.
25. Bernard Chevallier, *Napoléon*, exh. cat. 24 (Montréal, Musée Stewart, 1999), 107. For the payment to Chaudet, see Registre Vf 58 (1808), folios 2 verso (March 12) and 3 verso (March 24). Nine of these busts, including a slightly defective one, entered the salesroom during the Empire.
26. Carton T 1, liasse 2, dossier 4.
27. Registre Y 20, folio 40 verso, n° 38 bis. Production price 400 francs.
28. Registre Vbb 2, folio 98, November 20, 1809. It would appear that only one other bust of this type entered the salesroom during the Empire period, in March 1810, for 600 francs, also with a marble base (Registre Y 20, folio 42, n°17). For this model, see *Les Oeuvres de la Manufacture nationale de Sèvres*, vol. 1, *La Sculpture de 1738 à 1815* (Paris, n.d. [ca. 1932]), ill. n° 379, pl. 57.

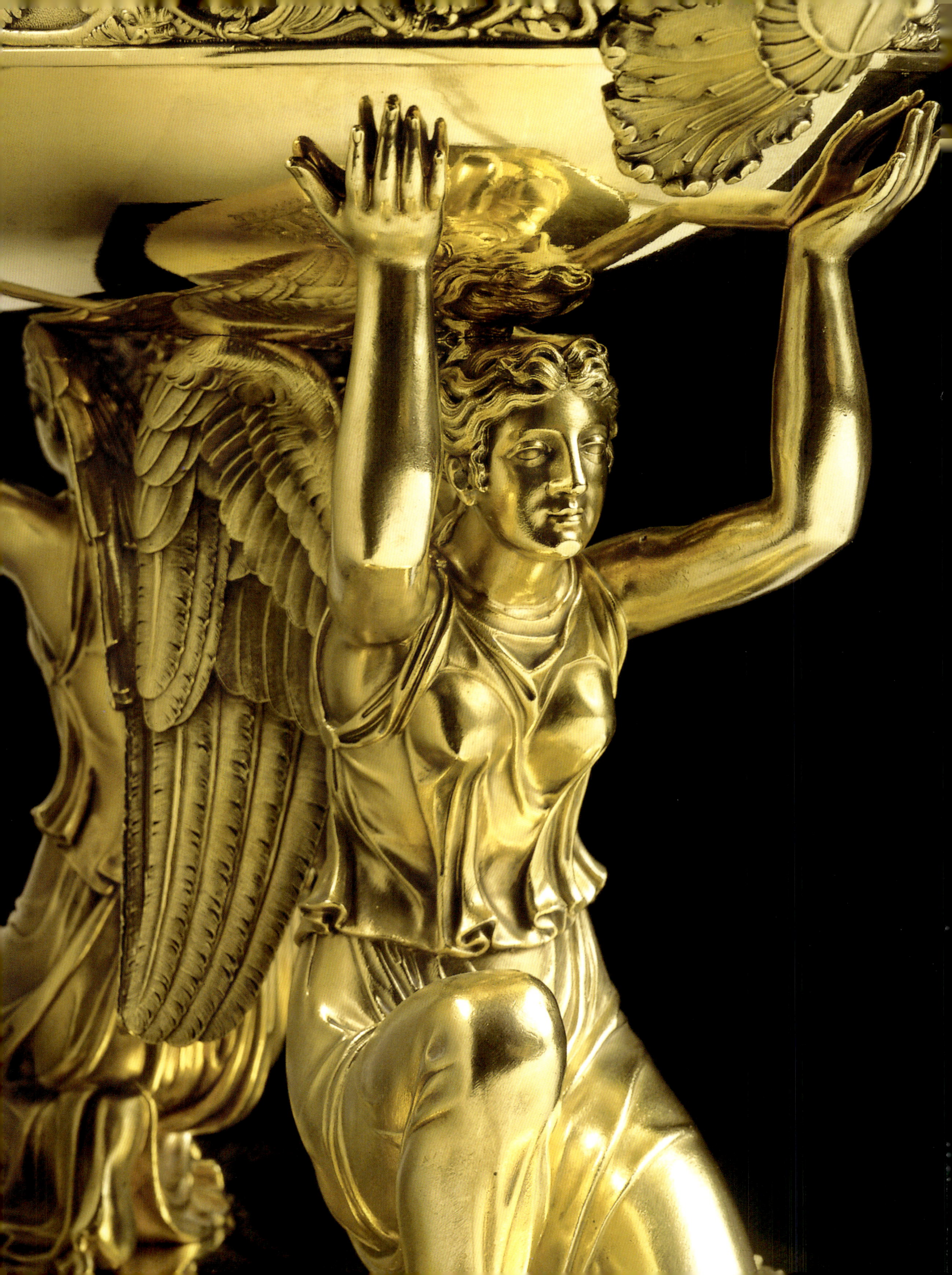

CHAPTER 9

CHRISTOPHER HARTOP

Empire Silver: A Gilded Age

JOSÉPHINE'S REFINED TASTE, combined with her insatiable appetite for *objets de luxe*, that became one of the driving forces in the adoption of the new taste for gilded silver in the first decade of the nineteenth century. So many silver vessels were gold-plated that, combined with the ormolu clocks, candelabra, and torchères from Thomire's workshop, and the ubiquitous gold-plated mounts on mahogany furniture, they ensured that the days of the Empire were truly an *age d'or*.

The taste for gold had its origins, like so many attributes of the empire, in ancient Rome.[1] Nero had seen the incorruptibility of gold as the symbol of immortality, and it was just such splendor that Napoléon needed to give a sense of permanence to his new regime. To gild entire dinner services, as became the norm during the Empire, would have been inconceivable before the Revolution. From the Middle Ages until the end of the eighteenth century, gilding had been a difficult and expensive process that was used sparingly on silver, sometimes to create a contrast with the white sheen on the body of a vessel but more often for the practical purpose of protecting silver from pitting or discoloration caused by the acid in fruit or wine, or by salt.

The dignified version of Neoclassicism that we know today as the Empire style, with its cool simplicity, was admirably suited to such lavish use of gold. Light and elegant classical outlines were found on the dining table, the dressing table, and even in those

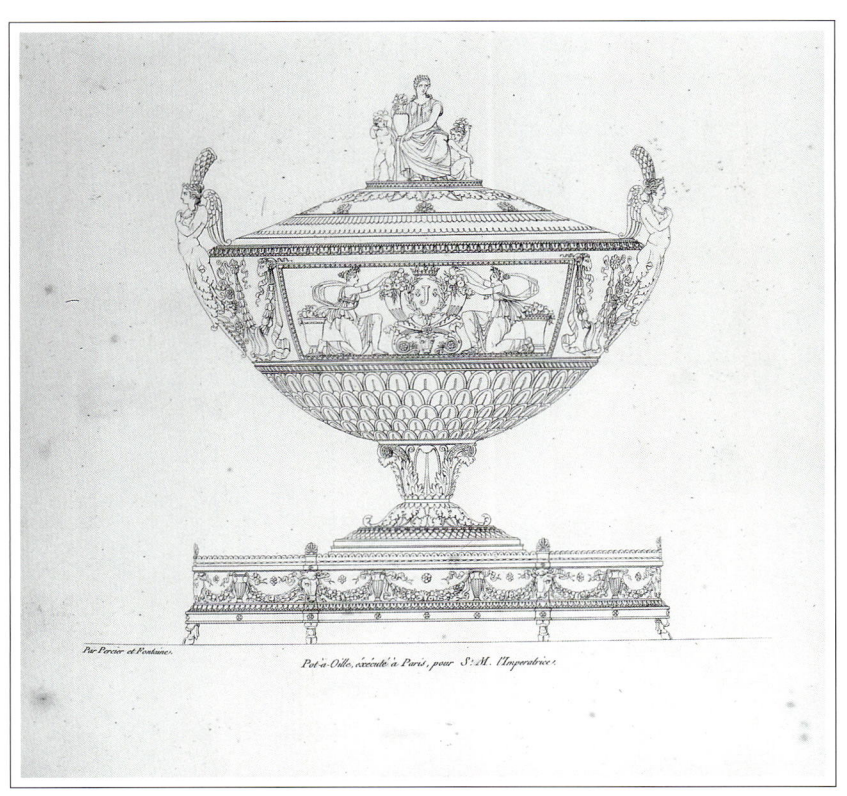

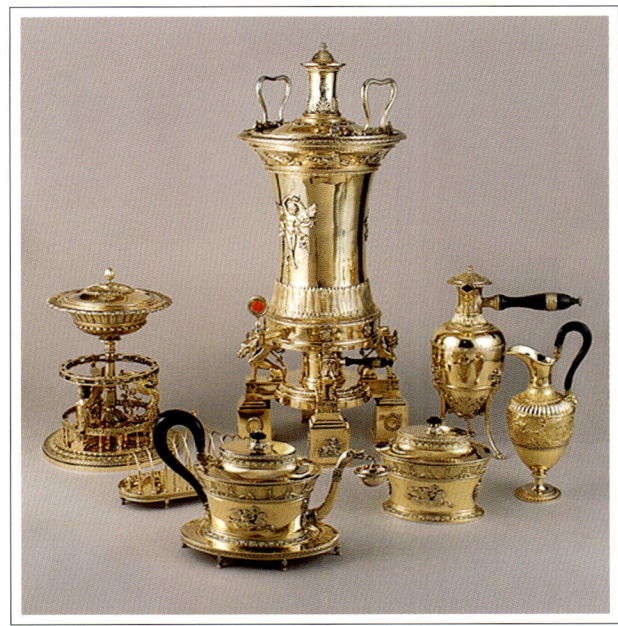

FIGURE 95.

Charles Percier (French, 1764–1838) and Pierre-François-Léonard Fontaine (French, 1762–1853), *Design for a Tureen and Stand for the Empress Joséphine*, French (Paris), 1812. Engraving from Percier and Fontaine, *Recueil de décorations intérieures* (Paris, 1812 ed.), plate 46. New York, Cooper-Hewitt Museum, Gift of the Council.

• • •

Percier and Fontaine's published designs document pieces made for Joséphine that disappeared long ago. Joséphine remained an enthusiastic patron of the designing partnership until her death.

FIGURE 96.

Tea Service, French (Paris). Made for Joséphine, supplied by Martin-Guillaume Biennais between 1796 and 1809. Maker's mark of Marie-Joseph-Gabriel Genu. Silver-gilt. Private collection.

• • •

Although ordered from Biennais over a period of some thirteen years, this service has the remarkable consistency of form and decoration that is a hallmark of Empire silver.

ravishing fitted traveling cases, called *nécessaires de voyage*, which became popular after Napoléon ordered one to take on his Egyptian campaign in 1798. Yet while Napoléon recognized the importance of splendor, and the power of a uniform style that could be equated with the new empire, his aesthetic sensibility by no means equalled Joséphine's. It was left to Joséphine to recognize the importance not only of surrounding the imperial court with gold but also in making the elegant classicism promoted by the architect-designers Charles Percier and Pierre-François-Léonard Fontaine the symbol of France's might.

Joséphine had been the first to use Percier and Fontaine for interior decoration, at her hotel in the rue Chantereine and, after 1800, at Malmaison. Percier and Fontaine also designed silver, and their influence on silverware during the period was extremely important, either through the drawings they supplied to the imperial silversmith Martin-Guillaume Biennais (1764–1843)—many of which have found their way into the Musée des Arts Décoratifs in Paris—or later through their engraved designs in *Recueil de décorations intérieures*, published in installments from 1801 to 1812 {FIGURE 95}.

The empress had always been an enthusiastic patron of silversmiths and, as Serge Grandjean has remarked, she "showed a pronounced taste, even a passion, for silverware in the same way as she did for jewels and clothes."[2] As early as 1800 she had ordered for Saint-Cloud a ewer and *bain de pieds* (foot bath) from Pierre-Joseph Dehanne—after she

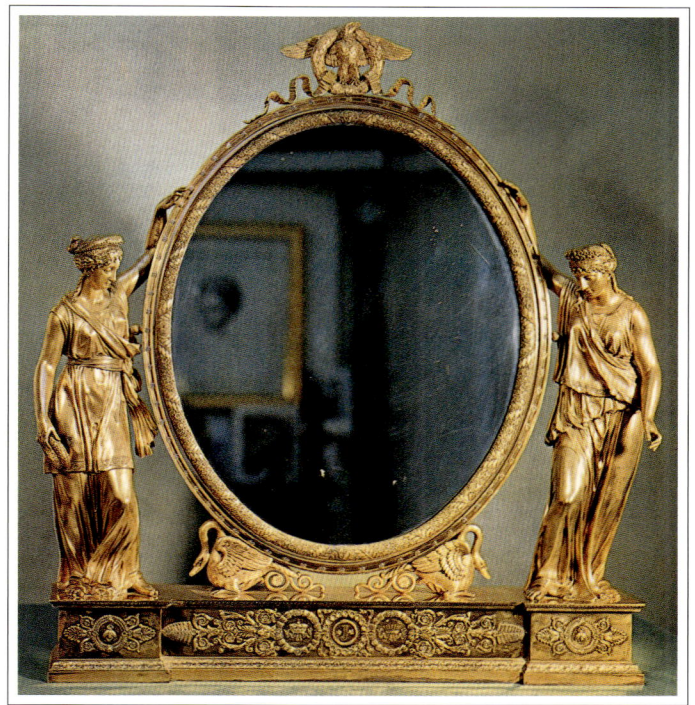

FIGURE 97.

Looking Glass, French (Paris), 1812.
Made for Joséphine by
Jean-Baptiste-Claude Odiot (1763–ca. 1850),
Silver-gilt, H: 97 cm (38 3/16 in.).
Private collection.

• • •

After her divorce in 1809, Joséphine was allowed to retain her title of empress and to maintain a household of imperial scale at Malmaison. This looking glass formed part of a toilet service of some twenty-nine pieces that, after the empress's death in 1814, passed to her son, Prince Eugène.

had approved his designs. After her death in 1814 it was found that Joséphine owed Biennais 58,232 francs and his rival Jean-Baptiste-Claude Odiot (1763–ca. 1850) another 6,043 francs.[3] In addition Napoléon had made her regular gifts of silver out of the 100,000 francs he set aside each year to buy silverware for the court. Starting in 1797 with a teapot and tray, he gradually amassed a sumptuous tea service for her, which was engraved in 1804 with the initial *J* and the imperial crown {FIGURE 96}. It must have made a startling contrast to the simple Sheffield plate service that had adorned her small but elegant house before her marriage to General Bonaparte.[4] For her bedroom at Malmaison, which was decorated like a campaign tent, a magnificent oval mirror flanked by two graceful female figures, perhaps designed by the painter Pierre-Paul Prud'hon, dominated the dressing table {FIGURE 97}. Ordered for the coronation in 1804 but not delivered until the following year, it still forms the nucleus of a stunning toilet service (now in a private collection) that includes jewel caskets and scent flagons. Luckily these pieces remained in Joséphine's possession at the time of her divorce and therefore escaped the melting pot in 1858 when Napoléon III had much of his great uncle's silver converted into a new table service by Cristofle.[5]

Although it has become synonymous with the imperial couple, the Empire style in silver was not, in fact, invented for them. It owed its origins to the *goût grec* (Greek taste) of the later years of Louis XVI's reign, which had been inspired by the writings of the archaeologist and art historian Johann Joachim Winckelmann (1717–1768). By the late 1780s, though, the ponderous forms drawn by the designer Jean-Charles Delafosse (1734–1789), which were used to such great effect in the celebrated Orloff service purchased by Catherine the Great from the royal silversmith Robert-Joseph Auguste (1723–1805), were giving way to lighter, more elegant ones based on slender vase and baluster shapes.

Much of the credit for this new, purer, form of classicism can be attributed to the sculptor Jean-Guillaume Moitte (1746–1810), who designed silver vessels with a richness that relies on line for effect, with horizontal bands of relief decoration set against highly burnished plain surfaces. Moitte supplied Auguste's son, Henry, with designs for silverware from the late 1780s onward. Some of the earliest examples of this style are a series of stylish basins and vase-shaped ewers, including a solid gold one, which Auguste made during the early years of the Revolution. But with the advent of the Terror, business in luxury goods all but dried up, and Auguste does not appear to have sold them. It may be that the client or clients who commissioned them were guillotined. Auguste had to wait until 1802 before he could sell them to the English aesthete and collector William Beckford. They are excellent examples of this new style, with its application of finely finished bands of architectural motifs taken directly from engravings of classical remains, giving the whole form a horizontality that was strikingly new.

Forced to lie dormant for much of the 1790s, the Empire style flowered with the patronage of the First Consul, and almost immediately it became the only one suitable for silver. Even Napoléon's enthusiasm for Egyptian art following the Nile campaign and the subsequent publication of Dominique-Vivant Denon's *Voyages dans la Bas et la Haute d'Egypt pendant les campagnes due général Bonaparte* (1802), which inspired stunning Sèvres porcelain during the early years of the new century, had little impact on Parisian silver. Curiously, it was only across the Channel, in London, that Egyptian-style silverware enjoyed any popularity—made popular there, ironically, by the French émigré designer Jean-Jacques Boileau (act. 1788–1851).

One of the secrets of the success of the Empire style was its interchangeability. The vase- and baluster-shaped outlines, set in contrast to horizontal straight lines, could be used just as easily for furniture and bronze work as for silverware, while the decoration in bas-relief could be used for gilt bronze as well as for silver. This meant that artists like Percier and Fontaine could design for any medium, and a total cohesiveness could be achieved, in which the silver on the table was in complete harmony with the other elements of the decor. Napoléon's rise had been too rapid for ambitious building works; instead the Empire style invaded existing rooms from the ancien régime, and silverware—perhaps the most easily moved of all the decorative arts—became the style's most effective ambassador, seen at close quarters on the tables of Napoléon's marshals and his far-flung family.

There were other reasons, too, why the Empire style swept the board so rapidly. With the rush of orders for table services, insignia, and decorations under the Consulate and Empire, it was a style that could be carried out on a large scale using industrial techniques. The breakdown of the guild system and deregulation of the arts brought about by the Revolution meant that there was a shortage of workers to maintain many of the craft traditions of the ancien régime. But it also meant that new men like Biennais, who had started as a *tabletier* (a supplier of small objects such as washstands and traveling sets), could enter the field of silversmithing without the restrictions of the old guild system. At its height under the Empire, Biennais' workshop employed almost two hundred artisans and used advanced techniques for mass production,[6] which in no way compromised the aesthetic quality of the silver. The borders of architectural motifs—such as honeysuckle, Greek keys, and stylized leaves—could be modeled, cast and finished separately, and then applied to the plain surfaces of the silver. Later, soldering was replaced by discrete nuts and bolts, visible only on the inside, which made components even more interchangeable and also heightened the contrast between the purity of the plain surfaces and the decorative borders.

One of Biennais' specialties in his early days as a *tabletier* had been the *nécessaire*, the silver components of which were supplied to him by freelance silversmiths. While the luxury goods trade was virtually nonexistent in the 1790s, with no orders for large-scale silver, the demand for personal items such as *nécessaires* remained steady from army officers. Tradition has it that Biennais owed his later appointment as *orfèvre de S. M. l'Empereur et Roi* (silversmith of His Majesty the Emperor and King) to the fact that he had supplied a *nécessaire* to Napoléon on the eve of the general's departure for Egypt in 1798 on the understanding that it would be paid for on his return. Napoléon ordered several *nécessaires* from Biennais during the Consulate and Empire. Like snuff boxes, these very personal objects made useful diplomatic presentations in an age when the more intimate the function of the object, the greater the honor of the gift. Napoléon gave a magnificent example, fitted with a myriad of medical and grooming tools as well as vessels for eating and drinking, to Czar Alexander I at their meeting at Erfurt. Napoléon's own *nécessaire* was captured in a symbolic moment by the Allies at Waterloo, and it may be the one by Biennais that was acquired, after many travels, by the Louvre {FIGURE 98}.

Another new object introduced under the Empire was the *déjeuner sur plateau tournant*, a form of lazy Susan in wood, fitted with silver-gilt dishes and cut-glass jars for condiments. Like the *nécessaire*, it was a product of the dissolution of the barriers between the

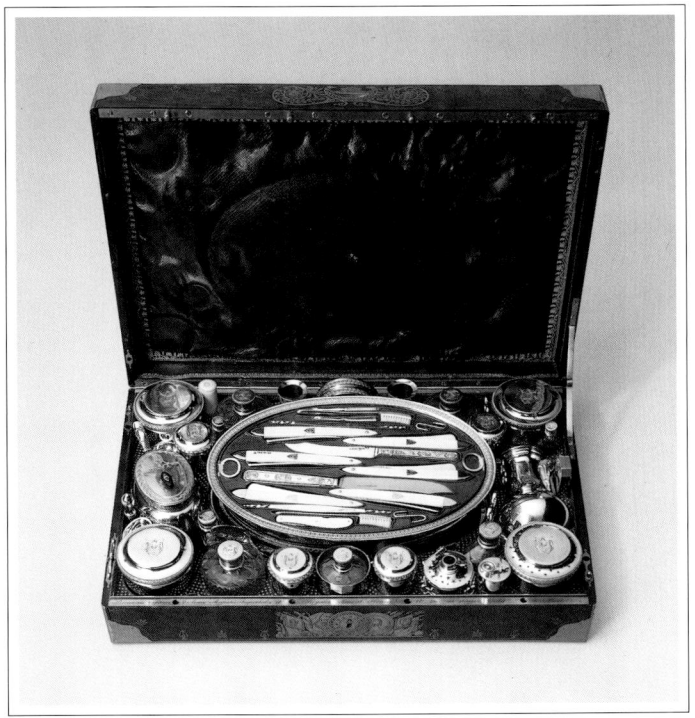

FIGURE 98.

Nécessaire (traveling box), French (Paris), 1806.
Made for Napoléon.
Maker's marks of Martin-Guillaume Biennais
and Pierre-Benoît Lorillon.
Silver-gilt, cut glass, mother-of-pearl, ivory, wood.
Paris, Musée du Louvre.

• • •

Napoléon purchased several of these traveling boxes from Biennais, the first on his departure for Egypt in 1796. Tradition has it that Biennais astutely gave the general credit until his return from the campaign, thus ensuring his future place as *orfèvre de S. M. l'Empereur et Roi* (silversmith of His Majesty the Emperor and King). This example may be the one he lost at Waterloo.

trades, for in Biennais' workshops the wood, glass, and silver could be worked on by specialists in each craft and fitted together into a harmonious whole. A sugar bowl in the form of a vase, on a stand with slots to hold six or a dozen spoons, was also first introduced in Biennais' shop, called Au Singe Violet, in the rue Saint Honoré. The commanding urn in Joséphine's tea service {see FIGURE 96} was another innovation, but this time one introduced from England along with a taste for tea among the fashionable. Ironically, while England and France fought off and on during the entire period of Napoléon's power, the fashionable in Paris continued to appreciate *le style anglais*, and in London the Prince Regent and aristocracy, with a bizarre fascination for "Boney," aped the splendors of Paris by surrounding themselves with opulent silver-gilt.

Other new types of silverware were the product of changes in dining customs under the Empire. Except possibly on the battlefield, nowhere else was the might of France felt as powerfully as at table. Yet it was paradoxical that the ceremonies of dining should have been so important to the regime, given the emperor's own lack of interest in food. He regarded eating as an interruption in the rhythm of the day and, according to his valet, spent an average of eight minutes eating lunch. He was prone to rise precipitously once he had eaten all he wanted and to stride out of the room, leaving his flustered aides to scurry, half-fed, after him. But Joséphine had recognized long before her marriage to Napoléon the importance not only of display but also of entertaining. To be invited to dine with the empress was not only a great honor for the invited but also a most effective means of persuasion. The great theatricality and formality of the court of Louis XIV had been diluted in the middle years of the eighteenth century by the introduction of a more relaxed atmosphere of elegant supper parties. Louis XV and later Louis XVI did not dine alone as often as the Sun King had, but their private dinners were limited to a small circle of courtiers. Under the Consulate and Empire, however, an invited guest might be a politician whose influence was sought, an officer needed for a delicate diplomatic mission, or, perhaps most important, a foreign emissary; and the idea of the guest as a participant, rather than merely a spectator at the table, was born.

The method of serving food *à la française*, in use since the seventeenth century, had dictated that all the dishes of a particular course were set out on the table and the diners either helped each other or, in more formal dinners, had servants do it for them. But with the growing influence of culinary authorities such as Carême, the types of dishes changed and so did the vessels required. Large oval tureens for soup {FIGURE 99} and slightly smaller ones for *oille*—a rich stew of game and fowl that had been introduced to the Bourbons by a Spanish marriage in the seventeenth century—continued to form the most elaborate elements of a formal dinner service. But for the next course, *service à la française* was replaced with *service à la russe*,[7] in which waiters brought food that had been carved and garnished in the kitchen. No longer was the food itself the table decoration; the stage was set for sculpture, not in pastry or sugar but in silver-gilt. Vases, often supported by elegant caryatids, held breathtaking displays of exotic flowers—Joséphine's great love—while compotes were arranged with neatly tiered arrangements of fruit. Moreover, as fashion had pushed the hour of dining later and later, the lack of daylight meant that space on the table

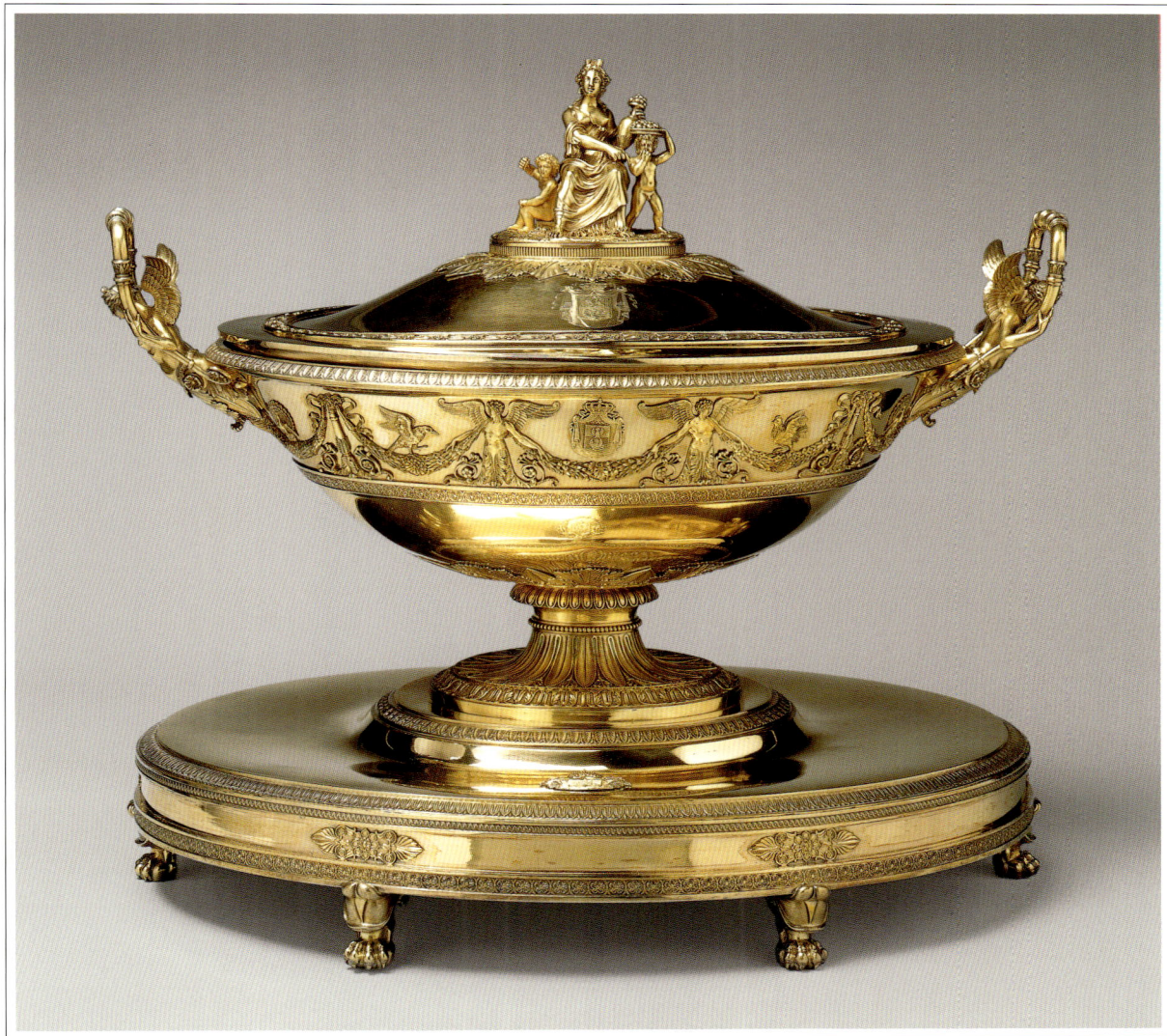

Figure 99.

Tureen, French (Paris), ca. 1805.
From the Borghese service, designed by
Charles Percier (French 1764–1838) and
Pierre-Françoise-Léonard Fontaine
(French, 1762–1853).
Maker's mark of Martin-Guillaume Biennais
(1764–1843).
Silver-gilt.
New York, The Metropolitan Museum of Art,
Joseph Pulitzer bequest.

• • •

Long thought to have been presented by Napoléon to his sister Pauline on her marriage to Prince Camillio Borghese in 1803, this service has many pieces that can be dated from their marks or inscriptions after 1805, suggesting it continued to be enlarged right into the 1820s by Italian as well as Parisian silversmiths.

had to be found for candlesticks and candelabra, whose form was based on Roman tripods.

Concurrent with this, however, was the need to reimpose the old ceremonial for the most important and public occasions, thereby using the past to give legitimacy to the new regime. For their coronation as emperor and empress in 1804, the city of Paris, following a tradition of the ancien régime, presented Napoléon and Joséphine with a massive silver-gilt dinner service numbering nearly eight hundred pieces of hollow ware and two hundred plates and dishes. It has always been known as the Grand Vermeil (literally, the "great silver-gilt"). The service was ordered from Henry Auguste, son of the last royal silversmith, on 2 *vendémiaire* year XIII (September 24, 1804) and was presented to the sovereigns at the banquet given for them by the city on December 16.

Most significant to this service was the inclusion of a *nef* and *cadinet* for the emperor and a matching pair for the empress {FIGURES 100, 101}. The *nef* was a medieval, boat-shaped receptacle into which a monarch's napkin, knife, salt, and anything else that could be

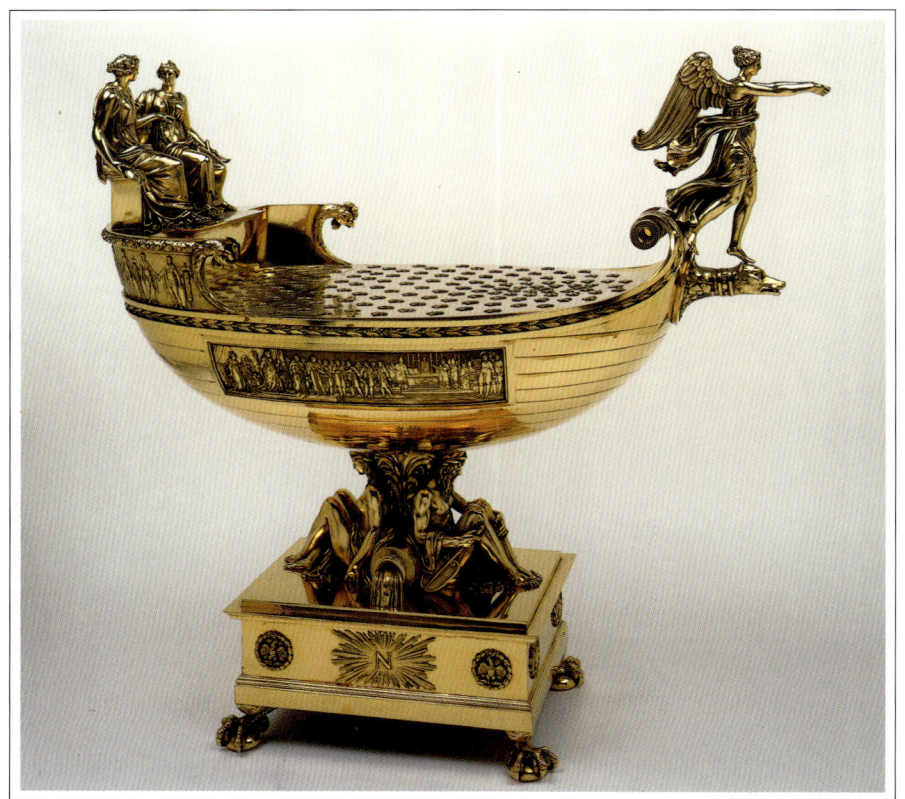

FIGURE 100.

"Nef de l'Impératrice" (The empress's *nef*),
French (Paris), delivered in 1804.
Maker's mark of Henry Auguste.
Silver-gilt.
Château de Fontainebleau:
depot du Mobilier national.

• • •

Originally made for Joséphine and used at the coronation banquet in 1804, the *nef* was also used by Marie-Louise at her wedding banquet.

FIGURE 101.

"Cadenas de l'Impératrice"
(*Cadinet* made for Joséphine),
French (Paris), delivered in 1804.
Maker's mark of Henry Auguste.
Silver-gilt.
Château de Fontainebleau:
depot du Mobilier national.

• • •

The *cadinet*, a medieval receptacle for safeguarding the monarch's spices, was, like the *nef*, re-created under the Empire. This and a matching one for Napoléon were made for the coronation in 1804. The Napoleonic emblems were removed at the Restoration, only to be reinstated by Napoléon III.

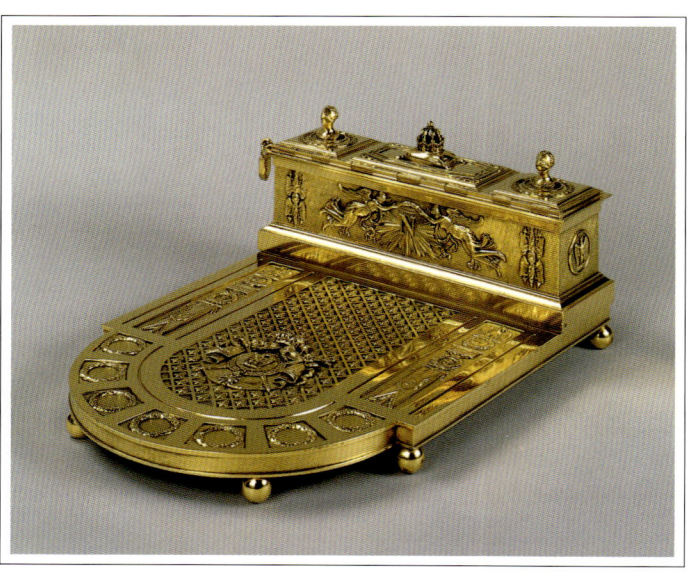

poisoned were deposited. The *cadinet*, a rectangular box, held his spices. Custom dictated that it was placed in front of the monarch with great ceremony at the commencement of every meal. No *nef* or *cadinet* of the French crown had survived, and by presenting the imperial couple with new ones, the city of Paris underlined Napoléon and Joséphine's royal status. Later, in 1810, at the banquet following the marriage of Napoléon and Marie-Louise in the Salle de Spectacle in the Tuilleries, the *nefs* and *cadinets* again appeared on the table, but the *nefs*, their original function long forgotten, were placed at each end of the table, well away from the imperial couple {FIGURE 102}.

The speed with which Henry Auguste was able to fill the order for the Grand Vermeil shows how rapidly the silver trade recovered under Napoléon. Auguste boasted that he used five hundred workers to complete it. Irascible and devious, he had argued incessantly with the architect Molinos (1743–1831) and the artist Pierre-Paul Prud'hon, who had been appointed to oversee the production. After the coronation, with the consent of the emperor, the service was placed on public display at the Hôtel de Ville, not only as an exhibition of what was held to be the greatest artistic achievement in silver but also as a demonstration of the manufacturing might of the French nation.

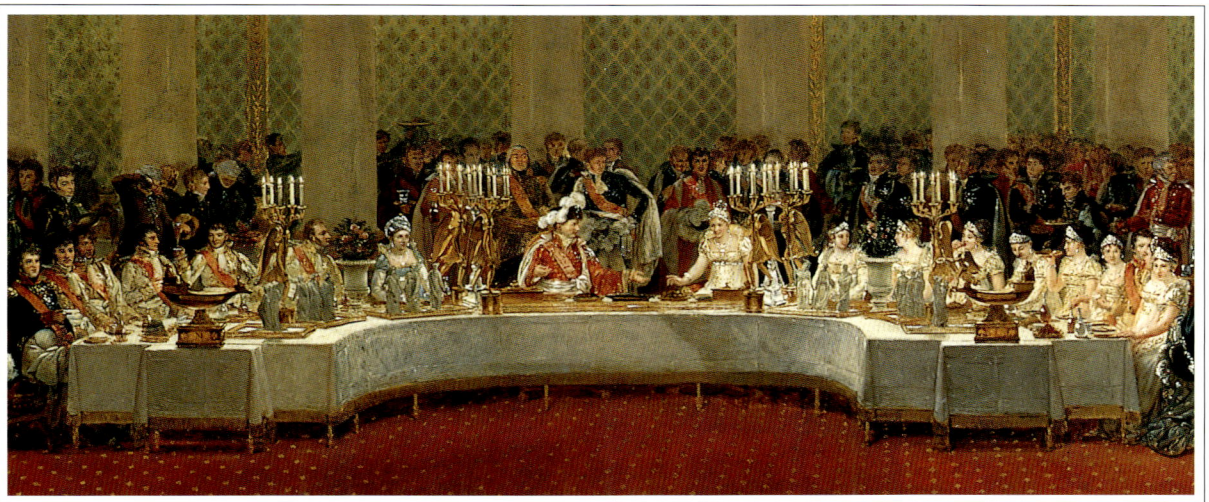

FIGURE 102.

Alexandre-Benoît-Jean Dufay, *dit* Casanova (1772–1844), *The Banquet of Napoléon and Marie-Louise* (detail), 1812.
Oil on canvas, 148 × 224.5 cm (58¼ × 88⅜ in.).
Château de Fontainebleau: depot du Musée national du Château de Versailles.

· · ·

The Grand Vermeil, the service presented to Napoléon by the city of Paris to commemorate his coronation in 1804, is shown on the table. The emperor's and empress's *nefs*—re-creations of the medieval boat-shaped vessel used to hold the monarch's napkin, salt cellar, and knife—have been incorrectly placed at each end of the table. They should be in front of Napoléon and Marie-Louise.

Other great dinner services were to follow. The orders, however, would go to Auguste's great rivals, Biennais and Odiot. Auguste found himself in financial difficulties in 1806, owing some 1,370,000 francs, and was given eight years by his creditors to put his affairs in order. Soon after, though, he was intercepted at Dieppe attempting to flee to England under an assumed name with what was left of his stock. He was sentenced to six years in irons in Martinique and ultimately died in Haiti in 1816. Auguste represented the old traditions and structure of the trade before the Revolution and clearly was unable to adapt to the new conditions. It had become impossible to maintain the huge workforce that his father had employed before the Revolution, and the days when the master of the workshop was also the chief designer, modeler, and chaser were over.

In contrast, the gifted entrepreneur Biennais used a network of contracting silversmiths who maintained their own establishments. This is why one often finds the marks of masters such as Marie-Joseph-Gabriel Genu (master 1788) and Jean-Charles Cahier on works engraved with Biennais' name. Cahier ultimately took over the business when Biennais retired in 1819.

Auguste's Grand Vermeil service is monumental and in some respects harks back to the sculptural quality of his father's great creations, like the service commissioned by George III of England for his Hanoverian dominion in the 1780s, now split between the Musée du Louvre and Waddesdon Manor. In contrast, it is in the output of Biennais' workshop where we see the true linear qualities of Empire silver being fully developed, in large part due to the designs of Percier and Fontaine. The Borghese service, the core of which was supplied by Biennais following the marriage of Napoléon's sister Pauline to Prince Camillo Borghese in 1803 and subsequently augmented to more than a thousand pieces by Odiot and Italian silversmiths, shows the lightness of form and decoration that could be achieved in the Empire style {see FIGURE 99}. The Borghese service exerted great influence over twentieth-century interpretations of the Empire style, especially in the United States.[8]

The Borghese service was one of a series of great dinner services used in Napoléon's satellite courts, which did so much not only to disseminate the Empire style but also to promote the excellence of French manufactories. On this last point Napoléon was adamant; only French workshops should be used. His brother Louis, king of Holland, to whom Napoléon sent a silver-gilt dinner service, was severely admonished when he patronized Dutch artists and artisans.[9] Services, for the most part by Biennais, were supplied to the emperor's mother, Letizia Bonaparte ("Mme Mère"), as well as to Jerome Bonaparte's court in Westphalia, Joaquim Murat's in Naples, and Elisa Bonaparte Bacciochi's in Tuscany. All these services are long since dispersed, the one made for Jérome, king of Westphalia having been most recently sold in Stuttgart in the 1950s. Apart from the Grand Vermeil, most of which is now at Fontainebleau, the only other imperial service to survive more or less intact is the one made by Biennais for Napoléon as king of Italy and sent to Eugène de Beauharnais, his viceroy in Milan. Only recently has this vast service, which descended to the Austrian royal house and has graced the table of the president of the Austrian republic since 1918, been recognized as a lost imperial treasure. This was by the chance discovery of the Italian royal arms under an applied Hapsburg cipher on a broken component.[10]

The Bernadotte court in Stockholm ordered a Biennais service, some of which survives today, while King Maximilian-Joseph of Bavaria—father of Eugène de Beauharnais's wife, Auguste—ordered a huge service from Odiot (still at the Residenz in Munich). Maria Feodorovna, mother of Czar Alexander I, ordered a service from Biennais of more than one thousand pieces that, despite sales in the 1920s, still stuns a visitor to the Hermitage. The fall of Napoléon does not seem to have lessened Europe's enthusiasm for silver in the Empire style. Louis XVIII may have been busy removing the Napoleonic *N* and King Childeric's bees from public buildings, but visitors to Paris enthusiastically ordered silver in the style that had been so much a part of the fallen empire. After the Restoration, many of the largest orders for silver appear to have gone to Odiot, and after Biennais' retirement in 1819 Odiot dominated the market for the next twenty years.

In the fifteen years following Waterloo, the Empire style became somewhat more ponderous but still retained its dignity. Odiot's use of the designs of the sculptor A.-L.-M. Cavelier meant that work from the Odiot workshop is of monumental forms, often supported by freestanding classical male and female figures, which have a sculptural, three-dimensional element often lacking in Biennais' elegant work. In 1817 Odiot supplied an extensive service to an "M. De Demidoff," who can be identified as Count Nikolai Demidoff, the Russian connoisseur who had fought against Napoléon at Borodino. It is ironic that many of the pieces of this service, which was dispersed at auction in New York in 1928,[11] follow the form and decoration of imperial pieces. No doubt the symbolism of Cavelier's kneeling Nike figures under the *pots-à-oilles* (stew pots) and *soupières* (soup tureens) was not lost on the count. Odiot reused many of Cavelier's designs two years later on the service he supplied to Count Branicki, a Polish francophile {FIGURE 103}. The Branicki service is perhaps the last of the great services in the pure Empire style. By the 1820s the vogue for naturalistic decoration, introduced from across the Channel, diluted the purity of the Neoclassicism that for nearly a quarter of a century had been the most potent symbol of the Napoleonic Empire. The elegance and lightness that we associate with Joséphine was gone forever.

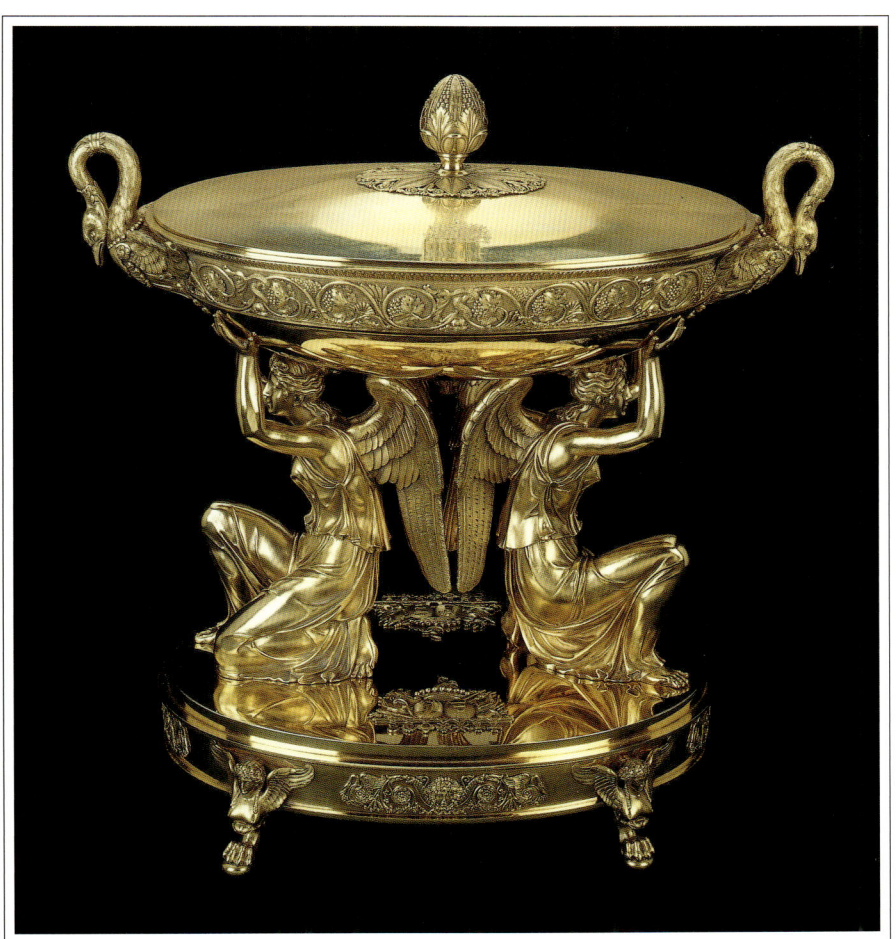

Figure 103.

Tureen and Cover, French (Paris), ca. 1819.
From the Branicki service.
Maker's mark of Jean-Baptist-Claude Odiot.
Silver-gilt.
The Indianapolis Museum of Art.

• • •

The Polish Countess Branicki was a woman of contrasts. Her great love of splendor is well illustrated by the silver-gilt dinner service she commissioned from Paris in 1819, but the interiors of her summer palace at Alexandrie and her winter residence at Belaia-Tzerkoff were paneled in plain wood. A significant portion of the service remains in Poland, but pieces from it appeared on the market in the twentieth century and may now be found in collections elsewhere in Europe and in America.

Notes

1. For a discussion of the use of gilding on early nineteenth-century silver, and the influence of Nero's *domus aurea*, see the excellent essay by Ubaldo Vitali, "A Quest for the *Domus Aurea* in the Resurgence of Gilding in A. Phillips and J. Sloane, *Antiquity Revisited: English and French Silver-Gilt from the Collection of Audrey Love*, exh. cat. (Christie's, New York, 1997), 17–27.
2. "De son côté, l'impératrice Joséphine a manifesté un gout prononcé, voire une passion, pour l'orfèvrerie comme pour les joyaux et les robes." Serge Grandjean, *L'Orfèvrerie du XIXe siècle en Europe* (Paris, 1964), 12.
3. Serge Grandjean, *Inventaire après décès de l'impératrice Joséphine à Malmaison* (Paris, 1964), 76.
4. Eleanor P. DeLorme, *Joséphine: Napoléon's Incomparable Empress* (New York, 2002), 33.
5. Following Joséphine's death both the toilet and tea services were inherited by her grandson, the duc de Leuchtenberg, who married a grand-duchess of Russia. The objects remained in Russia until 1919 when they were brought to Switzerland. In 1959 they were sold at auction and entered the Niarchos collection.
6. The mid-nineteenth-century silversmith François-Désiré Froment-Meurice recalled that his stepfather, who had worked in the Biennais workshop, spoke of six hundred craftsmen. This figure has been often repeated in books, but it appears to be an exaggeration. See Anne Dion-Tenenbaum, *L'Orfèvre de Napoléon, Martin-Guillaume Biennais*, exh. cat. (Musée du Louvre, Paris, 2003), 15.
7. *Service à la russe* was supposedly introduced by Alexandre Boriasovitch Kourakine, the Russian ambassador to Paris, whom Joséphine entertained at Malmaison.
8. The service was sold with the contents of the Borghese Palace in Rome in 1892 and ultimately was acquired by Edith Rockefeller McCormick, who lent it to the Art Institute of Chicago until her death in 1934 when it was sold in New York and split up into individual lots, many of them finding their way into American museums.
9. Timothy Wilson-Smith, *Napoléon and His Artists* (London, 1996), 232.
10. See Pierre Villard, "Service de Napoléon Ier, roi d'Italie ou le Grand Vermeil de la cour impériale de Vienne," in *Versailles et les tables royales en Europe XVIIème–XIXème siècles*, exh. cat. (Musée national des Châteaux de Versailles et de Trianon, 1993), 349–54.
11. The service was inherited by Demidoff's son Anatole, prince of San Donato, who ironically married Jérome Bonaparte's daughter. It was sold by him in 1863 and acquired through the London dealers Hancocks by Alfred de la Chapelle, an adventurer and gold miner. After his death it was sold by American Art Galleries in New York in 1928. Philippe Palasi recently identified de la Chapelle's arms, which had been applied on the service by Hancocks in 1863 and had long baffled experts. See Phillips and Sloane, *Antiquity Revisited*, 133.

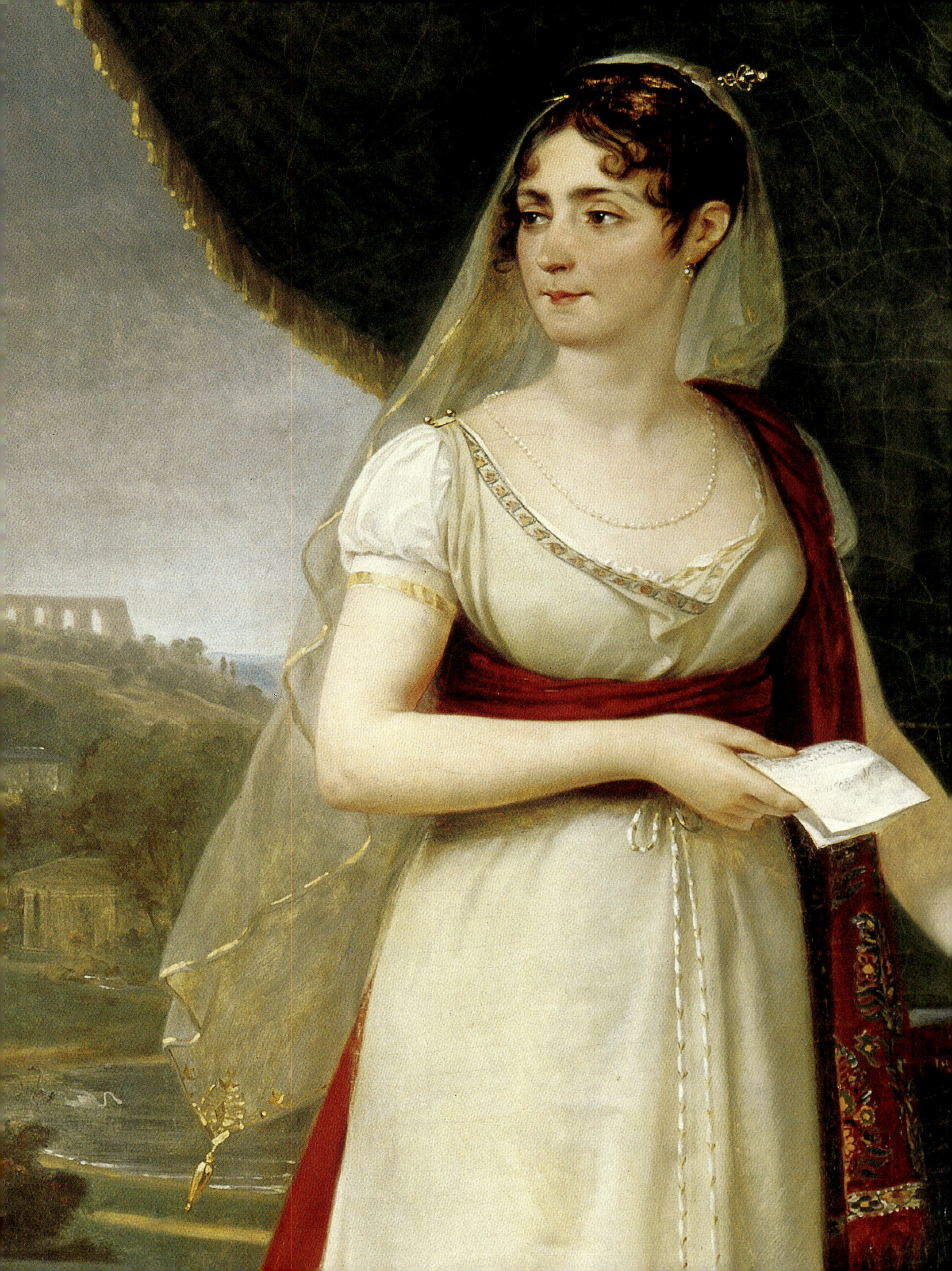

CHAPTER 10

KIMBERLY CHRISMAN-CAMPBELL

The Empress of Fashion: What Joséphine Wore

THE FRENCH REVOLUTION, THOUGH DAMAGING TO THE fashion industry, was a fertile period for fashion itself. Unwritten rules were relaxed, allowing new styles and fabrics to proliferate; archaic garments such as the hoop petticoat and the corset disappeared altogether. An anonymous print of 1797 compared the informal, politically charged fashions of the Revolution with the towering headdresses and three-dimensional trimmings of Louis XVI's court {FIGURE 104}. The new silhouette was natural and unembellished—the antithesis of the pinched, powdered, and padded styles of the ancien régime. Luxury and artifice became synonymous with tyranny and treason; instead, France embraced the democratic dress and politics of ancient Greece and Rome. Two portraits of Catherine Worlée before and after the Revolution illustrate the dramatic changes in dress and the remarkable adaptability of women like Worlée—and Joséphine—who weathered those turbulent times with style and grace {FIGURES 105, 106}.

It is difficult to imagine Joséphine wearing the cloying pastels, frothy lace, fussy ribbons, and gravity-defying hairstyles of the ancien régime, but she must have done so.[1] When Joséphine arrived in Paris in 1779 at age sixteen, Marie-Antoinette was at the height of her popularity, and every woman with any pretensions to fashion copied her gowns, jewels, hats, and hairstyles {FIGURES 107, 108}. The queen's taste and sartorial leadership had a lasting impact on Joséphine. Although the populace eventually turned against Marie-Antoinette, Joséphine sympathized with her and drew strength from her example. As

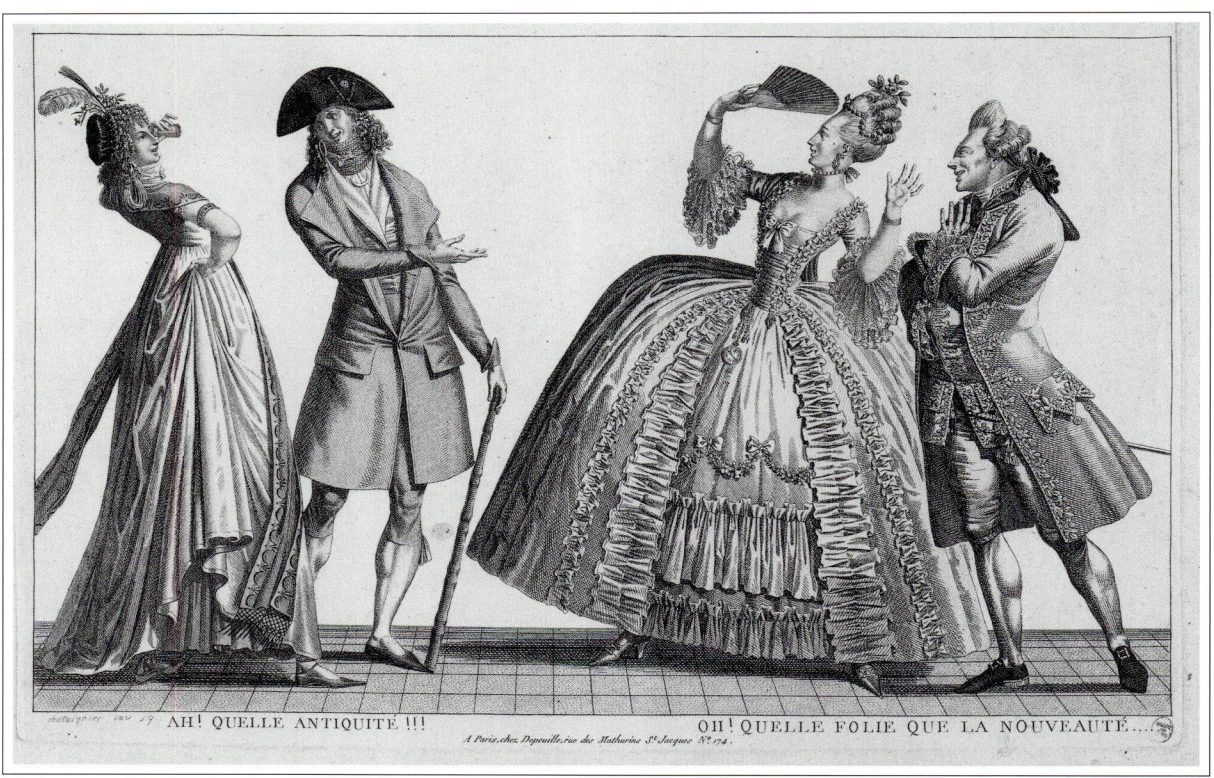

FIGURE 104.

Alexis Chataigner, *Ah! What Antiques!... Oh! What Follylike Novelty!*, ca. 1797.
Engraving, 24.2 × 39.8 cm (9½ × 15⅝ in.).
Paris, Musée Carnavalet.

• • •

The old regime meets the new in this caricature. The couple on the left wear politically correct post-Revolutionary dress while the couple on the right wear outmoded ancien régime finery of the 1770s. Interestingly, the artist does not choose sides, but suggests that each style is equally distinctive—and equally ridiculous—in its own way.

FIGURE 105.

Elisabeth Vigée-Lebrun (French, 1755–1842),
Catherine Worlée, Madame Grand, 1783.
Oil on canvas, 92 × 72.4 cm (36¼ × 28½ in.).
New York, The Metropolitan Museum of Art.

• • •

Mme Grand, age twenty-one, wears a silk *robe à l'anglaise* (English-style gown) trimmed with lace and a *parfait contentement* ("perfect contentment"), the evocative name given to a ribbon worn at the bosom. Her hair is dressed naturally by contemporary standards, and her modest accessories—ribbons and a simple silk gauze fichu—attest to the fashion for pastoral simplicity, also seen in figure 107. Vigée-Lebrun confessed to giving her sitters an abstracted expression when they had no distinct personality.

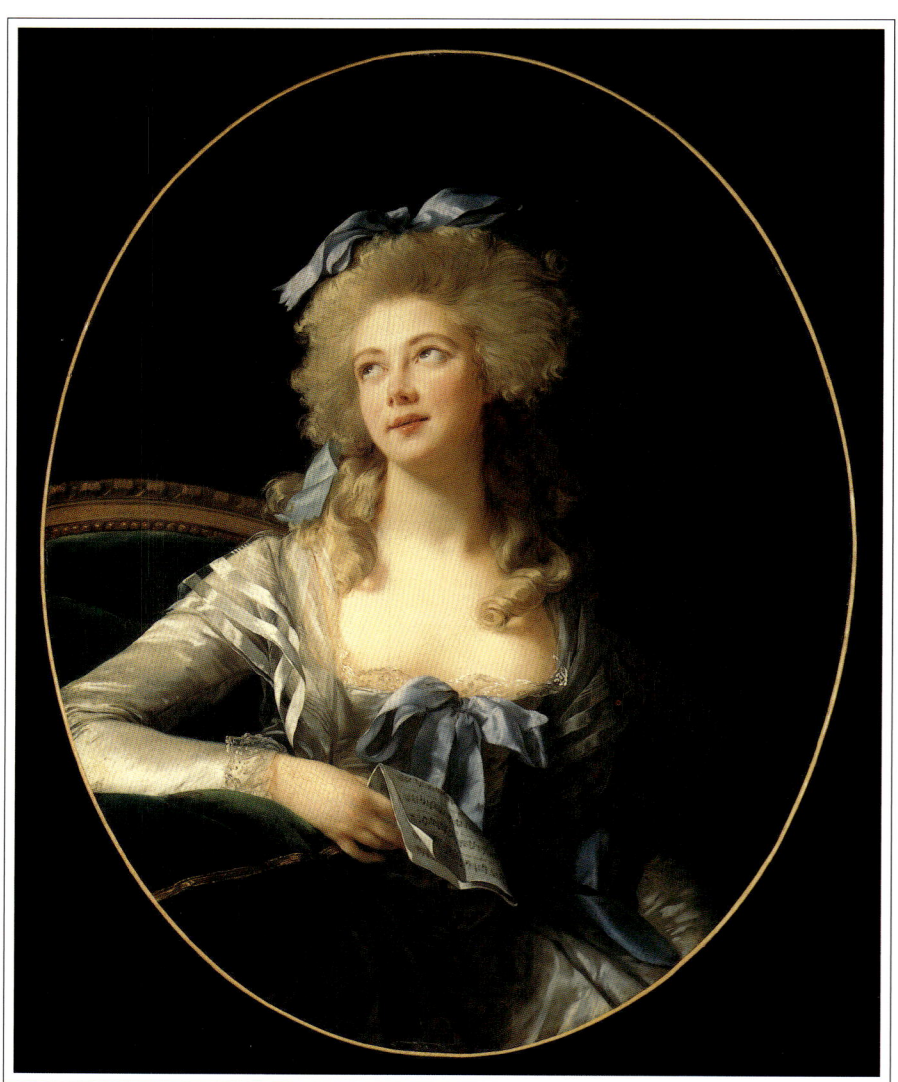

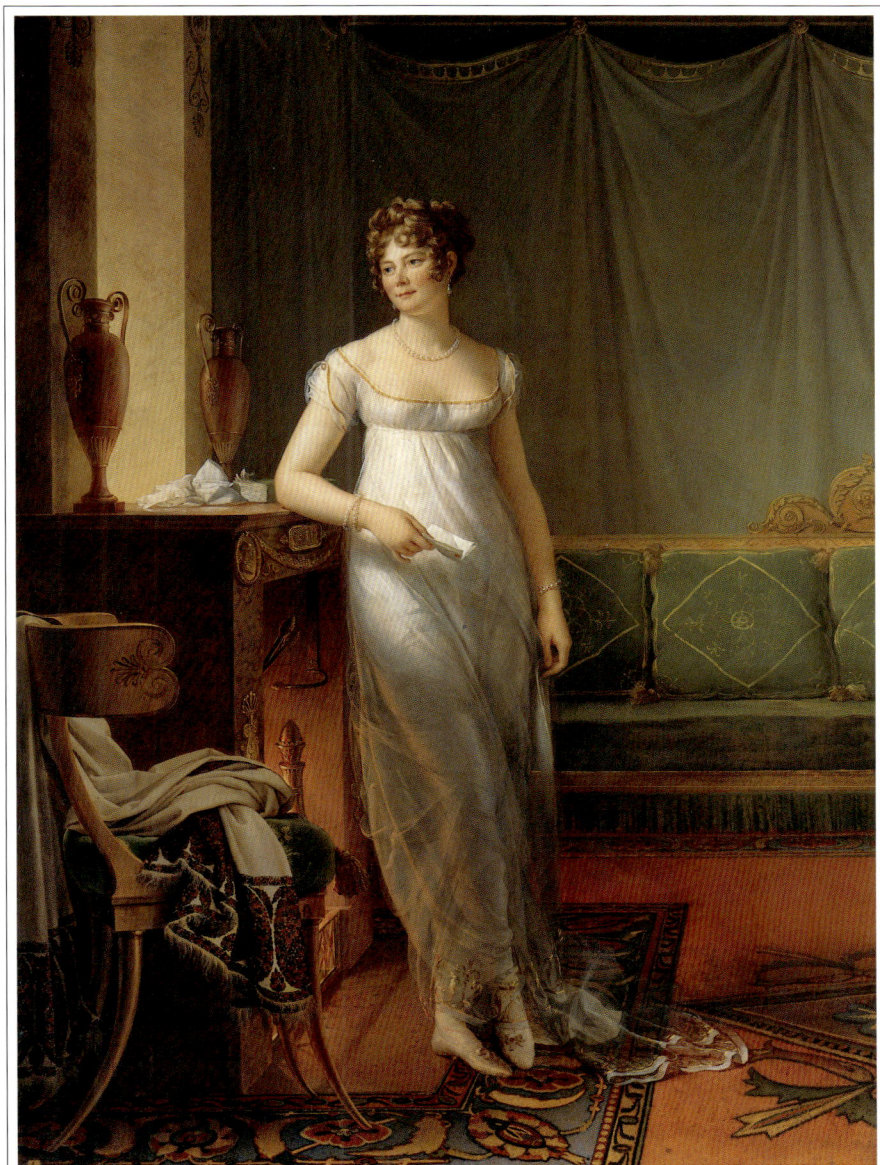

FIGURE 106.

Baron François Gérard (French, 1770–1837), *Catherine Worlée, Princess Talleyrand-Perigord*, ca. 1808.
Oil on unlined canvas, 225.7 × 164.8 cm (88⅞ × 64⅞ in.).
New York, The Metropolitan Museum of Art.

• • •

By this time, Worlée was the wife of the Prince de Talleyrand-Perigord, Napoléon's Minister of Foreign Affairs. Her clinging, diaphanous gown, bare arms, and coiffure *à l'antique* redefine sartorial simplicity for a new era, but the scale of the portrait and its tastefully composed domestic backdrop furnished with status symbols (including a pair of Greek vases and a cashmere shawl) attest to an eventful journey from the dreaming musician of figure 105 to a member of the emperor's inner circle.

empress, Joséphine inhabited the same rooms as the late queen, and "liked to surround herself with things that had belonged to Marie-Antoinette."[2] From her, Joséphine learned the value of luxury and the symbolic power of dress.

Although she was (and still is) regarded as the model of post-Revolutionary femininity, Joséphine's tastes remained firmly rooted in the eighteenth century. She preferred soft colors and delicate floral patterns to the bold hues and masculine geometric motifs promoted by the Revolution. Many of the fashion innovations attributed to her were actually revivals of eighteenth-century styles. While most women who had survived the Revolution looked back on the dress of the ancien régime with horror, Joséphine remained nostalgic for the fashions of her youth.[3] Among Joséphine's many talents, Mme de Chastenay counted "a perfect understanding of the ancien régime."[4] It was Joséphine's proximity to rather than her distance from the previous mode of fashion and culture that made her an effective and beloved ruler in the volatile cultural climate of the Consulate and the Empire.

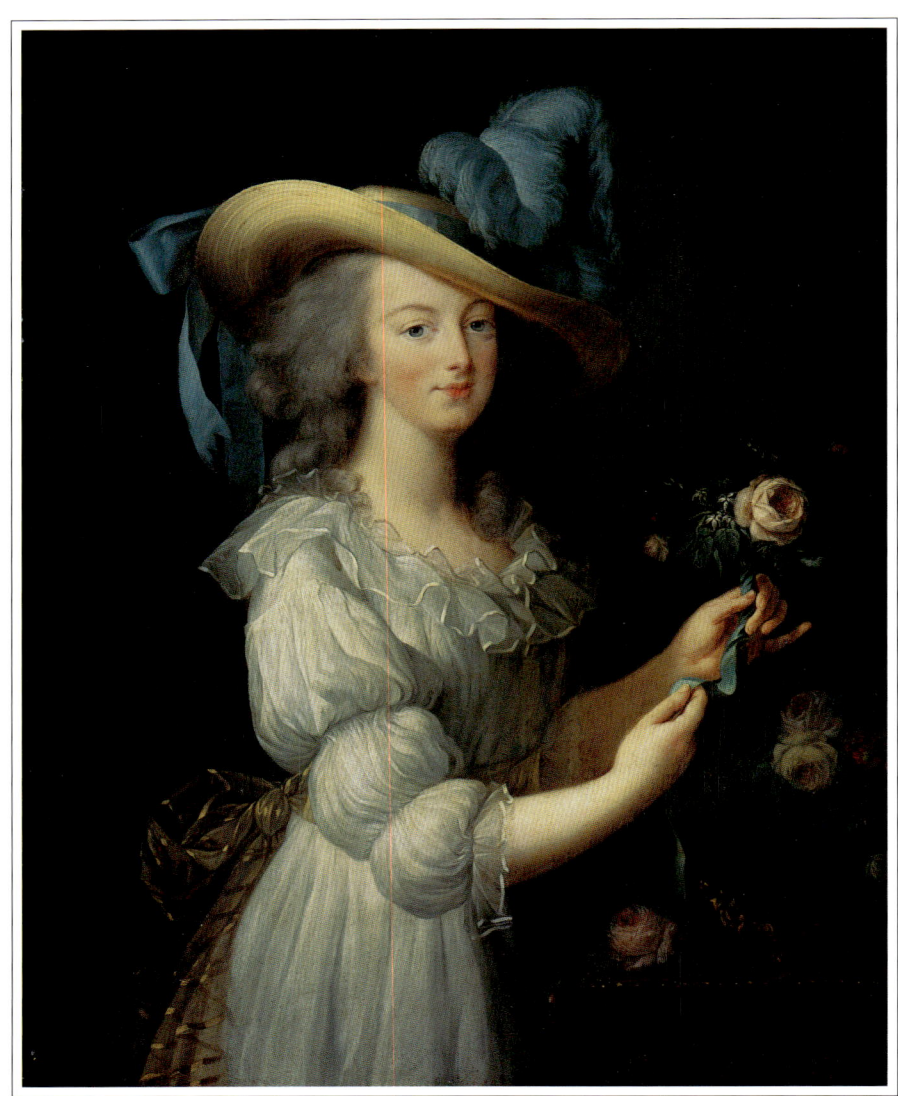

FIGURE 107.

Elisabeth Vigée-Lebrun (French, 1755–1842), *Marie-Antoinette in a Chemise Gown*, 1783. Oil on canvas, 92.7 × 73.1 cm (36½ × 28¾ in.). Washington, D.C., National Gallery of Art.

· · ·

This portrait caused a scandal at the Salon of 1783, as it was thought that the informal, somewhat rustic "chemise" gown and straw hat were inappropriate for a monarch. However, the chemise gown became the defining fashion trend of the 1780s, and it was the precursor to the Neoclassical *robes à l'antique* of Joséphine's era. Ironically, the fashion popularized by Marie-Antoinette was adopted as a badge of Republicanism during the French Revolution.

The Directoire: September 1795 to December 1799

Joséphine was released from prison in 1794 into a society that looked and behaved very differently from the one she had known before the Revolution. Foreign diaries and newspapers recorded the alarming (and mostly baseless) rumors that trickled out of Paris in the 1790s—that women were reportedly going half naked and shaving their heads, while men were literally *sans-culottes* (without breeches). The truth was less salacious, but no less cataclysmic. As a returning émigré remarked, "It was in this area, certainly, that the Revolution was complete."[5] The Revolution produced not only new garments but a new, more relaxed definition of elegance. "A light muslin gown with a bow of ribbon formed an exquisite outfit, and only very sullen old women missed powder, pockets, and high-heeled shoes."[6] This preference for informal, inexpensive gowns—made of imported muslins rather than native silks and velvets—had catastrophic consequences for the French fashion industry, which indirectly employed an estimated twenty-five thousand people in Paris alone.[7]

The establishment of the Directoire in 1795 paved the way for economic recovery. Luxury came back into fashion, thanks to the example of society hostesses such as Mme Tallien, Mme Recamier, and Mme (Joséphine) de Beauharnais, "whose elegant dress excited the notice and envy of all the women."[8] Balls, receptions, and other entertainments provided welcome opportunities to throw off one's Revolutionary rags. The costly tradition of the trousseau was revived.[9] Fashion magazines, which had disappeared during the Revolution, made a triumphant return in 1797, creating fervent interest in clothes and shopping.

A spirit of fantasy, ostentation, and artifice dominated Directoire fashion. For a morning concert in January 1797,

> The women were all in wigs, generally as different as possible from the true colour of their hair; their faces almost totally obscured. Their caps and hats had much gold and velvet, and very small feathers; their waists immoderately short, their faces daubed, their necks covered, their gowns muslin, with a great profusion of gold spangles and gold fringe.[10]

The beautiful Thérèse Tallien was the most notorious of these trendsetters. In November 1796, she attended the opera looking "very showy, with a spangled muslin gown and a scarlet cloak.... Her very black hair was plaited with gold ribbon, and ringlets fell over her forehead and neck; rather a short waist, her arms bare, and a great breadth of shoulders displayed. She was altogether very much *décolletée*, which is the fashion of the day."[11] Joséphine and Thérèse were close friends with the same taste in clothes; they often turned heads at balls by making an entrance in matching outfits.[12] But Joséphine discovered that she had to change her image when she became Mme Bonaparte.

The Consulate: December 1799 to May 1804

Napoléon found the low-cut, clinging gowns and outrageous sartorial excesses of the Directoire indecent, so, as first consul, he used his influence to reform female fashions. One evening at the Luxembourg palace, he ordered more logs to be heaped on the fire, declaring, "These ladies must be freezing." Joséphine and her scantily clad attendants took the hint, and thereafter they were careful to observe greater modesty in their dress.[13] It soon became known that the First Consul—and his elegant wife—disapproved of revealing fashions.[14]

Napoléon also manipulated fashion to defend French manufactures. He banned the wearing of muslin, which was imported from India via England, France's chief competitor in the textile market. Hortense de Beauharnais recalled,

> When my mother or I would come into the room wearing an elegant dress, his first question was, "Is that gown made of muslin?" We often replied that it was lawn from Saint-Quentin, but if a smile betrayed us he would instantly tear the guilty garment in two. This disaster having befallen our clothes several times, we were obliged to revert to satin or velvet.[15]

Domestically produced cambric and leno were acceptable alternatives to muslin, and those who wished to show allegiance to Napoléon ostentatiously patronized French textile manufacturers.[16]

In 1802, to create a demand for expensive textiles, Napoléon made formal dress mandatory for court receptions. "The First Consul liked women to be decorated," and the ladies of the court were more than happy to oblige.[17] Mme de Chastenay was struck by the sudden transformation: "It was no longer the muslin gown with the large flat ribbon; it was velvet and satin gowns, of every shade and every color. It took me some time to get used to it; I could not judge the price of fabrics, and the variegations of colors offended my eyes too strongly to appear magnificent to me."[18] But Napoléon must have been pleased with both the visual effect and its consequences for commerce and public opinion. An English visitor to Paris during the Peace of Amiens reported, "The Etiquette of a Court and Court dress are strictly observed, and everyone agrees that the splendour of the Court of the Tuilleries [*sic*] is much greater than ever was the old Court of France."[19]

The Coronation: December 2, 1804

With the proclamation of the Empire in May 1804, the question of what to wear at court took on new urgency. Louis XIV had introduced the concept of an exclusive court dress in the 1660s, but with the overthrow of the monarchy, court dress was no longer either needed or wanted. The leaders of the new regime took pride in wearing informal and even slovenly dress. This was not only inappropriate for an imperial court but also disastrous for France's weavers, embroiderers, and lace makers, who had grown dependent on the income generated by court costume. The coronation gave Napoléon an excuse to resurrect court dress—"which could scarcely have been introduced without very good reason in a Court which was yet entirely Republican"—and, in doing so, to revive France's textile industry.[20]

Throughout the eighteenth century, court dress had been trapped in the past. Women wore the *grand habit*, a stiff, awkward ensemble consisting of a boned bodice, a detachable train, and a skirt, worn over a large hoop petticoat {FIGURE 108}. Male courtiers wore the *habit habillée*, a richly embroidered suit consisting of a jacket, waistcoat, and breeches. These garments were adopted by courts throughout Europe, and they continued to be compulsory at court even as fashion rejected them in favor of simpler styles. While Napoléon favored a return to the styles of the ancien régime, Joséphine realized that for the new court dress to succeed, it would have to be fashionable and flattering as well as luxurious. Thus, imperial court dress was a compromise between tradition and modernity, formality and fashion. It combined a modern, high-waisted silhouette with traditional courtly accessories and opulence. As Mme de Rémusat sighed with relief, "There was no question of resuming the hoop."[21]

With the coronation, Napoléon sought to legitimize his claim to the throne while distinguishing himself from the deposed Bourbons, so he had David and Isabey delve into France's past to unearth visual cues that would establish the emperor's place in history and create an unforgettable tableau {see page viii and FIGURE 24}.[22] Napoléon borrowed elements of his coronation costume and regalia from national heroes such as Charlemagne and the fifth-century King Childeric.[23] In addition to inviting specific comparisons, these historical allusions conferred gravity and authority on their wearer.

Figure 108.

Elisabeth Vigée-Lebrun (French, 1755–1842), *Marie-Antoinette in a Grand Habit*, 1780. Oil on canvas, 273 × 193.5 cm (107½ × 76⅛ in.). Vienna, Kunsthistorisches Museum.

• • •

The Queen wears the *grand habit*, France's official female court dress from the reign of Louis XIV until the French Revolution. It consisted of a rigid boned bodice, a skirt worn over an enormous hoop petticoat, and a long, detachable train, worn with an array of courtly accessories. The *grand habit* was adopted by courts throughout Europe in the eighteenth century, only to be relinquished in favor of Napoléon's modern court dress.

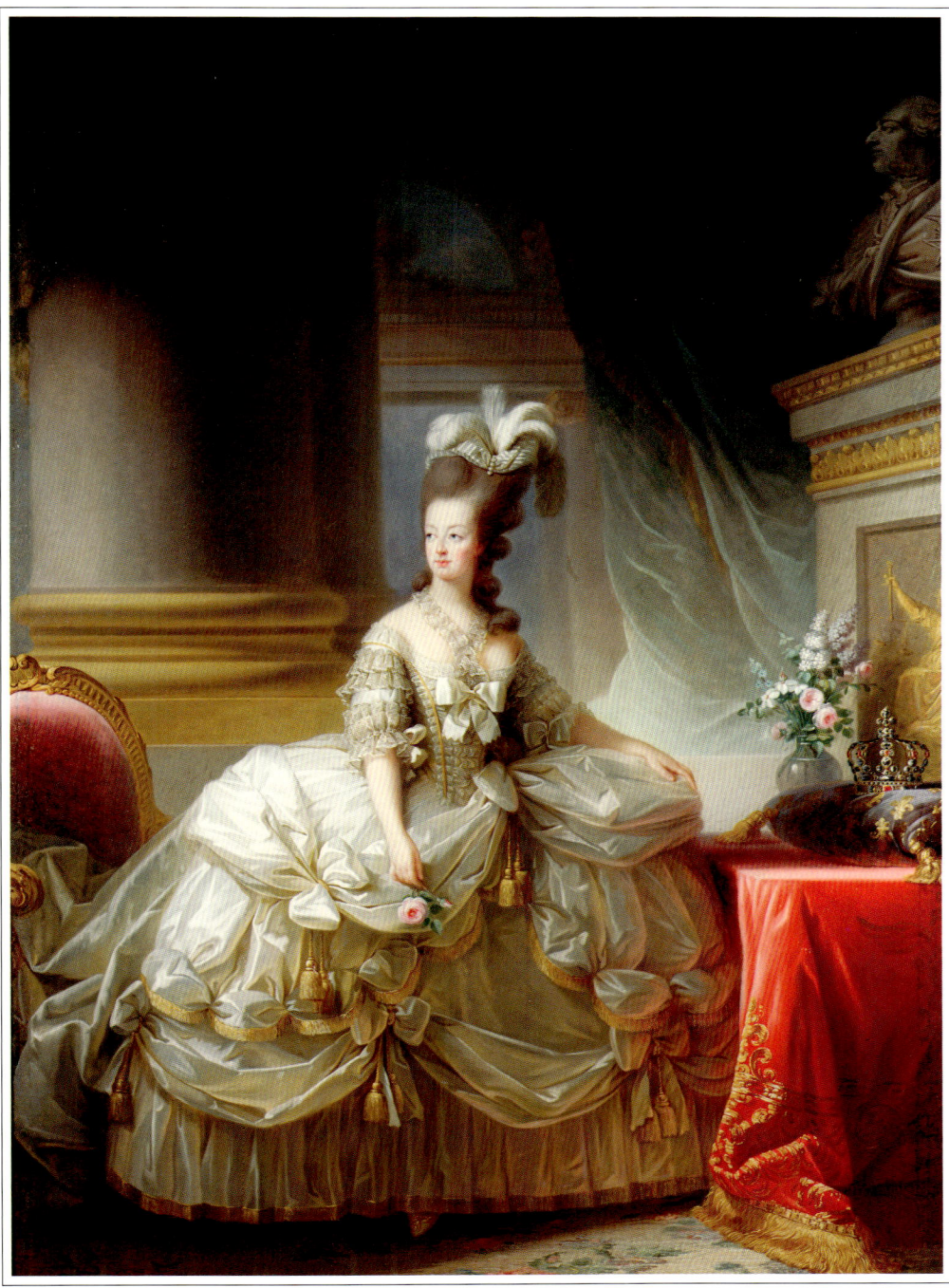

Formal and ceremonial dress is always based on the fashionable attire of the past; its survival is a measure of its importance. In contrast to fashion's constant, rapid permutations, the archaic court dress of the ancien régime was artificially, reassuringly stagnant, and its status and formality linked it visibly to the past. Although Napoleonic court dress was partially attuned to current fashions, it was equally dependent on the strength of tradition.

Joséphine's clothing was designed with similar concerns in mind {FIGURE 109}. The most recent precedent for a crowned queen of France was Marie de' Médicis in 1610. Thus Joséphine's coronation costume featured "a collar of silk lace, called a *chérusque*, which stood rather high behind the head...attached on the shoulders," also known as a Médicis collar.[24] This subtly identified Joséphine as the rightful successor to Marie de' Médicis (the Florentine wife of Henry IV) while framing her face and her famously elegant neck.[25] Other historical touches included knuckle-length sleeves that, along with the high waistline,

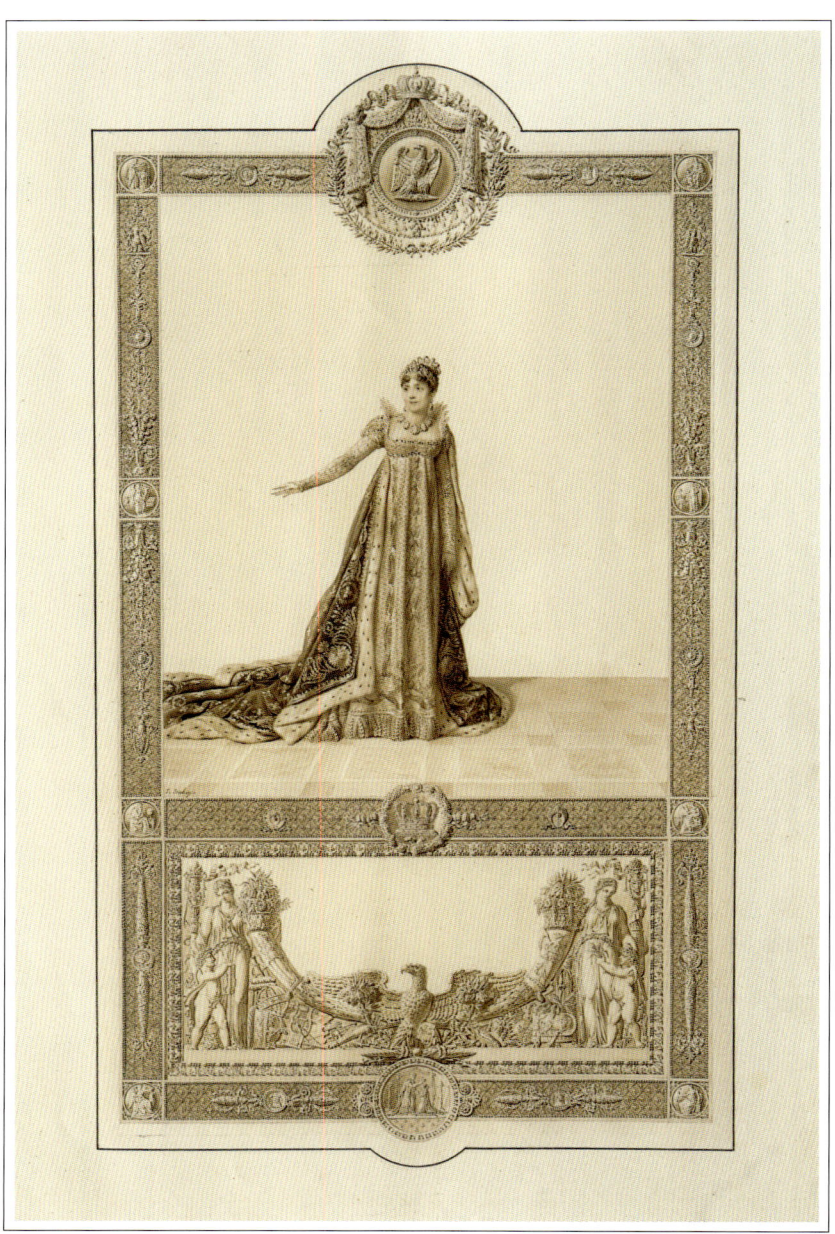

FIGURE 109.

Jean-Baptiste Isabey (French, 1767–1855),
Charles Percier (French, 1764–1838),
and Pierre-François-Léonard Fontaine
(French, 1762–1853),
Empress Joséphine in Coronation Costume,
from the *Livre du Sacre de S. M. l'Empereur Napoléon*
(Book of the Coronation), 1807.
Rueil-Malmaison, Musée national des Châteaux
de Malmaison et Bois-Préau.

• • •

Isabey's design, shaped by Napoléon and executed by LeRoy, would become the template for female court dress under the Empire, with one slight modification: for the coronation, the heavy train was anchored low on Joséphine's back by sturdy shoulder straps, rather than flowing asymetrically from the left shoulder. The text describes the gown as having "long sleeves of silver brocade scattered with gold bees, embroidered on the seams; the hem of the gown embroidered and trimmed with gold fringe; the bodice and the edges of the sleeves enriched with diamonds."

recalled the elongated silhouette of the late-Gothic period, and the upper part of the sleeve was puffed and cleverly embroidered to resemble the slashed, layered sleeves of the Renaissance. Both Isabey's costumes and David's painting were influenced by Rubens's well-known cycle of events from the life of Marie de' Médicis.

Joséphine's mantle required twenty-two meters (more than seventy-two feet) of crimson velvet embroidered with oak, laurel, and olive leaves, gold bees, and Napoléon's cipher at a cost of 614 francs; the ermine lining and border cost an additional 12,460 francs.[26] Isabey originally intended for it to hang from her left shoulder, creating a dramatic asymmetrical line that echoed the fall of Napoléon's imperial robe, which was worn open at the left shoulder. David's painting records that it was actually worn with shoulder straps, probably because, at eighty pounds, it was too heavy to wear any other way. Even with the straps, Joséphine had difficulty maintaining her balance. This precious garment was worn again only once, by Empress Marie-Louise.[27]

Joséphine's gown of white silk satin brocaded in silver cost ten thousand francs, not including its accessories.[28] It was trimmed with a band of gold fringe at the hem, echoing the fringe on Napoléon's tunic, and embroidered with gold bees and real diamonds to further embellish the sumptuous fabric.[29] Although its shape and color were consistent with the fashionable Neoclassical style, the gown's dense, buttery fabric set it apart from the diaphanous muslins and crêpes worn for everyday dress.[30] Thus, Joséphine's ensemble became the model for female court dress under the Empire {FIGURE 110}.

The establishment of the Empire sent the fashion industry into a frenzy of speculation and rivalry, which only intensified with the approach of the coronation. "The dressing room of the Empress was the aim of all the rivals, as the council room of the Emperor was of all the ambitious." The prize went to Louis Hippolyte LeRoy, Joséphine's usual *marchand de modes*, who executed Isabey's designs for Joséphine's coronation gown and mantle. "These objects were of a magnificence and taste which exceeded all imaginings."[31] Following the coronation, LeRoy instantly became the most sought-after dressmaker in Europe.

The day of the coronation was cold and misty; Joséphine and her ladies, dressed in low-cut court gowns more suitable for a heated drawing room, wore cashmere shawls for warmth but shed them at the entrance to Notre Dame. Amid all the costly apparel and carefully choreographed pageantry, onlookers were impressed by Joséphine's poise and humility as she knelt to receive her crown; her flawless performance launched a new fashion era.[32] Joséphine's grace and beauty made the new court dress seem deceptively flattering; what we now know as the "Empire style" was created for her, and no one wore it as well as she did. Indeed, it was fatal to those who lacked Joséphine's slim build, swanlike neck, and graceful arms. Nevertheless, women reveled in its unapologetic romanticism and luxury. Lace, jewelry, embroidery, and fur were officially acceptable again. Napoléon was forced to curb some of this extravagance by reintroducing a form of sumptuary law limiting the amount of embroidery on the border of a gown to four inches for those under the rank of princess; the men of Napoléon's court were soldiers, not wealthy aristocrats, and he did not wish to see them driven into poverty by extravagant wives.[33]

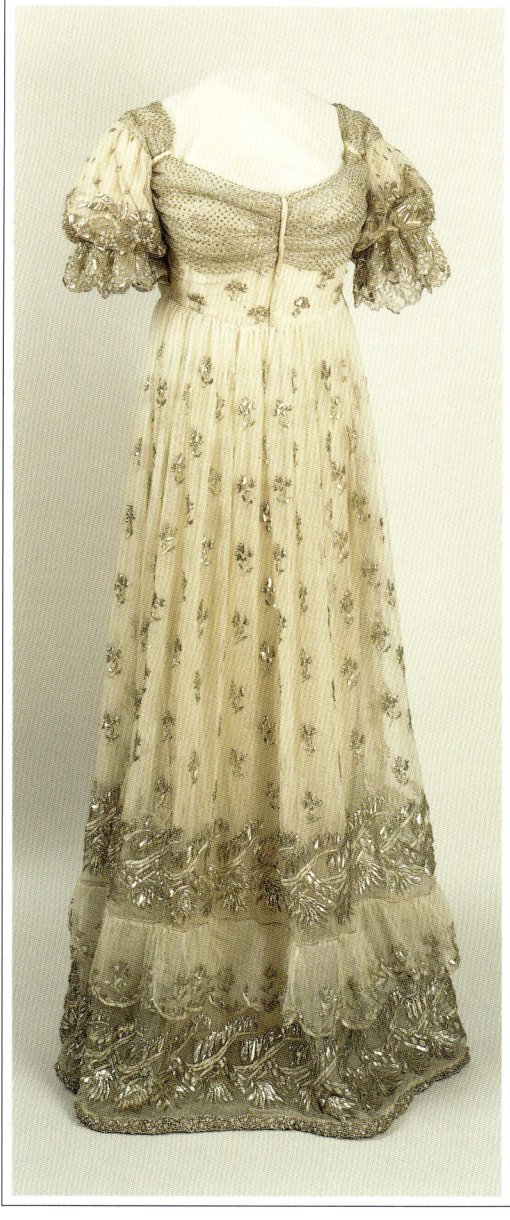

FIGURE 110.

Empress Joséphine's Court Gown, French, 1805. Silver gauze lamé ornamented with pattern of carnations, large border embroidered with flowers and palmettes. Rueil-Malmaison, Musée national des Châteaux de Malmaison et Bois-Préau.

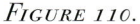

The art of embroidery had virtually died out during the Revolution, only to find new life in imperial court dress. It was executed not just in silk thread, but in genuine gold and silver thread mingled with glittering spangles, foil, and even real jewels. This lavishly embroidered gown, with its bodice covered in silver spangles, is reminiscent of the gown worn by Joséphine in Prud'hon's portrait of 1805 {see FIGURE 20}. The palmette was a fan-shaped decorative motif associated with ancient Greek architecture.

Thus, the eccentricity of the Directoire succumbed to the sophisticated allure of the Empire, and international press coverage of the coronation paid special attention to the new court dress. Although the outmoded *grand habit* was still in use at some European courts, it was increasingly discarded in favor of the captivating French styles. As Napoléon placed his relations on the thrones of Europe, his sartorial dominion expanded with his Empire. Once again, France shaped court dress throughout Europe.

THE EMPIRE: 1804–1814

Although "it can scarcely be imagined with what ease she stepped into the station of Queen," Joséphine was never entirely comfortable with court etiquette—or court costume.[34] "Elegant and simple in her dress, the Empress submitted with regret to the necessity of ceremonial dress."[35] Her 1809 wardrobe inventory reveals that most of her approximately two hundred gowns were cotton, not silk or velvet. Nevertheless, Joséphine understood that dress played an important role in shaping her image and, more important, her husband's. Moreover, she was an insatiable consumer of clothing and jewelry. "She bought everything, without ever asking the price, and, most of the time, forgot what she had bought."[36] Her annual budget for her wardrobe and personal expenses was 600,000 francs per annum; in 1809, she spent 920,816 francs, which was not unusual.[37] "The least little assembly, the least ball, was an occasion for her to order a new gown in spite of the numerous storerooms of rags ... in all the palaces."[38] Like Marie-Antoinette before her, Joséphine was careful not to appear in public in the same gown twice. She changed her linen three times a day, and wore only new stockings.[39] Many of her garments were worn once, then remodeled or given away to members of her family or her household.[40]

Napoléon took pride in his good taste in female dress, and would occasionally attend Joséphine's morning toilette, to the surprise of her ladies-in-waiting. "The Emperor sometimes came to the toilette of the Empress," one of them recalled, "and it was an extraordinary thing for us to see a man whose head was filled with such great things enter into the most minute details and decide on the gowns and jewels that he wanted the Empress to wear in this or that circumstance." He was equally fervent in his displeasure; he was known to stain with ink the gowns he disliked, or throw shawls into the fire.[41] "When he glimpsed ladies in his salon whose costume was not fresh, or whose toilette was badly done ... he reproached them."[42] If Joséphine is remembered as fashion icon, then Napoléon deserves some of the credit.

As hoped, the coronation revitalized the French fashion industry. Immediately afterward "there were great rivalries in toilettes. The Empress, as well as her sisters-in-law, always appeared with a new *parure*, and many pearls and jewels. ... One then began to wear many gold and silver spangled fabrics."[43] A surviving muslin gown worn by Joséphine has a bodice trimmed in silver spangles {see FIGURE 110}, and resembles the one she wears in her 1805 portrait by Prud'hon {see FIGURE 20}. However, the two fashion "innovations" most often associated with Joséphine were in fact drawn from the past: the classical age and the age of chivalry.

Fashions *à l'antique*

Fashions and hairstyles inspired by classical antiquity first appeared in France on the eve of the Revolution. "Greek" or "Etruscan" motifs replaced the undulating ribbons, flowers, and feathers of the ancien régime; cameos and gold armbands replaced diamonds and pearls. Thin, white muslin sheaths with high waistlines and low necklines imitated the clinging drapery of classical statues and bared the upper arms for the first time in centuries. The duchesse d'Abrantès complained, "No way to cheat nature any more. These days a plain woman tends to look even plainer, and a woman with a bad figure is lost. It is only the slender ones with a mass of hair and a small bosom who triumph."[44] Joséphine was among the lucky few.

Imaginative accessories completed the Hellenic tableau. High-heeled shoes were replaced by flat *cothurnes*—lightweight sandals laced up the leg, calling attention to bare flesh or flesh-colored stockings. Cropped, curled hair and wigs (called *à la Titus* after the Roman emperor) first appeared in 1798; women also copied the hairstyles of antique statues and medals. Joséphine collected antiquities, such as medals and engraved stones, and may have used these as inspiration for fashions and hairstyles.[45]

Cashmere shawls mimicked the drapery of antique statues and provided much-needed warmth; the traditional teardrop-shaped pinecone pattern and discreet floral motifs added visual interest to plain white gowns {see FIGURE 106}. Shawls first appeared in French fashion magazines and portraits in 1790, although they did not become available in appreciable quantities until Napoléon's campaigns in Egypt, where Indian shawls were easily obtained from traders.[46] As French soldiers returned home from Egypt laden with shawls, they became an essential female accessory, indoors and out. Joséphine was one of the first women in France to wear the shawl, and it would become her signature fashion statement.

Initially, Joséphine was skeptical of the shawls Napoléon sent her from Egypt. She confessed to her son Eugène, "I find them hideous. Their great advantage lies in their lightness, but I doubt very much if they will ever become fashionable."[47] But she was quickly converted to the new style, and her illustrious example helped to convert a generation of Frenchwomen. Joséphine herself possessed between three and four hundred shawls.[48] Not all of them were made of cashmere; her inventory of 1814 lists shawls and scarves of lace, gauze, and muslin, embroidered in gold and silver.[49]

> She always wore one in the morning which she draped over her shoulders more gracefully than anyone else I have ever seen.... She bought every shawl that was offered to her, whatever the price. She had some that were worth eight, ten and twelve thousand francs. But, indeed, these shawls were one of the great luxuries of this Court. The ladies scorned to appear in a shawl that had cost only fifty louis and boasted of the price of those they wore.[50]

In spite of his having thrown some into the fire, Napoléon gave Joséphine several shawls, including one worth more than ten thousand francs.[51] Joséphine developed creative uses for her surplus, turning them into gowns, bedcovers, and dog cushions.[52] LeRoy once cut up an expensive cashmere shawl to make a cloak for Joséphine.[53] In her 1809 portrait by Gros, the empress wears two cashmere shawls: one of unbleached white fabric made

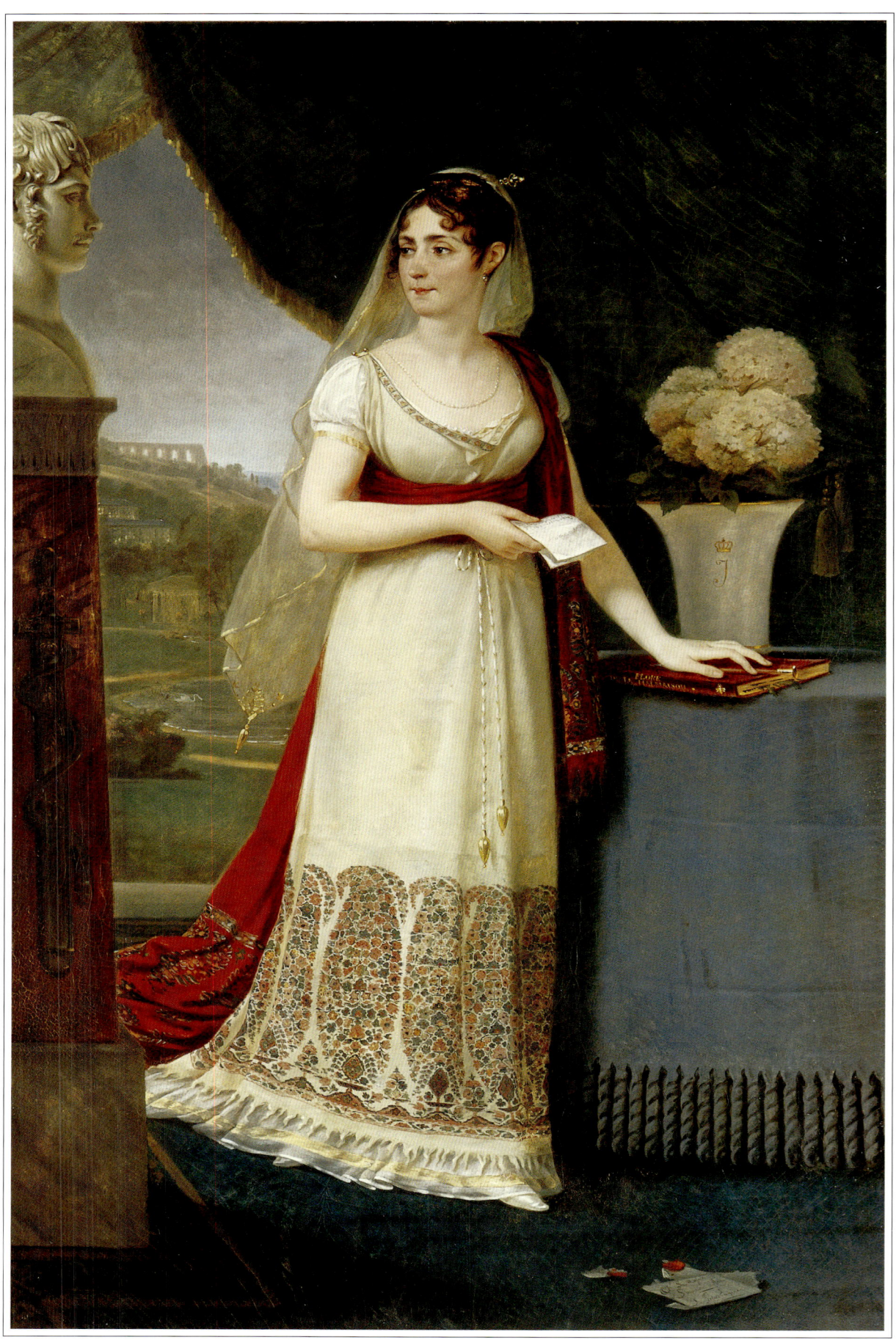

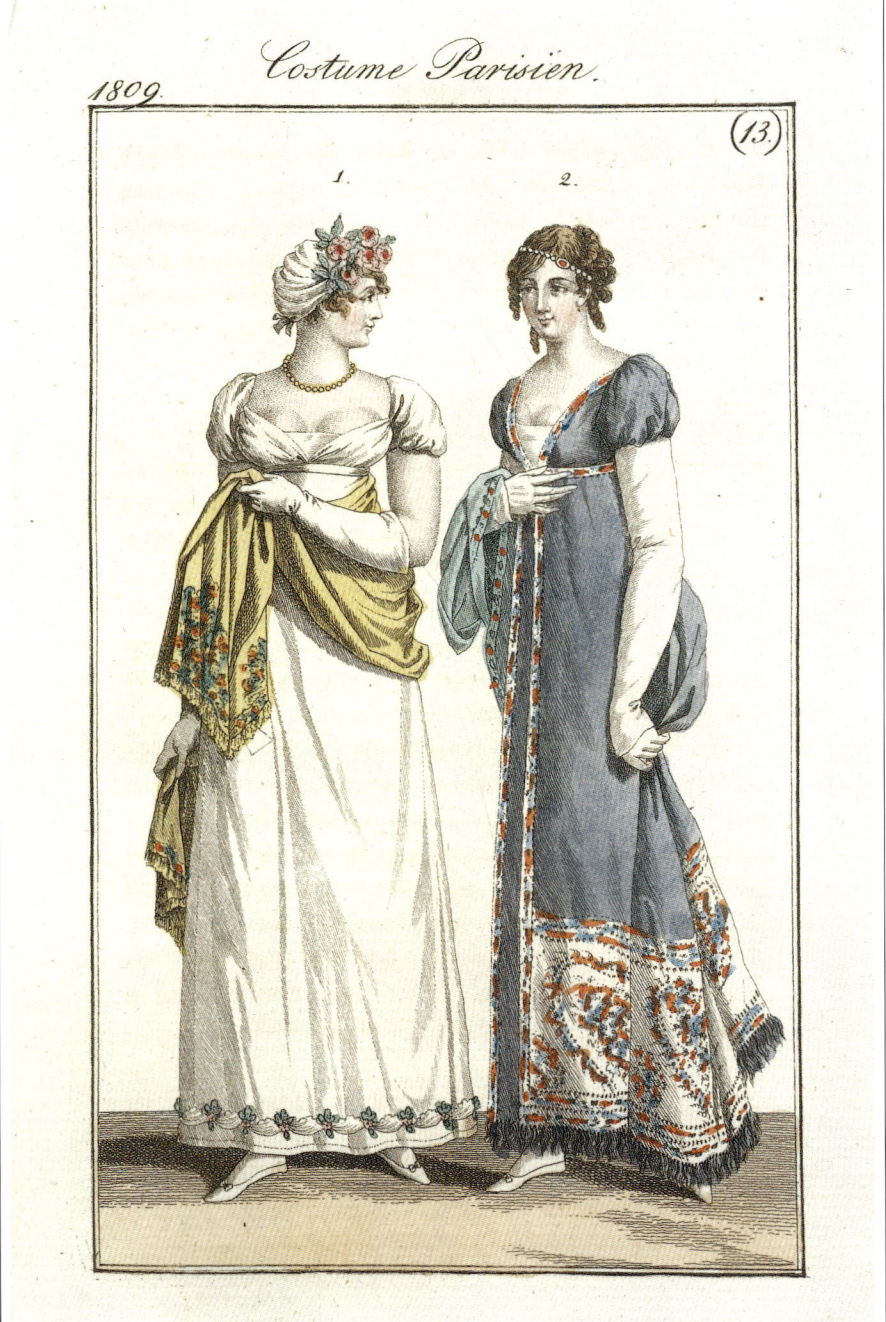

Figure 111.

Antoine-Jean Gros (French, 1771–1835), *Empress Joséphine*, 1808.
Oil on canvas, 217 × 141 cm (58½ × 55½ in.).
Nice, Musée d'Art et d'Histoire.

• • •

With hundreds of shawls at her disposal, Joséphine found creative uses for the precious textiles. Here she accessorizes a gown made of a shawl with another, contrasting shawl. Fashion magazines paid careful attention to her innovative attire, and reinterpreted it in fashion plates, ensuring that it had a widespread influence (see FIGURE 112).

Figure 112.

Anonymous, *Journal des dames et des modes*,
March 26, 1809, no. 13, plate 13.
Los Angeles, Los Angeles County Museum of Art.

• • •

In this fashion plate, the woman on the left wears a crêpe bonnet ornamented with roses, an amber necklace, a white gown trimmed with crêpe, flowers, and ribbons, an embroidered yellow silk shawl, white gloves, and white sandals. The woman on the right wears a coiffure "à la Ninon" decorated with pearls, a cashmere gown, an apple-green shawl, white gloves, and white sandals. A similar cashmere gown survives in the Musée historique des Tissus, Lyon.

into a tuniclike overdress, the other of vivid red, which she wrapped around her waist and draped over her left shoulder {FIGURE 111}. The fringed edge of the white shawl forms a decorative border at the hem of the gown. A similarly fringed cashmere gown appeared in the *Journal des dames et des modes* in March of the same year {FIGURE 112}.

The increasing availability of cheap European imitations helped to keep Indian-style shawls in vogue until the late nineteenth century, and they have been in and out of fashion ever since. Nevertheless, in the popular imagination, the cashmere shawl remains eternally associated with Joséphine.

Troubadour Style

Another trend often linked to Joséphine is the Troubadour, or Gothic, style. Joséphine collected paintings in the so-called *genre chevaleresque*, or Troubadour style (see chapter 1), and also wore fashions inspired by medieval and Renaissance dress. These had already been revived in the eighteenth century, for under Louis XV and Louis XVI elaborate costumes inspired by the age of chivalry—and specifically the glorious reign of Henri IV (1589–1610)—were worn for court balls. Although traditional court dress eventually triumphed over these costly, somewhat theatrical *habits à la Henri IV*, Marie-Antoinette (who enjoyed novels and plays set in the age of chivalry) continued to wear gowns evoking *le bon vieux temps* ("the good old times") at court balls. This ensured that the stylized elements of *le style troubadour*, reminiscent of the French poet-musicians who immortalized the age of chivalry, entered fashionable dress.[54]

Joséphine's enthusiastic patronage of art and fashions inspired by *le bon vieux temps* was manifested in her taste for long veils, slashed and puffed sleeves, ermine, and standing rufflike collars, shaped by the costume conventions of troubadour paintings. The jeweled headband she wears in her

Figure 113.

Antoine-Jean Gros, *Napoléon I Visiting the Salon of 1808* (detail), 1808. Oil on canvas, 350 × 640 cm (137¾ × 252 in.). Versailles, Musée national des Châteaux de Versailles et de Trianon.

• • •

Joséphine toured the Salon of 1808 at the Louvre wearing a vivid crimson velvet redingote trimmed with ermine, inspired by a medieval *sûrcote*. The details of her gown and those of her ladies echoed the historicized costumes of the troubadour paintings on display, including Jean-Baptiste Vermay's *Mary Stuart, Queen of Scotland, Receiving Her Death Sentence* {see FIGURE 114}.

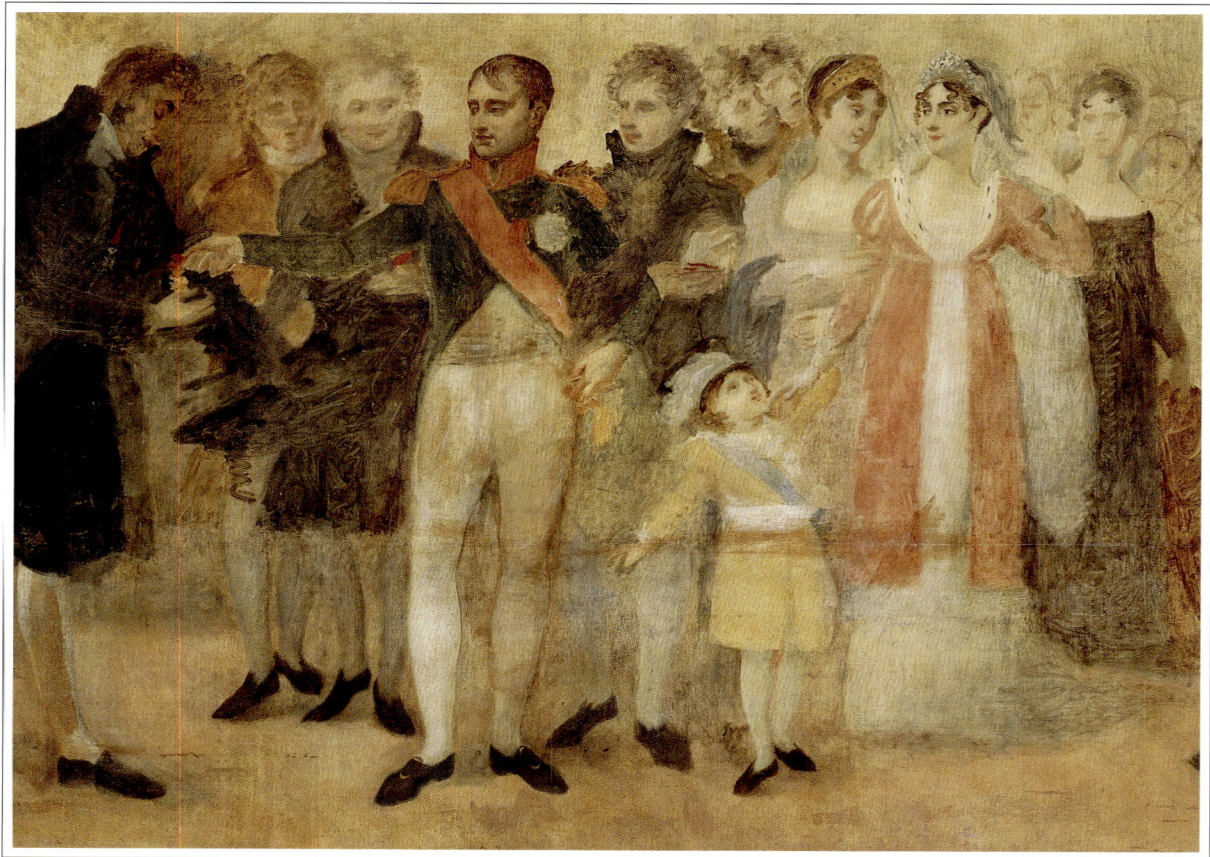

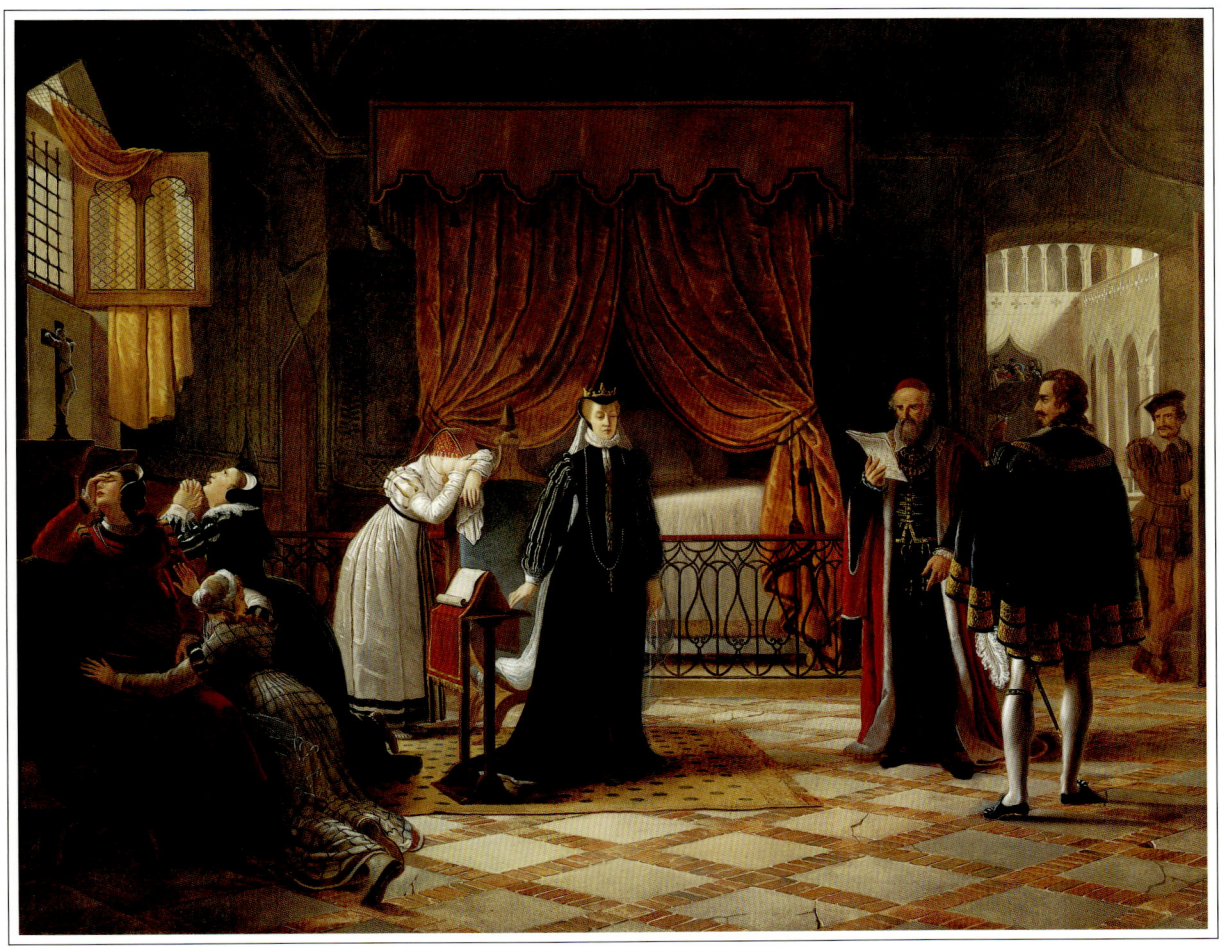

Figure 114.

Jean-Baptiste Vermay (French, ca. 1790–1833), *Mary Stuart, Queen of Scotland, Receiving Her Death Sentence,* ca. 1808. Oil on canvas, 129 × 162 cm (50¾ × 63¾ in.). Rueil-Malmaison, Musée national des Châteaux de Malmaison et Bois-Préau.

• • •

Vermay's painting in *le genre chevaleresque* reveals the extent to which imperial court dress influenced paintings and fashions in *le style troubadour*, and vice versa. The gowns worn by the Scottish queen and her ladies have the puffed and slashed sleeves, high waistlines, and long trains of Napoleonic court dress {see FIGURE 113}. Clearly, Joséphine approved of Vermay's romantic reinterpretation of Renaissance dress; she acquired this painting for her personal collection.

1805 portrait by Prud'hon {see FIGURE 20} recalls the so-called *ferronière* (jeweled chain) of the Renaissance. Joséphine also popularized ermine-trimmed velvet coats reminiscent of a *surcôte*, a tunic-like overgarment worn by both men and women in medieval times (and in Troubadour-style paintings). Ermine, formerly restricted to royalty, was a popular fashion fur under the Empire.[55] Joséphine wore one of these redingotes to the Salon of 1808, as illustrated in an unfinished painting by Gros {FIGURE 113}. It was at this Salon that she first saw Jean-Baptiste Vermay's *Mary Stuart, Queen of Scotland, Receiving Her Death Sentence* {FIGURE 114}, which she later added to her personal art collection. Scotland's history and literature provided numerous subjects for Troubadour artists. But Vermay may have found his inspiration closer to home; the gowns worn by the queen and her ladies bear a striking resemblance to Napoleonic court dress {FIGURE 115}.

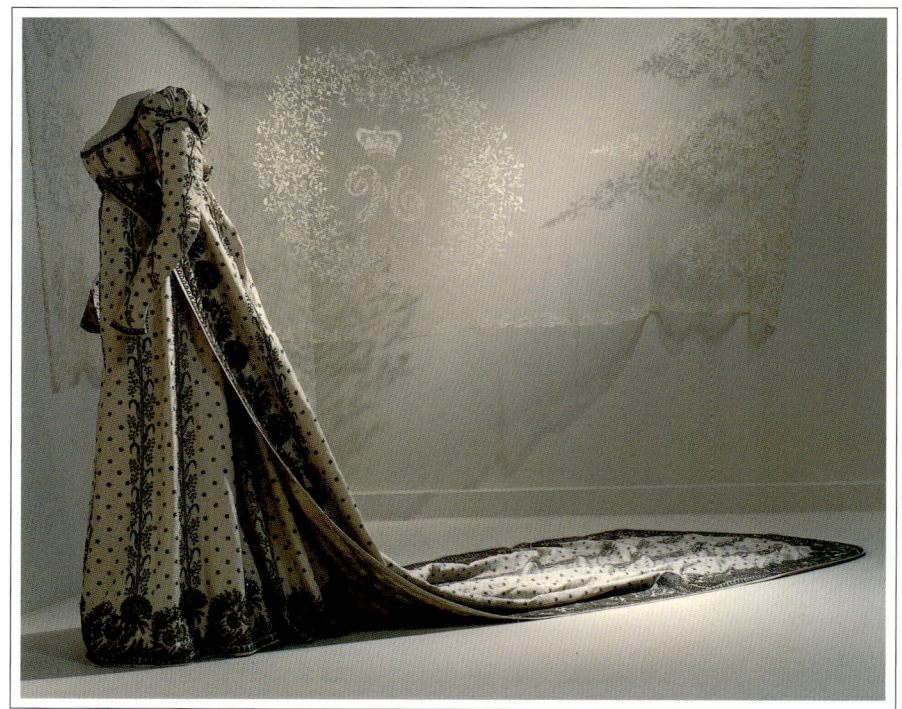

FIGURE 115.

Empress Joséphine's gown, French, 1804/9. Velvet, embroidered tulle, Brussels lace. Rueil-Malmaison, Musée national des Châteaux de Malmaison et Bois-Préau.

• • •

The sleeves of this court gown—puffed at the shoulders and reaching down to the knuckles—resemble those of Joséphine's coronation dress (see FIGURE 109). Bands of embroidery accentuate the strongly vertical lines of the gown and further ornament the already highly decorative confection of velvet, tulle, and Brussels lace. Napoléon had made the wearing of lace compulsory at court, but his attempts to promote French-made lace over the technically and stylistically superior Brussels product failed, even with his own wife.

DIVORCE AND DEATH: 1810–1814

After her divorce, Joséphine determinedly held on to her position at the forefront of fashion. "At Malmaison, she maintained the same luxury, and she dressed up, even when she did not have to receive anyone."[56] She employed a small army of ladies-in-waiting, chambermaids, and laundresses to look after her wardrobe. Napoléon ensured that she remained on the *liste civile*, so she could afford such indulgences. LeRoy continued to dress Joséphine until her death in 1814, but her purchases reflected her reduced income and infrequent public appearances.

Joséphine's idle life at Malmaison caused her to gain weight. "She had lost her slender figure; her features were altered; she was divested of that elegance which had once made her the most fascinating woman of Paris and of her Court. All that was left to her was a dignified deportment and great elegance of manners, and especially of dress. The last was always an important point with her."[57] It remained so until the very end, for "she died entirely covered with ribbons and rose-colored satin"—a fitting coda to her chic career.[58]

Joséphine had never been a great beauty, but she was blessed with perfect taste; her clothes, jewels, and hairstyles always suited her and the occasion perfectly. This, combined with her legendary kindness and charm, had the effect of making her seem like the most beautiful woman in the world. As Napoléon said of her: "All that which art could imagine to increase the attractions was put into use by her, but with such mystery, that one could hardly suspect it."[59] Despite their elegance and inventiveness, Joséphine's clothes never overshadowed the extraordinary woman who wore them.

Notes

1. Yvonne Deslandres, "Joséphine and La Mode," *Apollo*, July 1977, 44.
2. Denise Ledoux-Lebard, "Joséphine and Interior Decoration," *Apollo*, July 1977, 22.
3. Constant, *Mémoires intimes de Napoléon Ier*, ed. Maurice Dernelle (Paris, 1967), 209.
4. Mme de Chastenay, *Mémoires de Madame de Chastenay, 1771–1815*, ed. Alphonse Roserot (Paris, 1896), 2:364.
5. Chastenay, *Mémoires*, 1:302–3.
6. Chastenay, *Mémoires*, 1:302–3.
7. Daniel Roche, *The Culture of Clothing*, Jean Birrell, trans. (Cambridge, 1994), 279.
8. Laure Junot, *The Autobiography and Recollections of Laura, Duchess of Abrantès*, vol. 1 (London, 1893), 173.
9. For a description of a rich trousseau and corbeille, see Junot, *Autobiography and Recollections*, vol. 1, 393–97.
10. Henry Swinburne, *The Courts of Europe at the Close of the Last Century*, ed. C. White, vol. 2 (London, 1841), 181.
11. Swinburne, *The Courts of Europe*, vol. 2, 181; vol. 2, 139–40.
12. Deslandres, "Joséphine and La Mode," 46.
13. Christine Sutherland, *Marie Walewska: Napoleon's Great Love* (New York, 1979), 110–11.
14. Rev. Dawson Warren, *Journal of a British Chaplain in Paris*, ed. A. M. Broadley (London, 1913), 50.
15. Hortense de Beauharnais, *The Memoirs of Queen Hortense*, ed. Prince Napoléon, trans. Arthur K. Griggs and F. Mabel Robinson, vol. 1 (London, 1928), 56.
16. Junot, *Autobiography and Recollections*, vol. 3, 36.
17. Mme de Rémusat, *Mémoires de Madame de Rémusat* (Paris, 1968), 23.
18. Chastenay, *Mémoires*, 1:460.
19. Vere Foster, *The Two Duchesses* (London, 1898), 170.
20. Junot, *Autobiography and Recollections*, 3:36.
21. Rémusat, *Mémoires*, 157.
22. Aileen Ribeiro, *The Art of Dress: Fashion in England and France, 1750 to 1820* (New Haven, 1995), 156.
23. Katell le Bourhis, ed., introduction to *The Age of Napoleon: Costume from Revolution to Empire, 1789–1815* (New York, 1989), xii.
24. Rémusat, *Mémoires*, 157.
25. Junot, *Autobiography and Recollections*, 2:33.
26. Alphonse Maze-Sencier, *Les Fournisseurs de Napoléon Ier et des deux impératrices* (Paris, 1893), 4.
27. Ribeiro, *The Art of Dress*, 160.
28. Maze-Sencier, *Les Fournisseurs*, 3.
29. Ribeiro, *The Art of Dress*, 160.
30. With the health of the economy in mind, Napoléon had declared that only silk and velvet were sufficiently dignified for the imperial court and its representatives. See Musée national des Châteaux de Malmaison et Bois-Préau, *Soies tissées, soies brodées chez l'impératrice Joséphine* (Paris, 2002), 14.
31. Marie-Jeanne-Pierrette Avrillion, *Mémoires de Mlle Avrillion, première femme de chambre de l'imperatrice Joséphine*, ed. Maurice Derelle (Paris, 1986), 98–99.
32. Rémusat, *Mémoires*, 168.
33. Junot, *Autobiography and Recollections*, vol. 3, 34.
34. Junot, *Autobiography and Recollections*, vol. 1, 173.
35. Constant, *Mémoires*, 208.
36. Rémusat, *Mémoires*, 269–70.
37. Ribeiro, *The Art of Dress*, 120.
38. Rémusat, *Mémoires*, 270–71.
39. Rémusat, *Mémoires*, 270–71.
40. Fiona Ffoulkes, "'Quality Always Distinguishes Itself': Louis Hippolyte LeRoy and the Luxury Clothing Industry in Early Nineteenth-Century Paris," in *Consumers and Luxury: Consumer Culture in Europe, 1650–1850*, ed. Maxine Berg and Helen Clifford (Manchester, 1999), 194.
41. Avrillion, *Mémoires*, 91; Rémusat, *Mémoires*, 270.
42. Avrillion, *Mémoires*, 275–76.
43. Rémusat, *Mémoires*, 171.
44. Quoted in Sutherland, *Marie Walewska*, 111.
45. Constant, *Mémoires*, 215.
46. *Journal de la mode et du goût*, June 5, 1790.
47. Anny Latour, *Kings of Fashion* (London, 1958), 38.
48. Rémusat, *Mémoires*, 270.
49. Musée national des Châteaux de Malmaison et Bois-Préau, *Soies tissées, soies brodées chez l'impératrice Joséphine* (Paris, 2002), 72.
50. Rémusat, *Mémoires*, 270–71.
51. Philippe Séguy, "Costume in the Age of Napoleon," in Bourhis, ed., *The Age of Napoleon*, 81.
52. Rémusat, *Mémoires*, 270.
53. Ffoulkes, "'Quality Always Distinguishes Itself'," 190.
54. For a discussion of the taste for troubadour fashions at the court of Louis XVI, see Alice Mackrell, "Dress in Le Style Troubadour," *Costume* 32 (1998): 33–44
55. Lourdes Font and Michele Majer, "La Quatrième Unité: Costume and Fashion in Genre Historique Painting," in *Romance and Chivalry: History and Literature Reflected in Early Nineteenth-Century French Painting*, ed. Nadia Tscherny and Guy Stair Sainty (London, 1996), 202; and 198, 199.
56. Rémusat, *Memoires*, 272.
57. Junot, *Autobiography and Recollections*, vol. 4, 441.
58. Rémusat, *Mémoires*, 272.
59. Constant, *Mémoires*, 409.

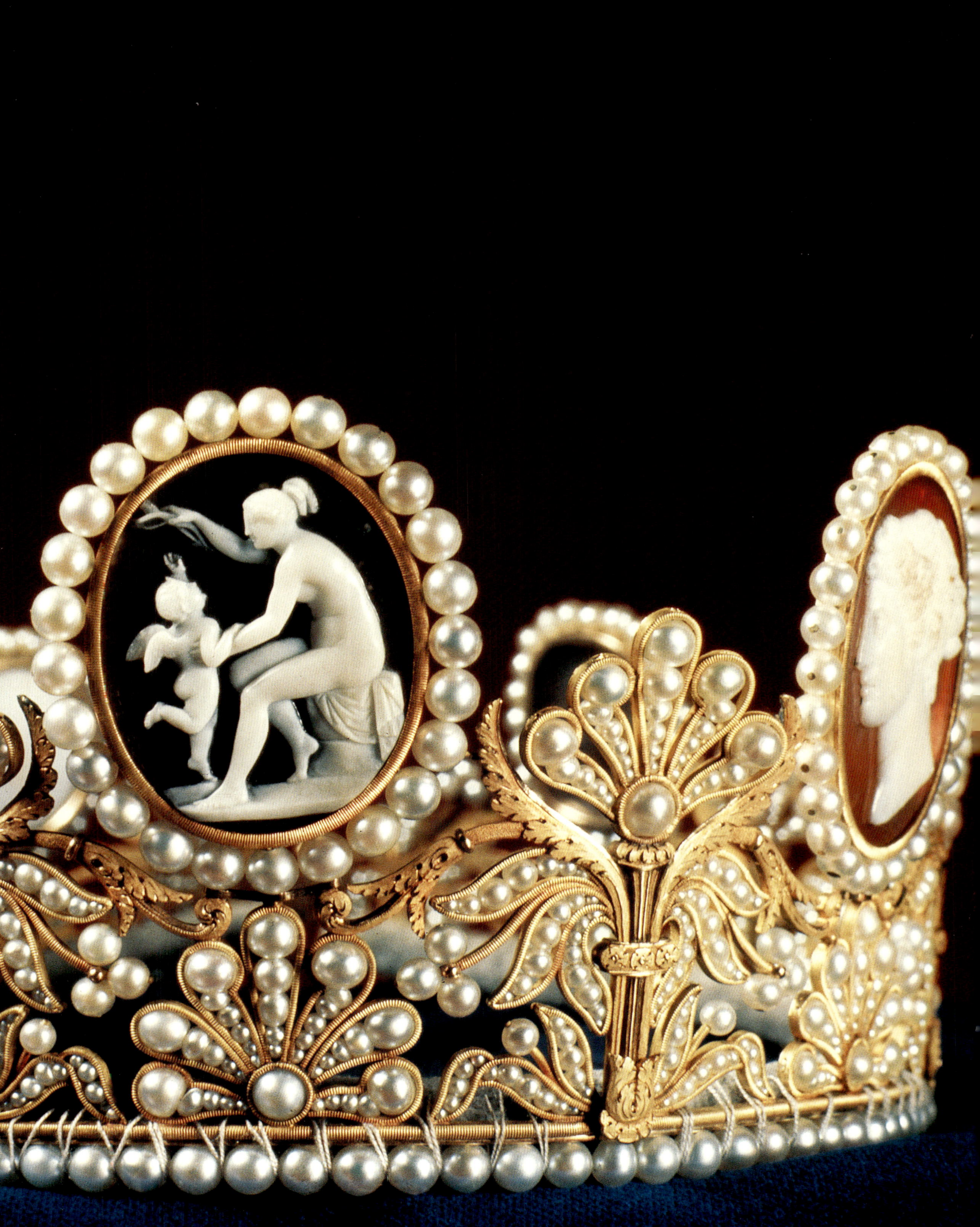

CHAPTER 11

Diana Scarisbrick

Love and Glory: Joséphine's Jewelry

Although there have been many biographies of the Empress Joséphine, even the best of these allots only a few pages to her jewelry. Yet her collection—which was vast—deserves special study, for it reveals much about her eclectic taste, love of novelty, extravagance, and warm heart, as well as the various phases of her extraordinary career.

As the Creole bride of Alexandre de Beauharnais, Joséphine was so delighted with the diamonds—a pair of girandole (three-drop) earrings, bracelets, watch, and chain—she received at her wedding in 1779,[1] that she carried them about in her pocket to show her friends.[2] Then came the Revolution of 1789, when she lost everything and narrowly escaped sharing her husband's fate at the guillotine.

A new era began in March 1796 when she married the young General Bonaparte, an event marked by his gift of a modest "alliance" ring with twin hearts.[3] In June of that year she joined her husband in Italy, remaining there until January 1798. Outside Milan, at the palace of Mombello, the couple established a brilliant court governed not by republican principles but by strict, quasi-royal protocol. Joséphine soon developed a taste not only for major works of art but also for the many other "pretty things for sale in Italy," which she acquired by gifts,[4] plunder, and purchases on an extravagant scale.[5] Through an agent, M. Sartoni, she bought hard-stone mosaics from Florence; coral and cameos from Naples; and glass mosaics, cameos, and intaglios from Rome; as well as copies of Greek and Roman jewels excavated from archaeological sites.[6]

These jewels struck just the right note in 1798 Paris, where, according to Count Miot de Melito, "women could indulge their passion for dress, fashion had regained its ascendancy, and there was a pronounced cult of antiquity."[7] A change of style began after November 1799 when, as the Consular court became ever more formal and splendid, Napoléon allowed Joséphine the use of the pearls and precious stones from the Trésor de la Couronne, which he was replenishing after the dispersals of the Revolution, and he encouraged her to buy all she wanted. Not only did Napoléon wish to assert his political authority through a display of grandeur, but he was determined to reinstate the Parisian jeweler to the preeminence lost in the years of anarchy after 1789. The stimulus thus given to trade was so successful[8] that immediately after the Treaty of Amiens in 1803, English travelers such as Lady Elgin and Mrs. Bertie Greathead had their jewels remounted in the latest Parisian fashion.[9]

To ensure that Joséphine always looked as imposing as he desired at the sumptuous festivities held at the Tuileries and elsewhere, Napoléon supervised her wardrobe.[10] Her display of magnificence became even more pronounced after the Senate proclaimed Napoléon emperor on May 18, 1804. Two months later Joséphine stood beside him at the Invalides where, after mass, the emperor distributed crosses to those appointed to the Legion of Honor. She eclipsed all others in a dress of pale pink tulle with gold and silver stars scintillating in the sun, her head crowned à la Cérès, with wheatears made of diamonds.[11] According to an inventory drawn up by the head *dame de la chambre*, Agatha Rible, for her successor, Mme Marco Besson de Saint Hilaire, Joséphine's private jewelry collection was already extensive.[12] The apotheosis came when she was crowned empress at Notre Dame {see FIGURE 24} on December 2, 1804, and all present applauded her grace and poise.[13] Her appearance at Napoléon's coronation in Milan cathedral in May 1805 was similarly impressive; there, too, she looked as if she had been born for her imperial destiny.

During the period between the coronation of 1804 and the divorce of 1809, the collection listed by Rible underwent considerable changes as new jewels were acquired and the old ones exchanged, modified, or dismantled. Thereafter, Josephine seems to have given some of her more important pieces to her children, Hortense and Eugène, but even so, she still owned an impressive amount at the time of her death in 1814. The posthumous inventory lists 130 items that, calculated at less than half the market value, still totaled 1,932,263 francs.[14] It seems too, from the large sums of money owed her jewelers, that she had continued to buy right up to the end. Kept in Joséphine's bedroom on the first floor at Malmaison, these jewels, which were then divided between the two children, are very difficult to identify and trace.

Her Jewelers

Joséphine must have inspired her jewelers, not only because of her looks, taste and elegance, but also because of her charm and extraordinary kindness. There is evidence that from the time of the Consulate she used her position on behalf of the sons-in-law of Edmé Marie Foncier, especially his successor, Bernard Armand Marguerite. Marie-Etienne Nitot also had cause to be grateful to her, according to a document describing an incident at

Malmaison.[15] It seems that Nitot's son, François-Regnault Nitot, established in a shop in the Place du Carrousel, never lost favor with the empress, as she owed him 73,722 francs (far more than any of her other creditors) in the year of her death.

Joséphine cast her net wide and also patronized other jewelers for their particular specialities.[16] Thus, following an introduction by the comtesse de Ségur, Joséphine bought snuff boxes and accessories as well as pearls and jewelry from François Mellerio of the rue Coq Saint Honoré, and from his cousin, Jean-Baptiste Mellerio of la Couronne de Fer in the rue Vivienne. Members of a dynasty established in France since the reign of Marie de Médicis, the Mellerios are credited with the invention of the acrostic jewel, which conveyed a message through the initials of the stones—for example, Ruby-Emerald-Garnet-Amethyst-Ruby-Diamond spells REGARD.[17]

However, even the very best that Paris could provide was not enough for Joséphine. She sent a special request to Count Daru, *intendant général* of Napoléon's military household, reminding him of her "taste for pretty things," and went on to ask him "if while on campaign you come across anything unusual in the way of pearls or gems, please buy them for me."[18]

Products of Italy

In another letter Joséphine tells Daru that Dominique-Vivant Denon, whom Napoléon had appointed director of museums, had assembled a collection of cameos and turquoises for her while on his travels. So she writes to Count Daru as follows: "The empress is no more exempt from a little coquetry than any other woman, but in her case it is excusable, given that all she desires is to please the emperor. I therefore beg you to authorize M. Denon to let me have these items as soon as possible."[19]

Mlle Avrillion remembered how much the empress enjoyed the company of Denon, a man of the world, "charming, with wonderful manners and brilliant conversation."[20] Since he acted as her agent abroad, these talks must have covered jewelry as well as painting and sculpture. Certainly such items as "chains, comb, earrings mounted with eleven scarabs with pearls...necklace with matching earrings of scarabs" and "two mummies mounted in gold," which were listed in her inventories, echo the excitement aroused by Napoléon's campaign in Egypt.

Yet however great her fascination with the civilization of the Nile, it could not compare with her enthusiasm for Greek and Roman art. In particular, she was captivated by sculpture not only of large scale in marble but also in miniature, namely cameos and intaglios. The empress and Denon are likely to have discussed the natural beauty of the hard and semi-precious stones used, the virtuoso engraving techniques, and the subjects depicted—divinities and heroes of mythology, and illustrious men and women of history—as well as their significance. Since the noble art of gem engraving had been patronized by Hellenistic and Roman rulers of the ancient world, and Napoléon liked to present himself as the successor to Alexander and Augustus, he associated the technique with his own regime and therefore approved of his wife's interest in it. In this spirit, after the French invasion of Rome, he gave Joséphine cameos of which the most famous was the double portrait of Augustus and Livia,[21] which had been removed from the Vatican collection in 1797. Modern cameos depicting the labors of Hercules are mounted in the bandeau and necklace she wears in a dramatic portrait by Jean-André Appiani {see FRONTISPIECE}. Further additions to Joséphine's collection came from victorious generals anxious to please her and from members of the imperial family traveling or residing in Italy.

To encourage contemporary work, Napoléon appointed Jean-Henri Simon (1752–1834) as engraver of the official seals, gave commissions to Romain Vincent Jeuffroy (1749–1826), instituted a biannual prize for medalists and gem engravers in 1803, and distributed the Prix de Rome from 1805 onward.[22]

Joséphine (who also patronized J.-H. Simon) was, like her husband, active in promoting the artists whose talents were bringing the great Roman tradition of gem engraving to a triumphant conclusion. She almost certainly owned gems cut by others besides those whose names are documented. These include Giuseppe Girometti (1779–1851), who engraved the Atlanta Cameo *opera di prima ordine*, which Pope Pius VII gave her when he arrived in France for Napoléon's coronation.[23] Through François-Regnault Nitot, Joséphine ordered from Luigi Pichler (1775–1854) a cornelian intaglio portrait of the pope, in which he is crowned with the papal tiara that Nitot had designed. She already owned another cornelian intaglio by Pichler, representing a sacrifice to the god Terminus.[24]

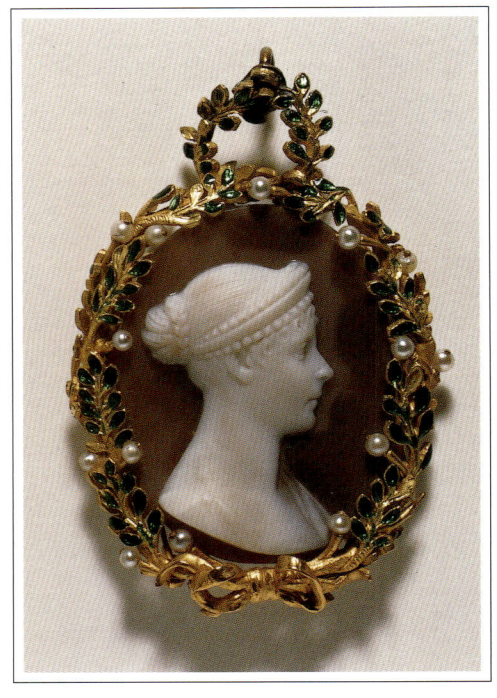

FIGURE 116.
Pendant with Cameo Portrait of the Empress Joséphine, cameo Italian, setting probably French, ca. 1804.
Gold with onyx cameo.
Nationalmuseum, Stockholm.

• • •

Crowned with a tiara, the empress is depicted in the tradition of ancient Roman cameo portraiture of the imperial family, an association further emphasized by the frame of enameled green laurel leaves and pearl berries. Whereas Napoléon, wishing to be seen as the new Augustus, patronized the art of gem engraving for political purposes, the empress's passion for both cameos and intaglios, ancient, Renaissance and contemporary, was purely aesthetic.

Several other Italian engravers are listed in the accounts, and portraits were frequently commissioned {FIGURE 116}. The Roman Gaspare Capparoni (1761–1808), for example, engraved the intaglio head of Napoléon after the life-size marble by Canova now at Apsley House;[25] and the Neapolitan Teresa Talani (1773–1844), a specialist in cameo and intaglio portraiture, is known for her double portrait of Napoléon and Joséphine, as well as one of the empress alone.[26] Her enthusiasm for cameo jewelry comes through in a letter to Hortense, in which she writes, "Eugène has put aside a necklace mounted with malachite cameos for you—I will bring it home with me. Meanwhile Mr. Berkheim is taking you another one, which I have just bought here in Milan. It is of engraved amethysts, which should look well with your lovely white skin. I'm sorry that I haven't had time to get a better setting for it."[27]

Napoléon demonstrated his belief in the political significance of cameo jewelry by asserting his right to the national collection of engraved gems housed in the Cabinet des Médailles. The eighty-two cameos and intaglios removed by imperial decree in 1808 were mounted with quantities of pearls by Nitot & Fils into a parure (matched set) of tiara, necklace, belt, and bracelets.[28] Unfortunately there are no portraits of Joséphine wearing it, perhaps because she never did so, as it might have been too heavy for comfort.[29] In any case, as state property, it was returned after the divorce to be used by Empress Marie-Louise.

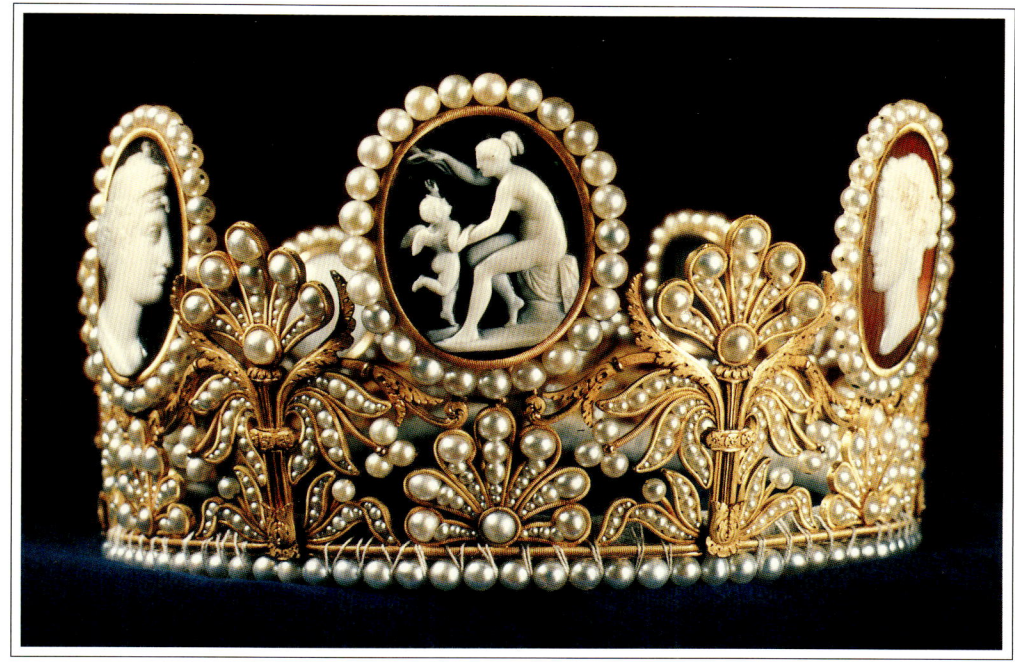

Whereas the inventories of 1804 and 1814 prove that Joséphine had a passion for cameos and intaglios, no details are given of the subjects represented, nor of signatures. The exception is an intaglio of the Three Graces, mounted as a seal to hang from a pearl, coral, and gold-bead necklace. The subject—a personification of grace, loyalty, and friendship—which she proposed to Antonio Canova in 1812, was especially meaningful to her after the divorce from Napoléon, whose regard she valued above all others.[30]

As for the settings of this type of jewel, it is clear that cameos and intaglios were often combined, that size determined the number of gems mounted in one ornament, and that although in some cases they were uniform in material, color, and iconography, this was not always the case. The gems in necklaces and bracelets were linked by single or double rows of gold chains in various patterns, such as Venetian and palmette, or by strings of seed pearls and gold beads twisted *en torsade*. Blue-black nicolo intaglios were, on rare occasion, mounted into a parure with strings of pearls with rubies. Sometimes the center of a necklace might be emphasized by a large gem, set as a plaque or hanging as a pendant. The frames might be plain gold with a matte border, perhaps outlined by a fillet of royal blue enamel or, for the most luxurious ornaments, embellished with pearls and diamonds wrought into motifs from classical art: Greek fret, leaves of olive or laurel, lyres, acanthus and vine scrolls, palmettes, or honeysuckles {FIGURE 117}.

Individual items listed in the inventories include tortoiseshell combs with high galleries centered on cameos in medallions {FIGURE 118} and pairs of earrings set with gems. Further, the belts, which emphasized the high-waisted Empire dress, might be mounted with cameos and intaglios all around or in the center plaque only, or perhaps with one large gem or as many as eleven smaller jewels clustered together. Many cameos and intaglios were intended for ring stones, and the empress had a large collection of these, attributed to ancient, Renaissance, and contemporary artists.

FIGURE 117.

Tiara, cameos Italian, setting French, attributed to F. R. Nitot, n.d.
Gold with stone cameos and pearls.
Royal Collection, Sweden.

• • •

This gold tiara features medallions set with cameos engraved by contemporary artists richly framed in pearl honeysuckles, scrolls, and palmettes, which complement the classical character of the engraved hard stones. This could be the tiara that the empress wears in a miniature painted by Ferdinand Quaglia shortly before her death (Wallace Collection, London). Her son, Eugène, gave it to his daughter Josefina, who married the future Oscar I of Sweden in 1823, and it has been worn by every queen of Sweden ever since.

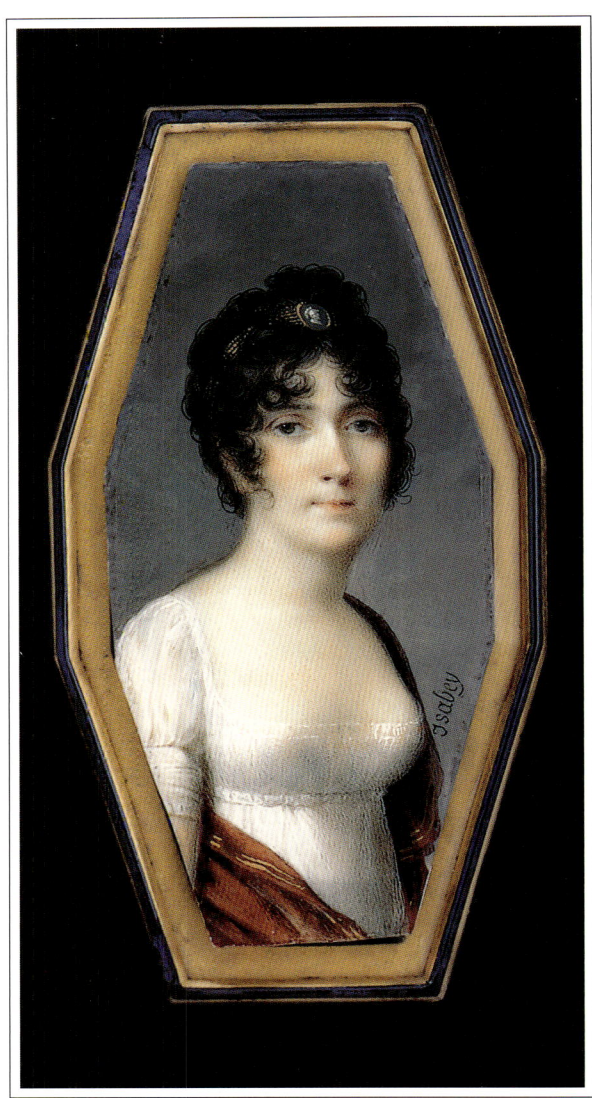

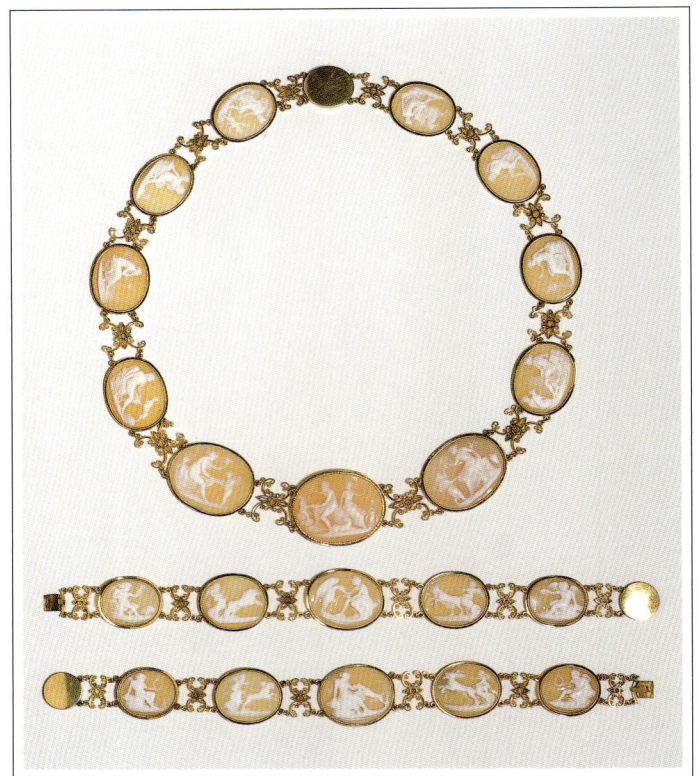

Figure 118.

Jean-Baptiste Isabey (French, 1767–1855).
Miniature of Joséphine, n.d.
Private collection.

• • •

This miniature of Joséphine, with cameo in center of a comb worn above the brow, is set in an octagonal frame with blue enamel border. With her excellent taste, the empress led the way in taking cameos and other specialities of Italy from the confines of the collector's cabinet into the world of luxury and fashion, setting an example that every *élégante* tried to follow.

Figure 119.

Necklace and Pair of Bracelets, cameos Italian, setting French or Italian, n.d.
Gold with shell cameo necklace, matching bracelets set with eleven and five cameos, respectively.
Private collection.

• • •

This was a gift from Empress Joséphine to one of her Tascher de la Pagerie cousins. Each came mounted in a narrow gold frame linked with addorsed C scrolls, representing an aspect of love: cupid in various guises interspersed with scenes depicting the loves of the gods for mortals, symbols of fidelity, and a widow's sorrow, personified by Agrippina grieving over the ashes of Germanicus. This is also the type of jewelry that Joséphine liked to wear when at home at Malmaison.

When a parure was set with gems that were linked iconographically—heads of emperors and empresses, illustrious men and women, Bacchanalian revels, or the loves of the gods—they were usually carved from shell, which was softer and therefore easier to work than the hard stones. Moreover, the white figures carved from the upper layer of the shell took a good polish and stood out well against the pale brown ground {FIGURE 119}. Joséphine, who found shell cameos difficult to resist, wrote from Milan in 1797, asking her brother-in-law, Joseph Bonaparte, to buy some for her.[31]

One of Joséphine's great pleasures when at Malmaison, with her ladies gathered around the fire, was to show them the cameos she was wearing that day. Then she would call for the boxes containing the rest of the collection to be brought out so that every piece could be examined.

Another Italian product of which the empress was very fond was coral, which she acquired in all shades from the richest red to the palest pink. Most came to her directly from the Genoese suppliers Oliva and Scotto. Sometimes coral was carved into cameo heads of divinities or shaped into round beads and drops of varying sizes and lengths,

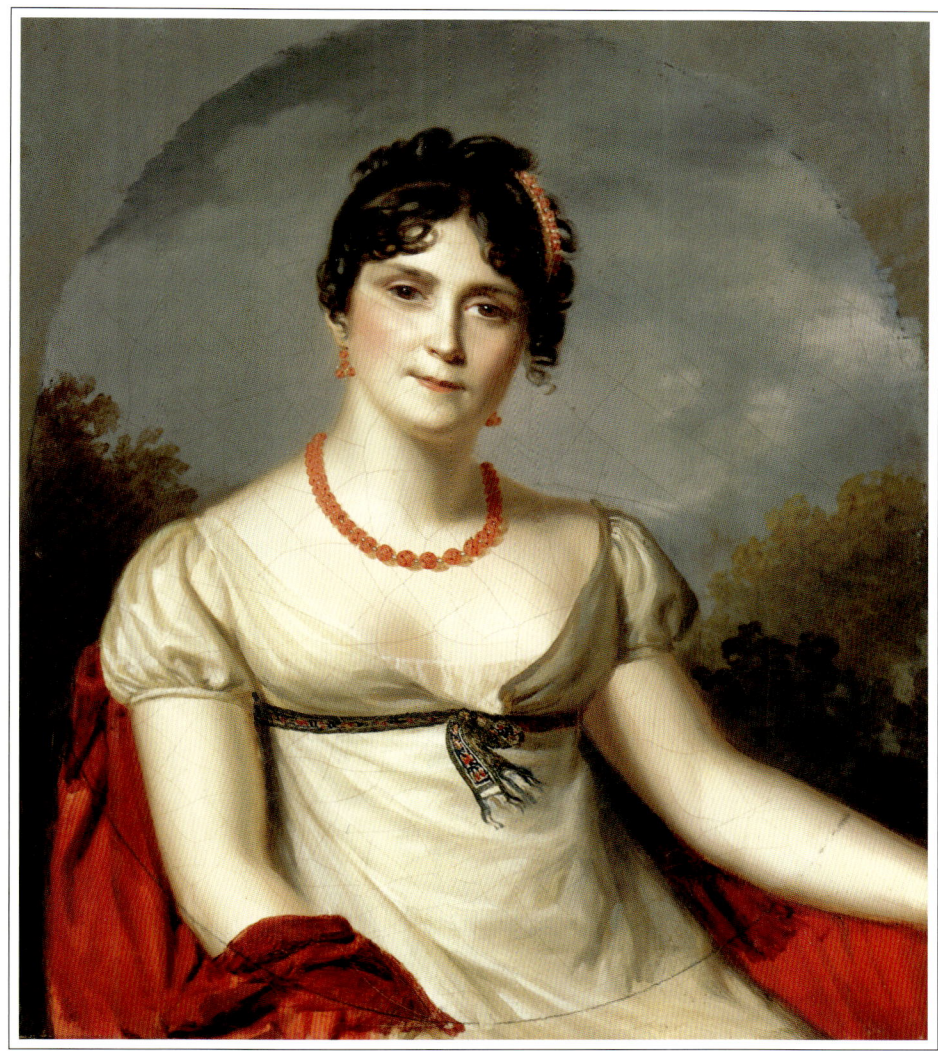

FIGURE 120.

Firmin Massot (French, 1766–1849),
Portrait of Empress Joséphine, ca. 1812.
Oil on canvas, 31 × 27.5 cm (12¼ × 10⅞ in.).
Rueil-Malmaison, Musée national des Châteaux
de Malmaison et Bois-Préau.

• • •

The empress not only bought coral jewelry of all shades from rich red to pale pink, mounted in jewelry for presentation on official visits and for weddings, but also acquired a large collection for her own use. Sometimes carved into cameo heads of divinities, it was more usually worn as seen here—in beads surmounting combs, hanging from the ears, and in strings around the neck.

either left smooth or faceted. The coral would then be mounted into parures; single ornaments for the head, neck, or wrists; or even into matching sets of buttons. The gold mounts admirably set off the beautiful color, as did the pearls with which the coral was sometimes combined. As it complemented the white muslin dresses then fashionable, Joséphine often chose to give coral jewelry as presents for weddings or official visits. It is clear from the number of items listed in her inventories that she also preferred coral for her own use. She wore it as necklaces of small and large beads strung into rows of different lengths, bracelets of up to six rows with a cameo centerpiece, and earrings carved into bunches of red currants or raspberries. Among the more important pieces she owned at the end of her life were a coral-and-pearl crown and a parure comprising a tiara, a comb, a necklace, earrings, bracelets, and a belt buckle {FIGURE 120}.

As with coral and cameos, Joséphine retained a love of mosaic jewelry. The beauty of mosaics representing the monuments of ancient Rome, scenes of Italian peasant life, idyllic views of the Campagna, or motifs from Pompeiian frescoes was enhanced by gold mounts, pearl frames, and settings that placed it among other pieces associated with the classical period. From Mellerio, who apparently specialized in this type of jewelry, she acquired rings set with mosaics in 1808.

Her Sentiments

Another group of jewels mirrors Joséphine's love for her children and her brilliant husband. Two rings at Malmaison recall her early life with Napoléon: one is enameled blue, bears the cipher *NB*, and is inscribed with the message AMOUR SINCERE; the other, with an oblong swivel bezel, displays a cipher above a picture of Cupid firing his arrow. She must have worn Napoléon's portrait in her rings not only out of love but also to express her pride in his great achievements. Thus she displays his miniature, pinned like a decoration to her red velvet gown, in Jean-Baptiste Isabey's portrait of her, painted in Strasbourg in 1805.[32]

Other portraits of her children and grandchildren were mounted as the centerpieces of belts and bracelets or as medallions, sometimes enclosing a lock of hair. Eugène sent his mother a cameo portrait in 1807, and in her note of thanks she expressed her eagerness to receive the portrait of the newest addition to his family. These cameos would almost certainly have been the work of Giovanni Beltrami (1777–1854) of Cremona, who was patronized by Prince Eugène. As a further sentimental reminder of her family, the empress wore acrostic bracelets with their names {FIGURE 121} and others with bands of hair plaited into a lacelike pattern similar to those supplied to her in 1813 by Mellerio.

Of the sentimental jewels she gave her children, one of the most touching was a gift to Hortense, who delayed her much-anticipated visit to her mother in the dreary château de Navarre at Evreux in 1811. To show that she was not offended, Joséphine gave her daughter a necklace, of which she wrote, "On it you will find three words that express my feelings for you, *JOSÉPHINE Á SA FILLE CHERIE*." The cross that hung from it was dated January 2, the day on which Hortense had been originally expected.[33]

FIGURE 121.

Pair of Acrostic Bracelets, French, n.d.
Royal Collection, Copenhagen.

These bracelets are set with colored stones whose initials spell out the names of the children of the Empress Joséphine: H(essonite) O(pal) R(uby) T(urquoise) E(merald) N(icolo) S(apphire) E(merald) for Hortense. The other shows initials E(merald) U(nakite) G(arnet) E(merald) N(icolo) E(merald) linked together by diamond clusters for Eugène. Acrostic jewelry, spelling out messages and the names of beloved individuals, was first introduced during the Empire period by the firm of Mellerio and enjoyed great success as a means of expressing sentiment.

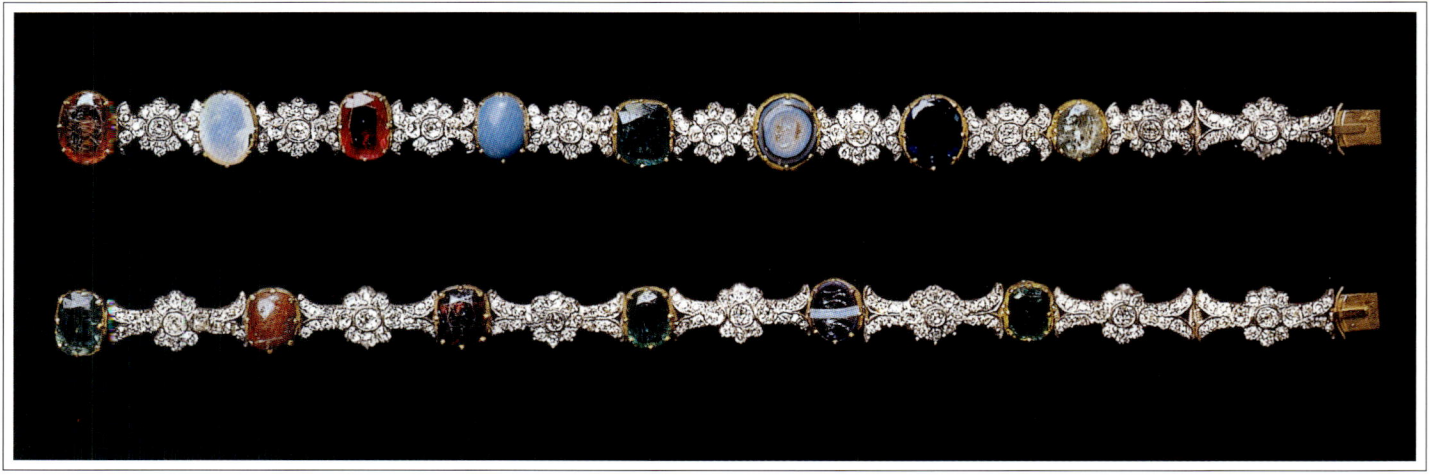

Her Pearls, Diamonds, and Colored Stones

The magnificence of her pearls {FIGURE 122}, diamonds, and colored-stone jewelry helped Joséphine play her role as queen and empress. She acquired a collection of pearls of the first water, either perfectly spherical or symmetrically pear-shaped with fine iridescent sheen or "orient," not only in various shades of cream and white but also in rose and black.

Nor did she stop at fine oriental pearls for, while taking the cure at Plombières, she so admired the river pearls fished from the river at Vologne that she brought back mussels from Vologne to farm in the pond at Malmaison. Although the transplant failed, it does prove that she had no prejudice against this type of pearl, which she must have also worn.[34] Her pearls were also combined with colored stones, framed cameos, plaques, and medallions. They were also mounted as linking pieces, inserted into chains for necklaces and bracelets, and threaded with gold mesh into waist bands.

For the very grandest occasions, diamonds were preferred because they reflected light with such intensity that the wearer stood out in any crowd. The emperor was keenly aware of this and was continually adding to her collection. However, what remained at her death was a mere shadow of what she had once possessed. The most important were a pair of pear-shaped earrings and the twenty-seven–stone collet necklace inherited by Hortense, who sold it in 1829 to the emperor of Russia.[35]

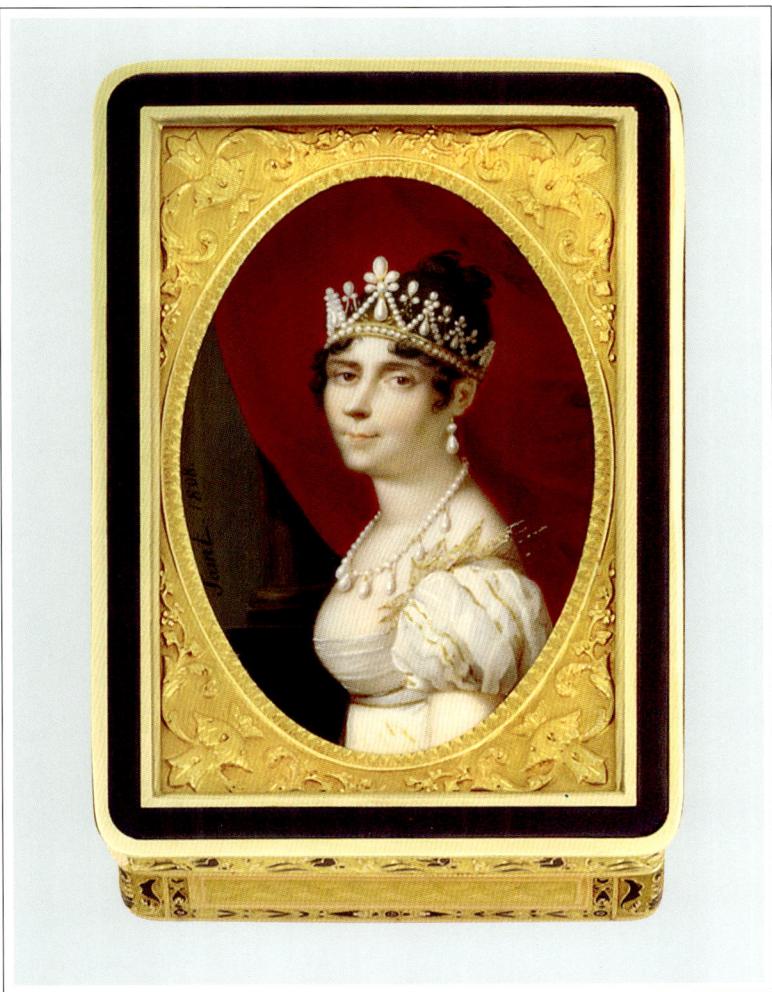

FIGURE 122.

Snuffbox, French, ca. 1808.
Cover set with miniature of Empress Joséphine by Daniel Saint (French, 1778–1847) after a painting by Jean-Baptiste Regnault (French, 1754–1829). Chased-gold and enameled box, painting on ivory, 8 × 5 × 2 cm (3⅛ × 2 × ¾ in.).
Private collection.

• • •

This snuffbox miniature shows Joséphine wearing a pearl parure comprised of a tiara with the pearls alternately arranged in high points or swinging in the round pearl arches below, a comb, and a necklace of round pearls hung with eight drops, bracelets, and a pair of "pendeloque" earrings. These magnificent pearls set off the beauty of her dark brown hair, worn low on the forehead, and of fine violet-blue eyes, which lit up her expressive face. More than very becoming, pearls were also evocative of the glories of the Versailles of Louis XIV, where they were the most prized of all precious gems. The empress is arrayed in the same set in the painting of the wedding of the king of Westphalia by J.-B. Regnault, 1808.

In some cases, diamonds were not the centerpiece but rather served to set off colored stones. As was usual with grand Empire jewelry, quantities of small diamonds were massed around large and semiprecious, colored stones mounted into the parures purchased in 1804 and those acquired over the following decade. Among the jewels in colored stones that Hortense inherited from Joséphine were pieces remaining from her ruby parure supplied by Nitot & Fils in 1809 and a set of sapphire ornaments later bought by the Duke and Duchess d'Orléans, the future Louis Philippe and Queen Marie-Amélie.[36]

Joséphine's taste was not limited to the intrinsically valuable, for she also owned matching sets mounted with relatively inexpensive lapis lazuli, yellow and red unengraved cornelians, amber and moss agate with inclusions fortuitously representing trees and even landscapes. A set of plum stones also demonstrates her eye for the unusual. Finally, there were somber jet and cut-steel parures for court and private mourning. Possessing jewels of such variety meant the empress did not need to appear twice in the same parure, as there was always something different to admire in her toilette.

The Types of Jewels

As for the many individual items of jewelry, like the sets, the pieces that Joséphine owned were almost all in the classical style, which the emperor had made his own and which the imperial architects Charles Percier and Pierre-François-Léonard Fontaine had brought to fruition in the Empire style. Applied to jewelry this meant using not only cameos but also clear outlines, symmetrical shapes, and motifs derived from antiquity {FIGURE 123}. Joséphine seems to have been forever on the alert for new ideas, and Mlle Avrillion relates that after a visit to the theater the empress asked Nitot & Fils to copy the tiara "quite different from any other" worn on stage by Mlle George.[37] Tiaras were for formal wear, whereas the tortoiseshell comb—with its high gallery embellished with gems, leaving the nape of the neck bare—was worn all the time. Joséphine had an extensive collection of combs, and one box alone contained twenty, all surmounted by pearls. The earrings framing her face were almost all simple-top and single- or triple-drop (girandole) design, which, since they were worn with both day and evening dress, came in a wide variety of materials {FIGURE 124}.

Low-cut gowns, framed by the *cherusque* (a high-standing, stiffened collar) at the back, left plenty of space for necklaces. Besides the opulent strings of pearls, *rivières* (diamond necklaces), and clusters of colored stones linked by jeweled chains worn for ceremonies, the empress owned many others for less formal attire. The usual design was of flat, oval, round, or lozenge-shaped, hard-stone plaques framed in small pearls linked by gold chains. The center might be emphasized by a

FIGURE 123.
Tiara, French.
Design of diamond and ruby laurel crowns.
Paris, Mauboussin Archives.

• • •

Echoing the tiaras of the empresses of ancient Rome, Joséphine wore her tiaras with such poise and dignity that ever since the Empire, this jewel, more than any other, has come to symbolize rank and authority. Not only have the classical designs been reproduced many times—particularly the laurel worn at the coronation of 1804—but so has her way of wearing them low on the brow, with very little hair showing. This particular design was a favorite in the Edwardian period.

FIGURE 124.
Pair of Earrings, French.
Pearl and diamonds.
Paris, Musée du Louvre.

• • •

These large, pear-shaped earrings once belonged to the Empress Joséphine. Uniting the brilliance of the diamond, which drew all eyes toward it, with the soft matte sheen of the pearl, they would light up the face attractively as well as complete the parure worn at formal events. According to *L'Hermite de la Chaussée d'Antin* (1811), the earrings of Nitot & Fils were the most elegant in Paris, and there is reason to suppose that these, as well as Joséphine's other important earrings, came from that firm.

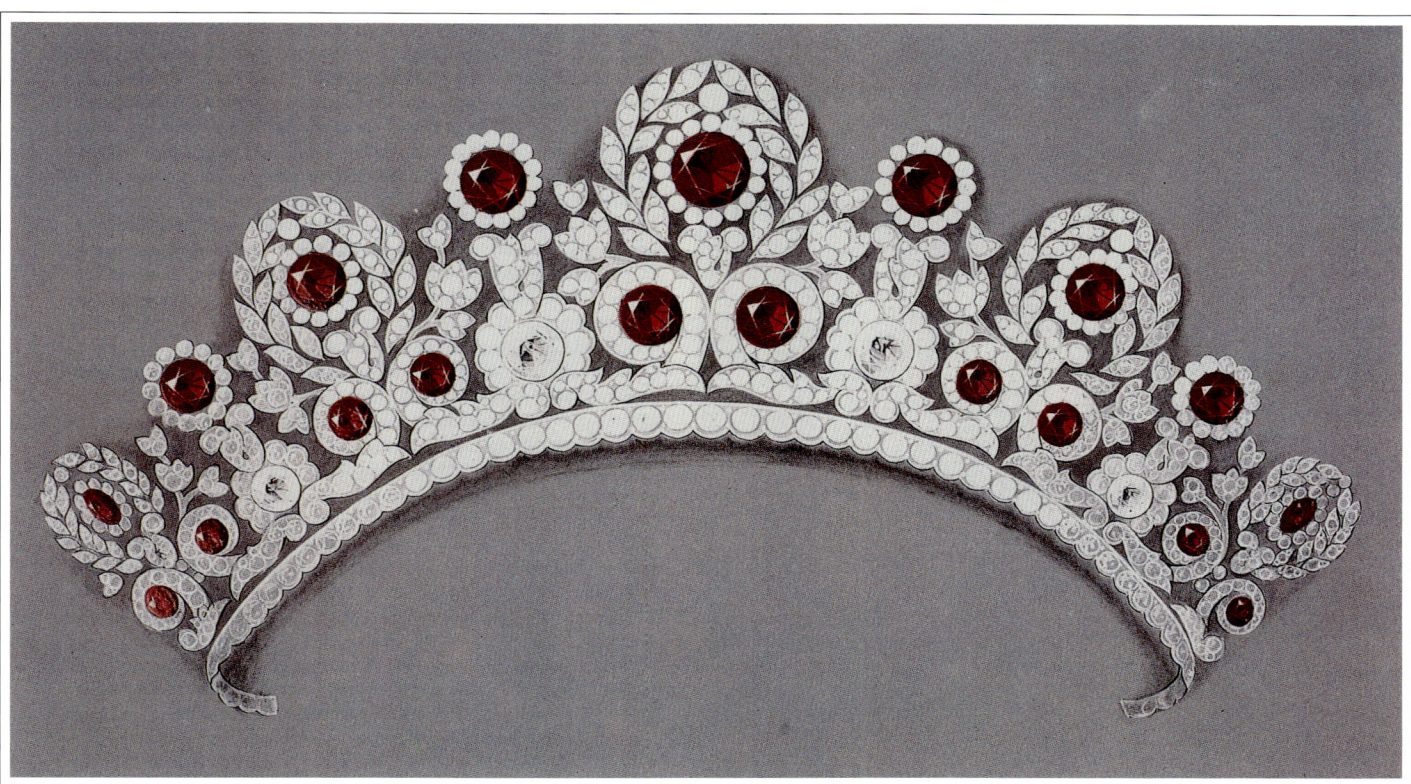

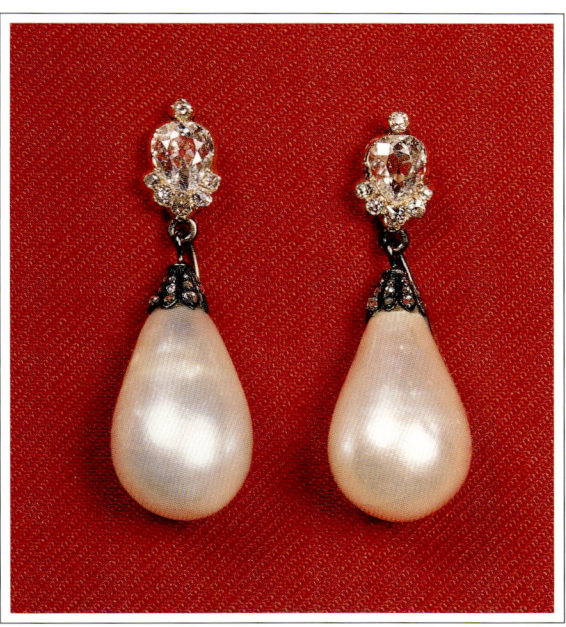

larger plaque or pendant such as the *petite chérubin en médaillon* (medallion of little angels; 1814) or by a cross. These varied in value from splendid diamond, ruby, emerald, and opal examples to the more modest type that was set with colored stones and suspended from an enameled, gold necklace. Her flat, round watches, sometimes hanging from the neck or from a chatelaine at the waist, were similarly enameled in various shades and bore her initial, *J*. Further emphasis was given to her excellent figure by the jeweled belt clasped round the high waist.

Narrow, ribbonlike bracelets on the arms, left bare by short sleeves, were always worn in pairs, the bands meeting at an ornamental centerpiece. Like Joséphine's necklaces, these came in pearls or precious stones and also in chains of assorted patterns clasped by enameled plaques.

It is Joséphine's rings that tell us most about the various aspects of her life — wife, mother, art lover, queen, and empress. Her coronation ring was set by Marguerite with a ruby, the emblem of joy, in contrast to Napoléon's ring set with an emerald, symbolizing "divine revelation."[38] She kept in reserve a group of rings bearing her miniature, as well as one with her diamond initial, *J*, and another with an emerald bee, a symbol adopted by Napoléon — these two presumably for presentation. Imperial grandeur was expressed by

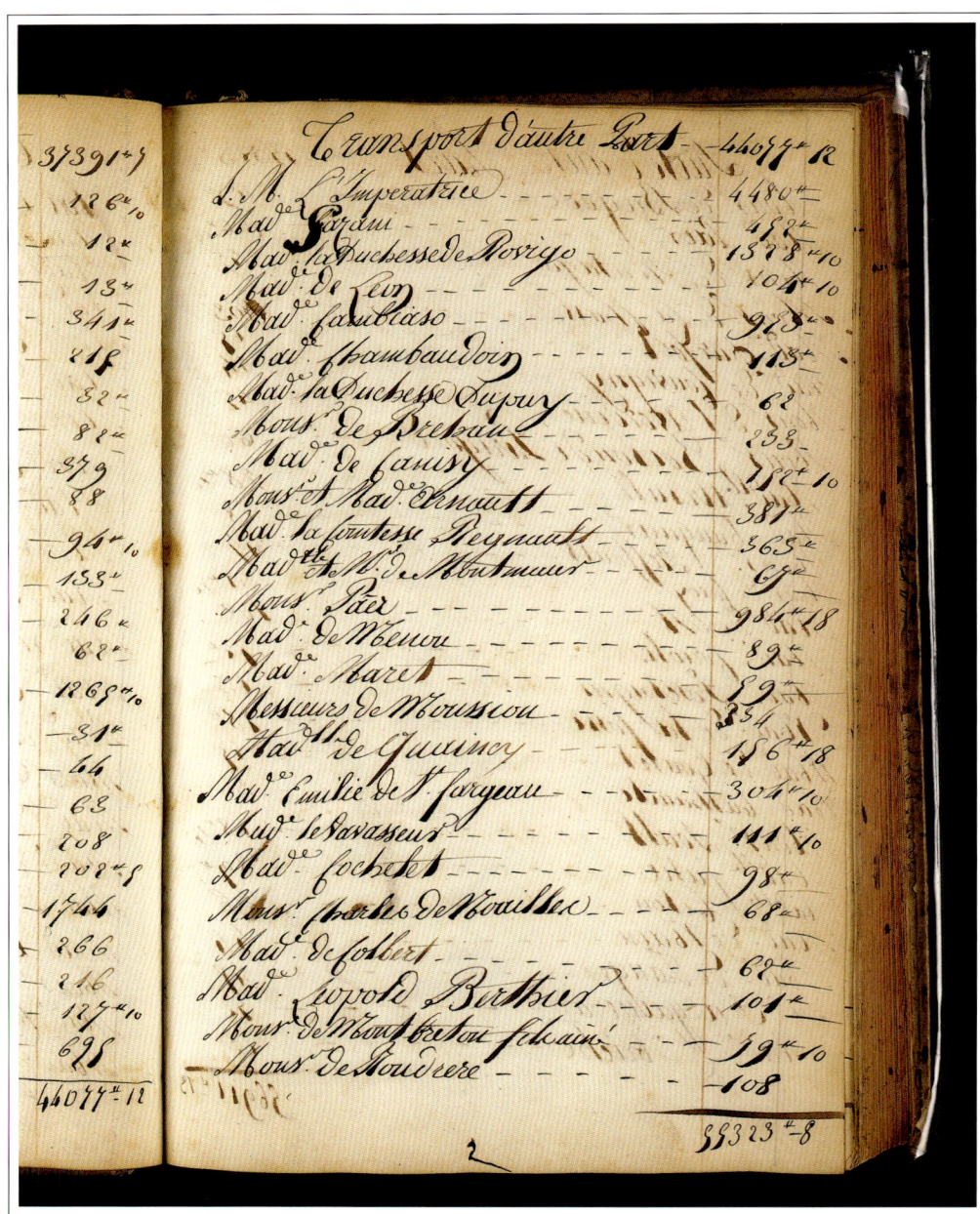

FIGURE 125.

Ledger Page.
Paris, Mellerio.

• • •

Page from the ledgers of Mellerio, the established Parisian jeweler, listing Empress Joséphine's name at the top, followed by those of the wives and daughters of the "new men" of the First Empire.

various diamond solitaires, huge turquoises, velvety blue sapphires, wine-red rubies, deep green emeralds, and rainbow-tinted opals often framed in brilliant, cut diamonds mounted as rings. These provided the finishing touch to Joséphine's splendid parures.

A final glimpse of her taste for the exotic and the new, represented by a mysterious Jèsopha stone, also comes from purchases recorded in the Mellerio archives. Her name appears in the Mellerio ledgers for other deliveries as well {FIGURE 125}. Some pieces were of the *style indiènne*, with gems gripped by lion's claws. Several others in the *style gothique* (1812, 1813) correspond to Joséphine's interest in the troubadour paintings, which opened the way for the Romantic movement that was to triumph soon after her death.

Notes

1. Bernard Chevallier, *Imperatrice Joséphine, Correspondance, 1782–1814*, annotations by Bernard Chevallier, Maurice Catinat, and Christophe Pincemaille (Paris, 1996), 12.
2. *Mémoires de Constant sur la vie privée de Napoléon* (Paris, 1909), 326.
3. B. Morel, *The French Crown Jewels* (Antwerp, 1998), 250.
4. E. Knapton, *Empress Josephine* (Cambridge, Mass., 1963), 154.
5. Knapton, *Empress Josephine*, 155–56.
6. Chevallier, *Imperatrice Joséphine*, 55.
7. Comte Miot de Melito, *Mémoires du Comte Miot de Melito*, vol. 1 (Paris, 1858), 223.
8. Serge Grandjean, "Jewellery under the First Empire," *Connoisseur* 193 (December 1976): 275.
9. J. Bury, ed., *An Englishman in Paris, 1803: The Journal of Bertie Greathead* (London, 1953), 30.
10. Mlle [Marie-Jean-Pierrette] Avrillion, *Mémoires*, vol. 1 (Paris, 1896), 95.
11. Mme de Rémusat, *Mémoires*, vol. 2 (Paris, 1893), 35.
12. Fréderic Masson, appendix to *Madame Bonaparte* (Paris, 1920), 372–84
13. Rémusat, *Mémoires*, 71.
14. Serge Grandjean, *Inventaire après le decès de l'Imperatrice Joséphine* (Paris, 1964).
15. R. Hurel and D. Scarisbrick, *Chaumet: Two Centuries of Fine Jewellery* (Paris, 1998), 25.
16. Also named in the surviving accounts or included in the list of Joséphine's creditors of 1814 are the following: Belhate, Cablat, Conrado, Despresle, Devoix of the quai des Orfèvres, Fister, Frièse, Grandcher of Au Petit Dunkerque, Hollander, Lignereux of the rue Taitbout, Lelong, the Frères Marx, Perret, Picot, Pitaux, Messin, Tourrier, and Vacher of the rue Vivienne. There were also the famous goldsmith Martin-Guillaume Biennais, and the watchmakers Breguet, Lepine, and Mugner Abroadi.
17. Etienne de Jouy, *L'Hermite de la Chaussée d'Antin*, 1811.
18. Chevallier, *Imperatrice Joséphine*, 187.
19. Chevallier, *Imperatrice Joséphine*, 194.
20. Avrillion, *Mémoires*, vol. 1, 78–79.
21. C. Brown, *Engraved Gems, Survivals and Revivals*, exh. cat., National Gallery of Art, Washington, D.C. (1997), 85–89.
22. E. J. Babelon, *Histoire de la gravure sur gemmes en France* (Paris, 1902), 223.
23. C. Pietrangeli, "Pio VII a Firenze e a Parigi 1804–5, I Doni del Papa," *L'Urbe* 5 (September–October 1982).
24. H. Rollett, *Die Drei Meister der Gemmoglypthik* (Vienna, 1874), 66–67, 173, and 197.
25. L. L. Pirzio Biroli, "Gaspare Capparoni, scultore in gemme," *Xenia* (n.p., 1981): 92.
26. In the collection of the Walters Art Museum, Baltimore, acc. no. 42.202.
27. Chevallier, *Imperatrice Joséphine*, 155
28. E. Babelon, *Catalogue des camées antiques et modernes de la Bibliothèque Nationale* (Paris, 1897), 169–72.
29. *Mémoires de Constant*, vol. 2, 172.
30. Timothy Clifford, ed., *The Three Graces* (Edinburgh, 1995), 36.
31. Chevallier, *Imperatrice Joséphine*, 55.
32. Collection Prince Napoléon. The empress is depicted holding a paper announcing the victory of Austerlitz.
33. Chevallier, *Imperatrice Joséphine*, 291.
34. G. Kunz, *The Book of the Pearl* (London, 1908), 170.
35. Morel, *The French Crown Jewels*, 264.
36. Avrillion, *Mémoires*, vol. 2, 409; but there is no proof that this is the set now in the Louvre.
37. Avrillion, *Mémoires*, vol. 2, 304.
38. Morel, *The French Crown Jewels*, 254.

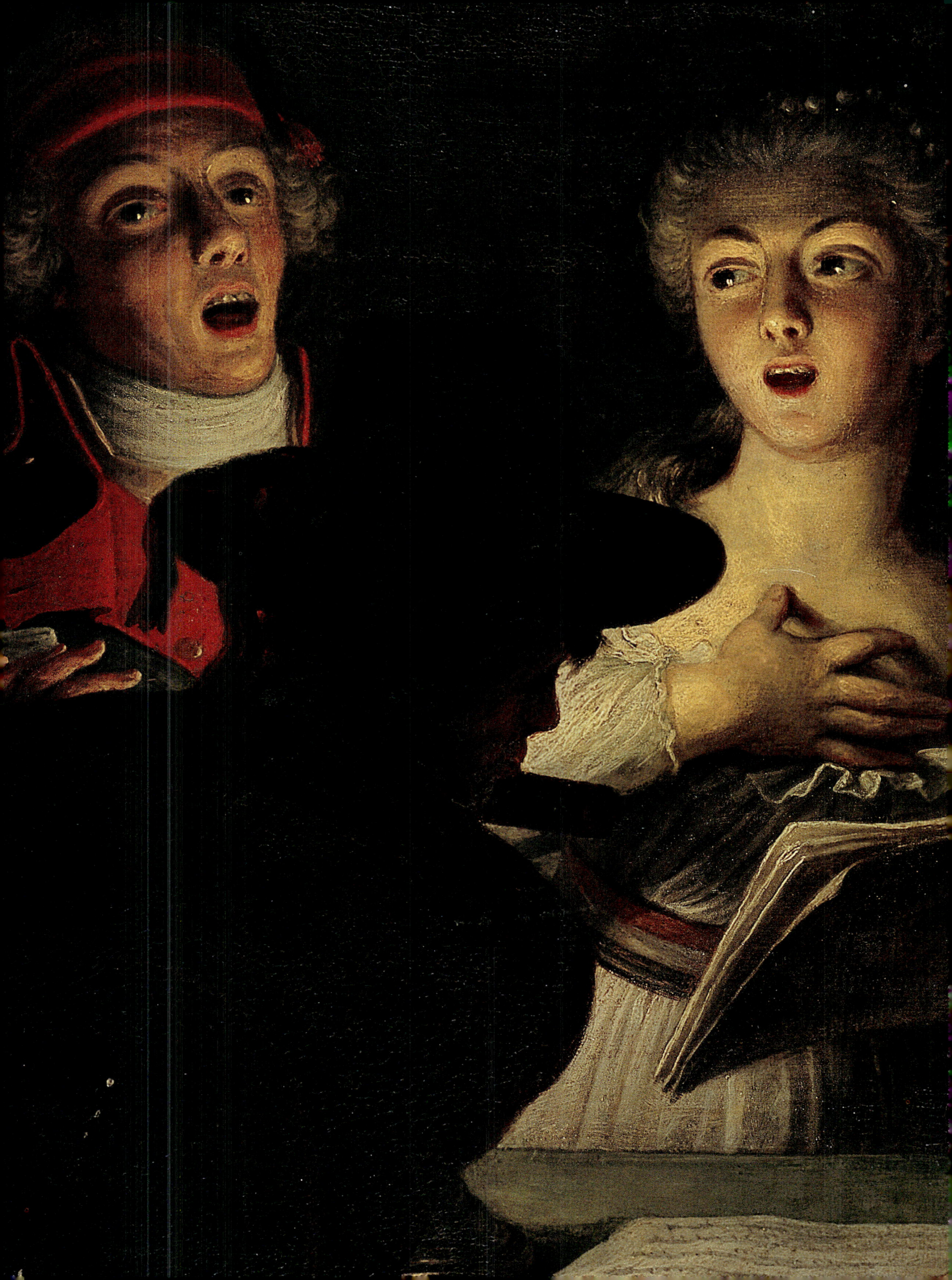

CHAPTER 12

DAVID GILBERT

The Music Joséphine Heard: From the "Plaisirs d'amour" to "Le Chant du départ"

UNLIKE PAINTING, ARCHITECTURE, OR THE DECORATIVE ARTS, music exists in time. Before the twentieth century, the only traces it passed down to history were notes on paper and the instruments that played them. Verbal descriptions and pictorial representations describe how the music sounded and show us where it was played, but none of this is the music itself. The sound of thousands of citizens singing "La Marseillaise" on the Champ de Mars, of Joséphine's daughter, Hortense, accompanying herself on the harp at Malmaison, or of Napoléon's First Grenadiers on parade is gone forever.

This chapter surveys the music that surrounded Joséphine in the course of her eventful life during the French Revolution and Empire period. Did she also hear the singing of African slaves as a girl on her native Martinique? If so, she left us no reaction to it. We do not know in particular whether she preferred Italian music to French (as did the emperor), what music she preferred to dance to, or the melodies she hummed and sang while she passed the time. We do know that she attended certain concerts, entertained musicians in her salon, had works dedicated to her, and in turn gave imperial support to musical institutions and composers. The music she heard is as varied and colorful as the personalities and events of her turbulent lifetime and, like the Revolution and Napoléon himself, greatly influenced the future. Given Joséphine's character and her zest for life, she very likely found something of interest in it all.

Revolutionary Songs and Festival Music

The Committee for Public Safety, and Maximilien Robespierre, who ruled France through the Reign of Terror, commanded a Festival of the Supreme Being for June 8, 1794 (or 20 *prairial*, year II of the Revolution). This festival was one of many vast civic ceremonies meant to replace religious worship and the pomp of monarchy, both of which had been quashed by the Revolution in 1792. Jacques-Louis David was in charge of production, and François Joseph Gossec (1734–1829) composed the music, "Hymne à l'Etre Suprême" (Hymn to the Supreme Being). The day before the festival, students and teachers of the Institut nationale de Musique fanned out across Paris and into the streets, markets, and meeting places to teach the words and music for the festival to the populace.[1] The next day, crowds of citizens descended on the Champ de Mars (the field where the Eiffel Tower stands today), and 2,400 voices led a mass performance of Gossec's hymn {FIGURE 126}. Although Joséphine was unable to attend the festival—for she was still in prison and in imminent danger of execution—no doubt she later attended many similar events and sang the patriotic songs and hymns composed for them.

FIGURE 126.

Pierre-Antoine Demachy (French, 1723–1807), *The Festival of the Supreme Being on the Field of Mars (20 prairial, year II—June 8, 1794).* Oil on canvas, 535 × 835 cm (208⅜ × 345⅛ in.). Paris, Musée Carnavalet.

• • •

The citizens of Paris crowd the Champ de Mars for the Festival of the Supreme Being where thousands sang Gossec's *Hymn to the Supreme Being*. This festival inaugurated the cult of the Supreme Being, a quasi religion combining deism, patriotism, and nationalism meant to replace traditional Christianity.

The makers of the Revolution enlisted all the forces of French culture to the cause, just as Napoléon would do for his Empire in the next decade. Even the most notable composers wrote music for public festivals, while popular songs and dances acquired new words that citizens sang in the streets and taverns, and at home. These Revolutionary songs and hymns not only instilled patriotism and "correct" political thinking but also celebrated French victories and the heroes of the Revolution. The crudest of them mocked the aristocracy and rejoiced at the demise of Louis XVI and his much maligned queen.

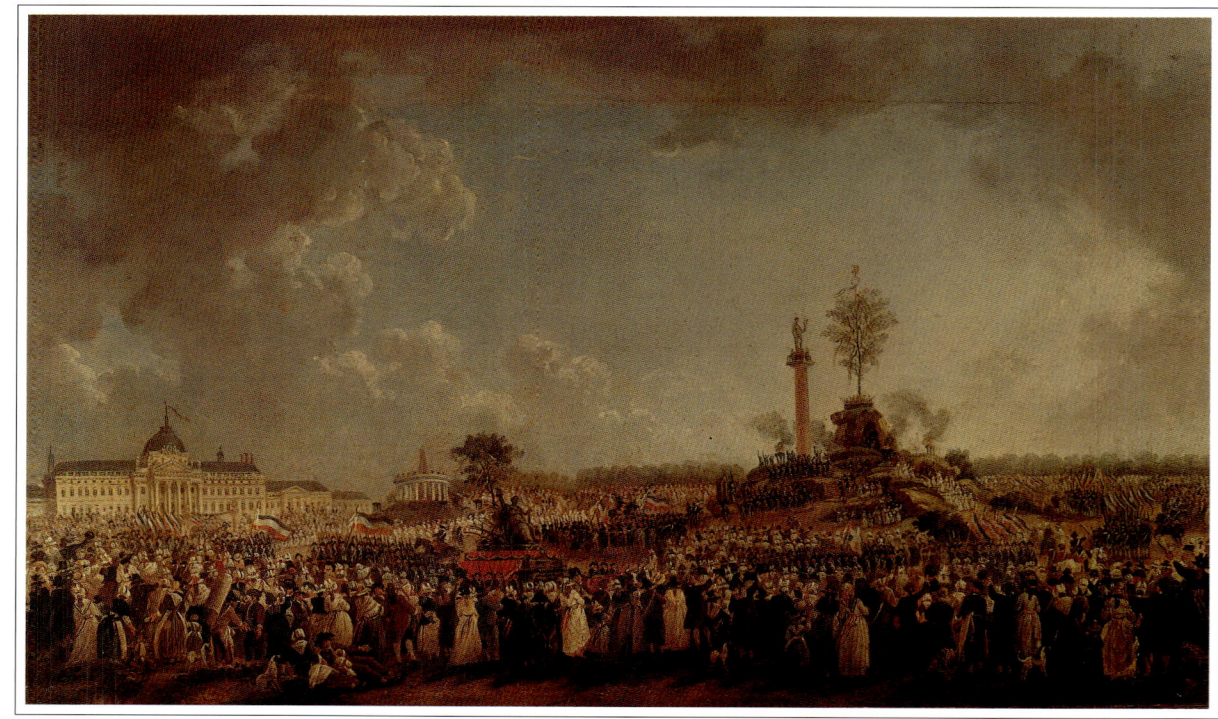

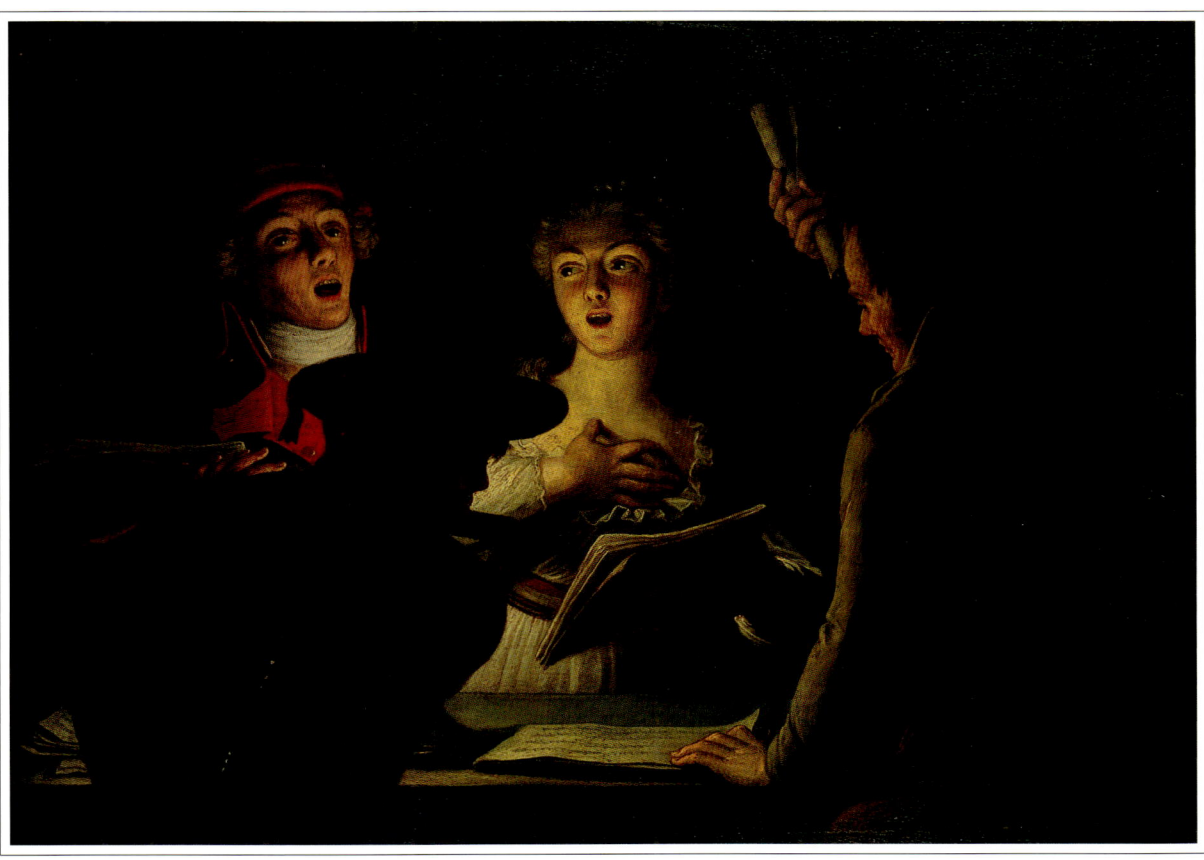

The song that became the French national anthem began as a popular Revolutionary song with all the characteristics of the style: a dotted-rhythm upbeat opening ("Allons enfants" [Come, children]), introducing a rousing, marchlike melody, which turns to the minor mode ("Ils viennent jus'-que dans nos bras" [They even come into our arms]) before a triumphant refrain ("Aux armes, Citoyens!" [To arms, citizens!]). "La Marseillaise" is atypical in that both the melody and words are original, written by Claude Joseph Rouget de Lisle (1760–1836), a soldier, engineer, librettist, composer, and friend of Joséphine's. In a fit of patriotic fervor and fortified by champagne, Rouget de Lisle composed the "Chant de guerre pour l'Armée du Rhin" (War Song of the Army of the Rhine), as it was originally called, on the night of April 15, 1792. It soon became the song of the regiment from Marseilles, which was commanded by Joséphine's first husband, Alexandre de Beauharnais, and thus acquired its familiar title, "La Marseillaise." Brought to Paris on the voices of the soldiers, the song became immensely popular and in 1795 obtained official sanction as the national song of the Republic. Although not favored by Napoléon, and certainly rankling to the Bourbons, the song nevertheless maintained its popularity with the people and in 1879 was proclaimed the official national anthem of France.

Music composed especially for public festivals, such as Gossec's "Hymn to the Supreme Being," was usually performed by professional musicians for a specific occasion but often composed so it could be easily enjoyed by amateurs and memorized by anyone {FIGURE 127}. The style has much in common with that of the popular songs described earlier.

FIGURE 127.

Dominique Doncre (French, 1743–1820), *La Marseillaise* (or *The Patriotic Singers*), 1792. Oil on canvas, 45 × 61 cm (17¾ × 24 in.). Paris, Musée Carnavalet.

Revolutionary songs were sung wherever two or three citizens gathered together in the name of the Revolution. Just as the festivals replaced religious ceremonies and patriotism replaced religious beliefs, the singing of revolutionary songs replaced household devotions.

Composers, no matter how sophisticated their tastes, training, or abilities, and no matter how chameleon-like their politics, knew what kind of music was required: relatively simple melodies, basic harmonies, and accompaniments adaptable to a variety of performance situations. The grandest of these odes, cantatas, hymns, and songs were written for performance on the Champs de Mars by two or three orchestras, wind bands, vocal soloists, and a chorus of thousands of singers. The large scale had a practical as much as a philosophical and artistic end: it was necessary for the populace, which was spread across the landscape, to hear and participate in the ceremony. This technique, which is sometimes called "architectural music," eventually found its most famous and successful practitioner in Hector Berlioz (1803–1869), who wrote the *Grande Messe des morts* (High Mass for the Dead) (1837) especially for the vast chapel of the Hôtel des Invalides. François Lesueur (1760–1837), Berlioz's teacher, is the composer most closely associated with this innovation; he, along with Gossec and other French composers, wrote music for the festivals. The many émigré composers living in Paris at the time contributed music to the Revolution as well—composers such as the Belgian master of *opéra comique*, André Grétry (1741–1813), and the Italian Luigi Cherubini (1760–1842).

The stirring beauty of "Le Chant du départ" (Departure Song) by Etiènne Nicolas Méhul (1763–1817) made this one of the most popular works composed for the festivals, rivaling at the time even "La Marseillaise" in number of performances and breadth of dissemination. Marie Joseph Chénier (1764–1811) composed seven of its verses to express the patriotic sentiments of the average French citizen or group of patriots. They tell of sacrifice for France: "Barra and Viala are dead, but they have conquered," declares a young boy. "Off to war, valiant husbands and ideal warriors, battles are your wedding celebrations," sings a group of young wives.[2] The refrain, sung first by the soloists and then by the crowd, calls all citizens to conquer or perish for the republic.

> La république nous appelle,
> Sachons vaincre ou sachons périr,
> Un français doit vivre pour elle,
> Pour elle un français doit mourir.
>
> [The Republic calls us,
> We know how to conquer or to die,
> A French citizen should live for her,
> For her a citizen should die.]

Méhul, one of the most lyrical composers of the period, imbued "Le Chant du départ" with memorable melodic gestures and a particularly expressive character. The setting for a variety of characters and the distinctive move to the minor mode turns each verse into a little drama, universally experienced.

Figure 128.

Nicholas Hoffman, "Musicians of the Imperial Guard," from the Album *Costumes militaire*, ca. 1805. Mounted, handcolored proof engravings, 48 × 36 cm (18⅞ × 14⅛ in.). Providence, Rhode Island, Brown University Library, Anne S. K. Brown Military Collection.

· · ·

A drum major, trumpeter, and cymbal player in the dress of Napoléon's First Granadiers, the largest and most ostentatious of the regimental bands. The instrumentalists played not only on the field of battle but also at official ceremonies and on parade. The musicians also supplemented the orchestras in the imperial chapel and theaters when necessary.

Military Music

Napoléon's love for Joséphine is legendary, but his heart was always with his troops on the battlefield. Although he frequently fell asleep at the opera and regarded the mass as a state necessity, he had a passion for military music. Each regiment of the army required a band, but the number of instruments and the extravagance of the uniforms depended on the wealth and prestige of the commanding officer. The largest and wealthiest, such as Napoléon's favorite First Grenadiers,[3] had a full complement of woodwinds and brass (doubled flutes, oboes, clarinets, trumpets, horns, trombones, and serpents) and "percussion à la Turk" (various drums, cymbals, a triangle, and a *chapeau-chinois*; FIGURES 128, 129).[4] The music the bands played and the signals they gave on the battlefield or on parade had to be totally new, since earlier ones would have brought to mind service to the king rather than to the Republic or the Empire. Military signals also had to be clear, memorable, easy to play under stress, while at the same time immediately distinguishable. A "pas de manoeuvre" (drill step) by Michel-Joseph Gebauer (1762–1812) has the following tune:[5]

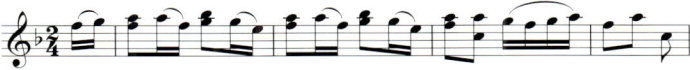

Gebauer played oboe and led the musicians of the First Grenadiers, the band that played for imperial ceremonies and at private concerts but, most important, on the battlefield. In fact, Gebauer himself perished during the disastrous retreat of Napoléon's army from Russia. His most famous composition, the march for the First Grenadiers, lived on, however, and resounded at the battle of Waterloo.

Bernard Sarrette (1765–1858), captain of the National Guard, deserves a special place in the history of French military music and, as is discussed later, in the history of music in general. In 1789 Sarrette, with the assistance of Lieutenant Gossec (the same who would

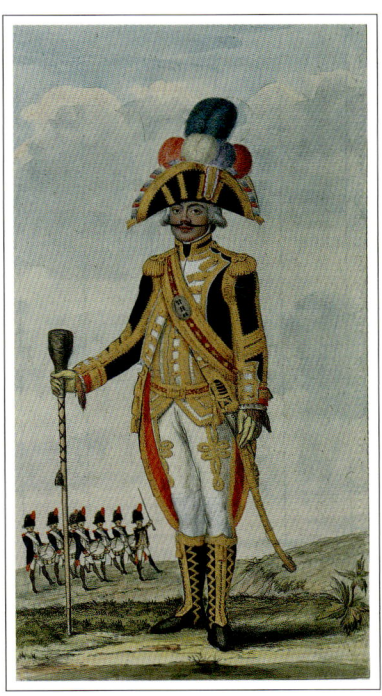
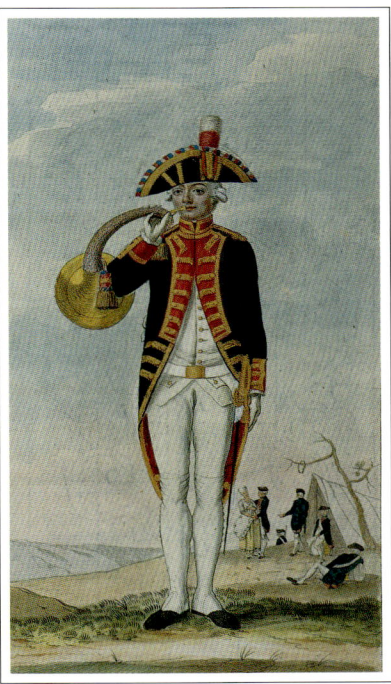
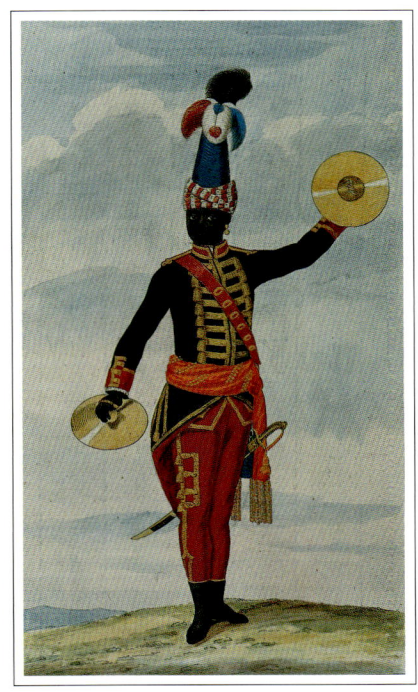

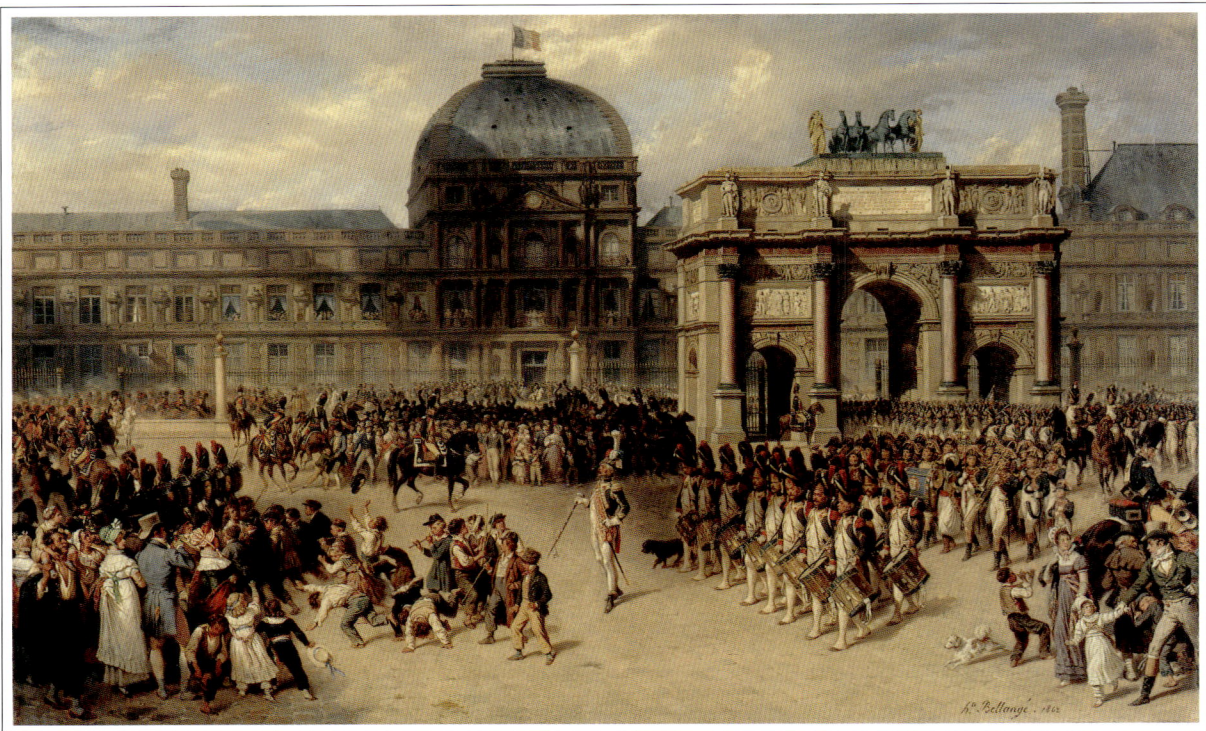

FIGURE 129.

Joseph Ballangé (French, 1800–1866),
*A Day of Review under the Empire (1810),
in the Background the Arc du Triomphe
du Carrousel and the Tuileries*, 1862.
Oil on canvas. 101 × 161 cm (39¾ × 63⅜ in.).
Paris, Musée du Louvre.

⋯

A regimental band in Napoléon's army passes the by the Tuileries Palace. Although painted during the reign of Joséphine's grandson, Napoléon III, typically the depiction is quite accurate. The large battery of percussion thundered across the battlefield and struck fear into the citizens of the cities Napoléon conquered.

later compose the "Hymn to the Supreme Being"), founded the National Guard band, which soon formed the core of musicians that performed at public festivals. In July 1792 Sarrette opened a school to train musicians for the army after convincing the government of the necessity for such an institution. Instruction was soon opened to civilians as well as the military, and in 1794 the school became the Institut nationale de Musique — the first public, secular school of music. Musicians from the institute played a large role in the music at the Festival of the Supreme Being, helping to convince the government of its usefulness. Finally, on a motion put forward to the Consulate by Chénier in the name of the Education Committee, Sarrette's institute became the Conservatoire national de Musique; thus the famous Paris Conservatoire began its venerable and distinguished history. Although frequently short of funds and commonly shortchanged by the emperor, the Conservatoire had a profound impact on French musical life and may be the most important musical legacy of the Revolution and Empire.

Church Music and Music for the Coronation

French church music was not at its apex during the final years of the monarchy. As early as the 1780s priests complained that composers were setting sacred texts to music taken from comic opera and vaudeville.[6] Still, the Revolution's ban on organized religion and the closing of the churches and monasteries brought to an end many ancient traditions unique to French Catholicism. Along with the cathedrals fell the *maîtrises*, the system of schools that had produced singers and composers for the Church since the Middle Ages. Napoléon's Concordat with Rome in July 1801 reopened the churches, but the recovery of earlier musical traditions or the creation of new ones was hampered by the shortage of trained church musicians.

Paris celebrated the Concordat on Easter Sunday, April, 18, 1802, with a mass at Notre Dame Cathedral and a *Te Deum* by Giovanni Paisiello (1740–1816), Napoléon's new *maître de chapelle* (music director). Napoléon had ordered Paisiello to Paris from Italy where he was already well known as a composer of Italian opera. His duties included organizing the imperial chapel, hiring the musicians, writing and conducting the music of the mass, and also composing works for important religious festivals and other official functions. Napoléon liked Paisiello's music because it was quiet and monotonous, a quality perhaps reflected in the composer's portrait {FIGURE 130}. Since the emperor probably used the time in the chapel and at the theater for rest and reflection, he preferred not to be challenged there musically. In 1804 Napoléon asked Paisiello to compose the music for his coronation.

Thanks to the scholarship of the musicologist Jean Mongrédien, we know a great deal about the role music played in the sumptuous coronation at Notre Dame on December 4, 1804. Most contemporary accounts describe the lavish ceremony and its jewel-bedecked participants, but the music receives only the most general comment. Archives, however, have yielded some fascinating details. The coronation itself cost close to five million francs, but the music only thirty thousand. Nevertheless, several soloists, two orchestras, and two choruses occupied the wings of the nave of the cathedral, requiring François Lesueur and four other conductors to coordinate the four hundred performers. Musicans and extra instruments were brought from the Tuileries chapel, the Opéra, other Paris theaters, and even Gebauer's military band had a role to play. Copyists produced 19,149 pages of music that lasts, in a contemporary performance, about one and one-half hours.[7]

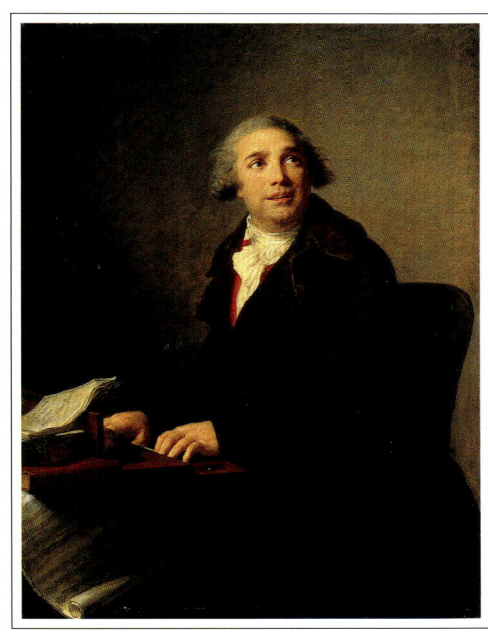

FIGURE 130.

Elisabeth Vigée-Lebrun (French, 1755–1824), *Portrait of Giovanni Paisiello (1741–1816), Composer*, 1791.
Oil on canvas. 130 × 100 cm (51¼ × 39⅜ in.).
Versailles, Musée National des Châteaux de Versailles et de Trianon.

. . .

Napoléon's favor for Paisiello suggests that his feeling for music was more practical than sophisticated. Joséphine's support of Spontini and other musicians shows her to have been the better judge of music.

Paisiello composed a coronation mass and a *Te Deum* for the occasion. Other music included two short motets and a *marche solennelle* (solemn march) by Lesueur, and a *Vivat in Aeternum* (Eternal Life) by the Abbé Roze (1775–1819), a minor composer of sacred music and Lesueur's former teacher. Lesueur's motet *Tu es Petrus* ("Thou art Peter, and upon this rock I will build my church," Matthew 16:18) accompanied the entrance and exit of Pope Pius VII, while his solemn march conveyed Napoléon and Joséphine in and out of Notre Dame. The musicians performed Roze's *Vivat* after the crowns were placed on the imperial heads and at other times during the ceremony.[8] Most of the music, including Paisiello's *Te Deum* (a revision of the work he had written to celebrate the Concordat) and the coronation mass, sound today like much ado about nothing. The music has only slight melodic interest and no dramatic direction, and the climaxes seem contrived and artificial. But Paisiello wrote brilliantly for

THE MUSIC JOSÉPHINE HEARD

the solo singers in the Italian bel canto style that appealed to Napoléon, and the composer's *Crucifixus* features a horn and harp duet, a favorite instrumental combination of the empress's. In the final *Domine salvum fac* Paisiello uses trumpets and drums for a stirring and noble finale to the ceremony.

Paisiello had left Paris and the emperor's service only a few weeks before the coronation. Humiliated by the reception of one of his comic operas at the Théâtre Italien, he asked for and received the emperor's permission to return to Italy. They remained on friendly terms, however, and Paisiello frequently sent music back to Paris in honor of his former patron's birthday or for other special occasions. Napoléon appointed Lesueur to be his new *maître de chapelle*, and so it was Lesueur who organized the music for the coronation and conducted Paisiello's music.

Public Concerts, Imperial Private Music, and the Salon

Paisiello not only was in charge of the imperial chapel but also was Napoléon's official composer. He wrote music and organized concerts and musical evenings for the imperial family at Malmaison as well as for other more formal occasions. He also composed operas for the emperor's private theaters. According to Claire de Rémusat, the emperor liked Paisiello's music for its monotony. "Impressions which repeat themselves are the only ones that take possession of us," Napoléon told Rémusat. To Cherubini, a composer whose music few would call dull, the emperor once remarked, "Speak to me like Paisiello, that is what lulls me gently."[9] Cherubini's opera *La Crescendo* (1810) concerns a man who cannot tolerate loud sounds or music and may well have been intended as a caricature of the emperor's musical preferences.[10] Napoléon appointed another Italian to succeed Paisiello in directing his private music, Ferdinando Paer (1771–1839), who in 1807 became imperial composer and music director for life.

Joséphine also had her musical establishment. She held weekly concerts in the Petite Galerie and Salon de Musique at Malmaison. There were also the more informal salons—gatherings of friends, members of the court, and a select set of savants who came together to debate philosophy, the arts, and the recent French victories. Music usually played a part in these evenings. Marie-Jeanne-Pierrette Avrillion, the empress's First Lady of the Chamber, recalled hearing the most accomplished virtuosos during these concerts and gatherings: the violinists Pierre Rode, Pierre Baillot, and Charles Auguste de Beriot; the harpist Joseph Nadermann, with Paer accompanying on the piano. Hortense, Eugène, and other members of the imperial family also participated in these soirées and hosted their own as well. "Eugène était fou de la musique" (Eugène is crazy about music), Mlle Avrillion reported,[11] although Hortense was the more genuinely talented. A rivalry existed between the members of this new aristocracy as to who could attract the more brilliant crowd and in whose house the cleverest conversation might be heard. Lucien Bonaparte, the emperor's brother, always tried to outshine Malmaison, according to Laura Junot, the Duchess d'Abrantès.[12] Lucien, also a lover of music, counted Luigi Boccherini (1743–1805) among his friends, and the composer dedicated a set of quartets to him.

Nevertheless, instrumental music has always been much less important in French musical life than vocal music. The bon mot "Sonate, que me veux-tu?" [Sonata, what do you want of me?] much repeated by thinkers such as Jean-Jacques Rousseau, expresses perfectly the incomprehensibility with which many sophisticated listeners responded to purely instrumental music. Moreover, some thought it could be dangerous: having no words or program to convey its meaning, pure instrumental music might hide an immoral message or even secret communications to the enemies of France. During the Revolution and Empire period, however, composers provided sonatas, string quartets, and even symphonies for the variety of public concert series that proliferated, although most were short lived. The art dealer Jean Baptiste Lebrun, husband of Elisabeth Vigée-Lebrun, sponsored the Concerts des Amateurs between 1799 and 1804. The orchestra, made up of both professionals and amateurs, performed Haydn and Méhul symphonies. The concerts at the Conservatoire, however, included the best, and its series was the longest lived and most influential.

The public recitals held in the conservatory auditorium provided the institution's teachers with an opportunity to show off their artistic talents as well as those of their student protégés. The first of these concerts took place in November 1801, and both Mme Mère and the future empress supported it and attended.[13] The program for the concert on February 9, 1802, included the following:

Symphony no. 85 ("La Reine") by Franz Joseph Haydn

Air from *Montano et Stéphanie* by Henri Berton

Concerto for Clarinet by Dacosta

Overture to *Elisa, or the Voyage to Mount Saint-Bernard* by Luigi Cherubini

Air [also from *Elisa*?]

Symphonie Concertante for Violin and Contrabass[14]

This musical potpourri of vocal, instrumental, and opera excerpts is typical of nineteenth-century concert programs. Haydn's symphony no. 85 is called "La Reine" (The Queen) after Marie-Antoinette, who patronized the concerts at the Paris Conservatory, where it was first performed in France. Although Haydn was definitely a man of the ancien régime he was nevertheless a favorite composer in Paris. It was on the way to a performance of his *Creation* that one of several attempts was made on Napoléon's life. Joséphine and Hortense proceeded to the concert but had to appear calm and collected in their box at the Opéra in spite of the recent narrow escape. When Napoléon and his conquering troops entered Vienna in 1809, the emperor immediately sent guards to protect the aged composer from being disturbed. Nevertheless, Haydn died only three weeks later at age seventy-seven, partly from the distress caused by the battle. Henri Berton (1767–1844) and Cherubini, whose works also appear on the conservatory program, were both teachers there, and Cherubini frequently directed the orchestra. The clarinet concerto, the two airs, and the Symphonie Concertante probably featured student soloists.

The primary vocal form for concert and salon performance, besides airs from opera, was the romance. This simple song form began its rise in the 1770s, reached its height of

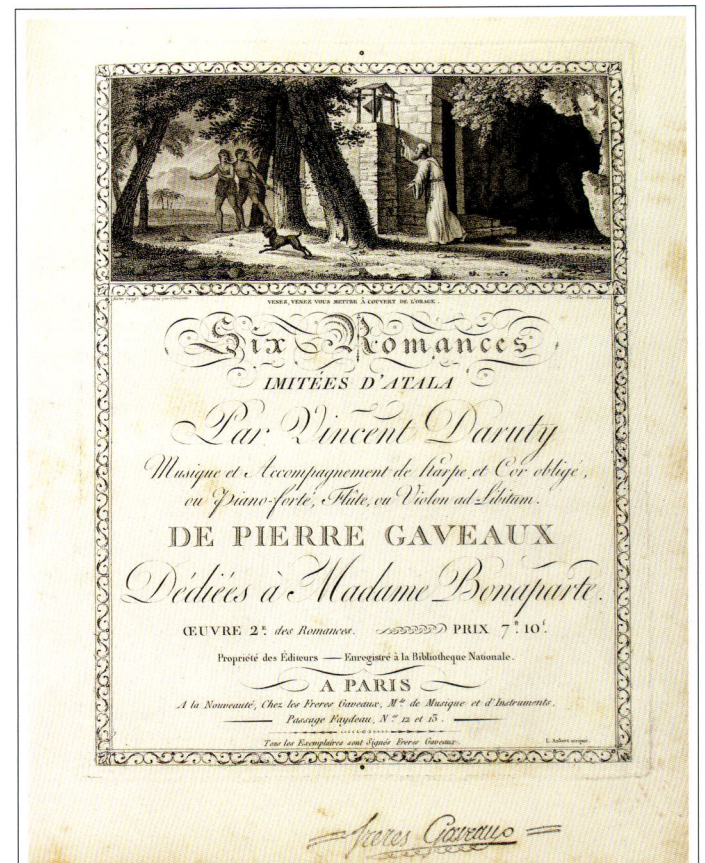

FIGURE 131.

Pierre Gaveaux (French, 1760–1825), Title Page of Score to *Six Romances after Atala*, [1812]. Lithograph, 26.5 × 19.5 cm (10⅜ × 7⅝ in.). Louisville, Kentucky, Southern Baptist Theological Seminary.

• • •

Joséphine probably received thousands of requests from writers and composers wishing to dedicate their work to her. These songs by Gaveaux invoke *Atala* (1801), an immensely popular novel by Chateaubriand that tells the story of a Christian girl who has taken a vow of celibacy but then falls in love with a Natchez Indian. The plot and theme are strikingly similar to Spontini's *La Vestale*, an opera that was performed only through the persistent intervention of the empress.

popularity and sophistication during the first decade of the nineteenth century, and remained popular through the 1820s. "Plaisirs d'amour" by Johann Paul Aegidius Martini (1741–1816) is the textbook example. Martini, a German, was another of the many émigré musicians living in Paris who had a great impact on French music. Texts chosen by composers of romances were not necessarily of the highest quality, and both the amateurs and professionals favored sentimental or pastoral themes about love and *la vie galante* (the courtly life). Easy-to-play accompaniments consisted generally of broken chords outlining simple harmonies, making the music amenable to performance on the piano, harp, or guitar. Short instrumental preludes and interludes, which were slightly more complex in style, sometimes set the tone. All of these characteristics made it possible for singers of romances to accompany their own performances.

Romances poured from the pens of musical amateurs, talented ladies, and professional singers who fancied themselves composers {FIGURE 131}. Marie-Antoinette composed at least one, "Ah! S'il est dans mon village." Hortense, who had studied piano with Daniel Steibelt and Hyacinthe Jadin, played the harp, sang, and devoted much of her leisure time to music. She composed more than 150 romances, which she published in small collections, often privately printed in luxurious editions and illustrated with prints of her own drawings and watercolors. She presented one such collection to her friends as a New Year's gift in 1813 and brought out another in 1828 to benefit the Greeks in their struggle for independence. Her work achieved a certain degree of popularity, not only due to her fame and aristocratic stature. Although she composed the melodies and fit them to the selected verse, the harmony and accompaniments were probably elaborated by her musicians and teachers, particularly Charles-Henri Plantade (1764–1835). Nevertheless, many of her romances show a true feeling for the genre and a genuine melodic gift. In her memoirs she recounts attempting to compose her own verses but confesses that the constraints of rhyme and meter defeated her.[15] Instead she found inspiration in the work of a variety of poets, including lyrics by her brother Eugène. She favored texts of a pastoral and neomedieval genre, telling stories of knights and troubadours or shepherds and shepherdesses.

Many romances, including those by Hortense, formed the basis for instrumental variations. Franz Schubert wrote a set for piano (*Variationen über ein französishes Lied* [Variations on a French Song], 1822), based on Hortense's "Le Bon Chevalier," and dedicated it to Beethoven. Contemporary virtuoso pianists often composed or improvised variations on well-known romances as "bonbons" for their concerts or to display their technique in the salons. Johann Nepomuk Hummel (1778–1837) composed a set on Hortense's "Sentinel"; and both Hummel and Jan Ladislaus Dussek (1760–1812), a Bohemian composer who spent much time in France before the Revolution and was a friend of Marie-Antoinette, used Hortense's most famous work, "The Beautiful Dunois," or "Departing for Syria," as a theme for variations. Later "Departing for Syria" became the anthem of the Bonapartistes during the Restoration and almost a second national song during the reign of Hortense's son, Napoléon III. It remained familiar well into the twentieth century, as Camille Saint-Saëns (1835–1921) quoted it in the "Fossils" movement of his *Carnival of the Animals* (1886).

Opera

Although talented amateurs continued to publish romances, almost all composers contributed them to the salon milieu, even the most important and serious of the era, including Luigi Cherubini and Gasparo Spontini (1774–1851). Opera, however, was the only true door to fame for composers and singers alike. The imperial family and their guests could enjoy opera at the Tuileries Palace theater and at their other residences. The public heard comic opera by Italian composers at the Théâtre Italien, French opéra comique at one or two other theaters in the city, and tragédie lyrique—a particularly French genre of serious opera—at the Académie de Musique, often simply called the Opéra.

For musical evenings at the Tuileries theater, imperial composer Ferdinando Paer often presented one act of a serious opera and one of a comic opera. Napoléon and Joséphine heard Paer's *Didone* at the Tuileries theater in 1806, featuring in the title role one of Napoléon's favorite singers (and briefly his mistress), Giuseppina Grassini (1773–1850). Mme Grassini was only one of the many internationally famous singers whose voice was "requested" for the emperor's or Joséphine's pleasure at the Tuileries, the chapel, or the music salon. Napoléon brought Mme Grassini to Paris in 1800 after hearing her at La Scala following the battle of Marengo. He selected her to perform that year at the national July 14 celebrations (a singular honor for a foreigner), and he eventually awarded her the title First Singer to His Majesty.

One of the last living castrati, Girolami Crescentini (1776–1846), also served the emperor. He and La Grassini performed together in Cherubini's *La Didone* at the Tuileries theater in 1809. Although the emperor much preferred Italian-trained singers along with his Italian music, French singers also appeared in the imperial concerts and in Joséphine's salon. The tenor Pierre Jean Garat (1762–1823) specialized in opéra comique and was a very popular performer and bon vivant. Pierre Gaveaux (1760–1825) was employed in the Tuileries chapel, but like many musicians he also sang in the emperor's theaters and at Joséphine's concerts.

In 1801 Mme Grassini proposed to Napoléon the idea of establishing an Italian opera company, but he gave the strictly controlled theater franchise to Mlle Montansier instead. Joséphine's protégé Gasparo Spontini became the director in 1804, and the theater where the Italian company performed, the Salle Louvois, became the Théâtre de l'Impératrice, which they shared with the Comédie Française. The opéra buffa of Spontini, Paisiello, Paer, and a host of lesser Italian composers enjoyed by the emperor and empress are almost completely (and many deservedly) forgotten today. Mozart's transformation of the genre with masterpieces such as *Le Nozze di Figaro* (The Marriage of Figaro, 1786) and *Così fan tutte* (Thus Do All Women, 1790) had not yet reached France. Until Rossini's more substantial works arrived in Paris, audiences chose Italian comic opera for an evening of light entertainment rather than anything challenging or thought provoking. Perhaps that explains its appeal to the emperor, who used his time at the theater and in chapel for needed relaxation.

The situation was quite different with French comic opera. Many composers turned away from the lyric tragedy and the Académie de Musique during the Revolution due to the strict rules and traditions surrounding the genre as much as the theater's aristocratic tinge. A ballet ended each act of a lyric tragedy, spoken dialogue was not allowed, and in spite of the name of the genre, a happy ending was de rigueur, frequently brought about by a deus ex machina. The purely entertaining elements of comic opera, the stock comedic characters and ballets, had begun to play a much smaller role in the works of André Grétry and other composers during the waning years of the monarchy, and Grétry's *Richard Coeur de Lion* (1784) had reached new expressive heights. Rather than the Elysian fields or the island of Naxos and gods descending from the clouds or riding in on fiery chariots, composers and audiences alike wanted at least a semblance of real people and everyday situations closer in time and place. The aims of composers also changed: rather than providing light, enchanting entertainment, they wanted to teach and edify their newly liberated audience. The action-packed stories, exotic settings, and mysterious and supernatural elements provided the spoonful of sugar.

Cherubini's *Medea* is the masterpiece of this subgenre of opéra comique, sometimes called "French revolutionary opera," even though the composer and librettist returned to classical literature for their story. Produced in 1797 at the Théâtre Feydeau (at this time one of two rival theaters staging French comic opera), the work portrays Medea's vengeance on Jason through her murder of their children. All comic elements have disappeared from the libretto, although the required ballets and spoken dialogue were retained. The sheer difficulty and unforgiving nature of the lead role, combined with Cherubini's mastery of orchestration, convey the heroine's extreme emotional states of jealousy, ferocity, tenderness, and love. Unfortunately, this work is most commonly performed today as a vehicle for soprano prima donnas in a form that destroys the dramatic pacing carefully crafted by Cherubini and his librettist, and with recitatives composed in 1854 by Franz Lachner to replace the spoken dialogue.

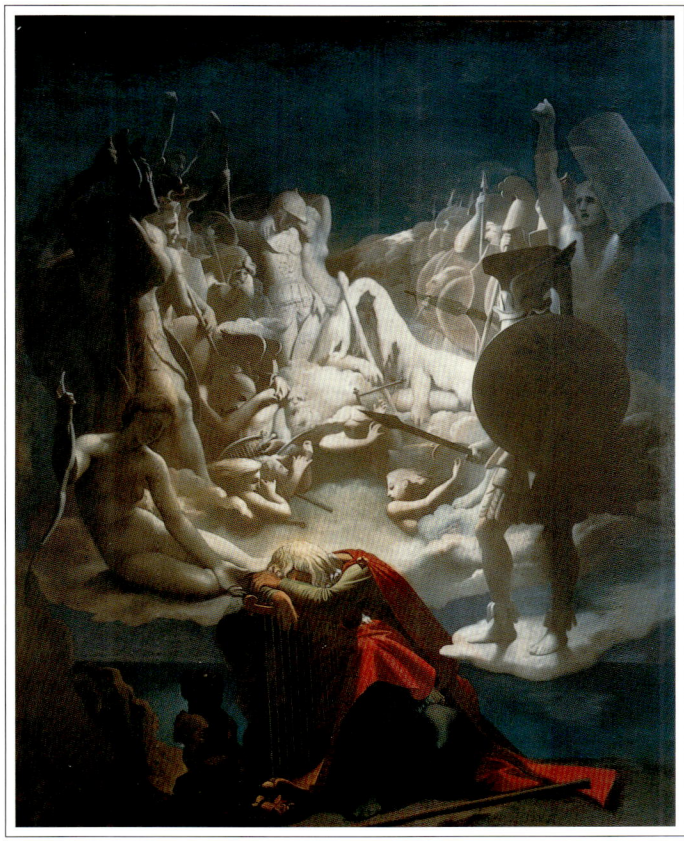

FIGURE 132.

Jean-Auguste-Dominique Ingres (1780–1867), *The Dream of Ossian*. 1813. Oil on canvas, 348 × 275 cm (137 × 108¼ in.). Montauban, Musée Ingres.

• • •

Ingres portrays a scene not found in Ossian's poetry but created by Lesueur and his librettist for the opera *Ossian*, or *The Bardes*. It is a precedent for the dreams, visions, and apparitions in later Romantic and Gothic operas such as Weber's *Der Freischütz* (1821), Marschner's *Der Vampyr* (1828), and Meyerbeers's *Robert le Diable* (1831).

The Empire restored the Opéra to its former glories, and Napoléon made it—along with his palaces, victories, and war booty—a symbol of his power. The Académie Impériale de Musique, as it was now called, soon boasted the best orchestra in France and mounted the most lavish productions, but the government exerted strict control over the works performed there, and every libretto had to pass through the censor. Works to celebrate the emperor's victories or bolster his image frequently squeezed out more legitimate works. In 1803 the facile Paisiello presented a lyric tragedy, *Proserpine*, portraying Napoléon as Jupiter. The most famous of the deification operas is *The Triumph of Trajan* by Louis Luc Loiseau de Persuis (1769–1819), a minor composer. No expense was spared for the production in October 1807; by 1814, during the Hundred Days, the opera received its one hundredth performance.[16] *The Triumph of Trajan*, however, was more pageant than music drama, and more appealing to the eye than to the ear.

The quality of the productions and prestige of the house—and a desire to please the emperor—sparked many composers' interest in writing tragédie lyrique during the Empire. Napoléon highly praised Lesueur's *Ossian, or the Bards* (1804), an opera based on the life of Ossian, the imaginary Scottish poet {FIGURE 132}. Lesueur recommended the use of twelve harps in the orchestra, and several aspects of the work achieve a full-blooded Romanticism: the invocation of the supernatural, the wild Highland setting, even at times Lesueur's music.[17] Méhul's *Uthal* (1806), another Ossianic opera, also exhibits proto-Romantic tendencies. Spontini, however, created the crowning operatic achievement of the decade when his tragédie lyrique, *La Vestale* {FIGURES 133, 134}, took the stage after withstanding many revisions, vicissitudes, and jealous cabals.

Spontini arrived in Paris in 1803 to make his way in the capital of Europe, first as a humble teacher of singing, although he was reputedly not a humble man. He was already well known in Italy as a composer of opéra buffa. He wrote several works for the Théâtre

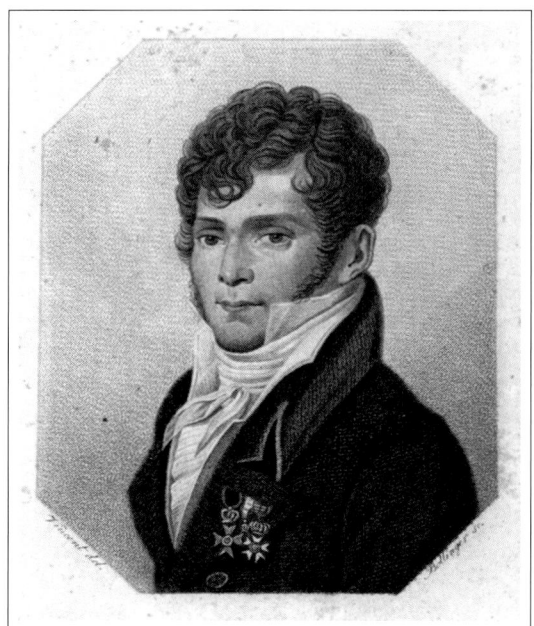
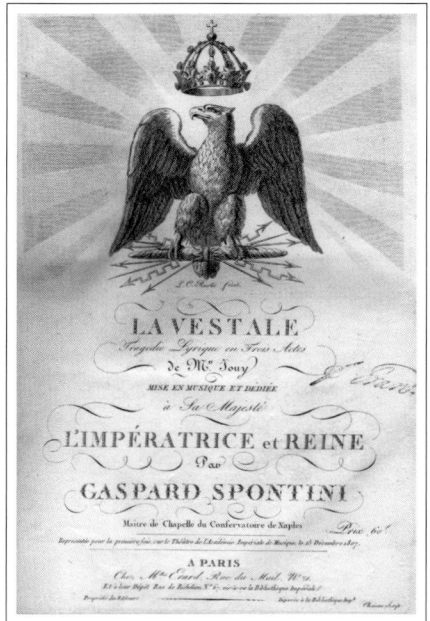

FIGURE 133.

Frederich Wilhelm Bollinger (German, 1777–1825)?,
Portrait of Gaspare Spontini, ca. 1820.
Engraving.
Millersville, Pennsylvania, Millersville University.

• • •

The opera *La Vestale* (1807) represented the apex of Spontini's career. His next tragédie lyrique, *Fernand Cortez* (1809), meant to flatter the emperor, unfortunately coincided with the long and ultimately unsuccessful subjugation of Spain. Out of favor and isolated during the Restoration, the failure of *Olimpie* (1819) finally caused Spontini to forsake Paris. He spent most of the rest of his career in Berlin and his final years in Italy.

FIGURE 134.

Title Page to Gasparo Spontini's *La Vestale*, 1807.
University of California, Los Angeles,
Music Library Special Collections.

• • •

The title page of Spontini's chef d'oeuvre, *La Vestale*, rightly bears a dedication to the empress, for without her the opera never would have taken the stage.

Italien and even tried his hand at opéra comique, although there his creations were decried by a faction favoring French composers for French music. Through advantageous social connections Spontini quickly brought himself to the attention of the imperial family, and by 1805 he was director of the empress's music and Joséphine's official composer. He produced several works for her, including a one-act comic opera, *Tout le monde a tort* (Everybody's Wrong), which was performed for her name day in 1806 at Malmaison by members of the imperial family. Joséphine's support provided Spontini with the time and inspiration to write a lyric tragedy for the Académie Impérial de Musique.

Without the empress's friendship, *La Vestale* would never have been heard, for the forces arrayed against it were formidable. Claques hired by those jealous of the influence of foreign musicians, composers waiting for their own operas to be produced at the academy, the Opéra's notorious political bureaucracy, even the emperor himself (who delayed its production three times) all had to be overcome. Joséphine worked tirelessly to champion Spontini's work, and *La Vestale* is probably her greatest musical legacy. After the wildly successful premiere on December 15, 1807, the opera quickly triumphed in the provincial opera houses and soon conquered the rest of Europe. By 1830 it had been produced at least two hundred times in Paris alone.[18]

La Vestale is in many ways the operatic icon of the Napoleonic Empire. Once again, a subject from antiquity takes the stage, but this time the source is Roman history rather than classical mythology, reflecting the common belief that the French Empire was the modern equivalent of the Roman one. Spontini successfully grafts the Italian bel canto style onto the French tragédie lyrique. The opera presents a personal drama—that of Julia, a vestal virgin, and her forbidden love for the Roman general, Licinius—against the pomp and splendor of religious ritual and public ceremony. Each act is designed as a huge crescendo from the personal to the public. In the end, the goddess Vesta herself relights the sacred flame of the temple (which Julia had allowed to die out), showing her forgiveness for the unfortunate priestess and bestowing her blessings upon the star-crossed couple

Unfortunately, no god descended from Olympus to grant Joséphine a child, just as no fire from heaven prevented Napoléon's final defeat at Waterloo. Even though Napoléon himself is a romantic figure and the seeds of Romanticism were sown in many works produced during his lifetime, Romanticism in France manifested itself principally in politics. The anarchy of the Revolution, the conservatism of the Empire, and the reactionary nature of the Restoration delayed the influence and arrival in France of the English and German Romantic ideas that had surfaced at the end of the eighteenth century. It was not until 1830—another year of revolution—that the political events of 1789 bore fruit in the performing arts in France with the double canon shot of Hector Berlioz's *Symphonie Fantastique* and Victor Hugo's *Hernani*. Given Napoléon's rather perfunctory appreciation of music and his choice of composers, it is fair to say that Joséphine would have been more prepared for that revolution than was her imperial husband.

Notes

1. Constant Pierre, *Les Hymnes et chansons de la Révolution: Aperçu général et catalogue* (Paris, 1904), 322.
2. "De Barra, de Viala le sort nous fait envie, Ils sont morts, mais ils ont vaincu," and "Partez, vaillants époux, les combats sont vos fêtes, Partez, modèles des guerriers." Joseph Barra (1779–1793) and Agricol Viala (1780–1793) were two *enfants héros* (child heroes). Barra was captured by royalists and killed because he would only say "Vive la République." Viala was killed after destroying a bridge over the Durance, preventing enemy troops from crossing.
3. Henry Lachouqe, *The Anatomy of Glory: Napoléon and His Guard, a Study in Leadership* (London, 1978), 210.
4. The serpent is a bass wind instrument with a brass mouthpiece, made of wood covered in leather, and bent into a curved serpentine shape. Unlike other brass instruments of the time, it was capable of playing a full chromatic scale. Serpent players were mostly employed in military bands and in churches to accompany the plain chant. The *chapeau-chinois* (literally, Chinese hat), or crescent, is a long pole with a hat or ornament on top (frequently a half-moon) with small bells, cymbals, and jingles attached to arms. It is played by shaking the pole or tapping the bottom against the ground.
5. Constant Pierre, *Musique des fêtes et cérémonies de la Révolution française: Oeuvres de Gossec, Cherubini, Lesueur, Méhul, Catel, etc.* (Paris, 1899), 558.
6. David Charlton, introduction to *Music and the French Revolution*, ed. Malcolm Boyd (Cambridge, 1992), 10.
7. A recording of excerpts is available on the compact disc *Sacre du Napoléon Premier* (Koch Schwann 3-1208-2), 1996.
8. This *Vivat*, with appropriate changes in text, was used throughout the Restoration to accompany the comings and goings of Louis XVIII and Charles X.
9. Claire Elisabeth Rémusat, Comtesse de Rémusat, *Memoires of Madame Rémusat, 1802–1808* (New York, 1880), 2.
10. Margaret Stone Selden, "Napoléon and Cherubini," *Journal of the American Musicological Society* 8, no. 2 (Summer 1955): 114.
11. Mlle [Marie-Jeanne-Pierrette] Avrillion, *Mémoires de Mlle Avrillion, première femme de chambre de l'Impératrice Joséphine*, ed. Maurice Derelle (Paris, 1986), 101.
12. Laure Junot Abrantès, Duchess of Abrantès, *Autobiography and Recollections of Laura, Duchess of Abrantès (widow of General Junot)*, vol. 2 (New York, 1964), 192.
13. Albert Lavignac and Lionel de La Laurencie, *Encyclopédie de la musique et dictionnaire du Conservatoire* (Paris, 1931), s.v. "L'Ensignement musical," and "Institut de France," 3448.
14. Lavignac and Laurencie, *Encyclopédie*, 3449.
15. Queen Hortense of Holland, quoted in Dorothea Baumann, "La Reine Hortense et la musique," in *La Reine Hortense, une femme artiste: La Présentation de l'exposition a été conçue par Frédéric Beauclair*, exh. cat., Musée national des Château de Malmaison et Bois-Préau, May 27–Sept. 27, 1993 (Paris, 1993), 22.
16. Jean Mongrédien, *La Musique en France des Lumières au Romantisme (1789–1830)*. (Paris, 1986), 60.
17. Edward Dent, *The Rise of Romantic Opera* (Cambridge, 1976), 87.
18. Mongrédien, *La Musique en France*, 80.

Index

NOTE: *Page numbers in italic indicate illustrations.*

Abrantès, Laure d'. *See* Junot, Laure
acrostic jewelry, 177, 182, *182*
Albrizzi, Giuseppe, 48
Alexander I (czar of Russia), 53, 54, 149
The Alliance of Wealth and the Arts (Prud'hon), 61
Amaryllis, Tuberoses, Reines Marguerites (Redouté), *93*
Anselme, Nicola-Pierre-Baptiste, 11
Appiani, Jean-André, 21–23, *21–23*, 178
Arneville, Marie-Blanche d', 87
"The Arrival of the Emperor at the Hôtel de Ville" (David), 36, *36*
Atala (Chateaubriand), 31, *198*
Audubon, John James, 101
Auguié, Adèle, 9
Auguste, Henry, 148, 151–53, *152*
Auguste, Robert-Joseph, 147, 148
Avrillion, Marie-Jeanne-Pierrette, 177, 184, 196

Bacciochi, Elisa Bonaparte, 154
Baillot, Pierre, 196
Ballangé, Joseph, *194*
The Banquet of Napoléon and Marie-Louise (Dufay), *153*
Barraband, Jacques, 100
Barras, Paul, 34
Barret, André, 16
Bartolozzi, Francesco, 97
Bataille, Laurent-Edmé, 74n9
The Battle of Austerlitz (Gérard), 27, *28*
The Battle of Marengo (Swebach), 135n7
Baudin, Nicolas, 85, 86, 100
Baudouin, Anoine-Thibaut, 119
Bauer, Ferdinand, 101
Beauharnais, Alexandre de, 1, 33–34, 57, 121, 175, 191
Beauharnais, Eugène de: childhood of, 1, 3; children of, 133–34; Desaix and, 22; dinner service of, 154; home of, *56*, 62–63, *63*, 74n9; marriage of, 3; in military, 8, 22; music and, 196; porcelain of, 133; sculpture of, 54; in works of art, 23, *23*, 27, 36, 182
Beauharnais, Hortense de: childhood of, 1, 3, 9; children of, 44; on fashion, 161; homes of, 57–62, *59–62*, 74n3; Isabey and, 13, 14, *14*; jewelry of, 182, 183, 184;

marriage of, 3; music by, 27, 78, 196, 198–99; in works of art, 14, *14*, 26, 27, *28*, 36
Beauharnais, Hôtel de, *56*, 62–63, *63*, 74n9
Beauharnais, Joséphine de: childhood of, 1; death of, 15, 20, 53, 73, 172; divorce of, 36, 44, 55n14, 117–19; first marriage of, 1, 33–34, 57, 175; marriage to Napoléon, 2–3; tomb of, 44; in works of art, 23, *24*, 24–25, 26, *29*, 30–31, 35–36, *41*, 41–42, *42*, 45, *140*, 140–42, *141*, 166
Beckford, William, 148
Bed Made in Paris for M. O. (Percier and Fontaine), 58, *59*
Bélanger, François-Joseph, 57–58, *59*
Belisarius (Gérard), 13
Beltrami, Giovanni, 182
Beriot, Charles Auguste de, 196
Berlioz, Hector, 192, 203
Berthault, Louis-Martin: and Compiègne, 117; and Malmaison, 72, 72–73, 74n3, 82–83, 119; and porcelain, 126, *127*
Berton, Henri, 197
Biennais, Martin-Guillaume, 146, *149*; works by, *146*, 147, *151*, 153, 154; workshop of, 148–49, 150, 155n6
Bignon, Mme, 130
Black Swans (Wailly), *84*
Blind Belisarius (A.-D. Chaudet), 45–46
Blondel, Merry-Joseph, 73, 75n43
Boccherini, Luigi, 196
Boileau, Jean-Jacques, 148
Boilly, Louis-Léopold, 10–12, *10–12*, 44, 97
Bollinger, Frederich Wilhelm, *202*
Bonaparte, Caroline, 48, 49, 55n22, 57
Bonaparte, Catherine, 3
Bonaparte, Jérôme, 3, 154
Bonaparte, Joseph, 3, 180
Bonaparte, Louis, 3, 44, 57; home of, 57–62, *59–62*, 74n3, 154
Bonaparte, Lucien, 10, 44, 57, 196
Bonaparte, Letizia, "Mme Mère," 154, 197
Bonaparte, Napoléon. *See* Napoléon I
Bonaparte, Napoléon-Charles, 44, 55n13, 55n14
Bonaparte, Pauline, 3, 153
Bonpland, Aimé (Goufau), 78, 83, 86
Borghese, Camille, 55n4, 153
Borghese, Pauline Bonaparte, 3, 153
Borghese dinner service, *151*, 153–54, 155n8

Bosio, François-Joseph, 42, *42*, 55n7, 142
Bosio, Jean-François, 42, 55n7
Boulard, Jean-Baptiste, 114
Boulard, Michel-Jacques, 70, 114
Bourgeois, Constant, 133
Bourrienne, Louis, 65
Boze, Joseph, 9, *9*
Branicki dinner service, *144*, 154, *155*
Brongniart, Alexandre, 57, 125–26, 137–42
Brookner, Anita, 61
Brutelle, Louis L'Héritier de, 97
The Bull (Potter), 8

Cahier, Jean-Charles, 153
Calmelet, Etiènne, 62, 74n22
cameos, 177–80, *178–80*, 182
Campan, Mme, 3, 9, *9*
Campbell, John, 49, 55n21
Candolle, Augustin-Pyramus de, 97
Canova, Antonio, 48–54; A.-D. Chaudet and, 47, 48; Prud'hon and, 29; works by, 2, 40, *48–52*, 48–54, 179
Capparoni, Gaspare, 178
Carême, Antonin, 65, 150
Carteaux, Jean-Baptiste-François, 70, 75n41
Cartellier, Pierre, 40, 43–44, *45*
Catherine Worlée (Gérard), *159*
Catherine Worlée (Vigée-LeBrun), *158*
Cavelier, A.-L.-M., 154
Champaigne, Philippe de, 8
Chanorier, Jean, 78, 89n5
"Le Chant du départ" (Méhul), 10, 192
Chantereine, rue, 103–5, *105*, 121–22, *122*, 134n1
Chaptal, Claude, 86
Chaptal, Jean-Antoine, 77–78
Charlemagne, 162
Charles X (king of France), 53–54
Chastenay, Mme de, 31, 37n27, 159, 161–62
Chataigner, Alexis, *158*
Chateaubriand, François-Auguste-René de, 31, 81, 87, 88–89, *198*
Chaudet, Antoine-Denis: works by, 40, 41, 45–47, 45–48, 115, *141*, 142
Chaudet, Elisabeth, 46, 55n16
Chénier, Marie Joseph, 192, 194
Cherubini, Luigi, 192, 196, 199, 200
Chevallier, Bernard, 4, 5n7
Childeric, 162
Chinard, Joseph, *41*, 41–42, 55n6
clothing, 157–72

204

Compiègne, *102*, *117*, 117–19, *118*
The Consecration of the Emperor Napoléon and the Coronation of Empress Joséphine (David), *34*, 35–36
conservatory, 86–88, *88*, 98
The Conservatory (Garnerey), *88*
Constantin, Guillaume-Jean, 30
coral, 180–81, *181*
coronation, 3; fashion at, 162–66, *164*; jewelry at, 176; music at, 195–96; paintings of, *34*, 35–36
Corot, Jean-Baptiste-Camille, 100
court dress, 161–63, *165*, 165–66, *170*, *172*
La Crescendo (Cherubini), 196
Crescentini, Girolami, 199
Cupid and Psyche (Canova), 47–49, *49*
Cupid Loosing His Arrows and Flying Away (F.-J. Bosio), 42, *43*
Cupid Playing with a Butterfly (A.-D. Chaudet), *46*, 47, 55n17
Cupid Playing with the Doves of Venus (Vassé), 39–40
Cyparissus Mourning His Fawn (A.-D. Chaudet), 40, *46*

Daedalus and Icarus (Canova), 48
Dael, Jan Frans van, 10–11, 97
Dagoty, Pierre-Louise, 130
Dancer with Her Hands on Her Hips (Canova), *50*, 50–51
Daru, Pierre, 111, 177
David, Jacques-Louis: in coronation, *34*, 35–36, 162, *164*; furniture designed by, 106–7; Gros and, 16, 18, 20; Jacob and, 104; music and, 190; works by, 8, 33–36, *34–36*
Day-Lily (Redouté), *99*
A Day of Review under the Empire (Ballangé), *194*
Dehanne, Pierre-Joseph, 146–47
Delacroix, Eugène, 4, 16, 18
Delafosse, Jean-Charles, 147
Demachy, Pierre-Antoine, *190*
Demarne, Jean-Louis, 130, 134
Demidoff, Anatole, 155n11
Demidoff, Nikolai, 154
Denon, Dominique-Vivant: advice on art from, 7, 100; Bosio and, 42; David and, 36; Gros and, 16–17, 19, 20; jewelry and, 177; at Malmaison, 83; as museum director, 2, 7; porcelain and, 124, 142, 148; on Redouté, 98; in Salons, 55n9; travels of, 2, 7, 125; in works of art, *25*, 25
Déperais, Claude-Antoine, 124
Dervieux, Mlle, 57, 58
Desaix, Louis-Charles-Antoine, 22, *22*
Deschamps, Jean-Marie, 51, 55n33
Desfontaines, René, 97
Desmazis, Alexandre, 111
diamonds, 175, 183–84
Dihl and Guérhard, 130–34, *132*, *133*

Dining Room in the House of Mlle Dervieux (Bélanger), *59*
Divoff, Mme, 65
Dodin, Charles-Nicholas, 123
Doncre, Dominique, *191*
Dou, Gerrit, 8
The Dream of Ossian (Ingres), *201*
Drolling, Martin, 10, 124, 130, 134
Dufay, Alexandre-Benoît-Jean, *153*
Duroc, Marshal, 20
Dussek, Jan Ladislaus, 199

Elgin, Lady, 176
Elysée Palace, 126–27, *128*
Empress Joséphine (Gros), *156*, 167–69, *168*
Empress Joséphine (Prud'hon), 29, 30–31, *166*, 170–71
The Empress Joséphine (F.-J. Bosio), 42, *42*
The Empress Joséphine (Chinard), *38*, 41, *41*
Empress Joséphine with an Herbarium (Lefèvre), *24*, 24–25
Endymion (Girodet-Trioson), *32*, 33

fashion, 157–72
Fénelon, Marie-Laure de, 122
Feodorovna, Maria, 154
Ferdinand IV (king of Naples), 39
The Festival of the Supreme Being (Demachy), *190*
The First Room of Modern Sculpture (Premazzi), *54*
Fitzgerald, F. Scott, 33
Foncier, Edmé Marie, 176
Fontaine, Pierre-François-Léonard: in Boilly's *Reunion*, 10–11; and dinnerware, *151*; and fashion, *164*; furniture of, 104, 106, 107, 110, *110*, 114–15; and Malmaison, 4, 66, 70, 79, 81, 106; and Musée Napoléon, 40–41; and silver, 146, *146*; style of, 58, *58*; and Tuileries Palace, 64
Fontainebleau: furniture at, 110–17, *112*, *113*, *117*; porcelain at, 123
Forbin, Auguste de, 33
Fouché, Joseph, 20
The Four Seasons (Prud'hon), 74n8
Fragonard, Alexandre-Evariste, 124, *139*
Fragonard, Jean-Honoré, 124
Frederick the Great (Carteaux), 70
Frochot, Nicolas, 31
The Funeral of Atala (Girodet-Trioson), 31, *32*
furniture, 103–19

Garat, Pierre Jean, 200
gardens, 77–89
Garnerey, Auguste: works by, *43*, *62*, 67–68, *68*, *80*, *82*, *83*, *88*, 89n15
Gaveaux, Pierre, *198*, 200
Gebauer, Michel-Joseph, 193, *195*
General Bonaparte at the Bridge of Arcole (Gros), 6, *18*, 18–19

General Louis-Charles-Antoine Desaix (Appiani), 22, *22*
Genu, Marie-Joseph-Gabriel, 153
George III (king of England), 153
Gérard, François, 26–27; in Boilly's *Reunion*, 10; David and, 34; Isabey and, 13, *13*, 26; Redouté and, 91; works by, 8, 26–27, *26–28*, 67, 140, *159*
gilding: on furniture, 111–19; silver, 145–55
Girodet-Trioson, Anne-Louis, 31–33; in Boilly's *Reunion*, 11; David and, 34; Gros and, 16, 31; works by, 2, 31–33, *32*, 67
Girometti, Giuseppe, 178
Glory Distributing Crowns (Cartellier), 43–44
gold, 145–46
Gossec, François Joseph, *190*, 192, 193–94
Goujon, Jean, 115–16
The Grand Salon of 1810 (Boilly), *11*, 12
Grand Vermeil service, 151–53, *152*, *153*, *154*
Grandjean, Serge, 146
Grassini, Giuseppina, 199, 200
Grétry, André, 192, 200
Greuze, Jean-Baptiste, 124
Gros, Antoine-Jean, 8, 16–20; Girodet-Trioson and, 16, 31; works by, 2, *17–19*, 17–20, *156*, 167–69, *168*, *170*, *171*
Guérin, Pierre-Narcisse, 13

Hamelin, Antoine, 21
Hamelin, Fortunée, *21*, 21–22
Haydn, Franz Joseph, 197
Hébé (Canova), 48, 49–50, *50*
Heem, J. D. de, 94
Hermitage Museum, 54, 69, 134
Hoffman, Nicholas, *193*
Hortensia, Jacinthe, Lis Saint Jacques, Chrysanthemum (Redouté), *90*, 96
Houdon, Jean-Antoine, 12, 41
Hubert, Gérard, 48, 73
Huet, Jean-Baptiste, 100
Hugo, Victor, 203
Humboldt, Alexander von, 78, 83, 86
Hummel, Johann Nepomuk, 199
The Hunting Party at the Pavilion of the Butard (J.-F. Robert), 135n7
Huysum, Jan van, 94
"Hymn to the Supreme Being" (Gossec), 190, *190*

Ingres, Jean-Auguste-Dominique, *201*
intaglios, 177–79
interiors, 57–73
Isabey, Jean-Baptiste, 13–15; and fashion, 162, 164, *164*; Gérard and, 13, *13*, 26; and porcelain, 141; works by, 8, 13–15, 65, *66*, *180*, *182*; in works of art, 10, 13, *13*

Jacob, Georges, 104, 105, 109
Jacob, Georges, II, 104, 109
Jacob-Desmalter, François-Honoré-
    Georges, 44, 68, 104, 106, 109, 115, *115*,
    117, 118
Jacob-Desmalter et Cie., 109–10
Jacob Frères, 104–10, *105*, *106*
Jadin, Hyacinthe, 198
Jaquotot, Marie Victoire, *140*, 141
Jardin des Plantes (Paris), 77, 78, 78n4, 85,
    86, 97
Jean-Baptiste Isabey (Vernet), 15, *15*
Jefferson, Thomas, 78
Jeuffroy, Romain Vincent, 178
jewelry, 175–86
Johns, Christopher, 54
Joséphine. *See* Beauharnais, Joséphine de
Julien, Pierre, 39
Juno in Her Chariot (Blondel), 73
Junot, Laure, 65, 80, 82, 114, 167, 196
Justice and Divine Vengeance Pursuing Crime
    (Prud'hon), *30*, 31

Kennedy, John, 86, 98

Laborde, Alexandre de, 78
Lachner, Franz, 200
Lafitte, Louis, 70
Lagarde, Joseph, 34
Lagrange, General, 7
Lagrange the Younger, 124
Lannoy, Hôtel de, 58–62, *59–62*, 74n3
Lavalette, Antoine, 18, 19
Laveissière, Sylvain, 61
Lebel, Nicolas-Antoine, 125, *126*
Lebrun, Charles, 64, 74n13
Lebrun, Jean Baptiste, 197
Lecomte, Felix, 63
Lee, James, 86, 98
Lefèvre, Robert, 13, *24*, 24–25, *25*
Leguay, Charles-Etienne, 130, 134
Lemot, François, 64
Lemoyne, Jean Louis, 80
Lenoir, Alexandre, 67, 82
LeRoy, Louis Hippolyte, *164*, 165, 167, 172
Lesueur, François, 192, 195, 196, 201
Licht, Fred, *50*, 53
Ligneureux, Martin-Eloi, 68, 108
Lilac, Capucines, and Fushia (Redouté), *95*
Les Lilacées (Redouté), 86, *87*, 92–93, *99*
Loo, Carle Van, 123
Lorrain, Claude, 83
Louis XIV (king of France), 81, 150, 162
Louis XV (king of France), 150
Louis XVI (king of France), 123, 125, 147,
    150
Louis XVIII (king of France), 126, 154
Louise (queen of Prussia), 128–29
Luini, Bernardino, 8, 23
Luxembourg Palace, 107

Macpherson, James, 33, 37n33
Madame Bonaparte (Appiani), 23
Madame Campan (Boze), 9, *9*
Madame Hamelin (Appiani), *21*, 22
Madame Pasteur (Gros), 16, *17*
mahogany furniture, 103–11, 118–19
Malmaison: acquisition of, 2–3, 78; conservatory at, 86–88, *88*, 98; fashion at, 172; furniture at, 68, 70, 105–7, 119; gardens at, 77, *79*, 79–89, *80*, *82*, *83*; interiors of, 4, 66–73, *68*, *69*, *71*, *72*, 75n27; jewelry at, 180, 182; music at, 196, 202; porcelain at, 123–26, *127*, 127, 129, 130, 134; sculpture at, 39, 53–54, 67; silver at, *147*, 147
Marguerite, Bernard Armand, 176, 185
Marie-Antoinette: Campan and, 9; fashion of, 157–59, *160*, *163*, 166, 170; furniture of, *112*, 113; homes of, 63, 65; interiors of, 3; music and, 197, *198*; porcelain of, 124; sculpture of, 39; in works of art, *160*, *163*
Marie-Antoinette in a Chemise Gown (Vigée-LeBrun), *160*
Marie-Antoinette in a Grand Habit (Vigée-LeBrun), *163*
Marie-Louise, 53, 118, 119, 152, 164, 178
"La Marseillaise" (Rouget de Lisle), 191, 192
La Marseillaise (Doncre), *191*
Martin, Joseph, 86
Martini, Johann Paul Aegidius, 198
Mary Stuart, Queen of Scotland (Vermay),
    171, 171
Massot, Firmin, *181*
Matsys, Quentin, 8
Maximilian-Joseph, 154
Maximilien de Leuchtenberg, 133–34
Mayer, Constance, 29, 67
Medea (Cherubini), 200
Médicis, Marie de', 163, 164
Méhul, Etiènne Nicolas, 10, 192, 197, 201
Melito, Miot de, 176
Mellerio, 181, 186, *186*
Mellerio, François, 177
Mellerio, Jean-Baptiste, 177
Mercer, Alexander, 73
Metsu, Gabriel, 12
Meulen, Adam Frans van der, 8
Meuricoffre, M. and Mme, 16
Micaud, Jacques-François, 124
Michaux, André, 84, 89n19
Michaux, François-André, 84
Michel, Marianne Roland, 100
Miel, Jan, *152*
Mies van der Rohe, Ludwig, 70
Miniature of Joséphine (Isabey), *180*
Mirbel, Charles-François Brisseau de, 98,
    100
Modesty (Cartellier), 40, 44, *45*
Moench, Frederic, 72
Moët, Jean-Remy, 14
Moitte, Jean-Guillaume, 104, 148
Molay, Jean-Jacques Le Couteulx du, 78
Molinos, 152

Mongrédien, Jean, 195
Montansier, Mlle, 200
Montesson, Mme de, 57
Moreau, Jean-Victor-Marie, 110–11
Moreau, Mme, *110*, 110–11, 113
Morel, Jean-Marie, 81, 89n12
Mozart, Wolfgang, 200
Murat, Caroline Bonaparte, 48, 49, 55n22, 57
Murat, Joaquim, 48, 49, 55n21, 154
music, 189–203; revolutionary, 190–92;
    romance, 197–99, *198*
The Music Salon at Malmaison (Garnerey),
    67–68, *68*
"Musicians of the Imperial Guard"
    (Hoffman), *193*

Nadermann, Joseph, 196
Napoléon (Gérard), 26–27, *27*
Napoléon I: on Canova, 53; David's work
    with, 34–35, 37n39; divorce of, 36, 44,
    55n14, 117–19; in exile, 88; fashion and,
    161–62, 165, 166, 167, 172; jewelry and,
    175–78; marriage to Joséphine, 2–3;
    marriage to Marie-Louise, 53, 118, 119,
    152, 164, 178; music and, 193, 195, 196,
    201; porcelain and, 125; rise of, 2–3; silver and, 147, 148, 149, *149*, 150, 154; in
    works of art, 17–20, *18*, *19*, 22, 26–27,
    27, 35–36, 42, 45, 48, *48*
Napoléon I, King of Italy (Appiani), 22
Napoléon I Visiting the Salon of 1808
    (Gros), *170*, 171
Napoléon III, 15, 147, 199
Napoléon as First Consul (Canova), 48, *48*,
    55n25
*Napoléon Bonaparte Visiting the Victims of
    the Plague at Jaffa* (Fros), *19*, 19–20
*Napoléon Decorating the Sculptor Cartellier
    at the Salon of 1808* (Boilly), *12*, 12, 44
*Napoléon Presenting the Newborn King of
    Rome to His Mother, the Empress Marie-
    Louise* (Isabey), 65, *66*
Nicholas I (czar of Russia), 133
Nicolle, Jean-Victor, *79*
Night (Prud'hon), 61, *61*
Night Thoughts (Young), 33
Nitot, François-Regnault, 177, 178
Nitot, Marie-Etienne, 176–77
Nitot & Fils, 184
Noon (Prud'hon), 61, *61*

*The Oath of the Army Made to the Emperor
    after the Distribution of Eagles* (David),
    35, 36
Odiot, Jean-Baptiste-Claude, 147, *147*, 153,
    154, *155*
opera, 193, 196, 199–203
Orléans, Gaston d', 97
Ossian, or the Bards (Lesueur), 201, *201*
Ossian (Forbin), 33
Ossian (Gérard), 26, 67
Ossian (Girodet-Trioson), 67
Ouvrard, Gabriel-Julien, *59*

Paer, Ferdinando, 196, 199
The Painter Isabey and His Daughter Alexandrine (Gérard), 13, *13*
paintings, 7–36
Paisiello, Giovanni, 195, *195*, 201
Paris (Canova), 51, *51*, 53, 54
Pasteur, Mme, 16, *17*
Peace (A.-D. Chaudet), 47, *47*
pearls, 183, *183*, 184, *185*
Percier, Charles: in Boilly's *Reunion*, 10–11; and dinnerware, *151*; and fashion, *164*; furniture of, 104, 106–8, *108*, 110, *110*, 115, *116*; and Malmaison, 4, 66, 70, 72, 79, 106; and Musée Napoléon, 40–41; and silver, 146, *146*; style of, 58, *58*; and Tuileries Palace, *64*
Persuis, Louis Luc Loiseau de, 201
Pichler, Luigi, 178
Pindemonte, Ippolito, 50
Pinks, Hyacinth, and Campanula (Redouté), *94*
Piranesi, Canaletto, 3
The Pissing Cow (Potter), 8
Pithou, Nicolas-Pierre, the Younger, 123, *123*
Pius VII (pope), 67, 110, 178, 195
Plantade, Charles-Henri, 198
porcelain, 121–42; botanical, 86, *87*, *120*, *129*, 129–30, *131*; with Joséphine's image, *136*, *140*, 140–42, *141*; Sèvres, 122–30, 134, 137–42
Portrait of Baron Dominique-Vivant Denon (Lefèvre), 25, *25*
Portrait of Empress Joséphine (Massot), *181*
Portrait of Eugène de Beauharnais (Appiani), 23, *23*
Portrait of Gasparo Spontini (Bollinger), *202*
Portrait of Giovanni Paisiello (Vigée-Lebrun), *195*
Portrait of Hortense (Gérard), 27, *28*
Potter, Paulus, 8
Pougetoux, Alain, 100–101
Premazzi, Luigi, 54
Prud'hon, Pierre-Paul, 29–31; in Boilly's *Reunion*, 10; and dinner service, 152; interiors of, 58–61, *60*, *61*, 74n8; wife of, 29; works by, 8, *29*, 29–31, *30*, 166, 170–71
Psyche and Cupid (Gérard), 26, *26*

Quaglia, Fernando, 130
Quatremère de Quincy, Antoine Chrysosthôme, 43, 48, 49, 50–51, 53
Queen Hortense (Isabey), 14, *14*
Queen Hortense's Boudoir (Garnerey), 62, *62*

Recamier, Juliette, 2, 13, 34, 75n34, 82, 104
Redouté, Pierre-Joseph, 91–101; in Boilly's *Reunion*, 11, 97; brothers of, 97; at Malmaison, 80, 86, 98; porcelain based on, 86, *87*, *120*, *129*, 129–30, *131*; reproductions of works, 92, 101; works by, 72, 73, 80, 86, *87*, 90, 91–101, *92*–*96*
Regnault, Jean-Baptiste, 24, *183*
Rémusat, Claire de, 36, 162, 196
Renaudin, Mme, 9
Reunion of Artists in Isabey's Studio (Boilly), *10*, 10–11, 97
Rible, Agatha, 176
Robert, Hubert, 40, 80, 89n8
Robert, Jean-François, 124, 135n7
Robespierre, 33, 34, 190
Rode, Pierre, 196
Rosentiel, 128, 129
Rossini, Gioacchino, 200
Rouget de Lisle, Claude Joseph, 191
Rousseau, Jean-Jacques, 197
Roze, Abbé, 195

Saint, Daniel, 141, *183*
Saint Catherine (Luini), 23
Saint-Cloud: furniture at, 107–9, *108*, *109*; interiors of, 65, 74n20, 74n21; porcelain at, 130; silver at, 146–47
Saint Hilaire, Marco Besson de, 176
Saint-Non, Abbé de, 133
Saint-Saëns, Camille, 199
The Salle des Saisons at the Louvre (H. Robert), 40
Salon of the Conservatory at Malmaison (Garnerey), 43
Salvi, Claudia, 100
Sarrette, Bernard, 193–94
Sartoni, M., 175
Sauvage, Piat, 130, 134
Schubert, Franz, 199
Scott, Sir Walter, 26–27
sculpture, 39–54
Sèvres porcelain, 122–30, 134, 137–42
shawls, 167–69, *168*, *169*
silver, 145–55
Simon, Jean-Henri, 178
Six Romances after Atala (Gaveaux), 198
Sleeping Hermaphrodite, 43, *43*, 45–46
Sowerby, James, 94
Spaendonck, Gerard van, 94, 96, 97
Spontini, Gasparo, 199, 200, 201–3, *202*
Staël, Germaine de, 13
Stearn, William T., 94
Steibelt, Daniel, 198
The Sultana Giving Her Order to the Odalisques (Pithou), 123
Swebach, Jacques-François Joseph, 10, 124, 130, 135n7

Talani, Teresa, 178
Tallien, Thérèse, 34, 161
Talma, François, 2, 11
Temple of Love (Garnerey), 83, *83*
Tender Is the Night (Fitzgerald), 33
Teniers, David, 8
tents, 67, 69, 70, 75n27, 75n28, 79, 80
Terborch, Gerard, II, 12

Thibault, Jean-Thomas, 81
Thiénon, Anne-Claude, 100
Thomire, Pierre-Philippe, 44, *59*, 109, *109*
The Three Graces (Canova), 51–53, *52*
tiaras, *174*, *179*, 184, *185*
Times of Day (Prud'hon), 61
The Toilette of the Sultana (Pithou), 123, *123*
The Tomb of Julie (Dael), 97
Töpffer, Adam, 100
The Torch of Venus (Mayer), 67
The Triumph of Trajan (Persuis), 201
Tuileries Palace, 3, 7; furniture at, 39, 107, *111*, 112, 114–16, *115*, *116*; interiors of, 4, 63–65, *64*; music at, 199, 200; porcelain at, 125, *126*; sculpture at, 43
Tulips and Roses (Redouté), 92

Uklanski, E. T. von, 87

Vassé, Louis-Claude, 39–40
Vautier, Achilles, 34
Vengeance of the Animals (Potter), 8
Verberckt, Jacques, 80
Verdonnet, comte de, 122
Vermay, Jean-Baptiste, 171, *171*
Vernet, Horace, 10, 15, *15*
La Vestale (Spontini), 201–3, *202*
View of the Facade of the Château on the Park Side (Garnerey), *80*
View of the Wooden Bridge (Garnerey), 76, *82*
Vigée-LeBrun, Elisabeth, 12, 55n16, *158*, 160, *163*, 195, 197
Vignon, Barthélemy, 81
Visconti, Ennio, 48
Voiart, Jacques-Philippe, 30, 37n26
Vue de la Cour d'honneur du château de la Malmaison (Nicolle), *79*

Wailly, Léon De, *84*, 100
Washington, George, 64, 74n12
Watteville, Nicolas-Rodolphe de, 130
Wealth (Prud'hon), 60, 60–61
Weisweiler, Adam, 62, 109, *109*
West, Alison, 42
Winckelmann, Johann Joachim, 147
Windus, Alfred, 135n7
Woman with Dropsy (Dou), 8
Worlée, Catherine, 157, *158*, *159*

Young, Edward, 33
Young Girl Feeding Her Chickens (E. Chaudet), 46
Young Girl Mourning the Death of Her Pigeon (E. Chaudet), 46
Young Oedipus Brought Back to Life by the Shepherd Phorbas (A.-D. Chaudet), 45, *46*

About the Authors

BERNARD CHEVALLIER is director of conservation at the Musée national des Châteaux de Malmaison et Bois-Préau in France and in 1997 was named director general of the Napoleonic museums of France. His books include *L'Art de Vivre au temps de Joséphine* and (with Christophe Pincemaille) *Napoléon* and *L'Impératrice Jósephine*.

KIMBERLY CHRISMAN-CAMPBELL is the Andrew W. Mellon Curatorial Fellow in French Art at The Huntington Library, Art Collections, and Botanical Gardens in San Marino, California. She is a graduate of the Masters Program in History of Dress at the Courtauld Institute of Art and received her Ph.D. from the University of Aberdeen.

ELEANOR P. DELORME is senior lecturer in art history at Wellesley College and has lectured at institutions including Harvard University; the Museum of Fine Arts, Boston; and Sotheby's Institute, New York. She is author of the biography *Joséphine: Napoléon's Incomparable Empress* and *Garden Pavilions and the Eighteenth-Century French Court*. She is a fellow of the International Napoleonic Society, which awarded *Joséphine* a first prize for "significant contributions to Napoleonic studies, outstanding research, originality, style, and interpretation."

DAVID GILBERT specializes in the music of Hector Berlioz and nineteenth-century France. He edited Berlioz's early cantata, *La Mort d'Orphée*, for its American premiere by the Boston Symphony Orchestra and has published articles on Berlioz, Gabriel Fauré, and music during the time of Napoléon. He is a music librarian at the University of California, Los Angeles.

CHRISTOPHER HARTOP is an independent art adviser and the author of *The Huguenot Legacy: English Silver, 1680–1760* and most recently *East Anglian Silver, 1550–1750* and *Royal Goldsmiths: the Art of Rundell & Bridge, 1797–1843*. From 1983 to 1999 he worked for Christie's, where he was head of the Silver Department and later executive vice president.

PETER MITCHELL is the owner of John Mitchell & Son, a paintings gallery founded in London in 1930. He is a graduate of the Courtauld Institute of Art, an authority in the field of flower and still life painting, and the author of *European Flower Painters*.

TAMARA PRÉAUD has written extensively on ceramics and is the author of *La Porcelaine de Vincennes* (with Antoine d'Albis) and *Ceramics of the 20th Century* (with Serge Gauthier) and contributing author to *The Sèvres Porcelain Manufactory: Alexandre Brongniart and the Triumph of Art and Industry, 1800–1847*. She is director of Archives and Documentation Services at the Manufacture nationale de Sèvres in Sèvres, France.

DIANA SCARISBRICK is a freelance historian of jewelry and engraved gems. She has published *Chaumet: Master Jewellers since 1780*, the story of the firm founded by M. E. Nitot, court jeweler to Napoléon; and more recently *Jewellery in Britain, 1066–1837*; *Jewelry, 1540–1940: From the Renaissance to Art Deco*; *Historic Rings: 4,000 Years of Craftsmanship*; and *Timeless Tiaras*. She organized the exhibition Napoléon Amoreux: Bijoux de l'Empire, held in Paris from September 21 to December 4, 2004.

JOHN D. WARD received his master's degree in the history of decorative arts from the Bard Graduate Center for Studies in the Decorative Arts and is assistant vice president of the Silver Department at Sotheby's, New York. He lectures internationally on the decorative arts.

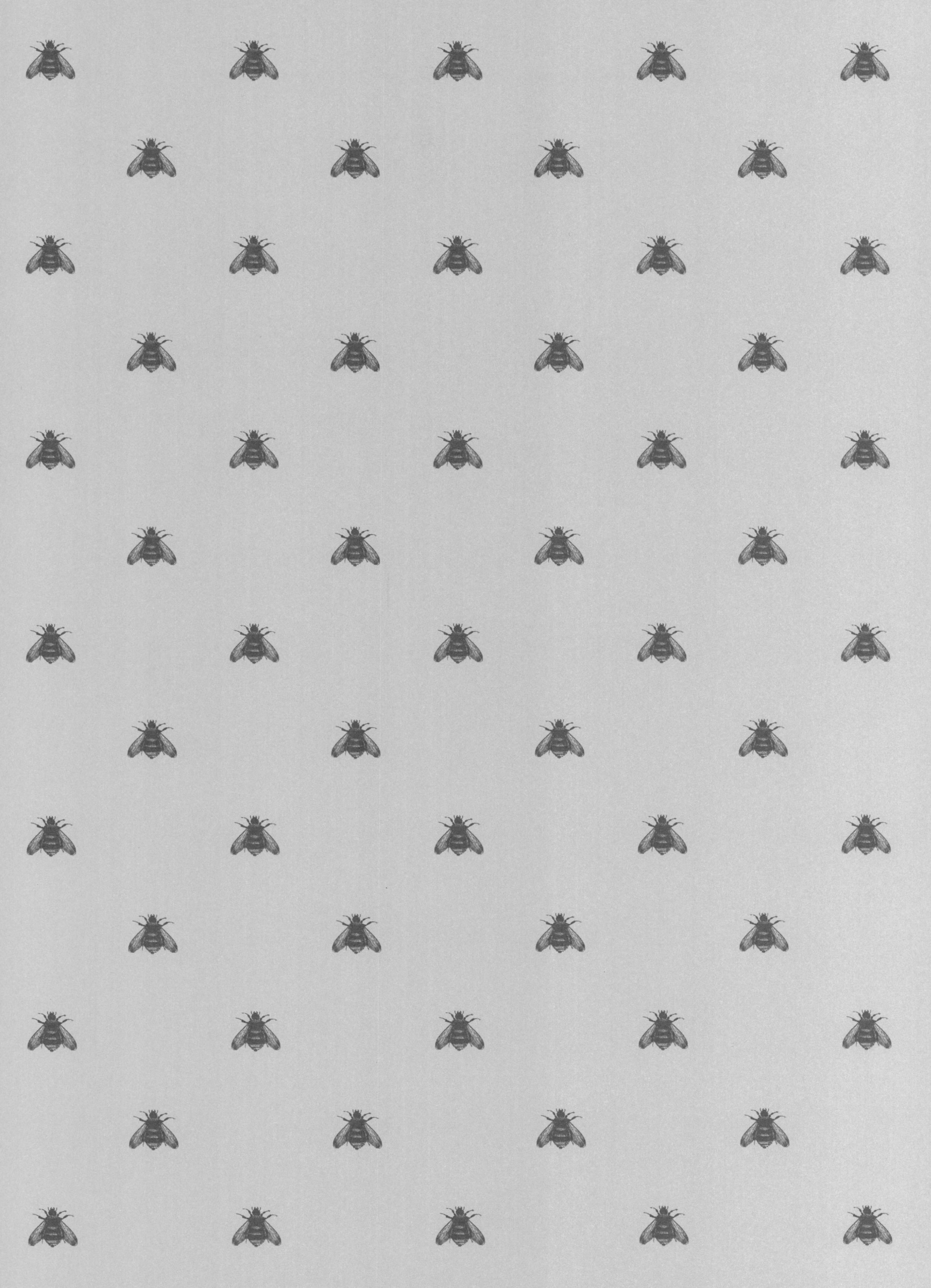

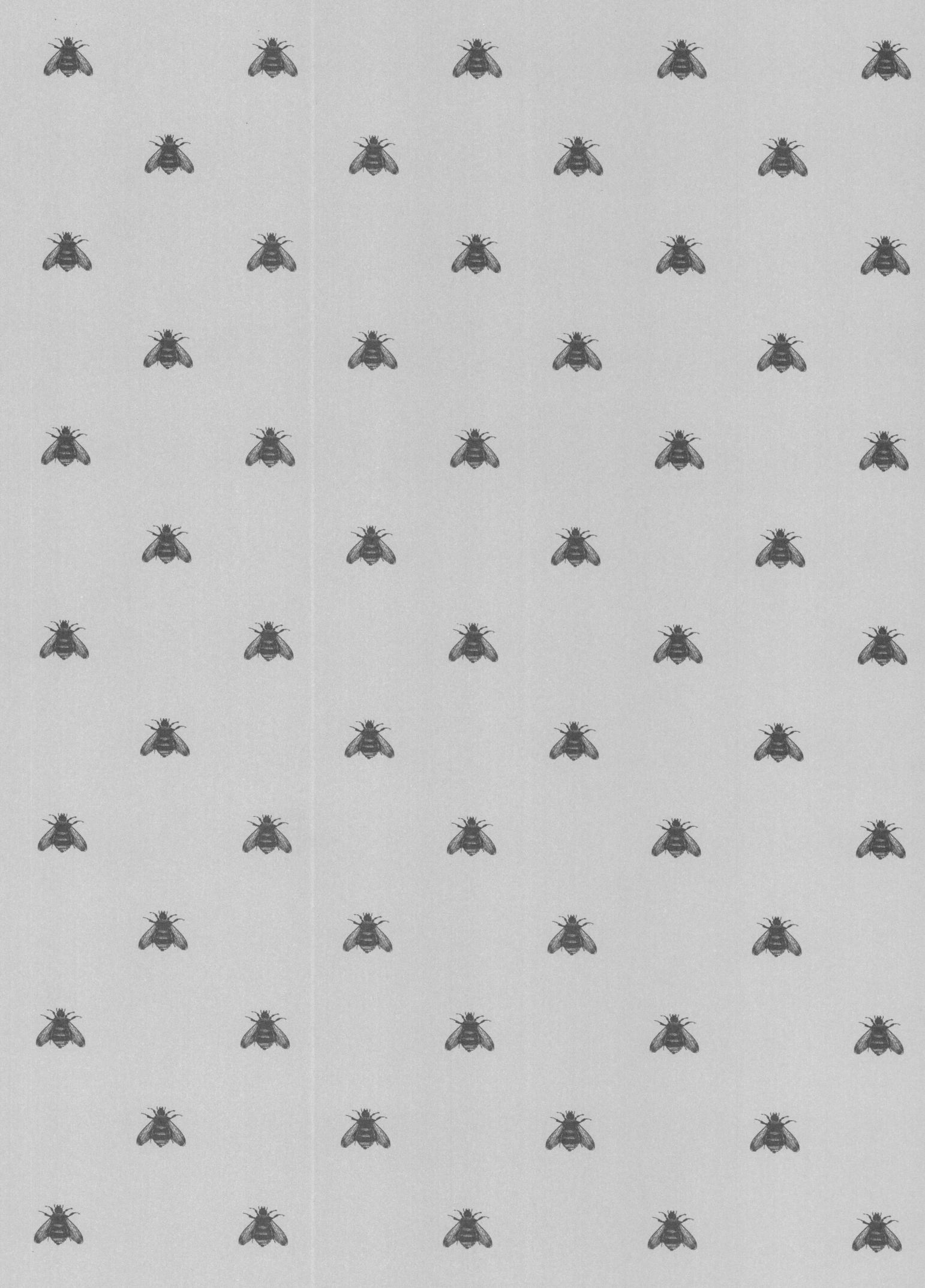